Olympiad ACE

A Comprehensive Practice Book

for School Olympiads & Talent Search Exams

MATHS

Class 11

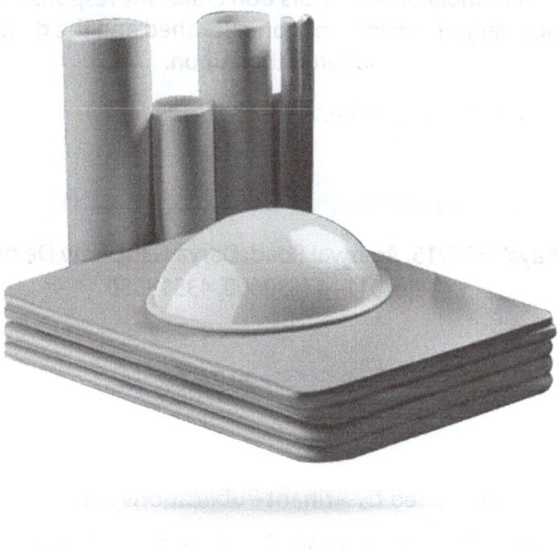

by
Rahul Jha

Olympiad ACE

BLOOM

Bloom Cap Edu Ventures Pvt. Ltd.

卐 **Administrative & Production Office**

'Ramchhaya' 4577/15, Agarwal Road, Darya Ganj, New Delhi -110002
Tele: 011- 47630600, 43518550

卐 **PRICE:** ₹175.00

Published by Arihant Publications (I) Ltd.

For further information about the books log on to
www.bloomcap.org

Follow us on

Preface

"Future belongs to those Who prepares for it today"

School Olympiads are National & International level competitions conducted by different Government, Non-Government & Educational Organisations with the purpose of making the children ready to face competitive exams. The challenging Questions asked in Olympiads motivate them to learn more & more and bring out the best result with improved academic performance. The Awards & Scholarship offered in Olympiads motivate children to aspire & strive for doing better and emerge out to be the best.

Maths Olympiads

Mathematics is an integral part of all competitive exams be it Aptitude or Commerce or Science. Maths Olympiads are meant to develop Mathematical aptitude in school students. They provide students with an opportunity to master their concepts and comprehend tricky questions effortlessly. Challenging Questions of Maths Olympiads encourage students to develop a logical approach to solve Mathematical Problems.

'Bloom Mathematics Olympiad Study Book Class 11' is a perfect resource to Study & Practice for Olympiad Exams and other National & State Level Talent Search Exams & Other Competitions.

Some Special Features of Bloom Maths Olympiad Study Books are;

- Chapterwise Exercises having different types of Objective Questions at par with the Olympiad Level.
- Detailed Explanation for each question.
- Olympiad Pattern Practice Sets at the end.

This book is prepared by Expert Panel with the utmost care, still if you have any suggestions regarding its improvement, then feel free to contact us at support@bloomcap.org. We will try to inculcate your suggestions in the further editions.

Contents

Chapter 01

Sets

MCQs 1 Mark Questions

1. The number of elements in the set $\{(a, b): 2a^2 + 3b^2 = 35, a, b \in Z\}$, where Z is the set of all integers is

(a) 2 (b) 4 (c) 8 (d) 12

2. Two finite sets have m and n elements. The total number of subsets of first set is 56 more than the total number of subsets of the second set. The values of m and n are

(a) 7 and 6 (b) 6 and 3
(c) 5 and 1 (d) 8 and 7

3. If a set A contains m $(m > 6)$ elements, then what is the number of subsets of A containing less than 6 elements?

(a) ${}^mC_5$ (b) ${}^mC_6$ (c) $\sum_{r=0}^{6} {}^mC_r$ (d) $\sum_{r=0}^{5} {}^mC_r$

4. If a set A contains 10 elements, then the number of subset of A containing all elements is

(a) 20 (b) 10^2 (c) 2^{10} (d) 200

5. Let $X = \{x : x \le 9, x \in N\}$ and let $Y = \{a, b, c\}$ be the subset of X, where $(a + b + c)$ is a multiple of 3. What is the largest possible number of subsets like Y?

(a) 12 (b) 21 (c) 27 (d) 30

6. Let $X = \{x \in R | -4 \le x < 4\}$

$Y = \{x \in R | -5 \le x \le 5\}$

$Z = \{x \in R | -7 \le x \le 10\}$

Then, which of the following is correct?

(a) $-7 \in (X \cap Y \cap Z)$
(b) $4 \in (X \cap Y \cap Z)$
(c) $-5 \in (X \cap Y \cap Z)$
(d) $-4 \in (X \cap Y \cap Z)$

7. If A, B and C are three sets such that $A \cup B = A \cup C$ and $A \cap B = A \cap C$, then which one of the following is correct?

(a) $A = B$ only (b) $B = C$ only
(c) $A = C$ only (d) $A = B = C$

8. If the sets X and Y are defined as

$X = \{(u, v) : v = \frac{1}{u}, u \ne 0, u \in R\}$

$Y = \{(u, v) : v = -u, u \in R\}$, then

(a) $X \cap Y = X$
(b) $X \cap Y = Y$
(c) $X \cap Y = \phi$
(d) None of these

9. Let $A = \{x^2 : x$ is a natural number$\}$ and $B = \{x^3 : x$ is a natural number$\}$. Which one of the following is not true?

(a) $A \cup B =$ Set of natural numbers
(b) $A \cap B$ is a finite set
(c) $\overline{(A \cup B)}$ is an infinite set
(d) $A \cap B \subseteq \{m^6 : m$ is a natural number$\}$

10. Let F_1 be the set of parallelograms, F_2 be the set of rectangles, F_3 be the set of rhombus and F_4 be the set of squares, then

(a) $F_1 = F_2 \cap F_3 \cap F_4$
(b) $F_1 = F_2 \cup F_3 \cup F_4$
(c) $F_1 = F_2 \cup F_3 \cap F_4$
(d) $F_1 = F_2 \cap F_3 \cup F_4$

11. If X is a set of multiple of 3, Y is a set of multiple of 4 and Z is a set of multiple of 12, then which one of the following is a null set?

(a) $(X - Y) \cup Z$ (b) $(X - Y) \cap Z$
(c) $(X \cap Y) \cap Z$ (d) $(X \cap Y) - Z$

12. Let A and B be two non-empty subsets of a set X such that A is not a subset of B, then

(a) A is always a subset of the complement of B
(b) B is always a subset of A
(c) A and B are always disjoint
(d) A and the complement of B are always non-disjoint

13. If U is the universal set and $A = B \cup C$, then the set $U - (U - (U - (U - (U - A))))$ is same as the set

(a) $\overline{B} \cup \overline{C}$ (b) $B \cup C$
(c) $\overline{B} \cap \overline{C}$ (d) $B \cap C$

14. If λ is the universal set and A is a subset of λ, then $(A - \lambda) \cup (\lambda - A) \cap A$ is equal to

(a) ϕ (b) A
(c) λ (d) None of these

15. If $P, Q, R \subseteq X$, where $P \neq \phi$, $Q \neq \phi$, $R \neq \phi$ such that $Q \cap R = P \cup Q$, which of the following is the strongest inference that can be derived?

(a) $P = Q = R$ (b) $P \subseteq Q = R$
(c) $P = Q \subseteq R$ (d) $P \subseteq Q \subseteq R$

16. Let $X = \{x : x = n^3 + 2n + 1, n \in N\}$ and $Y = \{x : x = 3n^2 + 7, n \in N\}$, then

(a) $X \cap Y \subseteq \{x : x = 3n + 5, n \in N\}$
(b) $X \cap Y \subseteq \{x : x = n^2 + n + 1, n \in N\}$
(c) $34 \in X \cap Y$
(d) $X \cap Y = \phi$

17. Let $X = \{1, 2, 3, 4, 5\}$. The number of different ordered pairs (Y, Z) that can be formed such that $Y \subseteq X, Z \subseteq X$ and $Y \cap Z = \phi$ is

(a) 2^5 (b) 3^5 (c) 5^3 (d) 5^2

18. Given, $A = \{x \mid x \text{ is a root of } x^2 - 1 = 0\}$ and $B = \{x \mid x \text{ is a root of } x^2 - 2x + 1 = 0\}$, then

(a) $A \cap B = A$ (b) $A \cup B = \phi$
(c) $A \cup B = A$ (d) $A \cap B = \phi$

19. If cardinality of set A is 4 and that of a set B is 3, then what is the cardinality of the set $(A - B) \cup (B - A)$?

(a) 5 (b) 1
(c) 7
(d) As, A and B are not known, so cannot be determined

20. Which one of the following is correct?

(a) $A \cup P(A) = P(A)$
(b) $A \cap P(A) = A$
(c) $A - P(A) = A$
(d) $P(A) - \{A\} = P(A)$

where, $P(A)$ is power set of set A.

21. For set A and B, $(A \cup B)' \cup (A' \cap B)$ equals

(a) A' (b) B'
(c) A (d) None of these

22. If A and B are two sets, then $A \cap (A \cup B)'$ is equal to

(a) A (b) B
(c) ϕ (d) None of these

23. If $A \cup B = (A - B) \cup (B - A)$, where $A, B \subseteq X$, then which one of the following is correct?

(a) $A \subset B$ (b) $A \subset (X - B)$
(c) $A = B$ (d) $B \subset A$

24. Consider the following statements for three non-empty sets A, B and C.

I. $A-(B-C)=(A-B)\cup C$

II. $(A-B)-C=A-(B\cup C)$

Which of the statements given above is/are correct?

(a) Only I (b) Only II

(c) Both I and II (d) Neither I nor II

25. What does the shaded region represent in the given figure?

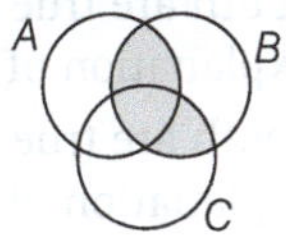

(a) $(A\cup B)-(A\cap C)$

(b) $A\cap(B\cap C)$

(c) $(A\cap B)\cap(A\cap C)$

(d) $(A\cap B)\cup(B\cap C)$

26. Which of the diagram indicates the best relationship between travelers, train and bus?

(a) 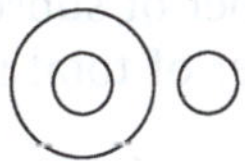 (b) 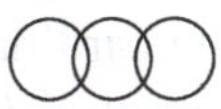

(c)  (d) 

27. The smallest set A such that $A\cup\{1,2\}=\{1,2,3,5,9\}$ is

(a) $\{2, 3, 5\}$ (b) $\{3, 5,9\}$

(c) $\{1, 2, 5, 9\}$ (d) None of these

28. The set $(A\cap B')'\cup(B\cap C)$ is equal to

(a) $A'\cup B\cup C$ (b) $A'\cup B$

(c) $A'\cup C'$ (d) None of these

29. Let S is the set of points inside the square. T is the set of points inside the triangle and C is the set of points inside the circle if triangle and circle intersect each other and are contained in the square, then which of the following is not true?

(a) $S\cap T\cap C\neq\phi$ (b) $S\cup T\cup C=C$

(c) $S\cup T\cup C=S$ (d) $S\cup T=S\cup C$

MCQs 2 Marks Questions

30. If the set A and B are defined as
$A=\{(x, y): y=e^x, x\in R\}$ and
$B=\{(x, y): y=x, x\in R\}$, then

(a) $B\subseteq A$ (b) $A\subseteq B$

(c) $A\cap B=\phi$ (d) $A\cup B=A$

31. Let A and B be two sets containing 3 elements and 4 elements, respectively. The number of subsets of $A\times B$ having 3 or more elements is

(a) 4017 (b) 4002 (c) 4096 (d) 4024

32. Suppose, $A_1, A_2, \ldots\ldots A_{30}$ are thirty sets each having 5 elements and $B_1, B_2, \ldots, B_n$ are n sets each with 3 elements, let $\bigcup_{i=1}^{30} A_i=\bigcup_{j=1}^{n} B_j=S$ and each element of S belongs to exactly 10 of the A_i's and exactly 9 of the B_j's, then n is equal to

(a) 15 (b) 45

(c) 3 (d) None of these

33. Two sets A and B are as under
$A=\{(a, b)\in R\times R: |a-5|<1$ and $|b-5|<1\}$; $B=\{(a, b)\in R\times R : 4(a-6)^2+9(b-5)^2\leq 36\}$, then

(a) A is a subset of B

(b) $A\cap B=\phi$ (null set)

(c) neither A is subset of B nor B is a subset of A

(d) B is a subset of A

34. Let $X=\{n\in N: 1\leq n\leq 50\}$. If $A=\{n\in X: n$ is a multiple of $2\}$ and $B=\{n\in X: n$ is a multiple of $7\}$, then the number of elements is the smallest subset of X containing both A and B is

(a) 23 (b) 25

(c) 26 (d) 29

35. The maximum number of sets obtainable from A and B by applying union and difference operations is

(a) 5 (b) 6

(c) 7 (d) 8

36. The value of $(A\cup B\cup C)\cap(A\cap B^c\cap C^c)\cap C^c$ is
(a) $B\cap C^c$
(b) $B^c\cap C^c$
(c) $B\cap C$
(d) $A\cap B\cap C$

37. Which of the following Venndiagram correctly illustrates the relationship among the class : Tennis fans, cricket players, students?

(a) 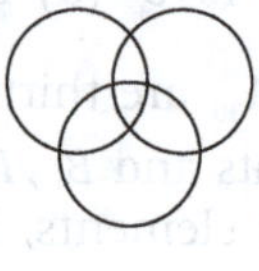 (b) 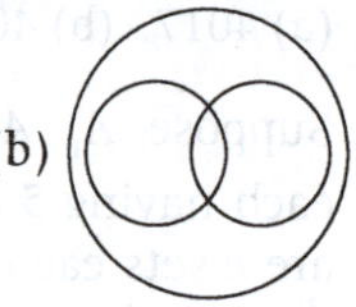

(c) 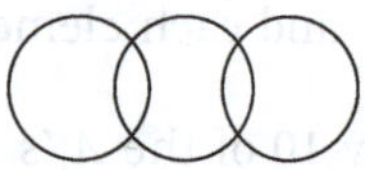 (d) 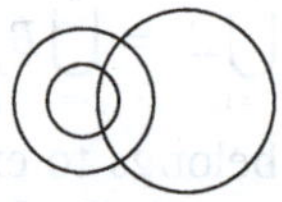

38. Let $A=\{a, b, c, d\}$ and $B=\{a, b, c\}$. Then, the number of sets X contained in A and not contained in B is
(a) 8 (b) 6
(c) 16 (d) 12

39. **Assertion** (A) For any two sets A and B, $A-B\subset B'$.
Reason (R) If A is any set, then $A\cap A'=\phi$
(a) A and R both are true and R is the correct explanation of A
(b) A and R both are true but R is not the correct explanation of A
(c) A is true but R is false
(d) A is false but R is true

40. **Assertion** (A) The subsets of the set $\{1, \{2\}\}$ are $\{\ \}$, $\{1\}$, $\{\{2\}\}$ and $\{1, \{2\}\}$
Reason (R) The total number of proper subset of a set containing n elements is 2^n.
(a) A and R both are true and R is the correct explanation of A
(b) A and R both are true but R is not the correct explanation of A
(c) A is true but R is false
(d) A is false but R is true

Directions (Q. Nos. 41 and 42) *Read the information carefully and answer the next two questions.*
The sum of cardinal number of two finite sets A and B is 9. The ratio of cardinal number of total number of subset of A is to the cardinal number of total number of subset of B is 8 : 1.

41. The cardinal number of set A is
(a) 2 (b) 3
(c) 6 (d) 8

42. The cardinal number of set B is
(a) 3 (b) 4
(c) 6 (d) 2

Darken your choice with HB Pencil

1.	ⓐ ⓑ ⓒ ⓓ	8.	ⓐ ⓑ ⓒ ⓓ	15.	ⓐ ⓑ ⓒ ⓓ	22.	ⓐ ⓑ ⓒ ⓓ	29.	ⓐ ⓑ ⓒ ⓓ	36.	ⓐ ⓑ ⓒ ⓓ
2.	ⓐ ⓑ ⓒ ⓓ	9.	ⓐ ⓑ ⓒ ⓓ	16.	ⓐ ⓑ ⓒ ⓓ	23.	ⓐ ⓑ ⓒ ⓓ	30.	ⓐ ⓑ ⓒ ⓓ	37.	ⓐ ⓑ ⓒ ⓓ
3.	ⓐ ⓑ ⓒ ⓓ	10.	ⓐ ⓑ ⓒ ⓓ	17.	ⓐ ⓑ ⓒ ⓓ	24.	ⓐ ⓑ ⓒ ⓓ	31.	ⓐ ⓑ ⓒ ⓓ	38.	ⓐ ⓑ ⓒ ⓓ
4.	ⓐ ⓑ ⓒ ⓓ	11.	ⓐ ⓑ ⓒ ⓓ	18.	ⓐ ⓑ ⓒ ⓓ	25.	ⓐ ⓑ ⓒ ⓓ	32.	ⓐ ⓑ ⓒ ⓓ	39.	ⓐ ⓑ ⓒ ⓓ
5.	ⓐ ⓑ ⓒ ⓓ	12.	ⓐ ⓑ ⓒ ⓓ	19.	ⓐ ⓑ ⓒ ⓓ	26.	ⓐ ⓑ ⓒ ⓓ	33.	ⓐ ⓑ ⓒ ⓓ	40.	ⓐ ⓑ ⓒ ⓓ
6.	ⓐ ⓑ ⓒ ⓓ	13.	ⓐ ⓑ ⓒ ⓓ	20.	ⓐ ⓑ ⓒ ⓓ	27.	ⓐ ⓑ ⓒ ⓓ	34.	ⓐ ⓑ ⓒ ⓓ	41.	ⓐ ⓑ ⓒ ⓓ
7.	ⓐ ⓑ ⓒ ⓓ	14.	ⓐ ⓑ ⓒ ⓓ	21.	ⓐ ⓑ ⓒ ⓓ	28.	ⓐ ⓑ ⓒ ⓓ	35.	ⓐ ⓑ ⓒ ⓓ	42.	ⓐ ⓑ ⓒ ⓓ

Chapter 02

Relations and Functions

MCQs 1 Mark Questions

1. Consider the following relations from P to Q, where
$P = \{a, b, c, d, e, f\}$, $Q = \{w, x, y, z\}$

I. $\{(a, w), (b, w), (c, w), (d, x), (e, x), (f, z)\}$

II. $\{(a, w), (b, x), (c, y), (f, z)\}$

III. $\{(a, z), (b, y), (c, x), (a, w), (b, x), (f, x)\}$

IV. $\{(a, x), (b, w), (c, z), (d, y), (e, x), (f, z)\}$

Which of the above relations are not functions?

(a) I and II (b) I and IV
(c) II and III (d) III and IV

2. A relation R is defined over the set of non-negative integers as xRy, $x^2 + y^2 = 36$. What is R?

(a) $\{(0, 6)\}$
(b) $\{(6, 0), (\sqrt{11}, 5), (3, 3\sqrt{3})\}$
(c) $\{(6, 0), (0, 6)\}$
(d) $\{(\sqrt{11}, 5), (2, 4\sqrt{2}), (5\sqrt{11}, 4\sqrt{2})\}$

3. $f:\{1,2,3\} \to \{4, 5\}$ is not a function if it is defined by which one of the following?

(a) $\{(2,4), (3,5), (1,5)\}$
(b) $\{(1,4), (2,5), (3,4)\}$
(c) $\{(1,4), (2,4), (3,4)\}$
(d) $\{(1,4), (1,5), (2,4), (2,5), (3,4), (3,5)\}$

4. R is a relation from $\{11,12,13\}$ to $\{8,10,12\}$ defined by $y = x - 3$. The relation R^{-1} is

(a) $\{(11,8), (13,10)\}$
(b) $\{(8,11), (10,13)\}$
(c) $\{(8,11), (9,12), (10,13)\}$
(d) None of the above

5. If R is a relation from a set A to the set B and S is a relation from B to C, then the relation SoR

(a) is from C to A (b) is from A to C
(c) does not exist (d) None of these

6. Let $R = \{(1, 3), (2, 2), (3, 2)\}$ and $S = \{(2, 1), (3, 2), (2, 3)\}$ be two relation on set $A = \{1, 2, 3\}$. Then, RoS is equal to

(a) $\{(3, 2), (1, 3)\}$
(b) $\{(1, 3), (2, 2), (3, 2), (2, 1), (2, 3)\}$
(c) $\{(2, 3), (3, 2), (2, 2)\}$
(d) $\{(2, 3), (3, 2)\}$

7. Let $X \neq \phi$ and $n(X) = m$. Then, number of relations on X is

(a) 2^{m^2} (b) 2^m (c) 2^{2m} (d) m^2

8. If $P, Q, R \neq \phi$ such that $P \cap R = \phi$, then $(P \times Q) \cap (R \times Q)$ is equal to

(a) $P \times R$ (b) $P \times Q$ (c) $Q \times R$ (d) ϕ

9. If set A contains 5 elements, then what is the number of elements in $A \times P(A)$?

(a) 32 (b) 150 (c) 160 (d) 128

10. Let $A = \{2, 5, 8\}$, $B = \{3, 6, 7\}$ and R be the relation 'one less than' from A to B, then how many elements will R contain?
(a) 2 (b) 3 (c) 5 (d) 9

11. Sets A and B have P elements in common. How many elements will $(A \times B)$ and $(B \times A)$ have in common?
(a) 0 (b) 1
(c) P (d) P^2

12. Consider the following with regard to a relation R on a set of real numbers defined by xRy, if $x + y = 4$
I. $0R4$ II. $1R\frac{1}{4}$ III. $-4R8$
Which of the above are correct?
(a) I and II (b) I and III
(c) II and III (d) I, II and III

13. The relation R defined on set
$A = \{x : |x| < 3, x \in I\}$
by $R = \{(x, y) : y = |x|\}$ is
(a) $\{(-2, 2), (-1, 1), (0, 0), (1, 1), (2, 2)\}$
(b) $\{(-2, -2), (-2, 2), (-1, 1), (0, 0), (1, -2), (1, 2), (2, -1), (2, -2)\}$
(c) $\{(0, 0), (1, 1), (2, 2)\}$
(d) None of the above

14. Consider the following statements
I. If $A \cap B = \phi$, then either $A = \phi$ or $B = \phi$
II. For $a \neq b$, $\{a, b\} = \{b, a\}$ and $(a, b) \neq (b, a)$.
III. If $A \subseteq B$, then $A \times A \subseteq (A \times B) \cap (B \times A)$.
IV. If $A \subseteq B$ and $C \subseteq D$, then $A \times C \subseteq B \times D$.
Which of these is/are correct?
(a) Only II (b) Only I
(c) Only IV (d) II, III and IV

15. If $0 < a < 1$, then the value of $\log_{10} a$ is negative. This is justified by
(a) negative power of 10 is negative
(b) negative power of 10 is positive
(c) negative power of 10 is between 0 and 1
(d) negative power of 10 is less than 1

16. The domain of definition of the function
$f(x) = \sqrt{\log_{10}\left(\frac{5x - x^2}{4}\right)}$ is
(a) $[1, 4]$ (b) $[1, 0]$
(c) $[0, 5]$ (d) $[5, 0]$

17. The domain of the function
$f(x) = \exp(\sqrt{5x - 3 - 2x^2})$ is
(a) $[3/2, \infty)$ (b) $[1, 3/2]$
(c) $(-\infty, 1]$ (d) $(1, 3/2)$

18. Domain of the function $\log|x^2 - 9|$ is
(a) R (b) $R - [-3, 3]$
(c) $R - \{-3, 3\}$ (d) None of these

19. If $\log_5(3x - 1) < 1$, then the value of x lies in the interval
(a) $(2, 4)$ (b) $\left(\frac{1}{3}, 2\right)$
(c) $\left(0, \frac{1}{3}\right)$ (d) None of these

20. The domain of the real valued function defined by $f(x) = \sqrt{x^2 + 1}$ is
(a) $x \in (1, \infty)$ (b) $x \in (-\infty, \infty)$
(c) $x \in (-\infty, -1)$ (d) $x \in (-\infty, \infty) - (-1, 1)$

21. The domain of the real valued function defined by $f(x) = \sqrt{x^2 - 1}$ is
(a) $x \in [1, \infty]$ (b) $x \in (-\infty, \infty)$
(c) $x \in (-\infty, -1]$ (d) $x \in (-\infty, \infty) - (-1, 1)$

22. The domain of the function
$f(x) = \sin^{-1}\left(\log_3 \frac{x}{3}\right)$ is
(a) $[-1, 9]$ (b) $[1, 9]$ (c) $[-9, 1]$ (d) $[3, 9]$

23. The domain of the function
$f(x) = \frac{1}{\sqrt{|x| - x}}$ is
(a) $(0, \infty)$ (b) $(-\infty, 0)$
(c) $(-\infty, \infty) - \{0\}$ (d) $(-\infty, \infty)$

24. The domain of the real valued function $f(x) = \sqrt{5 - 4x - x^2} + x^2 \log(x+4)$ is

(a) $-5 \le x \le 1$ (b) $-5 \le x$ and $x \ge 1$
(c) $-4 < x \le 1$ (d) ϕ

25. The domain of the function f defined by $f(x) = \sqrt{4-x} + \dfrac{1}{\sqrt{x^2-1}}$ is equal to

(a) $(-\infty, -1) \cup (1, 4]$ (b) $(-\infty, -1] \cup (1, 4]$
(c) $(-\infty, -1) \cup [1, 4]$ (d) $(-\infty, -1) \cup [1, 4)$

26. What is the range of $(\cos x - \sin x)$?

(a) $[2, 4]$ (b) $[-1, 1]$
(c) $[-\sqrt{2}, \sqrt{2}]$ (d) $(-\sqrt{2}, \sqrt{2})$

27. What is the range of the function

$$y = \frac{x^2}{1+x^2},\ x \in R?$$

(a) $[0, 1)$ (b) $[0, 1]$ (c) $(0, 1)$ (d) $(0, 1]$

28. If $f(x) = x - [x]$, where $[\cdot]$ denotes a greatest integer function, then range of $f(x)$ is

(a) $[0, 1)$ (b) $(0, 1)$ (c) $[0, 1]$ (d) $(0, 1]$

29. The range of the function $f(x) = \dfrac{x+2}{|x+2|}$ is

(a) $\{0, 1\}$ (b) $\{1, -1\}$
(c) R (d) $R - \{-2\}$

30. The range of $\cos\left(\dfrac{x}{9}\right)$ is

(a) $\left(-\dfrac{1}{9}, \dfrac{1}{9}\right)$ (b) $[-1, 1]$
(c) $\left(\dfrac{1}{9}, -\dfrac{1}{9}\right)$ (d) $(-9, 9)$

31. Range of the function $f(x) = \dfrac{1}{2 - \sin 2x}$ is

(a) $[1, 3]$ (b) $\left[\dfrac{1}{3}, 1\right]$ (c) $(1, 3)$ (d) $\left(\dfrac{1}{3}, 1\right)$

32. The function $f(x) = \log(x + \sqrt{(x^2+1)})$ is

(a) an even function
(b) an odd function
(c) a periodic function
(d) neither an even nor an odd function

33. Let $f(x) = \begin{cases} 2, & \text{if } 0 \le x \le 2 \\ 3, & \text{if } 2 < x \le 4 \end{cases}$, then f is

(a) a rational function
(b) a trigonometric function
(c) a step function
(d) an exponential function

34. The graph of the function $y = f(x)$ is symmetrical about the line $x = 3$, then

(a) $f(x) = -f(-x)$
(b) $f(x) = f(-x)$
(c) $f(3+x) = f(3-x)$
(d) $f(x+3) = f(x-3)$

35. Let $f: R \to R$ be defined as $f(x) = 2x + |x|$, then $f(2x) + f(-x) - f(x)$ is equal to

(a) $2x$ (b) $2|x|$ (c) $-2x$ (d) $-2|x|$

36. If $f(x) = \dfrac{x}{x-1}$, then $\dfrac{f(y)}{f(y+1)}$ is equal to

(a) $f(-y)$ (b) $f\left(\dfrac{1}{y}\right)$ (c) $f(y^2)$ (d) $f\left(\dfrac{-y}{y-1}\right)$

37. If $f: N \to N$ is defined by $f(x) = \sqrt{x}$, then $\dfrac{f(81)}{f(36) + f(49)}$ is equal to

(a) $\dfrac{3}{5}$ (b) $\dfrac{5}{3}$ (c) $\dfrac{13}{9}$ (d) $\dfrac{9}{13}$

38. If $f(x) = ax + b$, where a and b are integers, $f(-1) = -5$ and $f(3) = 3$, then a and b are equal to

(a) $a = -3, b = -1$ (b) $a = 2, b = -3$
(c) $a = 0, b = 2$ (d) $a = 2, b = 3$

39. If $f(x) = \cos(\log x)$, then $f(x)\, f(y) - \dfrac{1}{2}\left[f\left(\dfrac{x}{y}\right) + f(xy)\right]$ has the value

(a) -1 (b) $\dfrac{1}{2}$
(c) -2 (d) 0

40. If $f(x) - f(y) = f\left(\frac{x-y}{1-xy}\right)$ for $x, y \in (-1, 1)$, then $f(x)$ is equal to

(a) $\ln\left(\frac{1-x}{1+x}\right)$ (b) $\ln\left(\frac{2+x}{1-x}\right)$

(c) $\tan^{-1}\left(\frac{1-x}{1+x}\right)$ (d) $\tan^{-1}\left(\frac{1+x}{1-x}\right)$

41. If $2f(x) + f\left(\frac{1}{x}\right) = 2x$, then $f(2)$ is equal to

(a) $\frac{7}{2}$ (b) $\frac{2}{7}$ (c) $\frac{7}{3}$ (d) $\frac{3}{7}$

42. If $f(x) = 2x^3 + 3x^2 + 3x + 2$, then $x^3 f\left(\frac{1}{x}\right)$ is equal to

(a) $f(-x)$ (b) $\frac{1}{f(x)}$ (c) $\left(f\left(\frac{1}{x}\right)\right)^2$ (d) $f(x)$

43. Function $f(x) = \{x\}$, where $\{\cdot\}$ is fractional value function. This function is

(a) a periodic function with period 1/2
(b) not a periodic function
(c) a periodic function with period 1
(d) a periodic function with period 2

44. Which of the following functions is periodic?

(a) $f(x) = x - [x]$, where $[x]$ denotes the largest integer less than or equal to the real number x
(b) $f(x) = \sin\frac{1}{x}$, for $x \neq 0$, $f(0) = 0$
(c) $f(x) = x \cos x$
(d) None of the above

MCQs 2 Marks Questions

45. If $R = \{(x, y) : x, y \in Z, x^2 + 3y^2 \leq 8\}$ is a relation on the set of integers Z, then the domain of R^{-1} is

(a) $\{-1, 0, 1\}$ (b) $\{-2, -1, 1, 2\}$
(c) $\{-2, -1, 0, 1, 2\}$ (d) $\{0, 1\}$

46. Let Z be the set of integers of $A = \{x \in Z : 2^{(x+2)(x^2-5x+6)} = 1\}$ and $B = \{x \in Z : -3 < 2x - 1 < 9\}$, then the total number of relations of set A to set B is

(a) 2^{12} (b) 2^{18} (c) 2^{15} (d) 2^{10}

47. Domain of the function
$$f(x) = \frac{3}{4-x^2} + \log_{10}(x^3 - x) \text{ is}$$

(a) $(1, 2)$ (b) $(-1, 0) \cup (1, 2)$
(c) $(1, 2) \cup (2, \infty)$ (d) $(-1, 0) \cup (1, 2) \cup (2, \infty)$

48. The range of function $f(x) = \frac{x^2 - x + 1}{x^2 + x + 1}$ is

(a) R (b) $[3, \infty)$
(c) $\left[\frac{1}{3}, 3\right]$ (d) None of these

49. If $f(x) = ax^7 + bx^3 + cx - 5$, where a, b, c are real constants and $f(-7) = 7$, then range of $f(7) + 17\cos x$ is

(a) $[-34, 0]$ (b) $[0, 34]$
(c) $[-34, 34]$ (d) None of the above

50. Let $f(x) = \frac{9^x}{9^x + 3}$, then the value of
$$f\left(\frac{1}{2022}\right) + f\left(\frac{2}{2022}\right) + f\left(\frac{3}{2022}\right) + \ldots + f\left(\frac{2021}{2022}\right) \text{ is}$$

(a) 2022 (b) 1011 (c) 1011.5 (d) 1010.5

51. Match the following lists and then choose the correct code

	Function		Period of functions
(A)	$\sin 2x - \sqrt{3}\cos 2x$	(i)	4π
(B)	$\operatorname{cosec}^2 \frac{3}{4}x + \cot x$	(ii)	π
(C)	$2\sin 3x + 3\sin 2x$	(iii)	24π
(D)	$\sin\frac{\pi}{3}x + \sin\frac{\pi x}{4}$	(iv)	2π

Codes

	A	B	C	D
(a)	(i)	(iii)	(iv)	(ii)
(b)	(ii)	(i)	(iv)	(iii)
(c)	(ii)	(i)	(iii)	(iv)
(d)	(i)	(ii)	(iv)	(iii)

Directions (Q. Nos. 52-54) *Read the information carefully and answer next three questions.*

Let $f: R \to [0, \infty)$ be a function defined by $f(x) = |x|$ and $g(x) = f(x+1) + f(x-1)$, for all $x \in R$.

52. The value of $g(x)$ is

(a) $g(x) = \begin{cases} -2x, x < -1 \\ 2, -1 \le x < 1 \\ 2x, x \ge 1 \end{cases}$

(b) $g(x) = \begin{cases} -2x+1, x < -1 \\ -2x, -1 < x < 1 \\ 2x-1, x \ge 1 \end{cases}$

(c) $g(x) = \begin{cases} 2x, x < -1 \\ -2, -1 < x < 1 \\ -2x, x \ge 1 \end{cases}$

(d) $g(x) = \begin{cases} 2x-1, x < -1 \\ -2x, -1 < x < 1 \\ -2x+1, x \ge 1 \end{cases}$

53. Domain of $g(x)$ is

(a) $[-1, 1]$ (b) $(-\infty, -1] \cup [1, \infty)$

(c) R (d) $R - \{0\}$

54. The graph of $g(x)$ is

(a) 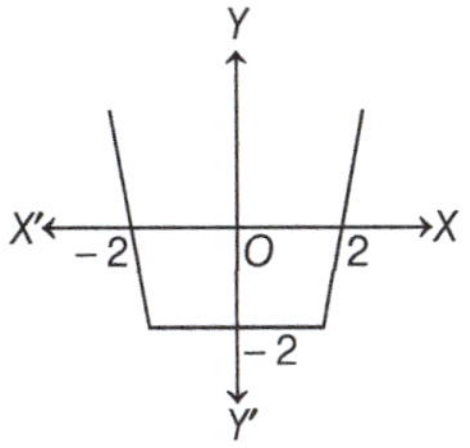

(b) 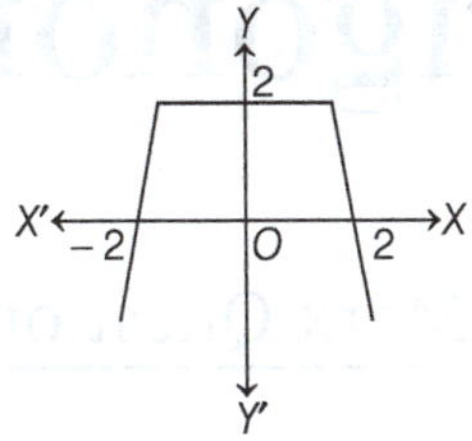

(c) 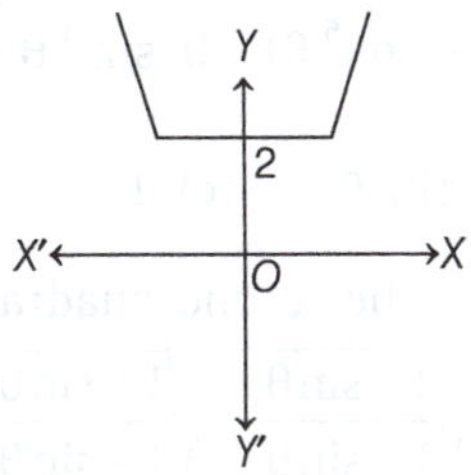

(d) 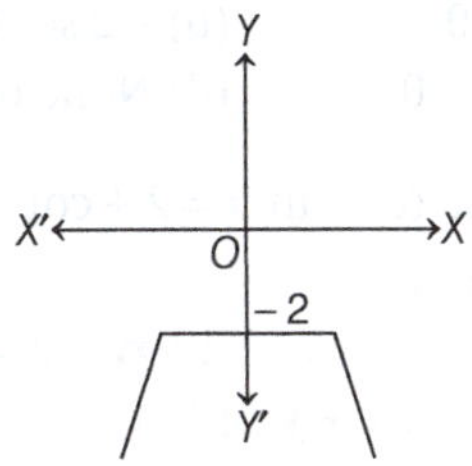

Darken your choice with HB Pencil

1.	(a) (b) (c) (d)	11.	(a) (b) (c) (d)	21.	(a) (b) (c) (d)	31.	(a) (b) (c) (d)	41.	(a) (b) (c) (d)	51.	(a) (b) (c) (d)
2.	(a) (b) (c) (d)	12.	(a) (b) (c) (d)	22.	(a) (b) (c) (d)	32.	(a) (b) (c) (d)	42.	(a) (b) (c) (d)	52.	(a) (b) (c) (d)
3.	(a) (b) (c) (d)	13.	(a) (b) (c) (d)	23.	(a) (b) (c) (d)	33.	(a) (b) (c) (d)	43.	(a) (b) (c) (d)	53.	(a) (b) (c) (d)
4.	(a) (b) (c) (d)	14.	(a) (b) (c) (d)	24.	(a) (b) (c) (d)	34.	(a) (b) (c) (d)	44.	(a) (b) (c) (d)	54.	(a) (b) (c) (d)
5.	(a) (b) (c) (d)	15.	(a) (b) (c) (d)	25.	(a) (b) (c) (d)	35.	(a) (b) (c) (d)	45.	(a) (b) (c) (d)		
6.	(a) (b) (c) (d)	16.	(a) (b) (c) (d)	26.	(a) (b) (c) (d)	36.	(a) (b) (c) (d)	46.	(a) (b) (c) (d)		
7.	(a) (b) (c) (d)	17.	(a) (b) (c) (d)	27.	(a) (b) (c) (d)	37.	(a) (b) (c) (d)	47.	(a) (b) (c) (d)		
8.	(a) (b) (c) (d)	18.	(a) (b) (c) (d)	28.	(a) (b) (c) (d)	38.	(a) (b) (c) (d)	48.	(a) (b) (c) (d)		
9.	(a) (b) (c) (d)	19.	(a) (b) (c) (d)	29.	(a) (b) (c) (d)	39.	(a) (b) (c) (d)	49.	(a) (b) (c) (d)		
10.	(a) (b) (c) (d)	20.	(a) (b) (c) (d)	30.	(a) (b) (c) (d)	40.	(a) (b) (c) (d)	50.	(a) (b) (c) (d)		

Chapter 03

Trigonometric Functions

MCQs 1 Mark Questions

1. The value of
$6(\sin^6\theta+\cos^6\theta)-9(\sin^4\theta+\cos^4\theta)+4$ is
(a) −3 (b) 0 (c) 1 (d) 3

2. If θ lies in the second quadrant, then the value of $\sqrt{\dfrac{1-\sin\theta}{1+\sin\theta}}+\sqrt{\dfrac{1+\sin\theta}{1-\sin\theta}}$ is equal to
(a) $2\sec\theta$ (b) $-2\sec\theta$
(c) $2\operatorname{cosec}\theta$ (d) None of these

3. Eliminate α from $x=2+\cot\alpha$ and $y=1+\tan\alpha$
(a) $xy+1=x+y$ (b) $xy+2=2y+x$
(c) $xy+1=2x+y$ (d) $xy+1=2y+x$

4. If $\sin\theta+\cos\theta=m$ and $\sec\theta+\operatorname{cosec}\theta=n$, then $n(m+1)(m-1)$ is equal to
(a) m (b) n (c) $2m$ (d) $2n$

5. If $\sec x+\sec^2 x=1$, then the value of $\tan^8 x-\tan^4 x-2\tan^2 x+1$ is equal to
(a) 0 (b) 1 (c) 2 (d) 3

6. The value of
$\cos^2\dfrac{\pi}{16}+\cos^2\dfrac{3\pi}{16}+\cos^2\dfrac{5\pi}{16}+\cos^2\dfrac{7\pi}{16}$ is
(a) 0 (b) 1 (c) −1 (d) 2

7. If $\sin\alpha+\cos\alpha=x$ and $\sin^3\alpha+\cos^3\alpha=y$, then $x(x^2-3)$ is equal to
(a) y (b) $2y$ (c) $-y$ (d) $-2y$

8. If $(1+\sin A)(1+\sin B)(1+\sin C)$
$=(1-\sin A)(1-\sin B)(1-\sin C)=P$
Then,
(a) $P=\sin A\sin B\sin C$
(b) $P=\pm\cos A\cos B\cos C$
(c) $P=\pm\sec A\sec B\sec C$
(d) $P=\pm\operatorname{cosec}A\operatorname{cosec}B\operatorname{cosec}C$

9. If $A=340°$, then $\sqrt{1-\sin A}-\sqrt{1+\sin A}$ is equal to
(a) $2\cos\dfrac{A}{2}$ (b) $2\sin\dfrac{A}{2}$
(c) $-2\cos\dfrac{A}{2}$ (d) $-2\sin\dfrac{A}{2}$

10. If $\alpha+\beta+\gamma=\pi$, then $\cos^2\alpha+\cos^2\beta+\cos^2\gamma$ is equal to
(a) $1+2\cos\alpha\cos\beta\cos\gamma$
(b) $1+2\sin\alpha\sin\beta\sin\gamma$
(c) $1-2\cos\alpha\cos\beta\cos\gamma$
(d) $1-2\sin\alpha\sin\beta\sin\gamma$

11. If x is real, then $\cos\theta=x+\dfrac{1}{x}$, then
(a) θ is an obtuse angle
(b) θ is right angle
(c) θ is an acute angle
(d) θ does not exist

12. $\tan\frac{\pi}{24}\cdot\tan\frac{3\pi}{24}\cdot\tan\frac{5\pi}{24}\cdot\tan\frac{7\pi}{24}\cdot\tan\frac{9\pi}{24}\cdot\tan\frac{11\pi}{24}$ is equal to

(a) 1 (b) -1 (c) $\sqrt{3}$ (d) $-\sqrt{3}$

13. $\tan 80° + \tan 40° - \sqrt{3}\tan 40° \tan 80°$ is equal to

(a) $\sqrt{3}$ (b) $-\sqrt{3}$ (c) $\frac{1}{\sqrt{3}}$ (d) $-\frac{1}{\sqrt{3}}$

14. If $\sin x + \sin y = \sqrt{3}(\cos y - \cos x)$, then $\sin 3x + \sin 3y$ is equal to

(a) 0 (b) 2 (c) 1 (d) $\frac{1}{2}$

15. $\frac{(1+\tan 13°)(1+\tan 32°)}{(1+\tan 12°)(1+\tan 33°)}$ is equal to

(a) 1 (b) 2 (c) 3 (d) 4

16. If $A+B=\frac{3\pi}{4}$, then $(1+\cot A)(1+\cot B)$ is equal to

(a) 1 (b) 2 (c) 3 (d) 4

17. The expression $\cos^2(A-B)+\cos^2 B - 2\cos(A-B)\cos A\cos B$ is

(a) dependent on B
(b) dependent on A and B
(c) dependent on A
(d) independent of A and B

18. In a ΔABC, $\angle B=\frac{\pi}{2}$, if $\tan\left(\frac{A}{2}\right)$ and $\tan\left(\frac{C}{2}\right)$ are the roots of the equation $ax^2+bx+c=0$ $(a\neq 0)$, then

(a) $a+b=c$ (b) $b+c=a$
(c) $a+c=b$ (d) $b=c$

19. The value of $\cos^2 48° - \sin^2 12°$ is equal to

(a) $\frac{\sqrt{5}+1}{2\sqrt{2}}$ (b) $\frac{\sqrt{5}+1}{5}$ (c) $\frac{\sqrt{5}-1}{8}$ (d) $\frac{\sqrt{5}+1}{8}$

20. $\sin 12° \sin 48° \sin 54°$ is equal to

(a) $\frac{1}{2}$ (b) $\frac{1}{4}$ (c) $\frac{1}{8}$ (d) $\frac{1}{16}$

21. If $\alpha+\beta-\gamma=\pi$, then $\sin^2\alpha+\sin^2\beta-\sin^2\gamma$ is equal to

(a) $2\sin\alpha\sin\beta\cos\gamma$
(b) $2\cos\alpha\cos\beta\cos\gamma$
(c) $2\sin\alpha\sin\beta\sin\gamma$
(d) $2\cos\alpha\cos\beta\sin\gamma$

22. If $\frac{\tan(A+B-C)}{\tan(A-B+C)}=\frac{\tan C}{\tan B}$ and $B\neq C$, then $\sin 2A+\sin 2B+\sin 2C$ is equal to

(a) 0 (b) 1 (c) 2 (d) $\frac{1}{2}$

23. $\sin A = x\sin\frac{A}{8}\cos\frac{A}{8}\cos\frac{A}{4}\cos\frac{A}{2}$, then x is equal to

(a) 2 (b) 4 (c) 6 (d) 8

24. If $\pi\le x\le\frac{3\pi}{2}$, then

$$\sqrt{4\sin^4 x+\sin^2(2x)}+4\cos^2\left(\frac{\pi}{4}-\frac{x}{2}\right)$$

is equal to

(a) 2 (b) -2 (c) 0 (d) 1

25. $\cos\alpha=\frac{2\cos\beta-1}{2-\cos\beta}$, $(0<\alpha,\beta<\pi)$ $\alpha+\beta=\pi$, then $\tan\frac{\alpha}{2}$ is equal to

(a) $3^{\frac{1}{2}}$ (b) 3 (c) 3^2 (d) $3^{\frac{1}{4}}$

26. If $\cos\theta=\cos A\cos B$, then $\tan\frac{\theta+A}{2}\tan\frac{\theta-A}{2}$ is equal to

(a) $\tan^2\frac{A}{2}$ (b) $\tan^2\frac{B}{2}$

(c) $\tan^2\frac{\theta}{2}$ (d) $\cot^2\frac{B}{2}$

27. If $\cos(\alpha+\beta)=\frac{4}{5}$, $\sin(\alpha-\beta)=\frac{5}{13}$ and α,β lies between 0 and $\frac{\pi}{4}$, then $\tan 2\alpha$ is equal to

(a) $\frac{16}{63}$ (b) $\frac{56}{33}$
(c) $\frac{28}{33}$ (d) None of these

28. If $\cos\alpha+\cos\beta=0=\sin\alpha+\sin\beta$, then $\cos 2\alpha+\cos 2\beta$ is equal to

(a) $2\cos(\alpha+\beta)$ (b) $-2\cos(\alpha+\beta)$
(c) $3\cos(\alpha+\beta)$ (d) None of these

29. The value of $\sin 20°\sin 40°\sin 60°\sin 80°$ is equal to

(a) $-\frac{3}{16}$ (b) $\frac{5}{16}$ (c) $\frac{3}{16}$ (d) $-\frac{5}{16}$

30. If $A+B+C=\pi$ and $\cos A=\cos B\cos C$, then $\tan B\tan C$ is equal to

(a) $\frac{1}{2}$ (b) 2 (c) 1 (d) $-\frac{1}{2}$

31. If $\alpha+\beta-\gamma=\pi$, then $\sin^2\alpha+\sin^2\beta-\sin^2\gamma$ is equal to

(a) $2\sin\alpha\sin\beta\cos\gamma$
(b) $2\cos\alpha\cos\beta\cos\gamma$
(c) $2\sin\alpha\sin\beta\sin\gamma$
(d) None of the above

32. The value of $\frac{\cos 12°-\sin 12°}{\cos 12°+\sin 12°}+\frac{\sin 147°}{\cos 147°}$ is equal to

(a) 1 (b) -1
(c) 0 (d) None of these

MCQs 2 Marks Questions

33. If $x=y\cos\frac{2\pi}{3}=z\cos\frac{4\pi}{3}$, then $xy+yz+zx$ is equal to

(a) -1 (b) 0 (c) 1 (d) 2

34. The value of k for which $(\cos x+\sin x)^2+k\sin x\cos x-1=0$ is an identity, is

(a) -1 (b) -2 (c) 0 (d) 1

35. The value of $\frac{1}{\sin 10°}-\frac{\sqrt{3}}{\cos 10°}$ is

(a) 0 (b) 1 (c) 2 (d) 4

36. If $\frac{\sin x}{\sin y}=\frac{1}{2}$, $\frac{\cos x}{\cos y}=\frac{3}{2}$, where $x,y\in\left(0,\frac{\pi}{2}\right)$, then the value of $\tan(x+y)$ is equal to

(a) $\sqrt{13}$ (b) $\sqrt{14}$ (c) $\sqrt{17}$ (d) $\sqrt{15}$

37. If $\tan(A+B)=p$ and $\tan(A-B)=q$, then the value of $\tan 2A$ is

(a) $\frac{p+q}{p-q}$ (b) $\frac{p-q}{1+pq}$ (c) $\frac{1+pq}{1-p}$ (d) $\frac{p+q}{1-pq}$

38. $\sin 47°+\sin 61°-\sin 11°-\sin 25°$ is equal to

(a) $\sin 36°$ (b) $\sin 7°$ (c) $\cos 36°$ (d) $\cos 7°$

39. If $\tan x=\frac{a}{b}$, then $b\cos 2x+a\sin 2x$ is equal to

(a) a (b) b (c) ab (d) $\frac{b}{a}$

40. If $\tan x=\frac{b}{a}$, then find the value of $\sqrt{\frac{a+b}{a-b}}+\sqrt{\frac{a-b}{a+b}}$.

(a) $\frac{2\cos x}{\sqrt{\cos 2x}}$ (b) $\frac{\cos x}{\sqrt{\cos 2x}}$
(c) $\frac{2\cos 2x}{\sqrt{\cos x}}$ (d) None of these

41. If $(a-b)\sin(\theta+\phi)=(a+b)\sin(\theta-\phi)$ and $a\tan\frac{\theta}{2}-b\tan\frac{\phi}{2}=c$, then the value of $\sin\phi$ is equal to

(a) $\dfrac{2ab}{a^2 - b^2 - c^2}$

(b) $\dfrac{2bc}{a^2 - b^2 - c^2}$

(c) $\dfrac{2bc}{a^2 - b^2 + c^2}$

(d) $\dfrac{2ab}{a^2 - b^2 + c^2}$

42. **Assertion** (A) The maximum value of $\sin\theta + \cos\theta$ is 2.

Reason (R) The maximum value of $\sin\theta$ is 1 and that of $\cos\theta$ is also 1.

(a) A and R both are true and R is the correct explanation of A
(b) A and R both are true but R is not the correct explanation of A
(c) A is true but R is false
(d) A is false but R is true

43. **Assertion** (A) The value of $\tan 6° \tan 42° \tan 66° \tan 78°$ is 1.

Reason (R)

$\tan\theta \tan(60° - \theta) \tan(60° + \theta) = \tan 3\theta$

(a) A and R both are true and R is the correct explanation of A
(b) A and R both are true but R is not the correct explanation of A
(c) A is true but R is false
(d) A is false but R is true

44. Consider the following statements

Statement I $\left(1 + \cos\dfrac{\pi}{8}\right)\left(1 + \cos\dfrac{3\pi}{8}\right)\left(1 + \cos\dfrac{5\pi}{8}\right)\left(1 + \cos\dfrac{7\pi}{8}\right) = \dfrac{1}{8}$

Statement II $\sin^2\theta = \dfrac{1}{2}(1 - \cos 2\theta)$

Choose the correct option.

(a) Statement I is true; Statement II is true; Statement II is a correct explanation for Statement I
(b) Statement I is true; Statement II is true; Statement II is not a correct explanation for Statement I
(c) Statement I is true; Statement II is false
(d) Statement I is false; Statement II is true

Directions (Q.Nos. 45-47) *Read the information carefully answer the next three questions.*

If $A = x\cos\theta - y\sin\theta$

and $B = x\sin\theta + y\cos\theta$ and

$A^2 + 4AB + B^2 = px^2 + qy^2, 0 \le \theta \le \dfrac{\pi}{2}$.

45. The value of $\cos 2\theta$ is

(a) 2 (b) 1 (c) 0 (d) −1

46. The value of p is

(a) 4 (b) 3 (c) 2 (d) 1

47. The value of q is

(a) −1 (b) 0 (c) 1 (d) 2

Darken your choice with HB Pencil

1.	ⓐ ⓑ ⓒ ⓓ	9.	ⓐ ⓑ ⓒ ⓓ	17.	ⓐ ⓑ ⓒ ⓓ	25.	ⓐ ⓑ ⓒ ⓓ	33.	ⓐ ⓑ ⓒ ⓓ	41.	ⓐ ⓑ ⓒ ⓓ
2.	ⓐ ⓑ ⓒ ⓓ	10.	ⓐ ⓑ ⓒ ⓓ	18.	ⓐ ⓑ ⓒ ⓓ	26.	ⓐ ⓑ ⓒ ⓓ	34.	ⓐ ⓑ ⓒ ⓓ	42.	ⓐ ⓑ ⓒ ⓓ
3.	ⓐ ⓑ ⓒ ⓓ	11.	ⓐ ⓑ ⓒ ⓓ	19.	ⓐ ⓑ ⓒ ⓓ	27.	ⓐ ⓑ ⓒ ⓓ	35.	ⓐ ⓑ ⓒ ⓓ	43.	ⓐ ⓑ ⓒ ⓓ
4.	ⓐ ⓑ ⓒ ⓓ	12.	ⓐ ⓑ ⓒ ⓓ	20.	ⓐ ⓑ ⓒ ⓓ	28.	ⓐ ⓑ ⓒ ⓓ	36.	ⓐ ⓑ ⓒ ⓓ	45.	ⓐ ⓑ ⓒ ⓓ
5.	ⓐ ⓑ ⓒ ⓓ	13.	ⓐ ⓑ ⓒ ⓓ	21.	ⓐ ⓑ ⓒ ⓓ	29.	ⓐ ⓑ ⓒ ⓓ	37.	ⓐ ⓑ ⓒ ⓓ	46.	ⓐ ⓑ ⓒ ⓓ
6.	ⓐ ⓑ ⓒ ⓓ	14.	ⓐ ⓑ ⓒ ⓓ	22.	ⓐ ⓑ ⓒ ⓓ	30.	ⓐ ⓑ ⓒ ⓓ	38.	ⓐ ⓑ ⓒ ⓓ	47.	ⓐ ⓑ ⓒ ⓓ
7.	ⓐ ⓑ ⓒ ⓓ	15.	ⓐ ⓑ ⓒ ⓓ	23.	ⓐ ⓑ ⓒ ⓓ	31.	ⓐ ⓑ ⓒ ⓓ	39.	ⓐ ⓑ ⓒ ⓓ		
8.	ⓐ ⓑ ⓒ ⓓ	16.	ⓐ ⓑ ⓒ ⓓ	24.	ⓐ ⓑ ⓒ ⓓ	32.	ⓐ ⓑ ⓒ ⓓ	40.	ⓐ ⓑ ⓒ ⓓ		

Chapter 04

Complex Numbers

MCQs 1 Mark Questions

1. Number of integral values of n for which the quantity $(n+i)^4$, where $i^2 = -1$ is an integer, is

(a) 1 (b) 2
(c) 3 (d) 4

2. If $a^2+b^2=1$, then $\frac{1+a+ib}{1+a-ib}$ is equal to

(a) 1 (b) 2 (c) $b+ia$ (d) $a+ib$

3. The conjugate of a complex number is $\frac{1}{i-1}$. Then, the complex number is

(a) $\frac{1}{i-1}$ (b) $\frac{-1}{i-1}$ (c) $\frac{1}{i+1}$ (d) $\frac{-1}{i+1}$

4. If $\text{Re}(z^2)=0$, then locus of z is

(a) parabola
(b) pair of lines
(c) pair of perpendicular lines
(d) circle

5. The locus of the point $z=x+iy$ satisfying the equation $\left|\frac{z-1}{z+1}\right|=1$ is given by

(a) $x=0$ (b) $y=0$
(c) $x=y$ (d) $x=-y$

6. If $f(z)=\frac{7-z}{1-z^2}$, where $z=1+2i$, then $|f(z)|$ is

(a) $\frac{|z|}{2}$ (b) $|z|$
(c) $2|z|$ (d) None of these

7. The complex number $\frac{2^n}{(1+i)^{2n}}+\frac{(1+i)^{2n}}{2^n}, n \in I$, is equal to

(a) 0 (b) 2
(c) $\{1+(-1)^n\}\cdot i^n$ (d) None of these

8. The imaginary part of $(3+2\sqrt{-54})^{1/2}-(3-2\sqrt{-54})^{1/2}$ can be

(a) $-\sqrt{6}$ (b) $-2\sqrt{6}$ (c) 6 (d) $\sqrt{6}$

9. Real part of $\frac{1}{1-\cos\theta+i\sin\theta}$ is

(a) $-\frac{1}{2}$ (b) $\frac{1}{2}$ (c) $\frac{1}{2}\tan\frac{\theta}{2}$ (d) 2

10. If $z(1+a)=b+ic$ and $a^2+b^2+c^2=1$, then $\frac{1+iz}{1-iz}$ is equal to

(a) $\frac{a+ib}{1+c}$ (b) $\frac{b-ic}{1+a}$
(c) $\frac{a+ic}{1+b}$ (d) None of these

11. Given, $z = \frac{q+ir}{1+p}$, then $\frac{p+iq}{1+r} = \frac{1+iz}{1-iz}$, if

(a) $p^2+q^2+r^2=1$

(b) $p^2+q^2+r^2=2$

(c) $p^2+q^2-r^2=1$

(d) None of the above

12. The complex number $z=1+i$ represented by the point P in argand plane and OP is rotated an angle of $\pi/2$ in counter clockwise direction, then the resulting complex number is

(a) $\bar{z}$ (b) $-z$

(c) $-\bar{z}$ (d) z

13. If $a+ib = \frac{3}{2+\cos\theta + i\sin\theta}$, then the value of $(a-3)(a-1)+b^2$ is equal to

(a) 1 (b) 2 (c) 0 (d) -1

14. Let z be a complex number such that $\left|\frac{z-2i}{z+i}\right| = 2, z \neq -i$, then z lies on the circle of radius 2 and centre

(a) (2, 0) (b) (0, 0)

(c) (0, 2) (d) (0, –2)

15. If $\left|z - \frac{4}{z}\right| = 2$, then the maximum value of $|z|$ is equal to

(a) $\sqrt{3}+1$ (b) $\sqrt{5}+1$

(c) 2 (d) $2+\sqrt{2}$

16. The equation $|z+i|-|z-i| = R$ represents a hyperbola, if

(a) $-3 < R < 2$ (b) $R > 2$

(c) $0 < R < 2$ (d) $R > 4$

17. If $x = p+q$, $y = p\omega + q\omega^2$ and $z = p\omega^2 + q\omega$, where ω is a complex cube root of unity, then xyz is equal to

(a) $p^2 - pq + q^2$ (b) $1+p^3+q^3$

(c) $p^3 - q^3$ (d) $p^3 + q^3$

18. If $\frac{z-1}{z+1}$ is a purely imaginary number $(z \neq -1)$, then the value of $|z|$ is

(a) –1 (b) 1 (c) 2 (d) –2

19. The complex numbers $\sin x + i\cos 2x$ and $\cos x - i\sin 2x$ are conjugate to each other for

(a) $x = n\pi$ (b) $x = \left(n+\frac{1}{2}\right)\pi$

(c) $x = 0$ (d) no value of x

20. If $z + \sqrt{2}|z+1| + i = 0$, then z equals

(a) $2+i$ (b) $-2+i$

(c) $-\frac{1}{2}+i$ (d) $-2-i$

21. The complex numbers z_1 and z_2 are such that $z_1 \neq z_2$ and $|z_1| = |z_2|$. If z_1 has positive real part and z_2 has negative imaginary part, then $\left(\frac{z_1+z_2}{z_1-z_2}\right)$ may be

(a) zero

(b) real and positive

(c) real and negative

(d) purely imaginary

22. Let a complex number $z, |z| \neq 1$, satisfy $\log_{\frac{1}{\sqrt{2}}}\left(\frac{|z|+11}{(|z|-1)^2}\right) \leq 2$. Then, the largest value of $|z|$ is equal to

(a) 8 (b) 7

(c) 6 (d) 5

23. If $|z-2| = \min\{|z-1|, |z-5|\}$, where z is a complex number, then

(a) $\text{Re}(z) = \frac{3}{2}$

(b) $\text{Re}(z) = \frac{7}{2}$

(c) $\text{Re}(z) \in \left\{\frac{3}{2}, \frac{7}{2}\right\}$

(d) None of the above

24. If for the complex numbers z_1 and z_2 $|1-\bar{z}_1 z_2|^2 - |z_1 - z_2|^2 = k(1-|z_1|^2)$ $(1-|z_2|^2)$, then k is equal to

(a) 1 (b) −1
(c) 2 (d) 4

25. The region of the complex plane for which $\left|\dfrac{z-a}{z+\bar{a}}\right| = 1\,[\text{Re}(a) \neq 0]$, is

(a) X-axis
(b) Y-axis
(c) the straight line $x = a$
(d) None of the above

26. If $(a_1 + ib_1)(a_2 + ib_2) \ldots (a_n + ib_n) = A + iB$, then $(a_1^2 + b_1^2)(a_2^2 + b_2^2) \ldots (a_n^2 + b_n^2)$ is equal to

(a) 1 (b) $A^2 + B^2$
(c) $A + B$ (d) $\dfrac{1}{A^2} + \dfrac{1}{B^2}$

27. If $\tan^{-1}(\alpha + i\beta) = x + iy$, then x is equal to

(a) $\dfrac{1}{2}\tan^{-1}\left(\dfrac{2\alpha}{1-\alpha^2-\beta^2}\right)$

(b) $\dfrac{1}{2}\tan^{-1}\left(\dfrac{2\alpha}{1+\alpha^2+\beta^2}\right)$

(c) $\tan^{-1}\left(\dfrac{2\alpha}{1-\alpha^2-\beta^2}\right)$

(d) None of the above

28. If z_1, z_2 and z_3 are complex numbers such that

$$|z_1| = |z_2| = |z_3| = \left|\frac{1}{z_1} + \frac{1}{z_2} + \frac{1}{z_3}\right| = 1, \text{then}$$

$|z_1 + z_2 + z_3|$ is

(a) equal to 1 (b) less than 1
(c) greater than 3 (d) equal to 3

29. If $|z - i\text{Re}(z)| = |z - \text{Im}(z)|$ (where $i = \sqrt{-1}$), then z lies on

(a) Re $(z) = 2$
(b) Im $(z) = 2$
(c) Re (z) + Im $(z) = 0$
(d) None of the above

30. Let z be a complex number such that $|z| + z = 3 + i$, (where $i = \sqrt{-1}$). Then, $|z|$ is equal to

(a) $\dfrac{\sqrt{34}}{3}$ (b) $\dfrac{5}{3}$
(c) $\dfrac{\sqrt{41}}{4}$ (d) $\dfrac{5}{4}$

31. Let $z = x + iy$ be a non-zero complex number such that $z^2 = i|z|^2$, where $i = \sqrt{-1}$, then z lies on the

(a) line $y = -x$ (b) imaginary axis
(c) line $y = x$ (d) real axis

32. If a, b, c, p, q, r are six complex numbers, such that $\dfrac{p}{a} + \dfrac{q}{b} + \dfrac{r}{c} = 1 + i$ and $\dfrac{a}{p} + \dfrac{b}{q} + \dfrac{c}{r} = 0$, where $i = \sqrt{-1}$, then the value of $\dfrac{p^2}{a^2} + \dfrac{q^2}{b^2} + \dfrac{r^2}{c^2}$ is

(a) 0 (b) −1
(c) $2i$ (d) $-2i$

33. If $|z| = 1$, then $\left(\dfrac{1+z}{1+\bar{z}}\right)$ equals

(a) z (b) $\bar{z}$
(c) z^{-1} (d) None of these

34. For $x_1, x_2, y_1, y_2 \in R$. If $0 < x_1 < x_2, y_1 = y_2$ and $z_1 = x_1 + iy_1$, $z_2 = x_2 + i\,y_2$, (where $i = \sqrt{-1}$) and $z_3 = \dfrac{1}{2}(z_1 + z_2)$, then z_1, z_2 and z_3 satisfy

(a) $|z_1| = |z_2| = |z_3|$
(b) $|z_1| < |z_2| < |z_3|$
(c) $|z_1| > |z_2| > |z_3|$
(d) $|z_1| < |z_3| < |z_2|$

35. If the multiplicative inverse of a complex number is $(\sqrt{3}+4i)/19$, (where $i=\sqrt{-1}$), then the complex number itself is

(a) $\sqrt{3}-4i$ (b) $4+i\sqrt{3}$
(c) $\sqrt{3}+4i$ (d) $4-i\sqrt{3}$

36. If $z=x-iy$ and $z^{1/3}=p+iq$, then $\left(\frac{x}{p}+\frac{y}{q}\right)\Big/(p^2+q^2)$ is equal to

(a) 1 (b) –1 (c) 2 (d) –2

37. If $\left(\frac{1+i}{1-i}\right)^x=1$, then

(a) $x=4n$, where n is any positive integer
(b) $x=2n$, where n is any positive integer
(c) $x=4n+1$, where n is any positive integer
(d) $x=2n+1$, where n is any positive integer

38. If ω is a complex cube root of unity, then for positive integral value of n, the product of $\omega\cdot\omega^2\cdot\omega^3\ldots\ldots\omega^n$ will be

(a) $\frac{1-i\sqrt{3}}{2}$ (b) $-\frac{1-i\sqrt{3}}{2}$
(c) 1 (d) Both (b) and (c)

MCQs 2 Marks Questions

39. Let $\left(-2-\frac{1}{3}i\right)^3=\frac{x+iy}{27}$ $(i=\sqrt{-1})$, where x and y are real numbers, then $y-x$ is equal to

(a) 91 (b) 85 (c) – 85 (d) – 91

40. If $a>0$ and $z=\frac{(1+i)^2}{a-i}$ have magnitude $\sqrt{\frac{2}{5}}$, then $\bar{z}$ is equal to

(a) $\frac{1}{5}-\frac{3}{5}i$ (b) $-\frac{1}{5}-\frac{3}{5}i$
(c) $-\frac{1}{5}+\frac{3}{5}i$ (d) $-\frac{3}{5}-\frac{1}{5}i$

41. If $\frac{z-\alpha}{z+\alpha}$ $(\alpha\in R)$ is a purely imaginary number and $|z|=2$, then the value of α is

(a) $\sqrt{2}$ (b) $\frac{1}{2}$
(c) 1 (d) 2

42. For what value of x, for which $\frac{1+i\cos x}{1-2i\cos x}$ is a real number?

(a) $2n\pi+\frac{3\pi}{2}, n\in Z$ (b) $2n\pi\pm\frac{\pi}{2}, n\in Z$
(c) $2n\pi+\frac{\pi}{4}, n\in Z$ (d) $2n\pi-\frac{3\pi}{2}, n\in Z$

43. The minimum value of $|z|+|z-2|$ is

(a) 0 (b) 2 (c) 4 (d) 8

44. If $z\geq 5$, then the least value of $\left|z+\frac{2}{z}\right|$ is

(a) $\frac{23}{5}$ (b) $\frac{24}{5}$
(c) 5 (d) $\sqrt{5}$

45. If Re $(z^2)=0, |z|=2$, then

(a) $z=\mp\sqrt{2}\pm i\sqrt{2}$ (b) $z=\mp\sqrt{3}\pm i\sqrt{3}$
(c) $z=\mp\sqrt{3}\pm i\sqrt{2}$ (d) None of these

46. If $x=a+ib$ is a complex number such that $x^2=3+4i$ and $x^3=2+11i$, where $i=\sqrt{-1}$, then $(a+b)$ is equal to

(a) 2 (b) 3 (c) 4 (d) 5

47. For all complex numbers z_1, z_2 satisfying $|z_1|=12$ and $|z_2-3-4i|=5$, the minimum value of $|z_1-z_2|$ is

(a) 0 (b) 2 (c) 7 (d) 17

48. Let $z \in C$ with Im $(z) = 10$ and it satisfies $\frac{2z-n}{2z-n} = 2i - 1$ for some natural number n, then

(a) $n = 20$ and $\text{Re}(z) = -10$
(b) $n = 40$ and $\text{Re}(z) = 10$
(c) $n = 40$ and $\text{Re}(z) = -10$
(d) $n = 20$ and $\text{Re}(z) = 10$

49. Assertion (A) If $z_1, z_2, z_3, \ldots, z_n$ are unimodular complex number, then
$|z_1 + z_2 + z_3 + \ldots + z_n| = \left|\frac{1}{z_1} + \frac{1}{z_2} + \ldots + \frac{1}{z_n}\right|$

Reason (R) For any complex number z, $z\bar{z} = |z|^2$.

(a) A and R both are true and R is the correct explanation of A
(b) A and R both are true but R is not the correct explanation of A
(c) A is true but R is false
(d) a is false but R is true

50. Assertion (A) If $\frac{5z_2}{11z_1}$ is purely imaginary, then $\left|\frac{2z_1 + 3z_2}{2z_1 - 3z_2}\right| = 1$

Reason (R) $|z| = |\bar{z}|$
i.e., $|a + ib| = |a - ib|, i = \sqrt{-1}$

(a) A and R both are true and R is the correct explanation of A
(b) A and R both are true but R is not the correct explanation of A
(c) A is true but R is false
(d) A is false but R is true

Directions (Q.Nos. 51-53) *Read the information carefully and answer next three questions.*

Let α, β, γ are three real numbers such that $\alpha^2 + \beta^2 + \gamma^2 - \gamma = 0$ and $z = \frac{\alpha + i\beta}{1 - \gamma}$.

51. $|z|^2$ is equal to

(a) γ (b) $1 - \gamma$
(c) $\frac{\gamma}{1-\gamma}$ (d) $\frac{1-\gamma}{\gamma}$

52. α is equal to

(a) $\frac{z + \bar{z}}{2(1 + |\bar{z}|^2)}$ (b) $\frac{(\bar{z} - z)i}{2(1 + |z|)^2}$
(c) $\frac{(z - \bar{z})i}{2(1 + |z|^2)}$ (d) None of these

53. β is equal to

(a) $\frac{z - \bar{z}}{2(1 + |z|^2)}$ (b) $\frac{(\bar{z} - z)i}{2(1 + |z|^2)}$
(c) $\frac{2}{2(1 + |z|^2)}$ (d) $\frac{2z}{1 + |z|^2}$

Darken your choice with HB Pencil

1.	ⓐ ⓑ ⓒ ⓓ	11.	ⓐ ⓑ ⓒ ⓓ	21.	ⓐ ⓑ ⓒ ⓓ	31.	ⓐ ⓑ ⓒ ⓓ	41.	ⓐ ⓑ ⓒ ⓓ	51.	ⓐ ⓑ ⓒ ⓓ
2.	ⓐ ⓑ ⓒ ⓓ	12.	ⓐ ⓑ ⓒ ⓓ	22.	ⓐ ⓑ ⓒ ⓓ	32.	ⓐ ⓑ ⓒ ⓓ	42.	ⓐ ⓑ ⓒ ⓓ	52.	ⓐ ⓑ ⓒ ⓓ
3.	ⓐ ⓑ ⓒ ⓓ	13.	ⓐ ⓑ ⓒ ⓓ	23.	ⓐ ⓑ ⓒ ⓓ	33.	ⓐ ⓑ ⓒ ⓓ	43.	ⓐ ⓑ ⓒ ⓓ	53.	ⓐ ⓑ ⓒ ⓓ
4.	ⓐ ⓑ ⓒ ⓓ	14.	ⓐ ⓑ ⓒ ⓓ	24.	ⓐ ⓑ ⓒ ⓓ	34.	ⓐ ⓑ ⓒ ⓓ	44.	ⓐ ⓑ ⓒ ⓓ		
5.	ⓐ ⓑ ⓒ ⓓ	15.	ⓐ ⓑ ⓒ ⓓ	25.	ⓐ ⓑ ⓒ ⓓ	35.	ⓐ ⓑ ⓒ ⓓ	45.	ⓐ ⓑ ⓒ ⓓ		
6.	ⓐ ⓑ ⓒ ⓓ	16.	ⓐ ⓑ ⓒ ⓓ	26.	ⓐ ⓑ ⓒ ⓓ	36.	ⓐ ⓑ ⓒ ⓓ	46.	ⓐ ⓑ ⓒ ⓓ		
7.	ⓐ ⓑ ⓒ ⓓ	17.	ⓐ ⓑ ⓒ ⓓ	27.	ⓐ ⓑ ⓒ ⓓ	37.	ⓐ ⓑ ⓒ ⓓ	47.	ⓐ ⓑ ⓒ ⓓ		
8.	ⓐ ⓑ ⓒ ⓓ	18.	ⓐ ⓑ ⓒ ⓓ	28.	ⓐ ⓑ ⓒ ⓓ	38.	ⓐ ⓑ ⓒ ⓓ	48.	ⓐ ⓑ ⓒ ⓓ		
9.	ⓐ ⓑ ⓒ ⓓ	19.	ⓐ ⓑ ⓒ ⓓ	29.	ⓐ ⓑ ⓒ ⓓ	39.	ⓐ ⓑ ⓒ ⓓ	49.	ⓐ ⓑ ⓒ ⓓ		
10.	ⓐ ⓑ ⓒ ⓓ	20.	ⓐ ⓑ ⓒ ⓓ	30.	ⓐ ⓑ ⓒ ⓓ	40.	ⓐ ⓑ ⓒ ⓓ	50.	ⓐ ⓑ ⓒ ⓓ		

Chapter 05

Linear Inequalities

MCQs 1 Mark Questions

1. The set of real values of x for which $\log_{0.5}\frac{x+2}{x}\le 1$ is
(a) $(-\infty, -2)$ (b) $(0, \infty)$
(c) $(-\infty, -2)\cup(0, \infty)$ (d) None of the above

2. The solution set for x of the inequality $\frac{2p+x}{3}\le\frac{4px-1}{2}$ is $x\ge\frac{3}{4}$, the value of the parameter p is
(a) $\frac{7}{10}$ (b) $\frac{9}{10}$
(c) $\frac{9}{11}$ (d) None of these

3. If x satisfies the inequalities $x+7<2x+3$ and $2x+4<5x+3$, then x lies in the interval
(a) $(-\infty, 3)$ (b) $(1, 3)$ (c) $(4, \infty)$ (d) $(-\infty, -1)$

4. If $|2x+3|<|x+6|$, then x belongs to
(a) $(-3, 3)$ (b) $\left(-6, \frac{-3}{2}\right)$
(c) ϕ (d) None of these

5. The set of real values of x satisfying $|x+1|\le 3$ and $|x+1|\ge 1$ is
(a) $[-4, 2]$ (b) $[2, \infty)$
(c) $[-4, -2]$ (d) $[-4, -2]\cup[0, 2]$

6. Solve for x : $\frac{|x+1|+x}{x-1}>1$
(a) ϕ (b) $(1, \infty)$
(c) $(0, 1)$ (d) $\{1\}$

7. The solution set of the inequality $|9^x-3^{x+1}-15|<2\cdot 9^x-3^x$ is
(a) $(-\infty, 1)$ (b) $(1, \infty)$
(c) $(-\infty, 1]$ (d) None of these

8. IQ of a person is given by the formula $IQ=\frac{MA}{CA}\times 100$, where MA = Mental age CA = Chronological age. If $100\le IQ\le 160$ for a group of 15 yr children, then the range of their mental age is
(a) $10\le MA\le 12$ (b) $20\le MA\le 24$
(c) $15\le MA\le 24$ (d) $100\le MA\le 200$

9. Consider the following statements

Statement I If $\frac{|x-2|}{x-2}\ge 0$, then $x\in(2, \infty)$.

Statement II x and b are real numbers. If $b>0$ and $|x|>b$, then $x\in(-b, \infty)$.

Choose the correct option.
(a) Statement I is true
(b) Statement II is true
(c) Both statements are true
(d) Both statements are false

10. The number of pairs of consecutive odd natural numbers both of which are larger than 15 such that their sum is less than 50 is

(a) 4 (b) 8 (c) 2 (d) 6

11. The range of values of y that satisfy the following system of equations is

$$-19 \le 2y - 9 \le -3, -22 \le 5y + 13 \le 3$$

and $-17 \le 3y + 10 \le -2$

(a) $[-5, -4]$ (b) $(-5, -3)$
(c) $[-5, -3)$ (d) $(-5, -4)$

12. The cost and revenue functions of a product are given by $C(x) = 5x + 80$ and $R(x) = 8x + 50$ respectively, where x is the number of items produced by the manufacturer. How many items the manufacturer must sell to realize some profit?

(a) More than 10
(b) More than 20
(c) More than 30
(d) More than or equal to 10

13. If $\log_{0.3}(x-1) < \log_{0.09}(x-1)$, then x lies in the interval

(a) $(2, \infty)$ (b) $(1, 2)$
(c) $(-2, -1)$ (d) None of these

14. The set of all real x satisfying the inequality $\dfrac{3-|x|}{4-|x|} > 0$

(a) $[-3, 3] \cup (-\infty, -4) \cup (4, \infty)$
(b) $(-\infty, -4) \cup (4, \infty)$
(c) $(-\infty, -3) \cup (4, \infty)$
(d) $(-\infty, -3) \cup (3, \infty)$
(e) $[-3, 3] \cup (4, \infty)$

15. The set of admissible values of x such that $\dfrac{2x+3}{2x-9} < 0$ is

(a) $\left(-\infty, -\dfrac{3}{2}\right) \cup \left(\dfrac{9}{2}, \infty\right)$
(b) $(-\infty, 0) \cup \left(\dfrac{9}{2}, \infty\right)$
(c) $\left(-\dfrac{3}{2}, 0\right)$ (d) $\left(-\dfrac{3}{2}, \dfrac{9}{2}\right)$

16. For $\dfrac{|x-1|}{x+2} < 1$, x lies in the interval

(a) $(-\infty, -2) \cup \left(-\dfrac{1}{2}, -\infty\right)$
(b) $(-\infty, 1) \cup [2, 3]$
(c) $(-\infty, -4)$ (d) $\left[-\dfrac{1}{2}, 1\right]$

17. The set of real x satisfying the inequality $\dfrac{5-2x}{3} \le \dfrac{x}{6} - 5$ is

(a) $(-\infty, 8)$ (b) $(8, \infty)$
(c) $[8, \infty)$ (d) $(-\infty, 8]$

18. Which of the following is the solution set of the inequality $\dfrac{x}{4} < \dfrac{(5x-2)}{3} - \dfrac{(7x-3)}{5}$?

(a) $(4, \infty)$ (b) $(-\infty, 4)$
(c) $[4, \infty)$ (d) $(-\infty, 4]$

19. If $5(2x-7) - 3(2x+3) \le 0$ and $2x + 19 \le 6x + 47$, then

(a) $x \in (-7, 11)$
(b) the solution on the number line is represented by

(c) Both (a) and (b)
(d) None of the above

MCQs 2 Marks Questions

20. Assertion (A) $|3x - 5| > 9$

$\Rightarrow \quad x \in \left(-\infty, -\dfrac{4}{3}\right) \cup \left(\dfrac{14}{3}, \infty\right)$.

Reason (R) The region containing all the solutions of an inequality is called the solution region.

(a) A and R both are true and R is the correct explanation of A
(b) A and R both are true but R is not the correct explanation of A
(c) A is true but R is false
(d) A is false but R is true

21. The range of x where $||x-3|-4|>3$ is
(a) $(-\infty, 4)$ (b) $(2, \infty)$
(c) $(-4, 2)$
(d) $(-\infty, -4) \cup (2, 4) \cup (10, \infty)$

22. Number of integral values of x satisfying the inequation $\frac{x}{x+2} \le \frac{1}{|x|}$ is
(a) 1 (b) 2 (c) 3 (d) 4

23. Which of the following is not the solution of $\frac{|x+3|+x}{x+2} > 1$?
(a) $(-5, -2)$ (b) $(-5, -1)$
(c) $(-1, \infty)$ (d) None of these

24. For the inequality, $0 < |3x+1| < \frac{1}{3}$ the solution is $(K_1, K_2) - \{+K_3\}$, then value of $K_1 + K_2 - K_3$ is
(a) $-\frac{1}{3}$ (b) $-\frac{2}{3}$ (c) $-\frac{2}{9}$ (d) $\frac{1}{3}$

25. The range of x satisfying the following inequality is

$$\log_2\{\log_3(4x+1)\} > \log_2\{\log_3(2x+3)\}$$

(a) $(-1, \infty)$ (b) $\left(-\frac{3}{2}, 0\right)$
(c) $\left(-\frac{1}{4}, \infty\right)$ (d) $(1, \infty)$

26. A technician measures an electric current which is 0.036 A with a possible error of ± 0.002 A. The inequality in the form of i, where i is the current, is
(a) $|i - 0.038| \le 0.034$
(b) $|i - 0.036| \le 0.002$
(c) $|i - 0.036| \le 0.02$
(d) $|i - 0.038| \le 0.002$

27. The solution set of the inequality

$$\log_{\frac{x+4}{2}}\left(\log_2 \frac{2x-1}{3+x}\right) < 0 \text{ is}$$

(a) $\left(\frac{1}{2}, \infty\right)$ (b) $(-\infty, -3)$
(c) $(-4, -3)$ (d) $(-4, -3) \cup \left(\frac{1}{2}, \infty\right)$

28. A manufacturer has 600 L of 30% solution of acid. The range of quantity of a 30% acid solution that must be added to it so that the acid content in the resulting mixture will be more than 15% but less than 18% is
(a) (120, 400) (b) (200, 300)
(c) (120, 450) (d) (120, 300)

29. If $a, b, c > 0$, then the minimum value of $\frac{a}{b+c} + \frac{b}{c+a} + \frac{c}{a+b}$ is
(a) 1 (b) $\frac{3}{2}$ (c) 2 (d) $\frac{5}{2}$

30. The number of positive integers satisfying the inequality ${}^{n+1}C_{n-2} - {}^{n+1}C_{n-1} \le 50$ is
(a) 9 (b) 8 (c) 7 (d) 6

Darken your choice with HB Pencil

1. ⓐ ⓑ ⓒ ⓓ	6. ⓐ ⓑ ⓒ ⓓ	11. ⓐ ⓑ ⓒ ⓓ	16. ⓐ ⓑ ⓒ ⓓ	21. ⓐ ⓑ ⓒ ⓓ	26. ⓐ ⓑ ⓒ ⓓ
2. ⓐ ⓑ ⓒ ⓓ	7. ⓐ ⓑ ⓒ ⓓ	12. ⓐ ⓑ ⓒ ⓓ	17. ⓐ ⓑ ⓒ ⓓ	22. ⓐ ⓑ ⓒ ⓓ	27. ⓐ ⓑ ⓒ ⓓ
3. ⓐ ⓑ ⓒ ⓓ	8. ⓐ ⓑ ⓒ ⓓ	13. ⓐ ⓑ ⓒ ⓓ	18. ⓐ ⓑ ⓒ ⓓ	23. ⓐ ⓑ ⓒ ⓓ	28. ⓐ ⓑ ⓒ ⓓ
4. ⓐ ⓑ ⓒ ⓓ	9. ⓐ ⓑ ⓒ ⓓ	14. ⓐ ⓑ ⓒ ⓓ	19. ⓐ ⓑ ⓒ ⓓ	24. ⓐ ⓑ ⓒ ⓓ	29. ⓐ ⓑ ⓒ ⓓ
5. ⓐ ⓑ ⓒ ⓓ	10. ⓐ ⓑ ⓒ ⓓ	15. ⓐ ⓑ ⓒ ⓓ	20. ⓐ ⓑ ⓒ ⓓ	25. ⓐ ⓑ ⓒ ⓓ	30. ⓐ ⓑ ⓒ ⓓ

Chapter 06

Permutations & Combinations

MCQs 1 Mark Questions

1. A man has 3 servants. The number of ways in which he can send invitation cards to 8 of his friends through the servants is
(a) 3^8 (b) 8^3
(c) $\frac{8!}{3!}$ (d) ${}^8P_3$

2. The value of $1\cdot3\cdot5\cdot\ldots\cdot(2n-1)2^n$ is equal to
(a) $\frac{(2n)!}{n}$ (b) $\frac{(2n)!}{n!}$
(c) $\frac{n!}{(2n)!}$ (d) $2n$

3. The value of $\sum_{r=1}^{n} r\cdot r!$ is equal to
(a) $(n+1)!+1$ (b) $(n-1)!+1$
(c) $(n+1)!-1$ (d) $(n+1)!$

4. The number of ways of permuting the letters of the word 'DELHI' so that neither 'D' is the first letter nor 'L' is the last letter is
(a) 36 (b) 78
(c) 42 (d) 114

5. If ${}^9P_5+5\cdot{}^9P_4={}^{10}P_r$, then r is equal to
(a) 3 (b) 4
(c) 5 (d) 6

6. 10 articles to be placed in 10 boxes one in each box, 5 of them are too big for four of the boxes. The number of arrangements is
(a) 10! (b) $5!\times4!$
(c) $6!\times5!$ (d) ${}^6P_4\times5!$

7. The number of words that can be formed using all the letters of the word 'KANPUR' when the vowels occupy even places is
(a) 36 (b) 24
(c) 48 (d) 144

8. The letter of the word 'KANPUR' are taken four at a time and arranged in all possible ways. The number of arrangements which begin with 'K' and ends with 'R' is
(a) 20 (b) 18
(c) 14 (d) 12

9. Find the number of positive integers greater than 6000 and less than 7000 which are divisible by 5, provided that no digit is to be repeated.
(a) 111 (b) 112
(c) 113 (d) None of these

10. The number of seven-digit integers with sum of the digits equal to 10 and formed by using the digits 1, 2 and 3 only is
(a) 77 (b) 35 (c) 42 (d) 82

11. The number of arrangements for three different rings can be worn by 4 fingers with atmost one ring in each of the fingers is

(a) 12 (b) 24 (c) 36 (d) 64

12. The number of ways in which 4 men, 3 boys, 2 girls be seated in a row so that the men, the boys and the women are not separated is

(a) $(4!)(3!)(2!)$
(b) $(4!)^2(3!)(2!)$
(c) $4!(3!)^2(2!)$
(d) $(4!)(3!)(2!)^2$

13. The family of 3 brothers and 4 sisters is to be arranged in a row. The number of ways in which they can be arranged, if all the sisters have to sit together is

(a) 720 (b) 144
(c) $(4!)^2$ (d) None of these

14. If a denotes the number of permutations of $x+2$ things taken all at a time, b denotes the number of permutations of x things taken 11 at a time and c is the number of permutations of $x-11$ things taken all at a time such that $a = 182bc$, then the value of x is

(a) 15 (b) 12
(c) 10 (d) 18

15. There are 5 white and 5 black balls marked with 1, 2, 3 4 and 5. The number of ways in which we can arrange these balls in a row such that neighbouring balls are of different colours is

(a) $5! \times 4!$ (b) $10!$
(c) $(5!)^2$ (d) $2 \times (5!)^2$

16. The number of ways in which the ten candidates A, B, C, D, E, F, G, H, I, J can be ranked, if 'A' is always above 'B' is

(a) $9!$ (b) $10!$
(c) $9! \times 2!$ (d) $\frac{10!}{2}$

17. The number of four-digit odd numbers that can be formed with 1, 2, 3, 4, 5, 6, 7, 8, 9 without repetition is

(a) 1680 (b) 1344
(c) 840 (d) 1050

18. The letters of the word 'DANGER' are arranged in all possible ways. The number of arrangements in which there are two letters between 'R' and 'D' is

(a) 720 (b) 144
(c) 120 (d) 24

19. The number of 4-digit number which are not divisible by 5 and which contains 4 odd digits is

(a) 96 (b) 120
(c) 24 (d) 32

20. A five-digit number is divisible by 6 is to be formed by using 0, 1, 2, 3, 4, 5 without repetition. The number of ways in which this can be done is

(a) 60 (b) 48
(c) 108 (d) 216

21. In the word 'ENGINEERING', if all E's are not together and N's come together, then number of permutations is

(a) $\frac{9!}{2!2!} - \frac{7!}{2!2!}$ (b) $\frac{9!}{3!2!} - \frac{7!}{2!2!}$

(c) $\frac{9!}{3!2!2!} - \frac{7!}{2!2!2!}$ (d) $\frac{9!}{3!2!2!} - \frac{7!}{2!2!}$

22. A man has invited 20 persons in a party. The number of arrangements in which they can be seated at a circular table with two particular persons seated on either side of the host is

(a) 18! 2! (b) 20! 2!
(c) 19! 2! (d) 18! 3!

23. The number of ways in which 6 men, 6 women and 10 children can sit around a circular table so that the children are always together is

(a) 5! 5! 10! (b) $13! \times 10!$
(c) $(12!)^2$ (d) $12! \times 10!$

24. There are 10 lamps in a room. Each one of them can be switched on independently. The number of ways in which the hall can be illuminated is

(a) 1024 (b) 1023
(c) $2^9 - 1$ (d) None of these

25. The number of different products that can be formed with 5 prime numbers is

(a) 23 (b) 24 (c) 25 (d) 26

26. Let A and B be the two sets containing 2 elements and 4 elements, respectively. The number of subsets of $A \times B$ having 3 or more elements is

(a) 256 (b) 220
(c) 219 (d) 211

27. The number of ways of distributing 12 identical balls in 3 distinct boxes so that none of the boxes is empty is

(a) ${}^{12}C_3$ (b) 55
(c) $12! \times 3!$ (d) $\frac{12!}{3!}$

28. The number of non-trivial divisors of 2160 is

(a) 36 (b) 37 (c) 38 (d) 40

29. If a polygon has 44 diagonals, then the number of its sides are

(a) 11 (b) 7
(c) 8 (d) None of these

30. If m parallel lines in a plane are intersected by n parallel lines the number of parallelograms formed is

(a) $\frac{m!n!}{(2!)^2}$

(b) $\frac{m!n!}{(m-2)!(n-2)!}$

(c) $\frac{m!n!}{(2!)^2 (m-2)!(n-2)!}$

(d) $\frac{(m+n)!}{(m+n-2)!2!}$

31. The number of ways in four numbers can be selected from 1 to 30 so as to exclude every selection of four consecutive numbers is

(a) 27378 (b) 27405
(c) 27399 (d) None of these

32. A committee of 5 men and 3 women is to be formed out of 7 men and 6 women, if two particular women are not to be together in the committee, the number of committees formed is

(a) 420 (b) 5040
(c) 336 (d) 216

33. A team of 9 players to be selected from the groups consisting 6 and 8 players, respectively. The number of ways to select team such that each selection contains atleast 4 players from the first group is

(a) 1400 (b) 1412
(c) 1414 (d) 1316

34. Out of 7 men and 4 women a committee of 5 is to be formed. The number of ways in which this can be done.

I. So, as to include exactly 2 women is 210.

II. So, as to include atleast 2 women is 301.

Which of the above statement is true?

(a) Only I (b) Only II
(c) Both I and II (d) Neither I nor II

MCQs 2 Marks Questions

35. The number of 4-digit number that can be formed from the digits 0, 1, 2, 3, 4, 5, 6, 7 without repetition so that each number contain digit 1 is

(a) 1225 (b) 1252
(c) 1522 (d) 750

36. The number of arrangements of the letter of the word 'SALOON', if the two O's do not occur together is

(a) 360 (b) 120
(c) 240 (d) 300

37. The rank of the word 'KRISHNA' when arranged in dictionary is

(a) 2709 (b) 2710
(c) 2711 (d) 2700

38. In a circus, there are ten cages for accomodating ten animals. Out of these four cages are so small that five out of ten animals cannot enter into them. In how many ways will it possible to accomodate ten animals in these ten cages?

(a) 66400 (b) 86400
(c) 96400 (d) None of these

39. How many different words can be formed by jumbling the letters in the word 'MISSISSIPPI' in which no two 'S' are adjacent?

(a) $7 \cdot {}^6C_4 \cdot {}^8C_4$ (b) $8 \cdot {}^6C_4 \cdot {}^7C_4$
(c) $6 \cdot 7 \cdot {}^8C_4$ (d) $6 \cdot 8 \cdot {}^7C_4$

40. There are 3 sections in a question paper and each section contains 5 questions. A candidate has to answer total of 5 questions, choosing atleast one question from each section. Then, the number of ways, in which candidate can choose the questions, is

(a) 3000 (b) 2255 (c) 1500 (d) 2250

41. In a chess tournament, participants were to play one game with another. Two chess players fell ill, having played 3 games each. If the total number of games played is 84, the number of participants in the beginning was

(a) 15 (b) 13 (c) 11 (d) 9

42. Given, six line segments of lengths 2, 3, 4, 5, 6, 7 units number of triangles that can be formed by these lines is

(a) 13 (b) 14 (c) 15 (d) 16

43. There are 10 lines lies in a plane, no two of which are parallel and no three are concurrent. The points of intersection are joined, then the number of fresh lines formed are

(a) 630 (b) 615
(c) 730 (d) 600

44. Which of the following statements is correct?

I. The number of ways of dividing 12 different objects into 3 equal groups is $\frac{12!}{(4!)^3}$.

II. The number of ways in which 52 cards can be distributed among 4 persons equally is $\frac{52!}{(13!)^4 \times 4!}$.

(a) Only I
(b) Only II
(c) Both I and II
(d) Neither I nor II

45. If ${}^nC_4, {}^nC_5$ and ${}^nC_6$ are in AP, then n can be

(a) 9 (b) 11 (c) 14 (d) 12

46. If $n = {}^mC_2$, then the value of ${}^nC_2$ is

(a) ${}^{m+1}C_4$ (b) ${}^{m-1}C_4$
(c) ${}^{m+2}C_4$ (d) $3\,{}^{m+1}C_4$

47. **Assertion** (A) The number of ways of arranging the letters of the word 'ASSOCIATION' such that the two S's come together and two I's are not together is $\frac{8!}{2!2!} \times 9P_2$.

Reason (R) If in the given n things and p things are alike of one kind and q things are alike of second kind, then the number of ways of arranging all the n things is $\frac{n!}{p!q!}$.

(a) A and R both are true and R is the correct explanation of A
(b) A and R both are true but R is not the correct explanation of A
(c) A is true but R is false
(d) A is false but R is true

48. **Assertion** (A) The value of

$$^{47}C_4 + \sum_{i=1}^{5} {}^{52-i}C_3 \text{ is } {}^{52}C_4$$

Reason (R) $^nC_{r-1} + {}^nC_r = {}^{n+1}C_r$

(a) A and R both are true and R is the correct explanation of A
(b) A and R both are true but R is not the correct explanation of A
(c) A is true but R is false
(d) A is false but R is true

Directions (Q.Nos. 49-51) *Read the information carefully and answer next three questions.*

In a certain city, all telephone numbers have seven digits. City is divided into 6 zones. Each zone is allotted a specific non-zero digit which is to be used as first digit of all telephone numbers of that zone.

49. How many different telephone numbers are there in city, if there is no restrictions?

(a) 6×9^6 (b) 6×10^6
(c) $6 \times {}^{10}P_6$ (d) $6 \times {}^9P_6$

50. How many different telephone numbers are there in city, if first two digits of different zone are 12, 23, 34, 45, 56 and 67?

(a) 6×10^5 (b) 6×8^5
(c) $6 \times {}^{10}P_5$ (d) $6 \times {}^8P_2$

51. How many different telephone numbers are there in each zone with all digits distinct?

(a) 9^6 (b) 10^6
(c) $^{10}P_6$ (d) $^9P_6$

Darken your choice with HB Pencil

1.	ⓐ ⓑ ⓒ ⓓ	**11.**	ⓐ ⓑ ⓒ ⓓ	**21.**	ⓐ ⓑ ⓒ ⓓ	**31.**	ⓐ ⓑ ⓒ ⓓ	**41.**	ⓐ ⓑ ⓒ ⓓ	**51.**	ⓐ ⓑ ⓒ ⓓ
2.	ⓐ ⓑ ⓒ ⓓ	**12.**	ⓐ ⓑ ⓒ ⓓ	**22.**	ⓐ ⓑ ⓒ ⓓ	**32.**	ⓐ ⓑ ⓒ ⓓ	**42.**	ⓐ ⓑ ⓒ ⓓ		
3.	ⓐ ⓑ ⓒ ⓓ	**13.**	ⓐ ⓑ ⓒ ⓓ	**23.**	ⓐ ⓑ ⓒ ⓓ	**33.**	ⓐ ⓑ ⓒ ⓓ	**43.**	ⓐ ⓑ ⓒ ⓓ		
4.	ⓐ ⓑ ⓒ ⓓ	**14.**	ⓐ ⓑ ⓒ ⓓ	**24.**	ⓐ ⓑ ⓒ ⓓ	**34.**	ⓐ ⓑ ⓒ ⓓ	**44.**	ⓐ ⓑ ⓒ ⓓ		
5.	ⓐ ⓑ ⓒ ⓓ	**15.**	ⓐ ⓑ ⓒ ⓓ	**25.**	ⓐ ⓑ ⓒ ⓓ	**35.**	ⓐ ⓑ ⓒ ⓓ	**45.**	ⓐ ⓑ ⓒ ⓓ		
6.	ⓐ ⓑ ⓒ ⓓ	**16.**	ⓐ ⓑ ⓒ ⓓ	**26.**	ⓐ ⓑ ⓒ ⓓ	**36.**	ⓐ ⓑ ⓒ ⓓ	**46.**	ⓐ ⓑ ⓒ ⓓ		
7.	ⓐ ⓑ ⓒ ⓓ	**17.**	ⓐ ⓑ ⓒ ⓓ	**27.**	ⓐ ⓑ ⓒ ⓓ	**37.**	ⓐ ⓑ ⓒ ⓓ	**47.**	ⓐ ⓑ ⓒ ⓓ		
8.	ⓐ ⓑ ⓒ ⓓ	**18.**	ⓐ ⓑ ⓒ ⓓ	**28.**	ⓐ ⓑ ⓒ ⓓ	**38.**	ⓐ ⓑ ⓒ ⓓ	**48.**	ⓐ ⓑ ⓒ ⓓ		
9.	ⓐ ⓑ ⓒ ⓓ	**19.**	ⓐ ⓑ ⓒ ⓓ	**29.**	ⓐ ⓑ ⓒ ⓓ	**39.**	ⓐ ⓑ ⓒ ⓓ	**49.**	ⓐ ⓑ ⓒ ⓓ		
10.	ⓐ ⓑ ⓒ ⓓ	**20.**	ⓐ ⓑ ⓒ ⓓ	**30.**	ⓐ ⓑ ⓒ ⓓ	**40.**	ⓐ ⓑ ⓒ ⓓ	**50.**	ⓐ ⓑ ⓒ ⓓ		

Chapter 07

Binomial Theorem

MCQs 1 Mark Questions

1. The number of terms in the expansion of $(2x+3y-4z)^n$ is
   (a) $n+1$
   (b) $n+2$
   (c) $\frac{(n+1)(n+2)}{2}$
   (d) $(n+1)(n+2)$

2. The number of terms in the expansion $(1+3x+3x^2+x^3)^{15}$ is.
   (a) 45 (b) 16
   (c) 46 (d) None of these

3. If $(1+nx)^a=1+8x+24x^2+\ldots$, then value of a and n are respectively,
   (a) 4 and 2 (b) 3 and 2
   (c) 6 and 3 (d) 2 and 1

4. If n is a positive integer, then $(\sqrt{2}+1)^{2n}-(\sqrt{2}-1)^{2n}$ is
   (a) a rational number other than positive integers
   (b) an even positive integer
   (c) an odd positive integer
   (d) an irrational number

5. In the expansion of $(x+a)^n$, sum of the odd terms is A and the sum of the even terms is B, then $4AB$ is equal to
   (a) $(x^2-a^2)^n$
   (b) $(x+a)^{2n}+(x-a)^{2n}$
   (c) $(x+a)^{2n}-(x-a)^{2n}$
   (d) $(x-a)^{2n}-(x+a)^{2n}$

6. The total number of terms in the expansion of $(x+a)^{51}-(x-a)^{51}$ after simplification is
   (a) 102
   (b) 25
   (c) 26
   (d) None of the above

7. The value of $\frac{1}{(1!)(n-1)!}+\frac{1}{(3!)(n-3)!}+\frac{1}{(5!)(n-5)!}+\ldots$ is
   (a) $\frac{2^n}{n!}$ (b) $\frac{2^n}{(n+1)!}$
   (c) $\frac{2^{n-1}}{n!}$ (d) $\frac{2^{n+1}}{n!}$

8. The value of $(\sqrt{5}+2)^4+(\sqrt{5}-2)^4$ is
   (a) 212 (b) 322
   (c) 218 (d) 328

9. The value of $\sum_{r=0}^{n}(-1)^r\cdot{}^nC_r$ is
   (a) -1 (b) 0
   (c) 2^r (d) 2^n

10. The value of

$^{13}C_2 + {}^{13}C_3 + {}^{13}C_4 + ... + {}^{13}C_{13}$ is

(a) $2^{13} - 13$

(b) $2^{13} - 14$

(c) an odd number $\neq 2^{13} - 14$

(d) None of the above

11. The value of $\sum_{r=0}^{n} r \cdot {}^nC_r$ is

(a) $n \cdot 2^n$

(b) 2^{n-1}

(c) $n \cdot 2^{n-1}$

(d) $(n+1)2^{n-1}$

12. Which one is larger in $(1.01)^{1000000}$ and 10000 ?

(a) $(1.01)^{1000000}$

(b) 10000

(c) Both are equal

(d) Cannot be determined

13. The remainder when 7^{103} is divided by 25 is

(a) 15 (b) 16

(c) 17 (d) 18

14. The remainder when $8^{2n} - (62)^{2n+1}$ is divided by 9 is

(a) 2 (b) 3

(c) 4 (d) 8

15. If 7 divides $32^{32^{32}}$, then remainder is

(a) 1 (b) 0

(c) 4 (d) 6

16. $(115)^{96} - (95)^{115}$ is divisible by

(a) 15 (b) 17

(c) 19 (d) 21

17. The last two digits of the number 3^{400} are

(a) 39 (b) 29

(c) 01 (d) 43

MCQs 2 Marks Questions

18. If $x \neq 0$, then $\left(x^2 + \frac{3}{x}\right)^4$ is equal to

(a) $x^8 + 12x^5 + \frac{108}{x} + \frac{81}{x^4}$

(b) $x^8 + 12x^5 + 54x^3 + \frac{180}{x} + \frac{81}{x^3}$

(c) $x^8 + 12x^5 + 54x^2 + \frac{108}{x} + \frac{81}{x^4}$

(d) None of the above

19. The value of $(100)^{50} + (99)^{50}$ is

(a) $> (101)^{50}$ (b) $= 101$

(c) $< (101)^{50}$ (d) > 101

20. The value of $(\sqrt{2}+1)^6 - (\sqrt{2}-1)^6$ is

(a) 140

(b) $140\sqrt{2}$

(c) $150\sqrt{2}$

(d) None of the above

21. Remainder when $(27)^{999}$ is divided by 7 is

(a) 4 (b) 5 (c) 3 (d) 6

22. The last digit in 7^{300} is

(a) 7 (b) 3 (c) 9 (d) 1

23. The sum of the series

$^{20}C_0 - {}^{20}C_1 + {}^{20}C_2 - {}^{20}C_3 + ... + {}^{20}C_{10}$ is

(a) $-{}^{20}C_{10}$ (b) $\frac{1}{2}\,{}^{20}C_{10}$

(c) 0 (d) $^{20}C_{10}$

24. The value of $\sum_{k=1}^{12} {}^{24}C_k$ is equal to

(a) $2^{23} - 1$

(b) $2^{24} - {}^{24}C_{12} - 1$

(c) $2^{23} + \frac{1}{2} \cdot {}^{24}C_{12} - 1$

(d) $2^{23} - \frac{1}{2} \cdot {}^{24}C_{12} + 1$

25. $2\cdot {}^nC_0 + 2^2\dfrac{{}^nC_1}{2} + 2^3\dfrac{{}^nC_2}{3} + \ldots + 2^{n+1}\cdot\dfrac{{}^nC_n}{n+1}$ is equal to

(a) $\dfrac{3^{n+1}-1}{2(n+1)}$ (b) $\dfrac{3^{n+1}}{n+1}$

(c) $\dfrac{3^n-1}{n+1}$ (d) $\dfrac{3^n+1}{n+1}$

26. If $(1+x-2x^2)^6$ $= 1 + a_1x + a_2x^2 + \ldots + a_{12}x^{12}$, then $a_2 + a_4 + a_6 + \ldots + a_{12}$ is equal to

(a) 29 (b) 30

(c) 31 (d) 32

Directions (Q. Nos. 27 and 28) *Read the information carefully, answer the next two questions.*

If $(1+x+x^2)^n = a_0 + a_1x + a_2x^2 + \ldots + a_{2n}x^{2n}$ for all $n \in N$.

27. The value $2(a_0 + a_1 + a_2 + \ldots + a_{n-1}) + a_n$ is

(a) 2^{2n-1} (b) 3^n

(c) $\dfrac{3^n}{2}$ (d) $\dfrac{3^n-2}{2}$

28. If $a_0^2 - a_1^2 + a_2^2 - a_3^2 + \ldots + a_{2n}^2 = K\cdot a_n$, then K is equal to

(a) 1 (b) 2 (c) $\dfrac{1}{3}$ (d) 0

Darken your choice with HB Pencil

1.	ⓐ ⓑ ⓒ ⓓ	6.	ⓐ ⓑ ⓒ ⓓ	11.	ⓐ ⓑ ⓒ ⓓ	16.	ⓐ ⓑ ⓒ ⓓ	21.	ⓐ ⓑ ⓒ ⓓ	26.	ⓐ ⓑ ⓒ ⓓ
2.	ⓐ ⓑ ⓒ ⓓ	7.	ⓐ ⓑ ⓒ ⓓ	12.	ⓐ ⓑ ⓒ ⓓ	17.	ⓐ ⓑ ⓒ ⓓ	22.	ⓐ ⓑ ⓒ ⓓ	27.	ⓐ ⓑ ⓒ ⓓ
3.	ⓐ ⓑ ⓒ ⓓ	8.	ⓐ ⓑ ⓒ ⓓ	13.	ⓐ ⓑ ⓒ ⓓ	18.	ⓐ ⓑ ⓒ ⓓ	23.	ⓐ ⓑ ⓒ ⓓ	28.	ⓐ ⓑ ⓒ ⓓ
4.	ⓐ ⓑ ⓒ ⓓ	9.	ⓐ ⓑ ⓒ ⓓ	14.	ⓐ ⓑ ⓒ ⓓ	19.	ⓐ ⓑ ⓒ ⓓ	24.	ⓐ ⓑ ⓒ ⓓ		
5.	ⓐ ⓑ ⓒ ⓓ	10.	ⓐ ⓑ ⓒ ⓓ	15.	ⓐ ⓑ ⓒ ⓓ	20.	ⓐ ⓑ ⓒ ⓓ	25.	ⓐ ⓑ ⓒ ⓓ		

Chapter 08

Sequence and Series

MCQs 1 Mark Questions

1. In the quadratic equation $ax^2 + bx + c = 0$, if $\Delta = b^2 - 4ac$ and $\alpha+\beta, \alpha^2+\beta^2, \alpha^3+\beta^3$ are in GP, where α, β are the roots of $ax^2 + bx + c = 0$, then

(a) $\Delta \neq 0$ (b) $b\Delta = 0$
(c) $c\Delta = 0$ (d) $\Delta = 0$

2. If $x, (2x+2), (3x+3), \ldots$ are in GP, then the next term of this sequence is

(a) 27 (b) -27
(c) 13.5 (d) -13.5

3. If the pth and qth terms of a GP are q and p respectively, then $(p+q)$th term is

(a) $\left(\frac{q^p}{p^q}\right)^{\frac{1}{p-q}}$ (b) $\left(\frac{q^q}{p^p}\right)^{\frac{1}{p-q}}$

(c) $\left(\frac{p^q}{q^p}\right)^{\frac{1}{p-q}}$ (d) None of these

4. If a, b, c, d and p are different real numbers such that $(a^2+b^2+c^2)p^2 - 2(ab+bc+cd)p + (b^2+c^2+d^2) \leq 0$, then a, b, c, d are in

(a) AP (b) GP
(c) HP (d) $ab = cd$

5. In an increasing, geometric series, the sum of the second and the sixth term is $\frac{25}{2}$ and the product of the third and fifth term is 25. Then, the sum of 4th, 6th and 8th terms is equal to

(a) 35 (b) 30
(c) 26 (d) 32

6. If the sum of the second, third and fourth terms of a positive term GP is 3 and the sum of its sixth, seventh and eighth terms is 243, then the sum of the first 50 terms of this GP is

(a) $\frac{1}{26}(3^{49}-1)$ (b) $\frac{1}{26}(3^{50}-1)$

(c) $\frac{2}{13}(3^{50}-1)$ (d) $\frac{1}{13}(3^{50}-1)$

7. The sum of the infinite series

$1 + \frac{2}{3} + \frac{7}{3^2} + \frac{12}{3^3} + \frac{17}{3^4} + \frac{22}{3^5} + \ldots$ is equal to

(a) $\frac{9}{4}$ (b) $\frac{15}{4}$

(c) $\frac{13}{4}$ (d) $\frac{11}{4}$

8. An infinite GP has the first term x and sum 5, then x belongs to

(a) $x < -10$ (b) $-10 < x < 0$
(c) $0 < x < 10$ (d) $x > 10$

9. If sum of the series $\sum_{n=0}^{\infty} r^n = S$, for $|r|<1$, then sum of the series $\sum_{n=0}^{\infty} r^{2n}$ is

(a) S^2 (b) $\frac{S^2}{2S+1}$

(c) $\frac{2S}{S^2-1}$ (d) $\frac{S^2}{2S-1}$

10. The sum of $(x+2)^{n-1} + (x+2)^{n-2}(x+1) + (x+2)^{n-3}(x+1)^2 + \ldots + (x+1)^{n-1}$ is equal to

(a) $(x+2)^{n-2} - (x+1)^n$

(b) $(x+2)^{n-1} - (x+1)^{n-1}$

(c) $(x+2)^n - (x+1)^n$

(d) None of the above

11. $(\underbrace{666\ldots6}_{n \text{ digits}})^2 + (\underbrace{888\ldots8}_{n \text{ digits}})$ is equal to

(a) $\frac{4}{9}(10^n - 1)$ (b) $\frac{4}{9}(10^{2n} - 1)$

(c) $\frac{4}{9}(10^n - 1)^2$ (d) None of these

12. In a geometric progression consisting of positive terms, each term equals the sum of the next two terms. Then, the common ratio of this progression is equal to

(a) $\frac{1}{2}(1-\sqrt{5})$ (b) $\frac{1}{2}\sqrt{5}$

(c) $\sqrt{5}$ (d) $\frac{1}{2}(\sqrt{5}-1)$

13. If the roots of the cubic equation $px^3 + qx^2 + rx + s = 0$ are in GP, then

(a) $r^3p = q^3s$ (b) $rp^3 = qs^3$

(c) $p^3q = r^3s$ (d) $pq^3 = rs^3$

14. Let $a_1, a_2, a_3, \ldots$ be a GP such that first term is negative. Sum of first two terms is 4 and sum of third and fourth terms is 16. If sum of first nine terms is $4k$, then k is equal to

(a) $\frac{511}{3}$ (b) -171

(c) 171 (d) $-\frac{5}{3}$

15. Let T_n be the nth term of a GP of positive terms. If $\sum_{n=1}^{100} T_{2n+1} = 200$ and $\sum_{n=1}^{100} T_{2n} = 100$, then $\sum_{n=1}^{200} T_n$ is equal to

(a) 300 (b) 175

(c) 225 (d) 150

16. In a GP of the terms for a fixed n, the nth term is equal to sum of the next two terms. Then, the common ratio of the GP is

(a) $\sin 18°$ (b) $\cos 18°$

(c) $2\sin 18°$ (d) $2\cos 18°$

17. The sum of infinite series of a GP is p and on squaring each term of it, the sum will be q, then the common ratio of the series is

(a) $\frac{p^2-q^2}{p^2+q^2}$ (b) $\frac{p^2+q^2}{p^2-q^2}$

(c) $\frac{p^2-q}{p^2+q}$ (d) $\frac{p^2+q^2}{p^2-q}$

18. If α and β are roots of the equation $x^2 - 3x + a = 0$ and γ and δ are roots of the equation $x^2 - 12x + b = 0$ and $\alpha, \beta, \gamma, \delta$ form an increasing GP, then the values of a and b are respectively

(a) 2, 16 (b) 4, 8

(c) 2, 32 (d) None of these

19. Let a, b, c, d and p be any non-zero distinct real numbers such that $(a^2+b^2+c^2)p^2-2(ab+bc+cd)p+(b^2+c^2+d^2)=0$. Then,

(a) a, c, p are in AP
(b) a, c, p are in GP
(c) a, b, c, d are in GP
(d) a, b, c, d are in AP

20. Let $a_1, a_2, \ldots, a_{10}$ be a GP. If $\frac{a_3}{a_1}=25$, then $\frac{a_9}{a_5}$ equals

(a) 5^3 (b) $2(5^2)$
(c) $4(5^2)$ (d) 5^4

21. Let a_n be nth term of the GP of positive numbers. Let $\sum_{n=1}^{100} a_{2n}=\alpha$ and $\sum_{n=1}^{100} a_{2n-1}=\beta$, such that $\alpha \neq \beta$, then the common ratio is

(a) $\frac{\alpha}{\beta}$ (b) $\frac{\beta}{\alpha}$
(c) $\sqrt{\frac{\alpha}{\beta}}$ (d) $\sqrt{\frac{\beta}{\alpha}}$

22. If $1+\lambda+\lambda^2+\ldots+\lambda^n = (1+\lambda)(1+\lambda^2)(1+\lambda^4)(1+\lambda^8)(1+\lambda^{16})$, then the value of n is (where $n \in N$)

(a) 32 (b) 16 (c) 31 (d) 15

23. The sum of first 10 terms of the sequence 0.7, 0.77, 0.777, ... is

(a) $\frac{7}{81}(89-10^{-10})$ (b) $\frac{7}{9}(49-10^{-10})$
(c) $\frac{7}{81}(89+10^{-10})$ (d) $\frac{7}{9}(49+10^{-10})$

24. The sum of the first 20 terms of the series $1+\frac{3}{2}+\frac{7}{4}+\frac{15}{8}+\frac{31}{16}+\ldots$ is

(a) $38+\frac{1}{2^{19}}$ (b) $38+\frac{1}{2^{20}}$
(c) $39+\frac{1}{2^{20}}$ (d) $39+\frac{1}{2^{19}}$

25. If the sum of the series $2+\frac{3}{x}+\frac{9}{x^2}+\frac{27}{x^3}+\ldots\infty$ is finite, then

(a) $|x|>3$ (b) $-3<x<3$
(c) $|x|<\frac{3}{2}$ (d) $|x|>\frac{3}{2}$

26. The value of

$$x=(0.36)^{\log_{0.25}\left(\frac{1}{3}+\frac{1}{3^2}+\frac{1}{3^3}+\ldots \text{ upto } \infty\right)}$$ is

(a) 0.9 (b) 0.8
(c) 0.6 (d) 0.25

27. If $x=1+a+a^2+\ldots\infty$, where $|a|<1$ and $y=1+b+b^2+\ldots\infty$, where $|b|<1$, then the value of $1+ab+a^2b^2+\ldots\infty$ is

(a) $\frac{xy}{x+y-1}$ (b) $\frac{xy}{x-y+1}$
(c) $\frac{xy}{x+y+1}$ (d) $\frac{-xy}{x+y-1}$

28. If $x=\sum_{n=0}^{\infty}(-1)^n \tan^{2n}\theta$ and $y=\sum_{n=0}^{\infty}\cos^{2n}\theta$ for $0<\theta<\frac{\pi}{4}$, then

(a) $y(1+x)=1$ (b) $x(1+y)=1$
(c) $y(1-x)=1$ (d) $x(1-y)=1$

29. If $1+\cos\alpha+\cos^2\alpha+\ldots\infty=2-\sqrt{2}$, then $\alpha, (0<\alpha<\pi)$ is

(a) $\frac{\pi}{8}$ (b) $\frac{\pi}{6}$ (c) $\frac{\pi}{4}$ (d) $\frac{3\pi}{4}$

MCQs 2 Marks Questions

30. The sum of the first three terms of a GP is S and their product is 27. Then, all such S lie in

(a) $(-\infty, 9]$ (b) $[-3, \infty)$
(c) $(-\infty, -9] \cup [3, \infty)$ (d) $(-\infty, -3] \cup [9, \infty)$

31. The first two terms of a geometric progression add upto 12. The sum of the third and the fourth terms is 48. If the terms of the geometric progression are alternately positive and negative, then the first term is

(a) 4 (b) −4
(c) −12 (d) 12

32. The value of the sum $\sum_{r=1}^{n} \sum_{s=1}^{n} S_{rs} 2^r 3^s$, where $S_{rs} = 0$, if $r \neq s$ and $S_{rs} = 1$, if $r = s$, is

(a) $\frac{(5^n - 1)}{4}$ (b) $\frac{6}{5}(6^n - 1)$
(c) $\frac{5^n 6^n}{n+1}$ (d) $\frac{5}{4}(5^n - 1)$

33. Let $n (> 1)$ be a positive integer, then the largest integer m such that $(n^m + 1)$ divides $(1 + n + n^2 + \ldots + n^{127})$, is

(a) 32 (b) 63 (c) 64 (d) 127

34. If x, y, z are in GP and $a^x = b^y = c^z$, then

(a) $\log_a c = \log_b a$ (b) $\log_b a = \log_c b$
(c) $\log_c b = \log_a c$ (d) None of these

35. The value of common ratio for which three successive terms of a GP are the sides of a triangle is

(a) $r > 0$
(b) $r \in (0, 1)$
(c) $r \in \left(\frac{\sqrt{5} - 1}{2}, \frac{\sqrt{5} + 1}{2}\right)$
(d) None of the above

36. Let α_1, β_1 are the roots of $x^2 - 6x + p = 0$ and α_2, β_2 are the roots of $x^2 - 54x + q = 0$. If $\alpha_1, \beta_1, \alpha_2, \beta_2$ form an increasing GP then, the value of $(q - p)$ is

(a) 500 (b) 520 (c) 540 (d) 560

37. If $\frac{1}{1^2} + \frac{1}{2^2} + \frac{1}{3^2} + \ldots$ upto $\infty = \frac{\pi^2}{6}$, then $\frac{1}{1^2} + \frac{1}{3^2} + \frac{1}{5^2} + \ldots$ upto ∞ is equal to

(a) $\frac{\pi^2}{4}$ (b) $\frac{\pi^2}{6}$
(c) $\frac{\pi^2}{8}$ (d) $\frac{\pi^2}{12}$

38. If S denotes the sum to infinite and S_n the sum of n terms of the series $1 + \frac{1}{2} + \frac{1}{4} + \frac{1}{8} + \cdots$ such that $S - S_n < \frac{1}{1000}$, then the least value of n is

(a) 8 (b) 9
(c) 10 (d) 11

39. The sum to the infinity of thc series

$$1 + \frac{2}{3} + \frac{6}{3^2} + \frac{10}{3^3} + \frac{14}{3^4} + \ldots \text{ is}$$

(a) 3 (b) 4
(c) 6 (d) 2

40. 5th term of a GP is 2, then the product of its 9 terms is

(a) 256 (b) 512
(c) 1024 (d) None of these

41. Let $\{a_n\}$ be a GP such that $\frac{a_4}{a_6} = \frac{1}{4}$ and $a_2 + a_5 = 216$. Then, a_1 is equal to

(a) 12 or $\frac{108}{7}$
(b) 10
(c) 7 or $\frac{54}{7}$
(d) None of the above

42. If $\sin\theta, \sqrt{2}(\sin\theta + 1), 6\sin\theta + 6$ are in GP, then the fifth term is

(a) 81

(b) $82\sqrt{2}$

(c) 162

d) None of the above

43. The value of $(0.16)^{\log_{2.5}\left(\frac{1}{3}+\frac{1}{3^2}+\frac{1}{3^3}+\ldots \text{ to } \infty\right)}$ is

(a) 4

(b) 0

(c) 2

(d) – 4

44. Let $a_1, a_2, a_3, \ldots$ be a GP such that $a_1 < 0$, $a_1 + a_2 = 4$ and $a_3 + a_4 = 16$. If $\sum_{i=1}^{9} a_i = 4\lambda$, then λ is equal to

(a) -171 (b) 171 (c) $\frac{511}{3}$ (d) -513

45. The product $2^{\frac{1}{4}} \cdot 4^{\frac{1}{16}} \cdot 8^{\frac{1}{48}} \cdot 16^{\frac{1}{128}} \ldots$ to ∞ is equal to

(a) $2^{\frac{1}{4}}$ (b) 2

(c) $2^{\frac{1}{2}}$ (d) 1

Darken your choice with HB Pencil

1.	ⓐ ⓑ ⓒ ⓓ	9.	ⓐ ⓑ ⓒ ⓓ	17.	ⓐ ⓑ ⓒ ⓓ	25.	ⓐ ⓑ ⓒ ⓓ	33.	ⓐ ⓑ ⓒ ⓓ	41.	ⓐ ⓑ ⓒ ⓓ
2.	ⓐ ⓑ ⓒ ⓓ	10.	ⓐ ⓑ ⓒ ⓓ	18.	ⓐ ⓑ ⓒ ⓓ	26.	ⓐ ⓑ ⓒ ⓓ	34.	ⓐ ⓑ ⓒ ⓓ	42.	ⓐ ⓑ ⓒ ⓓ
3.	ⓐ ⓑ ⓒ ⓓ	11.	ⓐ ⓑ ⓒ ⓓ	19.	ⓐ ⓑ ⓒ ⓓ	27.	ⓐ ⓑ ⓒ ⓓ	35.	ⓐ ⓑ ⓒ ⓓ	43.	ⓐ ⓑ ⓒ ⓓ
4.	ⓐ ⓑ ⓒ ⓓ	12.	ⓐ ⓑ ⓒ ⓓ	20.	ⓐ ⓑ ⓒ ⓓ	28.	ⓐ ⓑ ⓒ ⓓ	36.	ⓐ ⓑ ⓒ ⓓ	45.	ⓐ ⓑ ⓒ ⓓ
5.	ⓐ ⓑ ⓒ ⓓ	13.	ⓐ ⓑ ⓒ ⓓ	21.	ⓐ ⓑ ⓒ ⓓ	29.	ⓐ ⓑ ⓒ ⓓ	37.	ⓐ ⓑ ⓒ ⓓ		
6.	ⓐ ⓑ ⓒ ⓓ	14.	ⓐ ⓑ ⓒ ⓓ	22.	ⓐ ⓑ ⓒ ⓓ	30.	ⓐ ⓑ ⓒ ⓓ	38.	ⓐ ⓑ ⓒ ⓓ		
7.	ⓐ ⓑ ⓒ ⓓ	15.	ⓐ ⓑ ⓒ ⓓ	23.	ⓐ ⓑ ⓒ ⓓ	31.	ⓐ ⓑ ⓒ ⓓ	39.	ⓐ ⓑ ⓒ ⓓ		
8.	ⓐ ⓑ ⓒ ⓓ	16.	ⓐ ⓑ ⓒ ⓓ	24.	ⓐ ⓑ ⓒ ⓓ	32.	ⓐ ⓑ ⓒ ⓓ	40.	ⓐ ⓑ ⓒ ⓓ		

Chapter 09

Straight Lines

MCQs 1 Mark Questions

1. If the lines $y=-3x+4$, $\alpha y=x+10$ and $2y+\beta x+9=0$ represents three consecutive sides of a rectangle, then $\alpha\beta$ is equal to
(a) 15 (b) 18 (c) 21 (d) 24

2. If $x-3y-a=0$, $\alpha x+2y-b=0$ and $\alpha x+y=c$ form a right angled triangle, then
(a) $\alpha^2-6\alpha-12=0$ (b) $\alpha^2-9\alpha+12=0$
(c) $\alpha^2-9\alpha+18=0$ (d) $\alpha^2-6\alpha-18=0$

3. If a variable line drawn through the intersection of the lines $\frac{x}{3}+\frac{y}{4}=1$ and $\frac{x}{4}+\frac{y}{3}=1$, meets the coordinates axes at P and Q, $(P\neq Q)$, then the locus of the mid-point of PQ is
(a) $6xy=7(x+y)$
(b) $7xy=6(x+y)$
(c) $4(x+y)^2-28(x+y)+49=0$
(d) $14(x+y)^2-97(x+y)+168=0$

4. $A(x_1, y_1)$ lies on the line $y=6x-1$ and $B(y_1, x_1)$ lies on the line $2x=5(y+1)$, then the equation of line AB is
(a) $2x+y=3$ (b) $3x+2y=5$
(c) $x+y=6$ (d) $3x+y=7$

5. The straight line $\alpha x+\beta y+\gamma=0$ $(\alpha, \beta, \gamma\neq 0)$ will pass through the first quadrant and cut the positive X-axis, if
(a) $\alpha\gamma>0, \beta\gamma>0$
(b) $\alpha\gamma>0, \beta\gamma<0$
(c) $\alpha\gamma>0$ or $\beta\gamma>0$
(d) $\alpha\gamma<0$ or $\beta\gamma<0$

6. A straight line is such that it is at a distance of 5 units from the origin and its inclination is 135°. The intercepts of the line on the coordinate axes are
(a) 5, 5 (b) $\frac{5}{\sqrt{2}}, \frac{5}{\sqrt{2}}$
(c) $\sqrt{2}, \sqrt{2}$ (d) None of these

7. The equation of the sides of a triangle are $x-3y=0$, $4x+3y=5$ and $3x+y=0$. The line $3x-4y=0$ passes through the
(a) incentre (b) centroid
(c) orthocentre (d) circumcentre

8. The equation of straight line through the intersection of the lines $x-2y=1$ and $x+3y=2$ and parallel to $3x+4y=0$, is
(a) $3x+4y+5=0$
(b) $3x+4y-10=0$
(c) $3x+4y-5=0$
(d) $3x+4y+6=0$

9. Equation of a line passing through the line of intersection of lines $2x-3y+4=0$, $3x+4y-5=0$ and perpendicular to $6x-7y+3=0$, is

(a) $119x+102y+125=0$
(b) $119x+102y=125$
(c) $119x-102y=125$
(d) None of the above

10. The line $\frac{x}{a}-\frac{y}{b}=1$ cuts the X-axis at P. The equation of the line through P perpendicular to the given line is

(a) $x+y=ab$ (b) $x+y=a+b$
(c) $ax+by=a^2$ (d) $bx+ay=b^2$

11. Distance of origin from line $(1+\sqrt{3})y+(1-\sqrt{3})x=10$ along the line $y=\sqrt{3}x+m$ is

(a) 4 units (b) 5 units
(c) 6 units (d) 7 units

12. A point equidistant from the lines $4x+3y+10=0, 5x-12y+26=0$ and $7x+24y-50=0$ is

(a) (1, –1) (b) (1, 1)
(c) (0, 0) (d) (0, 1)

13. If $(-4,5)$ is one vertex and $7x-y+8=0$ is one diagonal of a square, then the equation of the other diagonal is

(a) $x+7y-31=0$
(b) $x+7y-15=0$
(c) $x+7y+8=0$
(d) $x+7y-35=0$

14. If α and β are the intercepts made by the straight line on the coordinate axes such that $\frac{1}{\alpha}+\frac{1}{\beta}=\frac{1}{\gamma}$, then the line passes through point

(a) (1, 1) (b) (γ, γ)
(c) $\left(\frac{1}{\gamma}, \frac{1}{\gamma}\right)$ (d) $\left(\frac{\gamma}{\alpha}, \frac{\gamma}{\alpha}\right)$

15. The sum of the intercepts cut-off by the axes on lines $x+y=p$, $x+y=pq$ and $x+y=pq^2$ is, where $p\neq 0$ and $q=\frac{1}{2}$

(a) $2p$ (b) $p\sqrt{2}$
(c) $2\sqrt{2}p$ (d) None of these

16. If one vertex of an equilateral triangle of side l lies at the origin and the other lies on the line $x=\sqrt{3}y$, then the coordinates of the third vertex are

(a) $\left(0, \frac{-l}{2}\right)$ (b) $(l, 0)$
(c) $\left(\frac{l\sqrt{3}}{2}, \frac{l}{2}\right)$ (d) $\left(\frac{l\sqrt{3}}{2}, \frac{-l}{2}\right)$

17. One side of an equilateral triangle is on $3x+4y=7$ and its vertex is (1, 2). Then, the length of the side of the triangle is

(a) $\frac{8\sqrt{3}}{15}$ units (b) $\frac{8\sqrt{3}}{17}$ units
(c) $\frac{8\sqrt{3}}{19}$ units (d) $\frac{7\sqrt{3}}{16}$ units

18. If a and b are lengths of the perpendiculars from the origin on the lines $x\sec\alpha - y\operatorname{cosec}\alpha = p$ and $x\cos\alpha + y\sin\alpha = p\cos 2\alpha$, then

(a) $4a^2+b^2=p^2$ (b) $a^2+b^2=p^2$
(c) $a^2+4b^2=p^2$ (d) $a^2+b^2=2p^2$

19. The equation of the line passing through (1, 2) and having a distance of 7 units from the point (8, 9) is

(a) $y=2$ (b) $x=2$
(c) $y=4$ (d) $x=4$

20. The vertices of a triangle are $A(-3,-1)$, $B(-1,-3)$ and origin O. The equation of the line parallel to AB and intersecting the sides OA and OB, whose perpendicular distance from O is $\frac{1}{2}$ is

(a) $x+y-\frac{1}{2}=0$ (b) $x+y-\frac{1}{\sqrt{2}}=0$

(c) $x+y+\frac{1}{2}=0$ (d) $x+y+\frac{1}{\sqrt{2}}=0$

21. Radius of the circle touching the lines $3x+4y-14=0$ and $6x+8y+7=0$ is

(a) $\frac{7}{4}$ units (b) $\frac{7}{2}$ units

(c) $\frac{5}{4}$ units (d) $\frac{5}{2}$ units

22. The line L is given by $\frac{x}{5}+\frac{y}{b}=1$ passes through the point (13, 32). The line K is parallel to L and has the equation $\frac{x}{c}+\frac{y}{3}=1$. Then, the distance between L and K is

(a) $\frac{17}{\sqrt{15}}$ units (b) $\frac{23}{\sqrt{17}}$ units

(c) $\frac{23}{\sqrt{15}}$ units (d) $\sqrt{15}$ units

23. If a, b and c are distinct, then $(b-c)x+(c-a)y+(a-b)=0$ and $(b^3-c^3)x+(c^3-a^3)y+(a^3-b^3)=0$ represent the same line, if

(a) $a+b+c=0$ (b) $a=b=c$

(c) $a^2+b^2+c^2=0$ (d) $a^3+b^3+c^3=0$

24. If the lines $x=\alpha+p$, $y=-2$ and $y=px$ are concurrent, then the least value of $|\alpha|$ is

(a) 2 (b) $\sqrt{2}$ (c) $2\sqrt{2}$ (d) 4

25. If the lines $\alpha x+\beta y+\gamma=0$, $\beta x+\gamma y+\alpha=0$ and $\gamma x+\alpha y+\beta=0$, $\alpha\neq\beta\neq\gamma$ are concurrent, then the point of concurrency is

(a) (0, 0) (b) (1, 1)

(c) (2, 2) (d) (–1, –1)

26. Consider the set of all lines $px+qy+r=0$ such that $3p+2q+4r=0$. Which one of the following statements is true?

(a) Each line passes through origin

(b) The lines are concurrent at the point $\left(\frac{3}{4},\frac{1}{2}\right)$

(c) All lines are parallel

(d) The lines are not concurrent

27. The range of a for which the points $(a, a+2)$ and $\left(\frac{3a}{2}, a^2\right)$ lie on opposite sides of the line $2x+3y-6=0$, is

(a) $(-\infty,-2)$

(b) (0, 1)

(c) $(-\infty,-2)\cup(0,1)$

(d) $(-\infty,1)\cup(2,\infty)$

28. If $L: 3x+4y=8$, then the points $(2,-5)$ and $(-5,2)$

(a) lie on L

(b) lie on same side of L

(c) lie on opposite sides of L

(d) equidistance from L

29. The acute angle bisector between the lines $3x-4y-5=0$ and $5x+12y-26=0$ is

(a) $7x-56y+32=0$

(b) $14x-112y+65=0$

(c) $9x-3y+13=0$

(d) $7x-13y+9=0$

30. The equation of the bisector of the angle between the lines $x-7y+5=0$, $5x+5y-3=0$, which is supplement of the angle containing the origin will be

(a) $x+3y-2=0$ (b) $x-3y+2=0$

(c) $3x-y+1=0$ (d) $3x+y+2=0$

31. Foot of the perpendicular from origin on the line joining the points $A(a\cos\alpha, b\sin\alpha)$ and $B(a\cos\beta, b\sin\beta)$ is

(a) $(\cos\alpha+\cos\beta, \sin\alpha+\sin\beta)$

(b) $(\cos\alpha-\cos\beta, \sin\alpha-\sin\beta)$

(c) $\left(\frac{a(\cos\alpha+\cos\beta)}{2}, \frac{b(\sin\alpha+\sin\beta)}{2}\right)$

(d) $(\cos\alpha\cos\beta, \sin\alpha\sin\beta)$

32. The equation of perpendicular bisectors of sides PQ, QR of ΔPQR are $x-y=5$, $x=-2y$, respectively and $P(1,-2)$, then coordinates of R are

(a) (1, 0) (b) (5, 0) (c) (−5, 0) (d) (4, 0)

33. The coordinates of the foot of the perpendicular drawn from the point (3, 4) on the line $2x+y-7=0$ are

(a) $\left(\frac{9}{5}, \frac{17}{5}\right)$ (b) (1, 5)

(c) (−5, 1) (d) (1, −5)

34. A ray of light coming from the point (1, 2) is reflected at a point A on the X-axis and then passes through the point (5, 3). The coordinates of the point A are

(a) $\left(\frac{13}{5}, 0\right)$ (b) $\left(\frac{5}{13}, 0\right)$

(c) (−7, 0) (d) None of these

35. The area bounded by $y=|x|-1$ $y=-|x|+1$ is

(a) 1 sq unit (b) 1.5 sq units

(c) 2 sq units (d) 2.5 sq units

36. The area enclosed by $2|x|+3|y|\le 6$ is

(a) 3 sq units (b) 3.5 sq units

(c) 4 sq units (d) 12 sq units

MCQs 2 Marks Questions

37. A point on the straight line $3x+5y=15$ which is equidistant from the coordinate axes will lie only in

(a) I quadrant (b) II quadrant

(c) Both (a) and (b) (d) I, II, IV quadrant

38. If the lines $y=3x+1$ and $2y=x+3$ are equally inclined with $y=mx+4$, then the value of m is

(a) $\frac{1+3\sqrt{2}}{7}$ (b) $\frac{1-3\sqrt{2}}{7}$

(c) $\frac{1\pm 3\sqrt{2}}{7}$ (d) $\frac{1\pm 5\sqrt{2}}{7}$

39. Let PQ be a diameter of the circle $x^2+y^2=9$. If α and β are the lengths of the perpendiculars from P and Q on the straight line, $x+y=2$ respectively, then the maximum value of $\alpha\beta$ is

(a) 7 (b) 8 (c) 9 (d) 5

40. The ray of light along $x+\sqrt{3}y=\sqrt{3}$ gets reflected upon reaching X-axis, the equation of the reflected ray is

(a) $x-y+\sqrt{3}=0$ (b) $x-\sqrt{3}y-\sqrt{3}=0$

(c) $3x-y-\sqrt{3}=0$ (d) $x-\sqrt{3}y-1=0$

41. Let L denotes the line in the XY-plane with x and y-intercepts as 3 and 1, respectively. Then, the image of the point $(-1,-4)$ in this line, is

(a) $\left(\frac{11}{5}, \frac{28}{5}\right)$ (b) $\left(\frac{29}{5}, \frac{11}{5}\right)$

(c) $\left(\frac{29}{5}, \frac{8}{5}\right)$ (d) $\left(\frac{8}{5}, \frac{29}{5}\right)$

42. A light ray coming along the line $3x+4y=5$ gets reflected from the line $\alpha x+\beta y=1$ and goes along the line $5x-12y=10$. Then,

(a) $\alpha=\frac{64}{115}, \beta=\frac{112}{15}$ (b) $\alpha=\frac{64}{115}, \beta=-\frac{8}{115}$

(c) $\alpha=\frac{4}{15}, \beta=\frac{3}{15}$ (d) $\alpha=1, \beta=\frac{12}{15}$

43. If the points $A(a, b)$, where $a=b^2$ lies in the region corresponding to the acute angle between the lines $y=\frac{x}{2}$ and $y=\frac{x}{4}$, then

(a) $b\in[2,4]$ (b) $b\in(2,4]$

(c) $b\in[2,5)$ (d) $b\in(2,4)$

44. The sides of a rhombus $PQRS$ are parallel to the lines, $x-y+2=0$ and $7x-y+3=0$. If the diagonals of the rhombus intersect at $A(1,2)$ and the vertex P(not at origin) is on the Y-axis, then the ordinate of P is

(a) $\frac{5}{2}$ (b) $\frac{7}{4}$ (c) 2 (d) $\frac{7}{2}$

45. Δ_1, Δ_2 and Δ_3 are the areas of the triangles with vertices $(0,0)$, $(a\tan\alpha, b\cot\alpha)$, $(a\sin\alpha, b\cos\alpha)$; (a, b), $(a\sec^2\alpha, b\,\mathrm{cosec}^2\alpha)$, $(a + a\sin^2\alpha$, $b + b\cos^2\alpha)$; $(0, 0)$, $(a\tan\alpha, -b\cot\alpha)$, $(a\sin\alpha, b\cos\alpha)$, then Δ_1, Δ_2 and Δ_3 are in GP for

(a) all values of α
(b) only one value of α
(c) finite number of values of α
(d) no value of α

46. If $f(x+y) = f(x)\,f(y)$, $\forall\, x, y$, if $f(1) = 2$, then area enclosed by $3|x| + 2|y| \le 8$ is

(a) $\frac{1}{3} f(6)$ sq units
(b) $\frac{1}{6} f(3)$ sq units
(c) $f(2)$ sq units
(d) $\frac{1}{2} f(4)$ sq units

47. The equation of a line L_1 is $x + y - 2 = 0$ and $L_2 \perp L_1$ passes through $\left(\frac{1}{2}, 0\right)$, then area of triangle (in sq units) formed by the Y-axis and the lines L_1, L_2 is

(a) $\frac{5}{4}$ (b) $\frac{25}{16}$ (c) $\frac{16}{25}$ (d) $\frac{4}{5}$

48. The distance of any point (x, y) from the origin is defined as $d(x, y) = \max\{|x|, |y|\}$, $d(x, y) = a$ non-zero constant the locus is

(a) a circle
(b) a straight line
(c) a square
(d) a triangle

49. The area bounded by the curve $\max\{|x|, |y|\} = 1$ is

(a) 2 sq units (b) 3 sq units
(c) 4 sq units (d) 8 sq units

50. P is a point on either of two lines $y - \sqrt{3}|x| = 2$ at a distance of 5 units from their point of intersection. The coordinates of the foot of perpendicular from P on the bisector of the angle between them are

(a) $\left(0, \frac{1}{2}(4 + 5\sqrt{3})\right)$ or $\left(0, \frac{1}{2}(4 - 5\sqrt{3})\right)$, (depending on which line the point P is taken)
(b) $\left(0, \frac{1}{2}(4 + 5\sqrt{3})\right)$
(c) $\left(0, \frac{1}{2}(4 - 5\sqrt{3})\right)$
(d) $\left(\frac{5}{2}, \frac{5\sqrt{3}}{2}\right)$

Darken your choice with HB Pencil

1.	ⓐ ⓑ ⓒ ⓓ	10.	ⓐ ⓑ ⓒ ⓓ	19.	ⓐ ⓑ ⓒ ⓓ	28.	ⓐ ⓑ ⓒ ⓓ	37.	ⓐ ⓑ ⓒ ⓓ	46.	ⓐ ⓑ ⓒ ⓓ
2.	ⓐ ⓑ ⓒ ⓓ	11.	ⓐ ⓑ ⓒ ⓓ	20.	ⓐ ⓑ ⓒ ⓓ	29.	ⓐ ⓑ ⓒ ⓓ	38.	ⓐ ⓑ ⓒ ⓓ	47.	ⓐ ⓑ ⓒ ⓓ
3.	ⓐ ⓑ ⓒ ⓓ	12.	ⓐ ⓑ ⓒ ⓓ	21.	ⓐ ⓑ ⓒ ⓓ	30.	ⓐ ⓑ ⓒ ⓓ	39.	ⓐ ⓑ ⓒ ⓓ	48.	ⓐ ⓑ ⓒ ⓓ
4.	ⓐ ⓑ ⓒ ⓓ	13.	ⓐ ⓑ ⓒ ⓓ	22.	ⓐ ⓑ ⓒ ⓓ	31.	ⓐ ⓑ ⓒ ⓓ	40.	ⓐ ⓑ ⓒ ⓓ	49.	ⓐ ⓑ ⓒ ⓓ
5.	ⓐ ⓑ ⓒ ⓓ	14.	ⓐ ⓑ ⓒ ⓓ	23.	ⓐ ⓑ ⓒ ⓓ	32.	ⓐ ⓑ ⓒ ⓓ	41.	ⓐ ⓑ ⓒ ⓓ	50.	ⓐ ⓑ ⓒ ⓓ
6.	ⓐ ⓑ ⓒ ⓓ	15.	ⓐ ⓑ ⓒ ⓓ	24.	ⓐ ⓑ ⓒ ⓓ	33.	ⓐ ⓑ ⓒ ⓓ	42.	ⓐ ⓑ ⓒ ⓓ		
7.	ⓐ ⓑ ⓒ ⓓ	16.	ⓐ ⓑ ⓒ ⓓ	25.	ⓐ ⓑ ⓒ ⓓ	34.	ⓐ ⓑ ⓒ ⓓ	43.	ⓐ ⓑ ⓒ ⓓ		
8.	ⓐ ⓑ ⓒ ⓓ	17.	ⓐ ⓑ ⓒ ⓓ	26.	ⓐ ⓑ ⓒ ⓓ	35.	ⓐ ⓑ ⓒ ⓓ	44.	ⓐ ⓑ ⓒ ⓓ		
9.	ⓐ ⓑ ⓒ ⓓ	18.	ⓐ ⓑ ⓒ ⓓ	27.	ⓐ ⓑ ⓒ ⓓ	36.	ⓐ ⓑ ⓒ ⓓ	45.	ⓐ ⓑ ⓒ ⓓ		

Chapter 10

Conic Sections

MCQs 1 Mark Questions

1. If A and B are points in the plane such that $\frac{PA}{PB} = \lambda$ (constant) for all P on a given circle, then the value of λ cannot be equal to

(a) 0 (b) 1
(c) π (d) e

2. A circle of area 16π sq units has two of its diameters along the lines $2x + y - 7 = 0$ and $x + 3y - 11 = 0$. Then, the equation of this circle is

(a) $x^2 + y^2 - 4x - 6y - 3 = 0$
(b) $x^2 + y^2 + 4x + 6y + 3 = 0$
(c) $x^2 + y^2 - 4x + 6y - 3 = 0$
(d) $x^2 + y^2 + 4x - 6y + 3 = 0$

3. A circle with centre $(6, k)$ touches X-axis and passes through the point $(5, -1)$. It also passes through the point

(a) (2, 6) (b) (7, −1)
(c) (0, 0) (d) (5, 1)

4. For all values of λ, the equation of a diameter of the circle

$$x^2 + y^2 - \lambda x - \lambda y + \frac{\lambda^2}{4} = 0 \text{ is}$$

(a) $x - y = \lambda$ (b) $x + 2y = \lambda$
(c) $2x + y = \lambda$ (d) $x + y = \lambda$

5. The equation of the image of the circle $x^2 + y^2 - 6x - 4y + 12 = 0$ by the mirror $x + y - 1 = 0$ is

(a) $x^2 + y^2 + 2x + 4y + 4 = 0$
(b) $x^2 + y^2 - 2x + 4y + 4 = 0$
(c) $x^2 + y^2 + 2x + 4y - 4 = 0$
(d) $x^2 + y^2 + 2x - 4y + 4 = 0$

6. If the two circles $x^2 + y^2 + 2ax + c = 0$ and $x^2 + y^2 - 2by - c = 0$ have equal radii, then locus of (a, b) is

(a) $x^2 + y^2 = c^2$ (b) $x^2 - y^2 = 2c$
(c) $x^2 - y^2 = c^2$ (d) $x^2 + y^2 = 2c^2$

7. If the point (1, 2) lies outside and the point $(-1, -2)$ lies inside the circle $x^2 + y^2 + 2x + 2y + p = 0$, then the set of all possible values of p is

(a) (1, 11) (b) (−11, −1)
(c) (−11, 1) (d) (−1, 11)

8. Two tangents are drawn from the origin to a circle with centre at $(2, -1)$. If the equation of one of the tangents is $3x + y = 0$, the equation of the other tangent is

(a) $3x - y = 0$ (b) $x + 3y = 0$
(c) $x - 3y = 0$ (d) $x + 2y = 0$

9. The length of the tangent from (1, 1) to the circle $x^2 + y^2 - 2x + y + 3 = 0$ is

(a) 4 units (b) 2 units
(c) 1 unit (d) $\sqrt{2}$ units

10. If the line $hx + ky = 1$ touches the circle $x^2 + y^2 = k^2$, then the locus of (h, k) is circle of radius

(a) $\frac{1}{k}$ (b) k^2

(c) k (d) $\frac{1}{k^2}$

11. *PQRS* is a square of unit area. A circle is tangent to two sides of *PQRS* and passes through exactly one of its vertices. The radius of the circle is

(a) $(\sqrt{2} - 1)$ units (b) $(2 - \sqrt{2})$ units

(c) $\sqrt{2}$ units (d) $\frac{1}{\sqrt{2}}$ units

12. If r and R are the radii of smallest and largest circles which passes through (5, 6) and touches the circle, $(x - 2)^2 + y^2 = 4$, then rR is equal to

(a) 41 (b) 4

(c) $\frac{41}{4}$ (d) $\frac{4}{41}$

13. If the tangent at the point A on the circle $x^2 + y^2 + 6x + 6y - 2 = 0$ meets a straight line $5x - 2y + 6 = 0$ at a point B on the Y-axis, then the length of AB is

(a) 4 units (b) $2\sqrt{5}$ units

(c) 5 units (d) $3\sqrt{5}$ units

14. The circles $x^2 + y^2 = \lambda x$ and $x^2 + y^2 = k^2 (k > 0)$ touch each other internally, then

(a) $|\lambda| = 2k$ (b) $2|\lambda| = k$

(c) $|\lambda| = k$ (d) $\lambda = 2k$

15. The coordinates of a point on the parabola $y^2 = 4x$, whose focal distance is 4 units, is

(a) $(\pm 2\sqrt{3}, 3)$ (b) $(2\sqrt{3}, 3)$

(c) $(3, 2\sqrt{3})$ (d) $(3, \pm 2\sqrt{3})$

16. The name of the conic represented by $\sqrt{\frac{x}{p}} + \sqrt{\frac{y}{q}} = 1$ is

(a) circle (b) parabola

(c) ellipse (d) hyperbola

17. The locus of centre of circle which touches $x^2 + y^2 = k^2$ and lines $x = a$ is

(a) parabola (b) circle

(c) ellipse (d) hyperbola

18. Let a be the length of the common chord of the curves $x^2 + y^2 = 9$ and $y^2 = 8x$ and b be the length of the latusrectum of $y^2 = 8x$, then

(a) $a > b$ (b) $a = b$

(c) $a < b$ (d) $\frac{a}{b} = \sqrt{2}$

19. A chord is drawn through the focus of the parabola $y^2 = 8x$ such that its distance from the vertex of this parabola is $\sqrt{3}$, then its slope can be

(a) $\frac{1}{\sqrt{3}}$ (b) $\sqrt{3}$ (c) $\sqrt{5}$ (d) $\frac{1}{\sqrt{5}}$

20. The length of focal chord of parabola $y^2 = 4ax$ makes an angle θ with the X-axis is

(a) $\operatorname{cosec}^2\theta$ (b) $4a \operatorname{cosec}^2\theta$

(c) $a \operatorname{cosec}^2\theta$ (d) $a \tan\theta$

21. The equation of the common tangent touching the circle $(x - 3)^2 + y^2 = 9$ and the parabola $y^2 = 4x$ above the X-axis is

(a) $\sqrt{3}y = 3x + 1$ (b) $\sqrt{3}y = -(x + 3)$

(c) $\sqrt{3}y = x + 3$ (d) $\sqrt{3}y = -(3x + 1)$

22. The equation of common tangent to the curves $y^2 = 8x$ and $xy = -1$ is

(a) $3y = 9x + 2$ (b) $y = 2x + 1$

(c) $2y = x + 8$ (d) $y = x + 2$

23. Consider the circle $C_1 : x^2 + y^2 - 6x + 1 = 0$ and parabola $C_2 : y^2 = 4x$, then

(a) C_1 and C_2 touch each other at one point
(b) C_1 and C_2 touch each other exactly at two points
(c) C_1 and C_2 intersect (but do not touch) at exactly two points
(d) C_1 and C_2 neither intersects nor touch each other

24. The equation of normal to curve $x^2 = 4y$, which passes through the point (1, 2) is

(a) $x + y = 3$ (b) $x - y = 3$
(c) $x - y = -3$ (d) $x + y = -3$

25. $\dfrac{x^2}{a^2 - a - 6} + \dfrac{y^2}{a^2 - 6a + 5} = 1$ will represents the ellipse, if a lies in the interval

(a) $(-\infty, -2) \cup (5, \infty)$
(b) $(3, \infty)$
(c) $(-2, 3)$
(d) $(1, \infty)$

26. Let $x^2 = 4ky, k > 0$ be a parabola with vertex A. Let BC be its latusrectum. An ellipse with centre on BC touches the parabola at A, and cuts BC at points D and E such that $BD = DE = EC$ $(B, D, E, C$ in that order). The eccentricity of the ellipse is

(a) $\dfrac{1}{\sqrt{2}}$ (b) $\dfrac{1}{\sqrt{3}}$ (c) $\dfrac{\sqrt{5}}{3}$ (d) $\dfrac{\sqrt{3}}{2}$

27. The equation $(5x+1)^2 + (5y+1)^2 = (\lambda - 1)^2(4x + 3y + 1)^2$ represents an ellipse, if $\lambda \in$

(a) (0, 1) (b) (0, 2) – {1}
(c) (1, 2) (d) (–1, 0)

28. If the distance between the foci of an ellipse is half the length of its latusrectum, then the eccentricity of ellipse is

(a) $\dfrac{1}{2}$ (b) $\dfrac{2\sqrt{2} - 1}{2}$
(c) $\sqrt{2} - 1$ (d) $\dfrac{\sqrt{2} - 1}{2}$

29. Ratio of the greatest and least focal distances of a point on the ellipse $4x^2 + 9y^2 = 36$ is

(a) $(3 + \sqrt{5}) : (3 - \sqrt{5})$
(b) $(3 - \sqrt{5}) : (3 + \sqrt{5})$
(c) $1 : \sqrt{3}$
(d) $\sqrt{3} : 1$

30. Equation of the largest circle with centre (1, 0) that can be inscribed in the ellipse $x^2 + 4y^2 = 16$ is

(a) $2x^2 + 2y^2 - 4x + 7 = 0$
(b) $x^2 + y^2 - 2x + 5 = 0$
(c) $3x^2 + 3y^2 - 6x - 8 = 0$
(d) $x^2 + y^2 - 2x = 0$

31. If q is length of the perpendicular from a focus on tangent at a point A of ellipse $\dfrac{x^2}{a^2} + \dfrac{y^2}{b^2} = 1$ and p is the distance of A from the focus, then $\dfrac{2a}{p} - \dfrac{b^2}{q^2}$ is equal to

(a) 0 (b) 1 (c) 2 (d) 5

32. The locus of a variable point whose distance from (2, 0) is $\dfrac{2}{3}$ times its distance from the line $x = -\dfrac{9}{2}$ is

(a) $\dfrac{x^2}{3} + \dfrac{y^2}{5} = 1$ (b) $\dfrac{x^2}{9} + \dfrac{y^2}{7} = 1$
(c) $\dfrac{x^2}{3} - \dfrac{y^2}{5} = 1$ (d) $\dfrac{x^2}{9} + \dfrac{y^2}{5} = 1$

33. The ellipse $\dfrac{x^2}{a^2} + \dfrac{y^2}{b^2} = 1$ and the straight line $y = mx + c$ intersects in real points only if

(a) $a^2m^2 < c^2 - b^2$ (b) $a^2m^2 > c^2 - b^2$
(c) $c^2 \le b$ (d) $a^2m^2 \ge c^2 - b^2$

34. The equation
$|\sqrt{(x-2)^2+(y-1)^2}-\sqrt{(x+2)^2+y^2}|=c$ will represent a hyperbola, if

(a) $0<c<6$ (b) $0<c<5$
(c) $0<c<\sqrt{17}$ (d) $0<c<\sqrt{19}$

35. If e_1 is the eccentricity of the ellipse $\frac{x^2}{25}+\frac{y^2}{b^2}=1$ and e_2 is the eccentricity of the hyperbola $\frac{x^2}{16}-\frac{y^2}{b^2}=1$ such that $e_1e_2=1$, then b is equal to

(a) ± 3 (b) ± 5
(c) ± 7 (d) ± 1

36. If $x-\sqrt{5}y+c=0$ is a tangent to the hyperbola $\frac{x^2}{25}-\frac{y^2}{4}=1$, then the value of c is

(a) $\pm 3\sqrt{5}$ (b) $\pm\sqrt{5}$
(c) $\pm 2\sqrt{5}$ (d) None of these

37. If two perpendicular tangents can be drawn from the point (a, b) to the hyperbola $x^2-y^2=k^2$, then (a, b) lies on

(a) $y=\pm x$ (b) $x^2+y^2=k^2$
(c) $x^2+y^2=2k^2$ (d) $y^2=4kx$

38. If the hyperbola $\frac{x^2}{b^2}-\frac{y^2}{a^2}=1$ passes through the focus of the ellipse $\frac{x^2}{a^2}+\frac{y^2}{b^2}=1$, then eccentricity of the hyperbola is

(a) $\sqrt{3}$ (b) $\frac{3}{2}$ (c) $\sqrt{2}$ (d) $\sqrt{\frac{3}{2}}$

39. If $\frac{x^2}{\lambda+3}+\frac{y^2}{2-\lambda}=1$ represents a hyperbola, then

(a) $\lambda\notin(2, 3)$ (b) $\lambda\notin(-2, 3)$
(c) $\lambda\notin(-3, 2)$ (d) $\lambda\notin(2, \infty)$

40. If the tangent and normal to $x^2-y^2=a^2$ at a point cut-off intercepts x_1, x_2 and y_1, y_2 on X and Y-axes, respectively, then $x_1x_2+y_1y_2$ is equal to

(a) 1 (b) -1
(c) 0 (d) Not defined

MCQs 2 Marks Questions

41. A circle touching the X-axis at (3, 0) and making a intercept of length 8 units on the Y-axis passes through the point

(a) (3, 10) (b) (3, 5)
(c) (2, 3) (d) (1, 5)

42. If the circles $x^2+y^2-16x-20y+164=r^2$ and $(x-4)^2+(y-7)^2=36$ intersect at two distinct points, then

(a) $0<r<11$ (b) $r>11$
(c) $1<r<11$ (d) $r=1$

43. Let C_1 and C_2 be the centres of the circles $x^2+y^2-2x-2y-2=0$ and $x^2+y^2-6x-6y+14=0$, respectively. If P and Q are the points of intersections of these circles, then the area (in sq units) of the quadrilateral PC_1QC_2 is

(a) 8 (b) 4 (c) 6 (d) 9

44. If the area of the triangle whose one vertex is at the vertex of the parabola, $y^2+4(x-a^2)=0$ and the other two vertices are the points of intersections of the parabola and Y-axis, is 250 sq units, then value of a is

(a) $5\sqrt{5}$ (b) 5
(c) $5(2^{1/3})$ (d) $10^{2/3}$

45. The radius of a circle having minimum area which touches the curve $y=4-x^2$ and the lines $y=|x|$ is

(a) $2(\sqrt{2}+1)$ (b) $2(\sqrt{2}-1)$
(c) $4(\sqrt{2}-1)$ (d) $4(\sqrt{2}+1)$

46. If the line $ax + y = c$, touches both the curve $x^2 + y^2 = 1$ and $y^2 = 4\sqrt{2}x$, then $|c|$ is equal to

(a) $\frac{1}{\sqrt{2}}$ (b) 2 (c) $\sqrt{2}$ (d) $\frac{1}{2}$

47. Let the length of the latusrectum of an ellipse with its major axis along X-axis and centre of origin be 8 units. If the distance between the foci of this ellipse is equal to the length of its minor axis, then which one of the following points lies on it?

(a) $(4\sqrt{2}, 2\sqrt{3})$ (b) $(4\sqrt{3}, 2\sqrt{2})$

(c) $(4\sqrt{2}, 2\sqrt{2})$ (d) $(4\sqrt{3}, 2\sqrt{3})$

48. If the line $x - y = 12$ is a tangent to the ellipse $\frac{x^2}{a^2} + \frac{y^2}{b^2} = 1$ at the point $\left(3, -\frac{9}{2}\right)$, then the length of the latusrectum of the ellipse is

(a) $8\sqrt{3}$ units (b) 18 units

(c) 5 units (d) $12\sqrt{2}$ units

49. Let $S = \left\{(x, y) \in R^2 : \frac{y^2}{1+r} - \frac{x^2}{1-r} = 1\right\}$, where $r \neq \pm 1$. Then, S represents

(a) a hyperbola whose eccentricity is $\frac{2}{\sqrt{1-r}}$, when $0 < r < 1$

(b) a hyperbola whose eccentricity is $\frac{2}{\sqrt{1+r}}$, when $0 < r < 1$

(c) an ellipse whose eccentricity is $\sqrt{\frac{2}{r+1}}$, when $r > 1$

(d) an ellipse whose eccentricity is $\frac{1}{\sqrt{r+1}}$, when $r > 1$

50. Let $0 < \theta < \frac{\pi}{2}$. If the eccentricity of the hyperbola $\frac{x^2}{\cos^2\theta} - \frac{y^2}{\sin^2\theta} = 1$ is greater than 2, then the length of its latusrectum lies in the interval.

(a) $\left(1, \frac{3}{2}\right]$ (b) $(3, \infty)$

(c) $\left(\frac{3}{2}, 2\right]$ (d) $(2, 3]$

51. Assertion (A) The curve $y = -\frac{x^2}{2} + x + 1$ is symmetrical with respect to the line $x = 1$.

Reason (R) A parabola is symmetric about its axis.

(a) A and R both are true and R is the correct explanation of A

(b) A and R both are true but R is not the correct explanation of A

(c) A is true but R is false

(d) A is false but R is true

52. Assertion (A) If the foci of a hyperbola are at (4, 1) and (− 6, 1) and eccentricity is $\frac{5}{4}$, then the length of its transverse axis is 4 units.

Reason (R) Distance between the foci of a hyperbola is equal to the product of its eccentricity and length of the transverse axis.

(a) A and R both are true and R is the correct explanation of A

(b) A and R both are true but R is not the correct explanation of A

(c) A is true but R is false

(d) A is false but R is true

53. Column I contains the equation of conics and Column II contains the equation of tangents at the positive end of the latusrectum. Match the columns

	Column I		Column II
A.	$\frac{x^2}{9}+\frac{y^2}{16}=1$	(i)	$\sqrt{41}\,x-4y-16=0$
B.	$\frac{x^2}{16}-\frac{y^2}{25}=1$	(ii)	$x-y-2=0$
C.	$x^2-y^2=4$	(iii)	$4x+\sqrt{7}y-16=0$
D.	$y^2=8(x-4)$	(iv)	$\sqrt{2}x-y-2=0$

	A	B	C	D		A	B	C	D
(a)	(ii)	(iv)	(i)	(iii)	(b)	(iii)	(ii)	(iv)	(i)
(c)	(iii)	(i)	(iv)	(ii)	(d)	(iii)	(i)	(ii)	(iv)

Directions (Q. Nos. 54 and 55) *Read the information carefully answer the next two questions.*

A parabola touches the bisectors of the angle obtained by the lines $x+2y+3=0$ and $2x+y+3=0$ at the point $(1, 1)$ and $(0,-2)$.

54. The focus of the parabola is

(a) $(2, 3)$ (b) $(-2, 3)$ (c) $\left(\frac{2}{5},\frac{7}{5}\right)$ (d) $\left(\frac{1}{5},-\frac{7}{5}\right)$

55. The length of latusrectum is

(a) $\frac{16}{5^{3/2}}$ units (b) $\frac{16\sqrt{2}}{5}$ units

(c) $\frac{16\sqrt{5}}{2^{3/2}}$ units (d) $\frac{16\sqrt{2}}{5^{3/2}}$ units

Directions (Q.Nos. 56-58) *Read the information carefully and answer the next three questions.*

Consider the ellipse $\frac{x^2}{9}+\frac{y^2}{4}=1$ and the parabola $y^2=2x$. They intersect at P and Q in the first and fourth quadrants, respectively. Tangents to the ellipse at P and Q intersect the X-axis at R and tangents to the parabola at P and Q intersects the X-axis at S.

56. The ratio of the areas of the ΔPQS and ΔPQR is

(a) 1 : 3 (b) 1 : 2 (c) 2 : 3 (d) 3 : 4

57. The area of quadrilateral (in sq units) $PQRS$ is

(a) $\frac{3\sqrt{15}}{2}$ (b) $\frac{15\sqrt{3}}{2}$ (c) $\frac{5\sqrt{3}}{2}$ (d) $\frac{5\sqrt{15}}{2}$

58. The equation of circle touching the parabola at upper end of its latusrectum and passing through its vertex is

(a) $2x^2+2y^2-x-2y=0$

(b) $2x^2+2y^2+4x-\frac{9}{2}y=0$

(c) $2x^2+2y^2+x-3y=0$

(d) $2x^2+2y^2-7x+y=0$

Darken your choice with HB Pencil

1.	ⓐ ⓑ ⓒ ⓓ	11.	ⓐ ⓑ ⓒ ⓓ	21.	ⓐ ⓑ ⓒ ⓓ	31.	ⓐ ⓑ ⓒ ⓓ	41.	ⓐ ⓑ ⓒ ⓓ	51.	ⓐ ⓑ ⓒ ⓓ
2.	ⓐ ⓑ ⓒ ⓓ	12.	ⓐ ⓑ ⓒ ⓓ	22.	ⓐ ⓑ ⓒ ⓓ	32.	ⓐ ⓑ ⓒ ⓓ	42.	ⓐ ⓑ ⓒ ⓓ	52.	ⓐ ⓑ ⓒ ⓓ
3.	ⓐ ⓑ ⓒ ⓓ	13.	ⓐ ⓑ ⓒ ⓓ	23.	ⓐ ⓑ ⓒ ⓓ	33.	ⓐ ⓑ ⓒ ⓓ	43.	ⓐ ⓑ ⓒ ⓓ	53.	ⓐ ⓑ ⓒ ⓓ
4.	ⓐ ⓑ ⓒ ⓓ	14.	ⓐ ⓑ ⓒ ⓓ	24.	ⓐ ⓑ ⓒ ⓓ	34.	ⓐ ⓑ ⓒ ⓓ	44.	ⓐ ⓑ ⓒ ⓓ	54.	ⓐ ⓑ ⓒ ⓓ
5.	ⓐ ⓑ ⓒ ⓓ	15.	ⓐ ⓑ ⓒ ⓓ	25.	ⓐ ⓑ ⓒ ⓓ	35.	ⓐ ⓑ ⓒ ⓓ	45.	ⓐ ⓑ ⓒ ⓓ	55.	ⓐ ⓑ ⓒ ⓓ
6.	ⓐ ⓑ ⓒ ⓓ	16.	ⓐ ⓑ ⓒ ⓓ	26.	ⓐ ⓑ ⓒ ⓓ	36.	ⓐ ⓑ ⓒ ⓓ	46.	ⓐ ⓑ ⓒ ⓓ	56.	ⓐ ⓑ ⓒ ⓓ
7.	ⓐ ⓑ ⓒ ⓓ	17.	ⓐ ⓑ ⓒ ⓓ	27.	ⓐ ⓑ ⓒ ⓓ	37.	ⓐ ⓑ ⓒ ⓓ	47.	ⓐ ⓑ ⓒ ⓓ	57.	ⓐ ⓑ ⓒ ⓓ
8.	ⓐ ⓑ ⓒ ⓓ	18.	ⓐ ⓑ ⓒ ⓓ	28.	ⓐ ⓑ ⓒ ⓓ	38.	ⓐ ⓑ ⓒ ⓓ	48.	ⓐ ⓑ ⓒ ⓓ	58.	ⓐ ⓑ ⓒ ⓓ
9.	ⓐ ⓑ ⓒ ⓓ	19.	ⓐ ⓑ ⓒ ⓓ	29.	ⓐ ⓑ ⓒ ⓓ	39.	ⓐ ⓑ ⓒ ⓓ	49.	ⓐ ⓑ ⓒ ⓓ		
10.	ⓐ ⓑ ⓒ ⓓ	20.	ⓐ ⓑ ⓒ ⓓ	30.	ⓐ ⓑ ⓒ ⓓ	40.	ⓐ ⓑ ⓒ ⓓ	50.	ⓐ ⓑ ⓒ ⓓ		

Introduction to 3-D Geometry

MCQs 1 Mark Questions

1. In the given figure, if P is (2, 4, 5), then the coordinates of F are

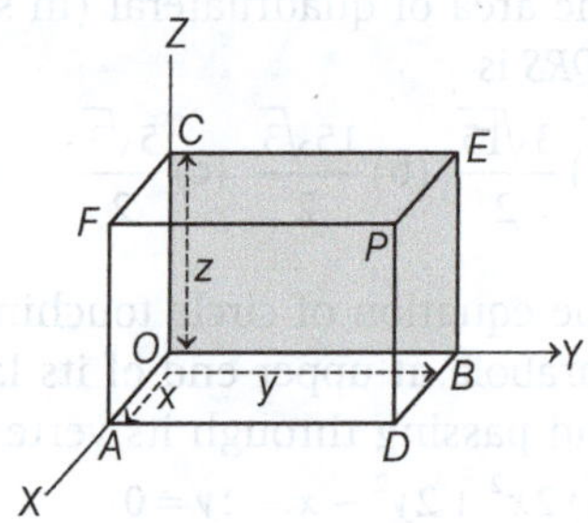

(a) (0, 2, 5) (b) (2, 0, 5)
(c) (0, 5, 2) (d) None of these

2. The equation of set of points P such that $PA^2 + PB^2 = 2k^2$, where A and B are the points (3, 4, 5) and (–1, 3, –7) respectively, is

(a) $2x^2 + 2y^2 + 2z^2 - 4x + 14y + 4z = 2k^2 + 109$

(b) $2x^2 + 2y^2 + 2z^2 - 4x - 14y + 4z = 2k^2 - 109$

(c) $3x^2 + 3y^2 + 3z^2 - 4x - 14y + 4z = 2k^2 + 109$

(d) None of the above

3. The locus of the points which is equidistant from YZ-plane and ZX-plane is
(a) $x + y = 0$
(b) $x^2 - y^2 = 0$
(c) $x^2 + y^2 + z^2 = 0$
(d) $x^3 - y^3 = 0$

4. The distance between the circumcentre and the orthocentre of the triangle formed by the points (2, 1, 5), (3, 2, 3) and (4, 0, 4) is
(a) 3 units (b) 2 units
(c) 1 unit (d) 0 unit

5. The perimeter of the triangle formed by (5, 0, 0), (0, 5, 0), (0, 0, 5) is
(a) $\sqrt{2}$ units (b) $5\sqrt{2}$ units
(c) $3\sqrt{2}$ units (d) $15\sqrt{2}$ units

6. If the extremities of a diagonal of a square are (1, – 2, 3) and (2, – 3 , 5), then the length of its side is
(a) $\sqrt{6}$ units (b) $\sqrt{3}$ units
(c) $\sqrt{5}$ units (d) $\sqrt{7}$ units

7. If $A(1, 2, 3)$, $B(3, 4, 5)$, $C(1, 0, 1)$, $D(3, 8, 6)$ are four points in a space, then point nearest to the origin is
(a) A (b) B (c) C (d) D

8. If a and b are the perpendicular distances from (3, 4, 5) to the X and Z-axes respectively, then ab is equal to

(a) $5\sqrt{41}$ units (b) 8 units

(c) $\sqrt{41}$ units (d) 12 units

9. The distance of a point $P(x, y, z)$ from its image in ZX-plane is

(a) $2|x|$ (b) $2|y|$

(c) $2|z|$ (d) $2\sqrt{x^2 + y^2 + z^2}$

10. The points $(-2, 3, 5)$, $(1, 2, 3)$ and $(7, 0, -1)$ form

(a) an isosceles triangle

(b) a right angled triangle

(c) an equilateral triangle

(d) collinear points

11. The equation of set of points which are equidistant from the point (1, 2, 3) and $(3, 2, -1)$ is

(a) $x - 2z = 0$ (b) $2x - z = 0$

(c) $2x + y = 0$ (d) $x - 2y = 0$

12. The circumcentre of the triangle formed by the points $(1, 2, 3)$, $(3, -1, 5)$, $(4, 0, -3)$ is

(a) (2, 2, 2) (b) (1, 1, 1)

(c) (3, 3, 3) (d) $\left(\frac{7}{2}, -\frac{1}{2}, 1\right)$

13. Which of the following pairs of points have a distance $\sqrt{43}$?

(a) (2, 3, 5) and (4, 3, 1)

(b) $(-3, 7, 2)$ and $(2, 4, -1)$

(c) $(-1, 3, -4)$ and $(1, -3, 4)$

(d) $(2, -1, 3)$ and $(-2, 1, 3)$

14. Which of the following statement(s) is/are correct?

(a) $(0, 7, -10)$, $(1, 6, -6)$ and $(4, 9, -6)$ are the vertices of an isosceles triangle

(b) $(0, 7, 10)$, $(-1, 6, 6)$ and $(-4, 9, 6)$ are the vertices of a right angled triangle

(c) $(-1, 2, 1)$, $(1, -2, 5)$ $(4, -7, 8)$ and $(2, -3, 4)$ are the vertices of a parallelogram

(d) All of the above

15. If the distance between the points $(a, 0, 1)$ and $(0, 1, 2)$ is $\sqrt{27}$, then the value of a is

(a) 5 (b) ± 5

(c) -5 (d) None of these

16. Distance of the point (1, 2, 3) from the coordinate axes are

(a) 13, 10, 5 (b) $\sqrt{13}, \sqrt{10}, \sqrt{5}$

(c) $\sqrt{5}, \sqrt{13}, \sqrt{10}$ (d) $\frac{1}{\sqrt{13}}, \frac{1}{\sqrt{10}}, \frac{1}{\sqrt{5}}$

17. If L, M and N are the feet of the perpendicular segments drawn from a point P (3, 4, 5) on the XY, YZ and ZX-planes respectively, then the coordinates of L, M and N are respectively

(a) (3, 0, 0), (0, 4, 5) and (3, 0, 5)

(b) (3, 4, 0), (0, 4, 5) and (3, 0, 5)

(c) (3, 4, 5), (0, 0, 3) and (3, 4, 0)

(d) None of the above

18. If (9, 1, 4) is centroid of the tetrahedron for which (2, 1, 5), (3, 2, 3) and (4, 0, 4) are three vertices, then the fourth vertex is

(a) (27, 1, 4) (b) (2, 3, 4)

(c) (4, 5, 16) (d) (2, 2, 12)

19. In a tetrahedron $ABCD$, $A = (2, 3, -1)$ and $G(2, 3, 4)$ is the centroid of the tetrahedron. If P is the centroid of ΔBCD, then AP is equal to

(a) $\frac{5}{3}$ (b) $\frac{20}{3}$ (c) 7 (d) 4

20. The equation of the set of points which are equidistant from the points $(1, 2, 3)$ and $(3, 2, -1)$ is

(a) $x - 3z = 0$ (b) $x - 2z = 0$

(c) $x - 4z = 0$ (d) $x + 2z = 0$

21. If the coordinates of the vertices of a ΔABC are $A(-1, 3, 2)$, $B(2, 3, 5)$ and $C(3, 5, -2)$, then $\angle A$ is equal to

(a) 45° (b) 60°

(c) 90° (d) 30°

MCQs 2 Marks Questions

22. If $x^2 + y^2 = 1$, then the distance from the point $(x, y, \sqrt{1 - x^2 - y^2})$ to the origin is

(a) 1 (b) -1
(c) 0 (d) 2

23. If a parallelopiped is formed by planes drawn through the points (5, 8, 10) and (3, 6, 8) parallel to the coordinate planes, then the length of diagonal of the parallelopiped is

(a) $2\sqrt{3}$ (b) $3\sqrt{2}$
(c) $\sqrt{2}$ (d) $\sqrt{3}$

24. If the sum of the squares of the distance of a point from the three coordinate axes be 36, then its distance from the origin is

(a) 6 (b) $3\sqrt{2}$
(c) $2\sqrt{3}$ (d) None of these

25. The point $A(1, -1, 3)$, $B(2, -4, 5)$ and $C(5, -13, 11)$ are

(a) collinear
(b) non-collinear
(c) Do not say anything
(d) None of the above

26. The area of the triangle, whose vertices are at the points (2, 1, 1), (3, 1, 2) and (– 4, 0, 1) is

(a) $\sqrt{19}$ (b) $\frac{1}{2}\sqrt{19}$
(c) $\frac{1}{2}\sqrt{38}$ (d) $\frac{1}{2}\sqrt{57}$

Directions (Q. Nos. 27 and 28) *Read the following information carefully and answer the next two questions.*

Consider the figure given below

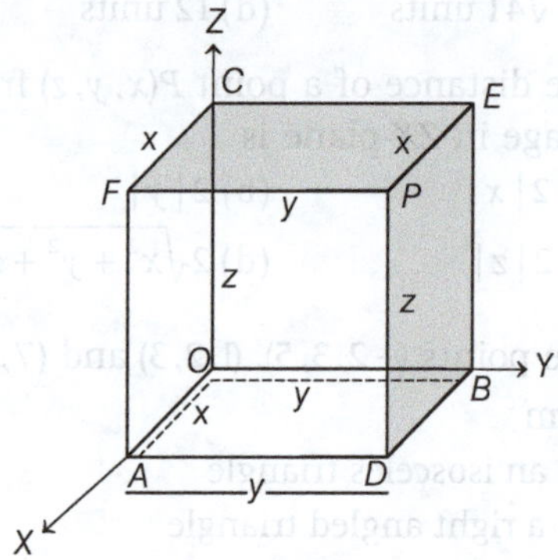

Here, a point P is shown in space, not in a coordinate plane and planes YZ, ZX and XY are meeting at the coordinate axes at the points A, B and C, respectively.

27. Based on the above information which among the following is said to be correct?

(a) $ADPF \parallel YZ$-plane
(b) $BDPE \parallel XZ$-plane
(c) $CFPE \parallel XY$-plane
(d) All of the above

28. Which of the following is/are not a pair of rectangular faces of the rectangular parallelopiped (as shown in the figure above)?

(i) ($ADPF$, $OBEC$)
(ii) ($BDPE$, $CFAO$)
(iii) ($AOEC$, $FPBD$)

(a) Only (i) (b) Only (ii)
(c) Only (iii) (d) Both (i) and (ii)

Darken your choice with HB Pencil

1.	ⓐ ⓑ ⓒ ⓓ	6.	ⓐ ⓑ ⓒ ⓓ	11.	ⓐ ⓑ ⓒ ⓓ	16.	ⓐ ⓑ ⓒ ⓓ	21.	ⓐ ⓑ ⓒ ⓓ	26.	ⓐ ⓑ ⓒ ⓓ
2.	ⓐ ⓑ ⓒ ⓓ	7.	ⓐ ⓑ ⓒ ⓓ	12.	ⓐ ⓑ ⓒ ⓓ	17.	ⓐ ⓑ ⓒ ⓓ	22.	ⓐ ⓑ ⓒ ⓓ	27.	ⓐ ⓑ ⓒ ⓓ
3.	ⓐ ⓑ ⓒ ⓓ	8.	ⓐ ⓑ ⓒ ⓓ	13.	ⓐ ⓑ ⓒ ⓓ	18.	ⓐ ⓑ ⓒ ⓓ	23.	ⓐ ⓑ ⓒ ⓓ	28.	ⓐ ⓑ ⓒ ⓓ
4.	ⓐ ⓑ ⓒ ⓓ	9.	ⓐ ⓑ ⓒ ⓓ	14.	ⓐ ⓑ ⓒ ⓓ	19.	ⓐ ⓑ ⓒ ⓓ	24.	ⓐ ⓑ ⓒ ⓓ		
5.	ⓐ ⓑ ⓒ ⓓ	10.	ⓐ ⓑ ⓒ ⓓ	15.	ⓐ ⓑ ⓒ ⓓ	20.	ⓐ ⓑ ⓒ ⓓ	25.	ⓐ ⓑ ⓒ ⓓ		

Chapter

12

Limits and Derivatives

MCQs 1 Mark Questions

1. If $\lim_{x \to 5} \frac{|x-5|}{x-5}$ is equal to

(a) 1 (b) −1

(c) does not exist (d) None of these

2. $\lim_{y \to 0} \frac{y\sqrt{x^2-(x-y)^2}}{\{\sqrt{8xy-4y^2}+\sqrt{8xy}\}^3}$ is equal to

(a) $\frac{1}{4x}$ (b) $\frac{1}{2}$

(c) $\frac{1}{128x}$ (d) None of these

3. If $f(x)=\begin{cases}\frac{1}{2-x}, & \text{when } x<1\\ 2-x, & \text{when } x>1\end{cases}$, then

(a) $\lim_{x\to 1^+} f(x)=0$ (b) $\lim_{x\to 1^-} f(x)=0$

(c) $\lim_{x\to 1^-} \neq \lim_{x\to 1^+} f(x)$ (d) None of these

4. The value of constants a and b so that $\lim_{x\to\infty}\left(\frac{x^2+1}{x+1}-ax-b\right)=0$ is

(a) $a=0, b=0$ (b) $a=1, b=-1$

(c) $a=-1, b=1$ (d) $a=2, b=-1$

5. $\lim_{x\to -1} \frac{1}{\sqrt{|x|-\{x\}}}$ is equal to [where, $\{\cdot\}$ denotes fractional part of x]

(a) 1 (b) $\frac{1}{2}$

(c) 0 (d) does not exist

6. The value of $\lim_{x\to 2} \frac{5^{x/2}-5}{5^x-25}$ is

(a) 0 (b) $\frac{1}{5}$

(c) $\frac{1}{10}$ (d) ln 5

7. $\lim_{x\to 1^+} \frac{\sqrt{x^2-1}+\sqrt{x-1}}{\sqrt{x^2-1}}$ is equal to

(a) $1+\frac{1}{\sqrt{2}}$ (b) $1-\frac{1}{\sqrt{2}}$

(c) $-1+\frac{1}{\sqrt{2}}$ (d) $-1-\frac{1}{\sqrt{2}}$

8. $f(x)=\begin{cases}x\sin\frac{1}{x}, & x\neq 0\\ 0, & x=0\end{cases}$, then $\lim_{x\to 0} f(x)$ is equal to

(a) 1 (b) 0

(c) −1 (d) does not exist

9. $\lim_{x\to 0} \frac{a^x-1}{\sqrt{1+x}-1}$ is equal to

(a) $2\log_e a$ (b) $\frac{1}{2}\log_e a$

(c) $a \log_e 2$ (d) None of these

10. The value of $\lim\limits_{x \to 1} \dfrac{\sqrt[3]{7+x^2} - \sqrt{3+x^2}}{x-1}$ is

(a) $-\dfrac{1}{3}$ (b) $\dfrac{3}{2}$ (c) $-\dfrac{1}{4}$ (d) $\dfrac{1}{4}$

11. The value of $\lim\limits_{x \to 2} \dfrac{\sqrt{x-2} + \sqrt{x} - \sqrt{2}}{\sqrt{x^2-4}}$ is

(a) 1 (b) 2 (c) $\dfrac{1}{2}$ (d) $\dfrac{1}{4}$

12. $\lim\limits_{x \to \infty} \dfrac{1^2 + 2^2 + 3^2 + \ldots + x^2}{x^3}$ is equal to

(a) $-\dfrac{1}{6}$ (b) $\dfrac{1}{6}$ (c) $\dfrac{1}{3}$ (d) $-\dfrac{1}{3}$

13. $\lim\limits_{x \to \infty} \left[\dfrac{1}{1-x^2} + \dfrac{2}{1-x^2} + \ldots + \dfrac{x}{1-x^2} \right]$ is equal to

(a) 0 (b) $-\dfrac{1}{2}$

(c) $\dfrac{1}{2}$ (d) None of these

14. $\lim\limits_{n \to \infty} \left[\dfrac{n!}{n^n} \right]^{\frac{1}{n}}$ is equal to

(a) e (b) $\dfrac{1}{e}$ (c) $\dfrac{\pi}{4}$ (d) $\dfrac{4}{\pi}$

15. $\lim\limits_{x \to 0} \dfrac{(1-\cos 2x)\sin 3x}{x^2 \sin 5x}$ is equal to

(a) $\dfrac{10}{3}$ (b) $\dfrac{3}{10}$ (c) $\dfrac{6}{5}$ (d) $\dfrac{5}{6}$

16. $\lim\limits_{x \to 1} (1-x)\tan\left(\dfrac{\pi x}{2}\right)$ is equal to

(a) $\dfrac{\pi}{2}$ (b) π (c) $\dfrac{2}{\pi}$ (d) 0

17. $\lim\limits_{x \to \frac{\pi}{2}} \left(\dfrac{1 - \tan\dfrac{x}{2}}{1 + \tan\dfrac{x}{2}} \right) \left(\dfrac{1 - \sin x}{(\pi - 2x)^3} \right)$ is equal to

(a) $\dfrac{1}{8}$ (b) $\dfrac{1}{32}$ (c) $\dfrac{1}{64}$ (d) $\dfrac{1}{128}$

18. $\lim\limits_{x \to \frac{\pi}{2}} \dfrac{\left(1 - \tan\dfrac{x}{2}\right)(1 - \sin x)}{\left(1 + \tan\dfrac{x}{2}\right)(\pi - 2x)^3}$ is equal to

(a) $\dfrac{1}{8}$ (b) 0 (c) $\dfrac{1}{32}$ (d) ∞

19. The value of $\lim\limits_{x \to \frac{1}{\alpha}} \dfrac{\sin(cx^2 + bx + a)}{x\alpha - 1}$ (where α and β are the roots of $ax^2 + bx + c = 0$) is

(a) $c\left(\dfrac{\beta - \alpha}{\alpha\beta}\right)$ (b) $\left(\dfrac{\beta - \alpha}{\alpha}\right)$

(c) $\dfrac{1}{\alpha}$ (d) $\dfrac{c}{\alpha}\left(\dfrac{1}{\alpha} - \dfrac{1}{\beta}\right)$

20. $\lim\limits_{x \to \frac{\pi}{2}} \dfrac{2^{\cot x} - 2^{\cos x}}{\cot x - \cos x}$ is equal to

(a) log 2 (b) 0 (c) 2 (d) log x

21. If $[\cdot]$ denotes the greatest integer function, then

$\lim\limits_{x \to 0} \dfrac{\tan([-2\pi^2]x^2) - x^2 \tan([-2\pi^2])}{\sin^2 x}$ is equal to

(a) – 20 + tan 20 (b) 20 + tan 20

(c) 20 (d) tan 20

22. $\lim\limits_{x \to 0} \dfrac{e^{ax} - e^{bx}}{x}$ is equal to

(a) $a + b$ (b) $\dfrac{1}{a} + b$ (c) $a^2 - b^2$ (d) $a - b$

23. $\lim\limits_{x \to 0} \dfrac{\log_e(1+2x) - 2\log_e(1+x)}{x^2}$ is equal to

(a) – 1 (b) 1 (c) 2 (d) – 2

24. $\lim\limits_{x \to 0} \dfrac{xe^x - \log(1+x)}{x^2}$ is equal to

(a) $\dfrac{2}{3}$ (b) $\dfrac{1}{3}$ (c) $\dfrac{1}{2}$ (d) $\dfrac{3}{2}$

25. Let $f(2) = 4$ and $f'(2) = 4$, then

$\lim\limits_{x \to 2} \dfrac{xf(2) - 2f(x)}{x-2}$ is equal to

(a) 2 (b) – 2
(c) – 4 (d) 3

26. If $f(x)=\sqrt{25-x^2}$, then $\lim_{x\to 1}\frac{f(x)-f(1)}{x-1}$ is equal to

(a) $\frac{1}{\sqrt{24}}$ (b) $\frac{1}{5}$ (c) $-\sqrt{24}$ (d) $-\frac{1}{\sqrt{24}}$

27. The value of the derivative of $|x-1|+|x+1|$ at $x=2$ is

(a) – 2 (b) 0
(c) 2 (d) not defined

28. If $2f(x)+f\left(\frac{1}{x}\right)=x+2$ and $y=3f(x)$, then $\frac{dy}{dx}$ at $x=1$ is

(a) 2 (b) 3 (c) 4 (d) 5

29. If $x^y=e^{x-y}$, then $\frac{dy}{dx}$ is equal to

(a) $\frac{\log x}{(1+\log x)^2}$ (b) $\frac{-\log x}{(1+\log x)^2}$

(c) $\frac{-\log x}{(1-\log x)^2}$ (d) $\frac{\log x}{(1-\log x)^2}$

30. $\frac{d}{dx}(\sqrt{\sin\sqrt{x}})$ is equal to

(a) $\frac{\cos\sqrt{x}}{4\sqrt{x\sin\sqrt{x}}}$ (b) $\frac{\sin\sqrt{x}}{4\sqrt{x\cos\sqrt{x}}}$

(c) $\frac{-\cos x\sqrt{x}}{4\sqrt{x\sin\sqrt{x}}}$ (d) $\frac{-\tan\sqrt{x}}{4\sqrt{x\cos\sqrt{x}}}$

31. If $y=e^{\cos^2 x+\cos^4 x+\cos^6 x+\ldots\infty}$, then $\frac{dy}{dx}$ is equal to

(a) $2y\cot x$ (b) $y\cot^2 x$
(c) $-2y\cot x\operatorname{cosec}^2 x$ (d) $2y\cot x\operatorname{cosec}^2 x$

32. If $f(x)=\log_x(\log x)$, then $f'(x)$ at $x=e$ is

(a) e (b) $\frac{1}{e}$ (c) 1 (d) $\frac{1}{e^2}$

33. If $\lim_{x\to 0}\left[1+x+\frac{f(x)}{x}\right]^{1/x}=e^3$, then $\lim_{x\to 0}\left[1+\frac{f(x)}{x}\right]^{1/x}$ is equal to

(a) e (b) e^2
(c) e^3 (d) None of these

34. $\lim_{x\to 1}(\log_2 2x)^{\log_x 5}$ is equal to

(a) $\log_2 5$ (b) $e^{\log_2 5}$
(c) e (d) 0

35. If $y=\cos x\cos 2x\cos 4x\cos 8x\cos 16x$, then $\frac{dy}{dx}$ at $x=\frac{\pi}{4}$ is

(a) $\sqrt{2}$ (b) $\frac{1}{\sqrt{2}}$
(c) 1 (d) None of these

36. If $y=\sqrt{\frac{1+\cos\theta}{1-\cos\theta}}$, then $\frac{dy}{d\theta}$ at $\theta=\frac{3\pi}{4}$ is

(a) $\sqrt{2}+2$ (b) $\sqrt{2}-2$
(c) 1 (d) – 1

37. The derivative of $\tan^{-1}\left(\frac{\sin x-\cos x}{\sin x+\cos x}\right)$ w.r.t. $\frac{x}{2}$, where $\left\{x\in\left(0,\frac{\pi}{2}\right)\right\}$ is

(a) 2 (b) –2 (c) 1 (d) –1

38. If $y=2^{2^x}$, then $\frac{dy}{dx}$ is equal to

(a) $y\cdot 2^x(\log 2)^2$ (b) $y\cdot 2^x\cdot\log 2$
(c) $(y\cdot 2^x)^2$ (d) $y\cdot 2^x$

39. If $y=(\log x)^x$, then $\frac{dy}{dx}$ is equal to

(a) $y\left[\log(\log x)+\frac{1}{\log x}\right]$

(b) $y\left[\log(\log x)-\frac{1}{\log x}\right]$

(c) $-y\left[\log(\log x)+\frac{1}{\log x}\right]$

(d) $-y\left[\log(\log x)-\frac{1}{\log x}\right]$

40. $\lim_{x\to 0}\frac{2^x-3^x}{x(2^x+3^x)}$ is equal to

(a) $\frac{1}{2}\log\frac{2}{3}$ (b) $\log\frac{2}{3}$

(c) $\frac{1}{2}\log\frac{3}{2}$ (d) $\log\frac{3}{2}$

MCQs 2 Marks Questions

41. If $a_1=1$ and $a_{n+1}=\frac{4+3a_n}{3+2a_n}, n\geq 1$ and if $\lim_{n\to\infty} a_n=n$, then the value of a is

(a) $\sqrt{2}$ (b) 2

(c) $-\sqrt{2}$ (d) None of these

42. $\lim_{y\to\infty}\left(\sqrt{y+\sqrt{y+\sqrt{y}}}-\sqrt{y}\right)$ is equal to

(a) 0 (b) log 2 (c) e^2 (d) $\frac{1}{2}$

43. $\lim_{x\to\frac{\pi}{2}}\frac{\cot x-\cos x}{(\pi-2x)^3}$ is equal to

(a) $\frac{1}{24}$ (b) $\frac{1}{16}$ (c) $\frac{1}{8}$ (d) $\frac{1}{4}$

44. If $y=\sum_{k=1}^{6}k\cos^{-1}\left\{\frac{3}{5}\cos kx-\frac{4}{5}\sin kx\right\}$, then $\frac{dy}{dx}$ at $x=0$ is

(a) 90 (b) 91 (c) 92 (d) 94

45. $\lim_{x\to y}\frac{\sin^2 x-\sin^2 y}{x^2-y^2}$ is equal to

(a) 0 (b) 1 (c) $\frac{\sin y}{y}$ (d) $\frac{\sin 2y}{2y}$

46. If α is the positive root of the equation $p(x)=x^2-x-2=0$, then the $\lim_{x\to\alpha^+}\frac{\sqrt{1-\cos(p(x))}}{x+\alpha-4}$ is equal to

(a) $\frac{1}{\sqrt{2}}$ (b) $\frac{1}{2}$ (c) $\frac{3}{\sqrt{2}}$ (d) $\frac{3}{2}$

47. The value of $\lim_{x\to 0^+}x^m(\log x)^n$, where $m, n\in N$ is

(a) 0 (b) $\frac{m}{n}$

(c) nm (d) None of these

48. $\lim_{x\to 2}\frac{\sin(e^{x-2}-1)}{\log(x-1)}$ is equal to

(a) -2 (b) -1 (c) 0 (d) 1

49. $\lim_{x\to 0}\frac{(729)^x-(243)^x-(81)^x+9^x+3^x-1}{x^3}=\lambda(\ln 3)^3$, then the value of λ is

(a) 4 (b) 5 (c) 6 (d) 9

50. For $x>1$, if $(2x)^{2y}=4e^{2x-2y}$, then $(1+\log_e 2x)^2\frac{dy}{dx}$ is equal to

(a) $\frac{x\log_e 2x+\log_e 2}{x(1+\log_e(2x))^2}$ (b) $\frac{x\log_e 2x-\log_e 2}{x(1+\log_e(2x))^2}$

(c) $x\log_e 2x$ (d) $\log_e 2x$

51. The differential coefficient of $\tan^{-1}\left(\frac{\sqrt{2ax-x^2}}{a-x}\right)$ w.r.t. x is

(a) $\frac{1}{\sqrt{2ax-x^2}}$ (b) $\frac{1}{\sqrt{2ax+x^2}}$

(c) $\frac{1}{\sqrt{ax+x^2}}$ (d) $\frac{1}{\sqrt{ax-x^2}}$

52. If $x=\sin^{-1}2^y$, then $\frac{dy}{dx}$ is equal to

(a) $\frac{\log 2}{\sqrt{1-x^2}}$ (b) $\frac{\sin x}{\log 2}$

(c) $\frac{\cot x}{\log 2}$ (d) $\frac{\tan x}{\log 2}$

53. If $y = \tan^{-1}\left(\dfrac{\cos x - \sin x}{\cos x + \sin x}\right)$, then $\dfrac{dy}{dx}$ is equal to

(a) $\dfrac{1}{2(1+x^2)}$ (b) $\dfrac{1}{1+x^2}$

(c) 1 (d) -1

54. If $x = t + \sin t$, $y = 1 - \cos t$ and $\dfrac{dx}{dy} = \cot p$, then p is equal to

(a) t (b) $2t$ (c) $\dfrac{t}{2}$ (d) $-t^2$

55. If $x = t - \dfrac{1}{t}$, $y = t + \dfrac{1}{t}$, then $\dfrac{dy}{dx}$ is equal to

(a) $\dfrac{x}{y}$ (b) $\dfrac{y}{x}$ (c) $-\dfrac{x}{y}$ (d) $-\dfrac{y}{x}$

56. Assertion (A) $\lim\limits_{x \to 0} \dfrac{\sqrt{1-\cos 2x}}{x}$ does not exist.

Reason (R) $|\sin x| = \begin{cases} \sin x, & 0 < x < \dfrac{\pi}{2} \\ -\sin x, & -\dfrac{\pi}{2} < x < 0 \end{cases}$

(a) A and R both are true and R is the correct explanation of A

(b) A and R both are true but R is not the correct explanation of A

(c) A is true but R is false

(d) A is false but R is true

Directions (Q.Nos. 57-61) *Read the information carefully and answer the next five questions.*

If $\lim\limits_{x \to 0^+} f(x) =$ finite, where

$$f(x) = \frac{\sin x + ae^x + be^{-x} + c\ln(1+x)}{x^3}$$ and

a, b, c are real numbers.

57. The value of a is

(a) $-\dfrac{1}{2}$ (b) 0 (c) $\dfrac{1}{2}$ (d) 1

58. The value of b is

(a) $-\dfrac{1}{2}$ (b) $\dfrac{1}{2}$ (c) 0 (d) 1

59. The value of c is

(a) $-\dfrac{1}{2}$ (b) $\dfrac{1}{2}$

(c) 0 (d) 2

60. The value of $\lim\limits_{x \to 0^+} f(x)$ is

(a) -2 (b) -1

(c) $-\dfrac{1}{2}$ (d) $-\dfrac{1}{3}$

61. For the same values of a, b, c as obtain above, then the value of $\lim\limits_{x \to 0^+} x^2 f(x)$ is

(a) 0 (b) 1 (c) 2 (d) 3

Darken your choice with HB Pencil

1.	ⓐ ⓑ ⓒ ⓓ	11.	ⓐ ⓑ ⓒ ⓓ	21.	ⓐ ⓑ ⓒ ⓓ	31.	ⓐ ⓑ ⓒ ⓓ	41.	ⓐ ⓑ ⓒ ⓓ	51.	ⓐ ⓑ ⓒ ⓓ
2.	ⓐ ⓑ ⓒ ⓓ	12.	ⓐ ⓑ ⓒ ⓓ	22.	ⓐ ⓑ ⓒ ⓓ	32.	ⓐ ⓑ ⓒ ⓓ	42.	ⓐ ⓑ ⓒ ⓓ	52.	ⓐ ⓑ ⓒ ⓓ
3.	ⓐ ⓑ ⓒ ⓓ	13.	ⓐ ⓑ ⓒ ⓓ	23.	ⓐ ⓑ ⓒ ⓓ	33.	ⓐ ⓑ ⓒ ⓓ	43.	ⓐ ⓑ ⓒ ⓓ	53.	ⓐ ⓑ ⓒ ⓓ
4.	ⓐ ⓑ ⓒ ⓓ	14.	ⓐ ⓑ ⓒ ⓓ	24.	ⓐ ⓑ ⓒ ⓓ	34.	ⓐ ⓑ ⓒ ⓓ	44.	ⓐ ⓑ ⓒ ⓓ	54.	ⓐ ⓑ ⓒ ⓓ
5.	ⓐ ⓑ ⓒ ⓓ	15.	ⓐ ⓑ ⓒ ⓓ	25.	ⓐ ⓑ ⓒ ⓓ	35.	ⓐ ⓑ ⓒ ⓓ	45.	ⓐ ⓑ ⓒ ⓓ	55.	ⓐ ⓑ ⓒ ⓓ
6.	ⓐ ⓑ ⓒ ⓓ	16.	ⓐ ⓑ ⓒ ⓓ	26.	ⓐ ⓑ ⓒ ⓓ	36.	ⓐ ⓑ ⓒ ⓓ	46.	ⓐ ⓑ ⓒ ⓓ	56.	ⓐ ⓑ ⓒ ⓓ
7.	ⓐ ⓑ ⓒ ⓓ	17.	ⓐ ⓑ ⓒ ⓓ	27.	ⓐ ⓑ ⓒ ⓓ	37.	ⓐ ⓑ ⓒ ⓓ	47.	ⓐ ⓑ ⓒ ⓓ	57.	ⓐ ⓑ ⓒ ⓓ
8.	ⓐ ⓑ ⓒ ⓓ	18.	ⓐ ⓑ ⓒ ⓓ	28.	ⓐ ⓑ ⓒ ⓓ	38.	ⓐ ⓑ ⓒ ⓓ	48.	ⓐ ⓑ ⓒ ⓓ	58.	ⓐ ⓑ ⓒ ⓓ
9.	ⓐ ⓑ ⓒ ⓓ	19.	ⓐ ⓑ ⓒ ⓓ	29.	ⓐ ⓑ ⓒ ⓓ	39.	ⓐ ⓑ ⓒ ⓓ	49.	ⓐ ⓑ ⓒ ⓓ	59.	ⓐ ⓑ ⓒ ⓓ
10.	ⓐ ⓑ ⓒ ⓓ	20.	ⓐ ⓑ ⓒ ⓓ	30.	ⓐ ⓑ ⓒ ⓓ	40.	ⓐ ⓑ ⓒ ⓓ	50.	ⓐ ⓑ ⓒ ⓓ	60.	ⓐ ⓑ ⓒ ⓓ
										61.	ⓐ ⓑ ⓒ ⓓ

Chapter 13

Statistics

MCQs 1 Mark Questions

1. The arithmetic mean of the series $^nC_0, {}^nC_1, {}^nC_2, \ldots, {}^nC_n$ is

(a) $\frac{2^n}{n}$ (b) $\frac{2^n}{n+1}$ (c) $\frac{2^{n+1}}{n}$ (d) $\frac{2^{n+1}}{n+1}$

2. The mean weight of all the students in a class is 60 kg. The mean weight of the boys from the class is 70 kg while that of the girls is 55 kg. The ratio of the numbers of boys to that of girls is

(a) 2 : 1 (b) 1 : 2 (c) 1 : 4 (d) 4 : 1

3. If AM of numbers $a_1, a_2, \ldots, a_n$ is K, then the AM of the numbers which are increased by 1, 2, 3, ..., n, respectively is

(a) $K + \left(\frac{n+1}{2}\right)$ (b) K

(c) $K + \frac{n(n+1)}{2}$ (d) $K - \left(\frac{n+1}{2}\right)$

4. The mean of 30 observations is 75. If each observation is multiplied by a non-zero number K and then each of them is decreased by 25, their mean remains the same. Then, K is equal to

(a) $\frac{10}{3}$ (b) $\frac{4}{3}$ (c) $\frac{1}{3}$ (d) $\frac{2}{3}$

5. The frequency distribution of daily working expenditure of families in a locality is as follows

Expenditure (in ₹) (x)	Number of families (f)
0-50	24
50-100	33
100-150	37
150-200	b
200-250	25

If the mode of the distribution is ₹ 140, then the value of b is

(a) 34 (b) 31 (c) 26 (d) 36

6. If the median and range of four numbers $\{x, y, 2x + y, x - y\}$, where $0 < y < x < 2y$, are 10 and 28 respectively, then mean of the numbers is

(a) 18 (b) 10 (c) 5 (d) 14

7. The median of 100 observations grouped in classes of equal width is 35. If the median class interval is 30-40 and the number of observations less than 30 is 45, then the frequency of median class is

(a) 10 (b) 20 (c) 15 (d) 12

8. The median of a set of 21 distinct observations is 18. If each of the largest 10 observations of the set is increased by 2, then the median of the new set

(a) remains the same as that of the original set
(b) is increased by 2
(c) is decreased by 2
(d) is two times the original median

9. The median of 27 observations of a variable is 18. Three more observations are made and the values of these observations are 16, 18 and 50. The median of these 30 observations is
(a) 18
(b) 19
(c) 25.5
(d) Cannot be determined due to insufficient data

10. Consider the following statements in respect of the below frequency distribution

Class interval	1-5	6-10	11-15	16-20
Frequency	3	7	6	5

I. The median is contained in the modal class.
II. The distribution is bell-shaped.

Which of the above statements is/are correct?
(a) Only I (b) Only II
(c) Both I and II (d) Neither I nor II

11. If in a frequency distribution, the mean and median are 21 and 22 respectively, then its mode is (approximately)
(a) 22.0 (b) 20.5 (c) 25.5 (d) 24.0

12. If the mean deviation of the numbers $1, 1+d, 1+2d, \ldots, 1+100d$ from their mean is 295, then d is equal to
(a) 10.5 (b) 11.5 (c) 11.68 (d) 11.55

13. The mean deviation from the mean of the AP $a, a+d, a+2d, \ldots, a+2nd$ is
(a) $n(n+1)d$ (b) $\frac{n(n+1)d}{2n+1}$
(c) $\frac{n(n+1)d}{2n}$ (d) $\frac{n(n-1)d}{2n+1}$

14. If the mean of 4, 7, 2, 8, 6 and x is 7, then the mean deviation about median is
(a) 1 (b) 3 (c) 5 (d) 8

15. If the mean deviation about median of the number $\{na\}_{n=1}^{50}$ is 50, then $|a|$ is equal to
(a) 3 (b) 2 (c) 4 (d) 5

16. The standard deviation of a variate y is σ_y. The standard deviation of the variable $\frac{cy+d}{a}$, where a, c and d are constants, is
(a) $\left(\frac{c}{a}\right)\sigma_y$ (b) $\left|\frac{c}{a}\right|\sigma_y$
(c) $\left(\frac{c^2}{a^2}\right)\sigma_y$ (d) None of these

17. The standard deviation of the following series is

Classes	0-10	10-20	20-30	30-40
f	1	3	4	2

(a) 81 (b) 7.6 (c) 9 (d) 2.26

18. If the standard deviation of -1, 1, 0 and k is $\sqrt{8}$ when $k>0$, then k is equal to
(a) $\sqrt{5}$ (b) $\sqrt{40}$ (c) $\sqrt{20}$ (d) $\sqrt{30}$

19. A student scores the following marks in five tests: 40, 45, 43, 42, 45. His score is not known for the sixth test. If the mean score is 45 in six test, then the standard deviation of marks in six tests is
(a) $\sqrt{21}$ (b) $\sqrt{22}$ (c) $\sqrt{23}$ (d) $\sqrt{24}$

20. If the standard deviation of the numbers 3, 2, 5, k and 10 is 4, then $40k$ is equal to
(a) 110 (b) -110 (c) 90 (d) -90

21. The mean and SD (standard deviation) of 10 observations are 20 and 2, respectively. Each of these 10 observations is multiplied by a and then reduced by b, where $x \neq 0$ and $y \neq 0$.

If the new mean and new standard deviation become half of their original values, then b is equal to

(a) -5 (b) 10 (c) -20 (d) -10

22. In a set of $2n$ observations, half of them are equal to p and the remaining half are equal to q, where $q = -p$. If the SD of all the observations is 4, then the value of $|p|$ is

(a) 4 (b) 2 (c) 16 (d) 8

23. The variance of first 5 natural numbers is

(a) 1 (b) 2 (c) 3 (d) 4

24. Five students have an average height of 150 cm and variance 18 cm^2. A new student joined them whose height is 156 cm. The variance of the height of six students will be

(a) 16 (b) 22 (c) 18 (d) 20

25. For two data sets, each of 5 observations, the variances are 4 and 5 and corresponding means are given to be 2 and 4, respectively. The variance of the combined data set is

(a) $\frac{11}{2}$ (b) 6 (c) $\frac{13}{2}$ (d) $\frac{5}{2}$

26. In an experiment, having 15 observations sum of observations is 170 and sum of their squares is 2830. If one observation 20 is replaced with 30, then new variance is

(a) 8.33 (b) 78.00
(c) 188.66 (d) 177.33

27. Suppose a population of 100 observations 101, 102, ..., 200 and another population of 100 observations 151, 152, ..., 250 has variance σ_x and σ_y respectively, then $\frac{\sigma_x}{\sigma_y}$ is equal to

(a) 1 (b) $\frac{9}{4}$ (c) $\frac{4}{9}$ (d) $\frac{2}{3}$

28. The variance of first 50 even natural numbers is

(a) $\frac{833}{4}$ (b) 833 (c) 437 (d) $\frac{437}{4}$

29. If the mean deviation of number $1, 1+d, 1+2d, \ldots, 1+100d$ from their mean is 255, then d is equal to

(a) 10.0 (b) 20.0 (c) 10.1 (d) 20.2

30. If $\bar{x}$ is the mean and σ^2 is the variance of n observations $x_1, x_2, \ldots, x_n$, then which of the following are true for the observations $ax_1, ax_2, ax_3, \ldots, ax_n$?

I. Mean of the observations is $\frac{\bar{x}}{a}$.

II. Variance of the observations is $\frac{\sigma^2}{a^2}$.

III. Mean of the observations is $a\bar{x}$.

IV. Variance of the observations is $a^2\sigma^2$.

(a) I and II are true
(b) I and IV are true
(c) II and III are true
(d) III and IV are true

MCQs 2 Marks Questions

31. If for some $x \in R$ the frequency distribution of the marks obtained by 20 students in a test is

Marks	2	3	5	7
Frequency	$(x+1)^2$	$2x-5$	x^2-3x	x

Then, the mean of the marks is

(a) 3.0 (b) 2.8
(c) 2.5 (d) 3.2

32. The mean of 20 observations is 15. On checking, it was found that two observations were mistakenly noted as 3 and 6. If wrong values are replaced by correct values 8 and 4, then the correct mean is

(a) 15.35 (b) 15.15
(c) 15 (d) 16

33. If the mean and the median of the following ten numbers in increasing order 10, 22, 26, 29, 34, x, 42, 67, 70, y are 42 and 35 respectively, then $\frac{y}{x}$ is equal to

(a) $\frac{19}{6}$ (b) $\frac{7}{2}$
(c) $\frac{8}{3}$ (d) $\frac{9}{4}$

34. If $\sum_{i=1}^{n}(x_i - 5) = n$ and $\sum_{i=1}^{n}(x_i - 5)^2 = 5n$, $(n > 1)$, then the standard deviation of n observations $x_1, x_2, \ldots, x_n$ is

(a) 4 (b) $n\sqrt{4}$
(c) $\sqrt{4n}$ (d) $\sqrt{4}$

35. If both mean and standard deviation of 50 observations $x_1, x_2, \ldots, x_{50}$ are equal to 16, then the mean of $(x_1 - 5)^2$, $(x_2 - 5)^2, \ldots, (x_{50} - 5)^2$ is

(a) 350 (b) 370
(c) 375 (d) 377

36. The mean of five observations is 5 and their variance is 9.20. If three of the given five observations are 1, 3 and 8, then a ratio of other two observations is

(a) 10 : 3 (b) 4 : 9 (c) 5 : 8 (d) 6 : 7

37. The sum of 100 observations is 400 and sum of their squares is 2475. Later on, it was found that three observations 3, 4 and 5 were incorrect. If incorrect observations are removed, then the variance of the remaining observations is

(a) 8.25 (b) 9.00 (c) 8.00 (d) 8.50

38. If the standard deviation of the numbers 2, 3, a and 11 is 3.5, then which of the following is true?

(a) $3a^2 - 26a + 55 = 0$
(b) $3a^2 - 32a + 84 = 0$
(c) $3a^2 - 34a + 91 = 0$
(d) $3a^2 - 23a + 44 = 0$

39. If mean and standard deviation of 5 observations x_1, x_2, x_3, x_4, x_5 are 10 and 3 respectively, then the variance of 6 observations x_1, x_2, x_3, x_4, x_5 and -50 is equal to

(a) 507.5 (b) 586.5
(c) 582.5 (d) 509.5

40. Let $x_1, x_2, x_3, \ldots, x_n$ be n observations and $\bar{x}$ be their arithmetic mean and σ^2 be the variance.

Assertion (A) Variance of $2x_1, 2x_2, 2x_3, \ldots, 2x_n$ is $4\sigma^2$.

Reason (R) Arithmetic mean of $2x_1, 2x_2, 2x_3, \ldots, 2x_n$ is $4\bar{x}$.

(a) A and R both are true and R is the correct explanation of A
(b) A and R both are true but R is not the correct explanation of A
(c) A is true but R is false
(d) A is false but R is true

Darken your choice with HB Pencil

1.	ⓐ ⓑ ⓒ ⓓ	8.	ⓐ ⓑ ⓒ ⓓ	15.	ⓐ ⓑ ⓒ ⓓ	22.	ⓐ ⓑ ⓒ ⓓ	29.	ⓐ ⓑ ⓒ ⓓ	36.	ⓐ ⓑ ⓒ ⓓ
2.	ⓐ ⓑ ⓒ ⓓ	9.	ⓐ ⓑ ⓒ ⓓ	16.	ⓐ ⓑ ⓒ ⓓ	23.	ⓐ ⓑ ⓒ ⓓ	30.	ⓐ ⓑ ⓒ ⓓ	37.	ⓐ ⓑ ⓒ ⓓ
3.	ⓐ ⓑ ⓒ ⓓ	10.	ⓐ ⓑ ⓒ ⓓ	17.	ⓐ ⓑ ⓒ ⓓ	24.	ⓐ ⓑ ⓒ ⓓ	31.	ⓐ ⓑ ⓒ ⓓ	38.	ⓐ ⓑ ⓒ ⓓ
4.	ⓐ ⓑ ⓒ ⓓ	11.	ⓐ ⓑ ⓒ ⓓ	18.	ⓐ ⓑ ⓒ ⓓ	25.	ⓐ ⓑ ⓒ ⓓ	32.	ⓐ ⓑ ⓒ ⓓ	39.	ⓐ ⓑ ⓒ ⓓ
5.	ⓐ ⓑ ⓒ ⓓ	12.	ⓐ ⓑ ⓒ ⓓ	19.	ⓐ ⓑ ⓒ ⓓ	26.	ⓐ ⓑ ⓒ ⓓ	33.	ⓐ ⓑ ⓒ ⓓ	40.	ⓐ ⓑ ⓒ ⓓ
6.	ⓐ ⓑ ⓒ ⓓ	13.	ⓐ ⓑ ⓒ ⓓ	20.	ⓐ ⓑ ⓒ ⓓ	27.	ⓐ ⓑ ⓒ ⓓ	34.	ⓐ ⓑ ⓒ ⓓ		
7.	ⓐ ⓑ ⓒ ⓓ	14.	ⓐ ⓑ ⓒ ⓓ	21.	ⓐ ⓑ ⓒ ⓓ	28.	ⓐ ⓑ ⓒ ⓓ	35.	ⓐ ⓑ ⓒ ⓓ		

Chapter 14

Probability

MCQs 1 Mark Questions

1. In a competition A, B and C took part. The probability of A's winning or B's winning each is three times the probability of C's winning. The probability of C's winning, if there is no tie is

(a) $\frac{4}{7}$ (b) $\frac{3}{7}$ (c) $\frac{2}{7}$ (d) $\frac{1}{7}$

2. The probability of obtaining K heads and $(n-K)$ tails, when we toss n unbiased coins is

(a) $\frac{K}{n}$ (b) $\frac{{}^nC_K}{2^n}$ (c) $\frac{{}^nC_K}{n}$ (d) $\frac{n-K}{K}$

3. 6 faces of a die are marked with the numbers 1, −1, 2, −2, 3 and 0. If such a die is thrown 3 times, the probability that the sum of numbers is 6, is

(a) $\frac{5}{108}$ (b) $\frac{1}{216}$ (c) 0 (d) $\frac{5}{27}$

4. Let S be the sample space of a throwing two dice (numbered from 1 to 6) and let $A_K = \{(a, b) \in S : ab = K\}$ for $K \geq 1$. If $P_K = P(A_K)$ for $K \geq 1$, then which of the following is correct?

(a) $P_1 < P_{30} < P_4 < P_6$

(b) $P_{36} < P_6 < P_2 < P_4$

(c) $P_1 < P_{11} < P_4 < P_6$

(d) $P_{36} < P_{11} < P_6 < P_4$

5. On a biased die, the probability of any face appearing is proportional to the number of points on its face. The probability of an odd number, if it is thrown once is

(a) $\frac{1}{7}$ (b) $\frac{2}{7}$ (c) $\frac{3}{7}$ (d) $\frac{4}{7}$

6. The probability that the birthdays of 5 girls will fall on 5 different calender months of a year, is

(a) $\frac{1}{(12)^5}$ (b) $\frac{{}^{12}C_5}{(12)^5}$ (c) $\frac{{}^{12}P_5}{(12)^5}$ (d) $\frac{1}{(12)^4}$

7. Consider the system of equations $px + qy = 0$, $rx + sy = 0$, where $p, q, r, s \in \{0, 1\}$. The probability that the system of equations has a unique solution, is

(a) $\frac{1}{8}$ (b) $\frac{1}{2}$ (c) $\frac{3}{4}$ (d) $\frac{3}{8}$

8. Two children were picked at random and found to have born in 1996, then the probability that exactly one of them is born on 29th February, is

(a) 0 (b) $\frac{1}{366 \times 365}$

(c) $\frac{365}{(366)^2}$ (d) $\frac{365}{366 \times 183}$

9. Numbers 1, 2, 3, ..., $2n$ (where n is a natural number) are printed on $2n$ cards. The probability of drawing a number K is proportional to K, then the probability of drawing an even number in one draw is

(a) $\frac{n+2}{n+3}$ (b) $\frac{n+1}{n+3}$

(c) $\frac{1}{2}$ (d) $\frac{n+1}{2n+1}$

10. The probability that 13th day of a randomly chosen month is a Friday, is

(a) $\frac{1}{12}$ (b) $\frac{1}{7}$

(c) $\frac{1}{84}$ (d) None of these

11. An ellipse of eccentricity $\frac{2\sqrt{2}}{3}$ is inscribed in a circle and a point within the circle is chosen at random. The probability that this point lies outside the ellipse, is

(a) $\frac{2}{3}$ (b) $\frac{1}{3}$ (c) $\frac{4}{3}$ (d) $\frac{5}{3}$

12. An integer is chosen at random. The probability that the sum of digits of its square is 24, is

(a) $\frac{1}{39}$ (b) $\frac{2}{39}$ (c) $\frac{1}{11}$ (d) 0

13. The probability that India wins a match against Australia in a cricket match is $\frac{1}{3}$. India and Australia played 3 matches

I. The probability that India wins atleast one match is $\frac{4}{27}$.

II. The probability that India losses all the three matches is $\frac{8}{27}$.

Which of the above statements is correct?

(a) Only I
(b) Only II
(c) Both I and II
(d) Neither I nor II

14. Four houses are available in a locality, four persons apply for the houses. Each person applies for one house. The probability that all four apply for the same house, is

(a) $\frac{1}{16}$ (b) $\frac{3}{16}$

(c) $\frac{1}{64}$ (d) None of these

15. If the letters of the word 'MISSISSIPPI' are arranged at random, the probability that all the 4S's appear consecutively, is

(a) $\frac{8!\times 2!}{11!}$ (b) $\frac{4!\times 2!}{11!}$

(c) $\frac{8!\times 4!}{11!}$ (d) $\frac{6!\times 2!}{11!}$

16. There are P persons in a row. Two of them are randomly selected. The probability that the two selected persons are together, is

(a) $\frac{{}^{P-1}C_2}{{}^{P}C_2}$ (b) $\frac{P-1}{{}^{P}C_2}$

(c) $\frac{P-3}{{}^{P}C_2}$ (d) $1-\frac{{}^{P-1}C_2}{{}^{P}C_2}$

17. Two squares of a chess-board having 8×8 squares are selected at random the probability that they have a side common, is

(a) $\frac{56}{{}^{64}C_2}$ (b) $\frac{168}{{}^{64}C_2}$

(c) $\frac{112}{{}^{64}C_2}$ (d) None of these

18. Three electric bulbs are to be fitted in a room. Three bulbs are chosen at random from 8 bulbs having 5 good bulbs. The chance that the room is lighted, is

(a) $\frac{1}{30}$ (b) $\frac{1}{56}$

(c) $\frac{55}{56}$ (d) 1

19. Two letters are taken at random from the word 'HOME'. The probability that atleast one is a consonant, is

(a) $\frac{5}{6}$ (b) $\frac{3}{5}$

(c) $\frac{1}{6}$ (d) $\frac{1}{3}$

20. In a well shuffled pack of cards, four cards are accidentally dropped. The probability that the cards dropped are one from each suit, is

(a) $\frac{(13)^4}{^{52}C_4}$ (b) $\frac{^{13}C_4}{(13)^4}$

(c) $\frac{13!}{^{13}C_4}$ (d) None of these

21. There are three locks on the door and the keys are among the five different ones that you carry in your pocket. You dropped one somewhere in a hurry. The probability that you can still open the door, is

(a) $\frac{1}{2}$ (b) $\frac{1}{4}$ (c) $\frac{1}{3}$ (d) $\frac{2}{5}$

22. A person draws 2 cards from a well shuffled pack of cards, then put it back after noting their colour. Then, another person draws 2 cards after shuffling the pack. The probability that there are exactly one common card, is

(a) $\frac{50}{663}$ (b) $\frac{25}{663}$

(c) $\frac{100}{663}$ (d) $\frac{75}{663}$

23. If the papers of 5 students can be checked by any one of the eight teachers, then the probability that all the five papers are checked by exactly two teachers, is

(a) $\frac{105}{8^4}$ (b) $\frac{1}{8^4}$

(c) $\frac{59}{8^7}$ (d) None of these

24. A five-digit number is chosen at random. The probability that all the digits are distinct and digits at odd places are odd and digits at even places are even, is

(a) $\frac{1}{25}$ (b) $\frac{1}{37}$

(c) $\frac{25}{567}$ (d) $\frac{1}{74}$

25. In a game called odd man out, $n (n > 2)$ persons toss a coin who will buy refreshments for the entire group. A person who gets an outcomes different from that of the rest of the members of the group is called the odd man out. If the probability that there is a loser in any game is $\frac{1}{2}$, then the value of n is

(a) 1 (b) 2 (c) 3 (d) 4

26. From a bag containing 30 tickets numbered 1, 2, 3,..., 30. Three tickets are selected at random without replacement. Suppose these tickets are arranged as $x_1 < x_2 < x_3$. The probability that $x_2 = 15$ and $x_3 > 20$ is

(a) $\frac{1}{29}$ (b) $\frac{1}{7}$

(c) $\frac{1}{19}$ (d) $\frac{1}{11}$

27. From a set of 100 cards numbered from {1, 2, 3,..., 100}, one card is drawn at random. The probability that the number obtained on the card is divisible by 6 or 8 but not by 24, is

(a) $\frac{1}{5}$ (b) $\frac{1}{4}$

(c) $\frac{1}{6}$ (d) $\frac{2}{5}$

28. An electric bulb will last for 100 days or more with probability 0.7 and it will last for atmost 120 days with probability 0.8. The probability that the bulb will last between 100 and 120 days, is

(a) 0.2 (b) 0.3 (c) 0.4 (d) 0.5

29. Three events A, B and C have probabilities $\frac{2}{5}, \frac{1}{3}$ and $\frac{1}{2}$, respectively. Also, given that $P(A \cap C) = \frac{1}{5}$ and $P(B \cap C) = \frac{1}{4}$, then the value of $P(A' \cap C')$ is

(a) $\frac{3}{10}$ (b) $\frac{3}{4}$

(c) $\frac{3}{5}$ (d) $\frac{1}{2}$

30. Let A and B be two events such that $P(A \cup B) \geq \frac{3}{4}$ and $\frac{1}{8} \leq P(A \cap B) \leq \frac{3}{8}$, then $P(A) + P(B)$ is greater than equal to

(a) $\frac{2}{3}$ (b) $\frac{3}{8}$ (c) $\frac{11}{8}$ (d) $\frac{7}{8}$

31. A and B throw a pair of dice alternatively. A wins the game, if he gets a total of 6 and B wins, if step gets a total of 8. If A starts the game, then the probability of winning the game by A in third throw of the pair of dice is

(a) $\left(\frac{31}{36}\right)^3$ (b) $\frac{(31)^2 \times 5}{(36)^3}$

(c) $\frac{(31)^2}{(36)^3}$ (d) $\frac{3 \times (31)^2}{(36)^2}$

32. If $P(A \cup B) = P(A \cap B)$, then the relation between $P(A)$ and $P(B)$ is

(a) $P(A) \subset P(B)$ (b) $P(A) = P(B)$

(c) $P(A) \neq P(B)$ (d) None of these

MCQs 2 Marks Questions

33. If the sum of the ordinate and the abscissa of a point $P(x, y)$ is $2n$, where x and y are natural numbers, then probability that the point does not lie on $y = x$, is

(a) $\frac{n-1}{n+3}$ (b) $\frac{2n-2}{2n-1}$

(c) $\frac{2n+1}{2n+3}$ (d) None of these

34. Let x be a non-zero real number. A determinant is chosen from the set of all determinants of order 2 with enteries x or $-x$ only. The probability that the value of determinant is non-zero, is

(a) $\frac{3}{16}$ (b) $\frac{1}{4}$

(c) $\frac{1}{2}$ (d) $\frac{1}{8}$

35. A number x is chosen at random from the set $S = \{1, 2, 3, \ldots, 100\}$. Then, the probability that the expression $\sqrt{\frac{x-15}{(x-10)(x-20)}}$ is a positive real number, is

(a) $\frac{11}{25}$ (b) $\frac{7}{25}$

(c) $\frac{21}{25}$ (d) $\frac{17}{25}$

36. A person throws two fair dice. He wins ₹ 15 for throwing a doublet (same numbers on the two dice) wins ₹ 12 when the throws results in the sum of 9 and loses ₹ 6 for any other outcome on the throw. The expected gain/loss (in ₹) of the person is

(a) $\frac{1}{2}$ gain (b) $\frac{1}{4}$ loss

(c) $\frac{1}{2}$ loss (d) 2 gain

37. An urn contains x white balls and y black balls. Two players A and B alternatively draw a ball with replacement from the urn. The player who draws a white ball first wins the game. If B begins the game, then the probability of his winning the game is

(a) $\frac{x}{x+y}$ (b) $\frac{x+y}{x+3y}$

(c) $\frac{x+y}{x+2y}$ (d) $\frac{x+y}{x^2+y}$

38. There are four machines and it is known that exactly two of them are faulty. They are tested one by one in a random order till both the faulty machines are identified. Then, the probability of that only two tests are needed, is

(a) $\frac{1}{3}$ (b) $\frac{1}{6}$

(c) $\frac{1}{2}$ (d) $\frac{1}{4}$

39. A bag contains 3 white, 3 black and 2 red balls. One by one 3 balls are drawn without replacing them for only the 3rd ball to be red the probability is

(a) $\frac{1}{28}$ (b) $\frac{5}{28}$

(c) $\frac{7}{28}$ (d) $\frac{3}{28}$

40. There are 2 urns one of which contains 3 black and 4 white balls, while the other contains 4 black and 3 white balls. *A* die is thrown, if face 1 or 3 turns up a ball is taken from the first bag, if any other face turns up a ball is taken from the second bag. The probability of drawing a black ball is

(a) $\frac{5}{21}$ (b) $\frac{10}{21}$

(c) $\frac{11}{21}$ (d) $\frac{6}{21}$

41. The probability that *A* speaks truth is $\frac{4}{5}$, while the probability for *B* is $\frac{3}{4}$. The probability that they contradict each other when asked to speak on a fact, is

(a) $\frac{3}{20}$ (b) $\frac{7}{20}$

(c) $\frac{1}{5}$ (d) $\frac{4}{5}$

42. Two students Akash and Anil appeared in an examination. The probability that Anil will qualify the examination is 0.05 and that of Akash is 0.10. The probability that both will qualify the examination is 0.02. The probability that only one of them will qualify the examination is

(a) 0.11 (b) 0.10 (c) 0.13 (d) 0.12

43. For three events *A*, *B* and *C*, if *P* (exactly one of *A* or *B* occurs) = *P* (exactly one of *B* or *C* occurs) = *P* (exactly one of *C* or *A* occurs = $\frac{1}{4}$ and *P* (all three events occurs simultaneously) = $\frac{1}{16}$, then probability of atleast one of them occurs is

(a) $\frac{7}{32}$ (b) $\frac{7}{16}$

(c) $\frac{7}{54}$ (d) $\frac{3}{16}$

Darken your choice with HB Pencil

1. (a) (b) (c) (d)	9. (a) (b) (c) (d)	17. (a) (b) (c) (d)	25. (a) (b) (c) (d)	33. (a) (b) (c) (d)	41. (a) (b) (c) (d)
2. (a) (b) (c) (d)	10. (a) (b) (c) (d)	18. (a) (b) (c) (d)	26. (a) (b) (c) (d)	34. (a) (b) (c) (d)	42. (a) (b) (c) (d)
3. (a) (b) (c) (d)	11. (a) (b) (c) (d)	19. (a) (b) (c) (d)	27. (a) (b) (c) (d)	35. (a) (b) (c) (d)	43. (a) (b) (c) (d)
4. (a) (b) (c) (d)	12. (a) (b) (c) (d)	20. (a) (b) (c) (d)	28. (a) (b) (c) (d)	36. (a) (b) (c) (d)	
5. (a) (b) (c) (d)	13. (a) (b) (c) (d)	21. (a) (b) (c) (d)	29. (a) (b) (c) (d)	37. (a) (b) (c) (d)	
6. (a) (b) (c) (d)	14. (a) (b) (c) (d)	22. (a) (b) (c) (d)	30. (a) (b) (c) (d)	38. (a) (b) (c) (d)	
7. (a) (b) (c) (d)	15. (a) (b) (c) (d)	23. (a) (b) (c) (d)	31. (a) (b) (c) (d)	39. (a) (b) (c) (d)	
8. (a) (b) (c) (d)	16. (a) (b) (c) (d)	24. (a) (b) (c) (d)	32. (a) (b) (c) (d)	40. (a) (b) (c) (d)	

Practice Set 01

Time : 60 Mins. Max. Marks : 60

General Instructions

1. This question paper contains 50 questions.
2. All questions are compulsory. There is no negative marking.
3. This question paper is divided into two parts; In first part, there are 40 MCQs of 1 mark each while in second part, there are 10 MCQs of 2 marks each.
4. Use HB pencil / Blue ball point pen to mark your choice of answer by darkening the circles on the OMR Sheet.

MCQs 1 Mark Questions

1. If $A=\{1,2,3,4\}$, $B=\{2,3,5,6\}$ and $C=\{3,4,6,7\}$, then

(a) $A-(B\cap C)=\{1,3,4\}$

(b) $A-(B\cap C)=\{1,2,4\}$

(c) $A-(B\cup C)=\{2,3\}$

(d) $A-(B\cup C)=\phi$

2. If $X=\{4^n-3n-1:n\in N\}$ and $Y=\{9(n-1):n\in N\}$, where N is the set of natural numbers, then $X\cup Y$ is equal to

(a) N

(b) $Y-X$

(c) X

(d) Y

3. Set $A=\{0, 7, 26, 63\}$ in set-builder form B

(a) $\{x: x\in N, x=n^3-1 \text{ and } \le 7\}$

(b) $\{x: x\in N, x=n^2-1 \text{ and } n\le 5\}$

(c) $\{x: x\in N, x=n^2-1 \text{ and } n<4\}$

(d) $\{x: x\in N, x=n^3-1 \text{ and } n\le 4\}$

4. If $f(x)=(ax^2+b)^3$, then the function g such that $f\{g(x)\}=g\{f(x)\}$ is given by

(a) $g(x)=\left(\dfrac{b-x^{1/3}}{a}\right)^{1/2}$

(b) $g(x)=\dfrac{1}{(ax^2+b)^3}$

(c) $g(x)=(ax^2+b)^{1/3}$

(d) $g(x)=\left(\dfrac{x^{1/3}-b}{a}\right)^{1/2}$

5. The range of the function $f(x)=\dfrac{x}{1+x^2}$ is

(a) $(-\infty,\infty)$ (b) $[-1,1]$

(c) $\left[-\dfrac{1}{2},\dfrac{1}{2}\right]$ (d) $[\sqrt{-2},\sqrt{2}]$

6. If $f(x)=\log_e\left(\dfrac{1+x}{1-x}\right)$, then $f\left(\dfrac{2x}{1+x^2}\right)$ is equal to

(a) $[f(x)]^2$ (b) $[f(x)]^3$

(c) $2f(x)$ (d) $3f(x)$

7. The value of $\lim_{x \to 2} \dfrac{\sin(e^{x-2}-1)}{\log_e(x-1)}$ is

(a) 0 (b) −1 (c) 2 (d) 1

8. If $x + iy = (1+i)(1+2i)\ldots(1+ni)$, then the value of $x^2 + y^2$ is equal to

(a) $2.5 \ldots (1+n^2)$ (b) $2.4 \ldots (1+n^2)$

(c) $2.5 \ldots (1-n^2)$ (d) None of these

9. If θ lies in second quadrant, then $\sqrt{\dfrac{1-\sin\theta}{1+\sin\theta}} + \sqrt{\dfrac{1+\sin\theta}{1-\sin\theta}}$ is equal to

(a) $2\cos\theta$ (b) $2\sec\theta$

(c) $-2\cos\theta$ (d) $-2\sec\theta$

10. The value of $\sin 20°\cdot\sin 40°\cdot\sin 60°\cdot\sin 80°$ is

(a) $\dfrac{-3}{16}$ (b) $\dfrac{5}{16}$ (c) $\dfrac{3}{16}$ (d) $\dfrac{1}{16}$

11. If $\tan A = \dfrac{1}{2}$ and $\tan B = \dfrac{1}{3}$, then the value of $A + B$ is

(a) 45° (b) 60° (c) 30° (d) 0°

12. α and β are different complex numbers with $|\beta| = 1$, then $\left|\dfrac{\beta-\alpha}{1-\bar{\alpha}\beta}\right|$ is equal to

(a) 1 (b) 2 (c) 4 (d) 3

13. The set of admissible values of x such that $\dfrac{2x+3}{2x-9} < 0$, is

(a) $\left(-\infty, \dfrac{-3}{2}\right) \cup \left(\dfrac{9}{2}, \infty\right)$

(b) $\left(\dfrac{-3}{2}, 0\right)$

(c) $\left(0, \dfrac{9}{2}\right)$

(d) $\left(\dfrac{-3}{2}, \dfrac{9}{2}\right)$

14. The solution set of the inequality $|x+1| + |x| > 3$ is

(a) $(-\infty, -2)$ (b) $(1, \infty)$

(c) $(-\infty, -2) \cup (1, \infty)$ (d) $(-\infty, -2] \cup [1, \infty)$

15. The range of the function $f(x) = {}^{7-x}P_{x-3}$ is

(a) $\{1, 2, 3\}$ (b) $\{1, 2, 3, 4, 5, 6\}$

(c) $\{1, 2, 3, 4\}$ (d) $\{1, 2, 3, 4, 5\}$

16. The number of ways of placing 18 mice in two experimental groups and one control group, with all group equally large, are

(a) $\dfrac{18!}{(6!)^3}$ (b) $\dfrac{18!}{6!6!}$

(c) $\dfrac{12!}{(6!)^2}$ (d) None of these

17. The value of ${}^{50}C_4 + \sum_{r=1}^{6} {}^{56-r}C_3$ is

(a) ${}^{56}C_4$ (b) ${}^{56}C_3$

(c) ${}^{55}C_3$ (d) ${}^{55}C_4$

18. The number of terms in the expansion of $(x^2 - 2xy + y^2)^{10}$ is

(a) 11 (b) 15

(c) 20 (d) 21

19. If 7 divides $32^{32^{32}}$, then remainder is

(a) 1 (b) 0

(c) 4 (d) 6

20. If the first term of a GP is 1 and the sum of the third term and fifth term is 90, then the possible common ratio of the GP are

(a) ± 4 (b) ± 2

(c) ± 6 (d) ± 3

21. In a GP of positive terms, if any term is equal to the sum of the next two terms, then the common ratio of the GP is

(a) $\sin 18°$ (b) $2\cos 18°$

(c) $\cos 18°$ (d) $2\sin 18°$

22. If a denotes the number of permutations of $x+2$ things taken all at a time, b the number of permutations of x things taken 11 at a time and c the number of permutations of $x-11$ things taken all at a time such that $a=182\,bc$, then the value of x is

(a) 15 (b) 12
(c) 10 (d) 18

23. If $0<\phi<\frac{\pi}{2}$, $x=\sum_{n=0}^{\infty}\cos^{2n}\phi$, $y=\sum_{n=0}^{\infty}\sin^{2n}\phi$ and $z=\sum_{n=0}^{\infty}\cos^{2n}\phi\sin^{2n}\phi$, then

(a) $xyz = xz + y$ (b) $xyz = xy + z$
(c) $xyz = x + y + z$ (d) $xyz = yz + x$

24. A ray of light coming from the point (1, 2) is reflected at a point A on the X-axis and then passes through the point (5, 3). Then, the coordinates of the point A are

(a) (13, 0) (b) $\left(\frac{13}{5},0\right)$
(c) $\left(\frac{17}{2},0\right)$ (d) (17, 0)

25. If t_1 and t_2 are roots of the equation $t^2+\lambda t+1=0$, where λ is an arbitrary constant, then the line joining the points $(at_1^2, 2at_1)$ and $(at_2^2, 2at_2)$ always passes through a fixed point (m, n), where m and n respectively are

(a) $a, 0$ (b) $0, a$
(c) $-a, 0$ (d) $0, -a$

26. If the distance between a focus and corresponding directrix of an ellipse be 8 and the eccentricity be 1/2, then length of the minor axis is

(a) 3 (b) $4\sqrt{2}$
(c) 6 (d) None of these

27. If the perpendicular bisector of the line segment joining the points $P(1, 4)$ and $Q(k, 3)$ has y-intercept equal to -4, then a value of k is

(a) $\sqrt{15}$ (b) -4
(c) $\sqrt{14}$ (d) -2

28. The points (5, −1, 1), (7, −4, 7), (1, −6, 10) and (−1, −3, 4) are

(a) the vertices of a rectangle
(b) the vertices of a square
(c) the vertices of a rhombus
(d) None of the above

29. The equation of normal to the circle $x^2+y^2-5x+2y-48=0$ at the point (5, 6) is

(a) $14x-5y+40=0$
(b) $14x+5y+40=0$
(c) $14x-5y-40=0$
(d) $14x+5y-40=0$

30. Equation $(4m-3)x^2+my^2+10x-8y+16=0$ represents a circle for $m=$

(a) 3 (b) $\frac{3}{4}$
(c) 1 (d) -1

31. The coordinates of the foot of the perpendicular drawn from the point $P(3, 4, 5)$ on the YZ – plane are

(a) (3, 4, 0) (b) (0, 4, 5)
(c) (3, 0, 5) (d) (3, 0, 10)

32. If the distance between the points (0, 0, 1) and (0, 1, 2) is $\sqrt{27}$, then the value of a is

(a) 5
(b) ± 5
(c) -5
(d) None of the above

33. $\lim\limits_{x \to 0} \dfrac{\cos ax - \cos bx}{\cos cx - 1}$ is equal to $\dfrac{m}{n}$, where m and n are respectively

(a) $a^2 + b^2, c^2$ (b) $c^2, a^2 + b^2$

(c) $a^2 - b^2, c^2$ (d) $c^2, a^2 - b^2$

34. $\lim\limits_{x \to 1} [x - 1]$, where $[\cdot]$ is greatest integer function, is equal to

(a) 1 (b) 2

(c) 0 (d) Does not exist

35. If $f(x) = \begin{cases} \dfrac{\sin[x]}{[x]}, [x] \neq 0 \\ 0 [x] = 0 \end{cases}$ where $[\cdot]$ denotes the greatest integer function, then $\lim\limits_{x \to 0} f(x)$ is equal to

(a) 1 (b) 0

(c) −1 (d) Does not exist

36. The mean age of a combined group of men and women is 25 yrs. If the mean age of the group of men is 26 and that of the group of women is 21, then the ratio of men and women in the group is

(a) 1 : 4 (b) 4 : 1

(c) 3 : 1 (d) 1 : 3

37. Every body in a room shakes hands with everybody else. The total number of hand shakes is 66. The total number of persons in the room is

(a) 11 (b) 12

(c) 13 (d) 14

38. Let A and B be two events such that the probability that exactly one of them occurs is $\dfrac{2}{5}$ and the probability that A or B occurs is $\dfrac{1}{2}$, then the probability of both of them occur together is

(a) 0.10 (b) 0.20

(c) 0.01 (d) 0.02

39. An integer is chosen at random from the numbers 1,2,...,25. The probability that the chosen number is divisible by 3 or 4, is

(a) $\dfrac{2}{25}$ (b) $\dfrac{11}{25}$

(c) $\dfrac{12}{25}$ (d) $\dfrac{14}{25}$

40. Three of the six vertices of a regular hexagon are chosen at random. Then, the probability that the triangle formed with these vertices is equilateral, is

(a) $\dfrac{3}{10}$ (b) $\dfrac{3}{20}$

(c) $\dfrac{1}{20}$ (d) $\dfrac{1}{10}$

MCQs 2 Marks Questions

41. The variance of 20 observations is 5. If each observation is multiplied by 2, then the new variance of the resulting observations is

(a) $2^3 \times 5$

(b) $2^2 \times 5$

(c) 2×5

(d) $2^4 \times 5$

42. Consider the first 10 positive integers. If we multiply each number by (−1) and then add 1 to each number, the variance of the numbers so obtained is

(a) 8.25 (b) 6.5

(c) 3.87 (d) 2.87

43. If two dice are thrown simultaneously, then the probability that the sum of the numbers which come up on the dice to be more than 5 is

(a) $\dfrac{5}{36}$ (b) $\dfrac{1}{6}$

(c) $\dfrac{5}{18}$ (d) $\dfrac{13}{18}$

44. If $A = \{(x, y) : x^2 + y^2 = 25\}$ and $B = \{(x, y) : x^2 + 9y^2 = 144\}$, then $A \cap B$ contains

(a) one point (b) two points
(c) three points (d) four points

45. If a, b, c are pth, qth and rth terms of a GP, then $(q - r) \log a + (r - p) \log b + (p - q) \log c$ is equal to

(a) $p + q + r$ (b) 1
(c) $-pqr$ (d) 0

46. The complex numbers $\sin x + i \cos 2x$ and $\cos x - i \sin 2x$ are conjugate to each other for

(a) $x = n\pi$ (b) $x = \left(n + \frac{1}{2}\right)\pi$
(c) $x = 0$ (d) No value of x

47. If $(1 + x)^{15} = {}^{15}C_0 + {}^{15}C_1 x + {}^{15}C_2 x^2$ ...... ${}^{15}C_{15} x^{15}$, then the value of ${}^{15}C_0 + 2\,{}^{15}C_1 + 3\,{}^{15}C_2 + 4\,{}^{15}C_3 + 5\,{}^{15}C_4 + \ldots\ldots + 16\,{}^{15}C_{15}$ is

(a) 62144 (b) 278528
(c) 524288 (d) None of these

48. If $\cos x + \cos y + \cos\alpha = 0$ and $\sin x + \sin y + \sin\alpha = 0$, then $\cot\left(\frac{x + y}{2}\right)$ is equal to

(a) $\sin\alpha$
(b) $\cos\alpha$
(c) $\cot\alpha$
(d) $\sin\left(\frac{x + y}{2}\right)$

49. The points whose coordinates are $x = x_1 + t(x_2 - x_1)$, $y = y_1 + t(y_2 - y_1)$ divides the join of (x_1, y_1) and (x_2, y_2) in the ratio

(a) $\frac{t}{(1 + t)}$ (b) $\frac{(1 + t)}{t}$
(c) $\frac{t}{(1 - t)}$ (d) $\frac{(1 - t)}{t}$

50. If $\left(m_i, \frac{1}{m_i}\right)$, $i = 1, 2, 3, 4$ are concyclic points, then the value of $m_1 m_2 m_3 m_4$ is

(a) 1
(b) -1
(c) 0
(d) None of these

Darken your choice with HB Pencil

1.	ⓐ ⓑ ⓒ ⓓ	10.	ⓐ ⓑ ⓒ ⓓ	19.	ⓐ ⓑ ⓒ ⓓ	28.	ⓐ ⓑ ⓒ ⓓ	37.	ⓐ ⓑ ⓒ ⓓ	46.	ⓐ ⓑ ⓒ ⓓ
2.	ⓐ ⓑ ⓒ ⓓ	11.	ⓐ ⓑ ⓒ ⓓ	20.	ⓐ ⓑ ⓒ ⓓ	29.	ⓐ ⓑ ⓒ ⓓ	38.	ⓐ ⓑ ⓒ ⓓ	47.	ⓐ ⓑ ⓒ ⓓ
3.	ⓐ ⓑ ⓒ ⓓ	12.	ⓐ ⓑ ⓒ ⓓ	21.	ⓐ ⓑ ⓒ ⓓ	30.	ⓐ ⓑ ⓒ ⓓ	39.	ⓐ ⓑ ⓒ ⓓ	48.	ⓐ ⓑ ⓒ ⓓ
4.	ⓐ ⓑ ⓒ ⓓ	13.	ⓐ ⓑ ⓒ ⓓ	22.	ⓐ ⓑ ⓒ ⓓ	31.	ⓐ ⓑ ⓒ ⓓ	40.	ⓐ ⓑ ⓒ ⓓ	49.	ⓐ ⓑ ⓒ ⓓ
5.	ⓐ ⓑ ⓒ ⓓ	14.	ⓐ ⓑ ⓒ ⓓ	23.	ⓐ ⓑ ⓒ ⓓ	32.	ⓐ ⓑ ⓒ ⓓ	41.	ⓐ ⓑ ⓒ ⓓ	50.	ⓐ ⓑ ⓒ ⓓ
6.	ⓐ ⓑ ⓒ ⓓ	15.	ⓐ ⓑ ⓒ ⓓ	24.	ⓐ ⓑ ⓒ ⓓ	33.	ⓐ ⓑ ⓒ ⓓ	42.	ⓐ ⓑ ⓒ ⓓ		
7.	ⓐ ⓑ ⓒ ⓓ	16.	ⓐ ⓑ ⓒ ⓓ	25.	ⓐ ⓑ ⓒ ⓓ	34.	ⓐ ⓑ ⓒ ⓓ	43.	ⓐ ⓑ ⓒ ⓓ		
8.	ⓐ ⓑ ⓒ ⓓ	17.	ⓐ ⓑ ⓒ ⓓ	26.	ⓐ ⓑ ⓒ ⓓ	35.	ⓐ ⓑ ⓒ ⓓ	44.	ⓐ ⓑ ⓒ ⓓ		
9.	ⓐ ⓑ ⓒ ⓓ	18.	ⓐ ⓑ ⓒ ⓓ	27.	ⓐ ⓑ ⓒ ⓓ	36.	ⓐ ⓑ ⓒ ⓓ	45.	ⓐ ⓑ ⓒ ⓓ		

Practice Set 02

Time : 60 Mins. Max. Marks : 60

General Instructions

1. This question paper contains 50 questions.
2. All questions are compulsory. There is no negative marking.
3. This question paper is divided into two parts; In first part, there are 40 MCQs of 1 mark each while in second part, there are 10 MCQs of 2 marks each.
4. Use HB pencil / Blue ball point pen to mark your choice of answer by darkening the circles on the OMR Sheet.

MCQs 1 Mark Questions

1. If $P = \{\theta : \sin\theta - \cos\theta = \sqrt{2}\cos\theta\}$ and $Q = \{\theta : \sin\theta + \cos\theta = \sqrt{2}\sin\theta\}$ are two sets. Then,

(a) $P \subset Q$ and $Q - P \neq \phi$

(b) $Q \not\subset P$

(c) $P \not\subset Q$

(d) $P = Q$

2. Universal set,
$U = \{x : x^5 - 6x^4 + 11x^3 - 6x^2 = 0\}$,
$A = \{x : x^2 - 5x + 6 = 0\}$ and
$B = \{x : x^2 - 3x + 2 = 0\}$.
Then, $(A \cap B)'$ is equal to

(a) $\{1, 3\}$ (b) $\{1, 2, 3\}$

(c) $\{0, 1, 3\}$ (d) $\{0, 1, 2, 3\}$

3. If $f(x) = \frac{1}{2} - \tan\left(\frac{\pi x}{2}\right), -1 < x < 1$ and $g(x) = \sqrt{3 + 4x - 4x^2}$, then domain $(f + g)$ is given by

(a) $\left[\frac{1}{2}, 1\right]$ (b) $\left[\frac{1}{2}, -1\right)$

(c) $\left[-\frac{1}{2}, 1\right)$ (d) $\left[-\frac{1}{2}, -1\right]$

4. Let $f : (1, 3) \to R$ be a function defined by $f(x) = \frac{x[x]}{1 + x^2}$, where $[x]$ denotes the greatest integer $\leq x$. Then, the range of f is

(a) $\left(\frac{2}{5}, \frac{3}{5}\right] \cup \left(\frac{3}{4}, \frac{4}{5}\right)$

(b) $\left(\frac{2}{5}, \frac{4}{5}\right]$

(c) $\left(\frac{3}{5}, \frac{4}{5}\right)$

(d) $\left(\frac{2}{5}, \frac{1}{2}\right) \cup \left(\frac{3}{5}, \frac{4}{5}\right]$

5. The sum of the first three terms of a GP is S and their product is 27. Then, all such S lie in

(a) $(-\infty, 9]$ (b) $[-3, \infty)$

(c) $(-\infty, -9] \cup [3, \infty)$ (d) $(-\infty, -3] \cup [9, \infty)$

6. $3 + 3\alpha + 3\alpha^2 + \ldots = \frac{45}{8}$, then the value of α is

(a) $\frac{15}{23}$ (b) $\frac{7}{15}$

(c) $\frac{7}{8}$ (d) $\frac{15}{7}$

7. Let $S_1, S_2, \ldots$ be squares such that for each $n \geq 1$, the length of a side of S_n equals the length of a diagonal of S_{n+1}. If the length of a side of S_1 is 10 cm, then for which of the following values of n, the area of S_n less than 1 sq cm ?

(a) 7 (b) 6 (c) 9 (d) None of these

8. If x, y, z, are in GP and $a^x = b^y = c^z$, then

(a) $\log_b a - \log_a c$ (b) $\log_c b = \log_a c$
(c) $\log_b a = \log_c b$ (d) None of these

9. Let $i = \sqrt{-1}$, define a sequence of a complex number by $z_1 = 0$, $z_{n+1} = z_n^2 + i$ for $n \geq 1$. In the complex plane, how far from the origin is z_{111}?

(a) 1 (b) $\sqrt{2}$ (c) $\sqrt{3}$ (d) $\sqrt{110}$

10. If $z = \dfrac{7-i}{3-4i}$, then $|z|^{14}$ is

(a) 2^7 (b) $2^7 i$ (c) -2^7 (d) $-2^7 i$

11. If $4x + i(3x - y) = 3 - 6i$, then the value of x and y are

(a) $x = 3, y = 4$ (b) $x = \dfrac{3}{4}, y = \dfrac{33}{4}$
(c) $x = 4, y = 3$ (d) $x = 33, y = 4$

12. There are three coplanar parallel lines. If any p points are taken on each of the lines, the maximum number of triangles with vertices on these points is

(a) $3p^2(p-1)+1$ (b) $3p^2(p-1)$
(c) $p^2(4p-3)$ (d) None of these

13. A man X has 7 friends, 4 of them are ladies and 3 are men. His wife Y also has 7 friends, 3 of them are ladies and 4 are men. Assume X and Y have no common friends. Then, the total number of ways in which X and Y together can throw a party inviting 3 ladies and 3 men, so that 3 friends of each of X and Y are in this party, is

(a) 485 (b) 468 (c) 469 (d) 484

14. The value of $(99)^5$ is

(a) 9509900490 (b) 9509900495
(c) 9509900499 (d) None of these

15. The remainder left out when $8^{2n} - (62)^{2n+1}$ is divided by 9 is

(a) 0 (b) 2
(c) 7 (d) 8

16. If $m \sin\theta = n \sin(\theta + 2\alpha)$, then $\tan(\theta + \alpha)\cot\alpha$ is equal to

(a) $(m+n)(m-n)$ (b) $\dfrac{m-n}{m+n}$
(c) $\dfrac{m+n}{m-n}$ (d) $2(m+n)(m-n)$

17. If $\cos(\alpha+\beta) = \dfrac{4}{5}$, $\sin(\alpha-\beta) = \dfrac{5}{13}$ and α, β lies between 0 and $\dfrac{\pi}{4}$, then $\tan 2\alpha$ is equal to

(a) $\dfrac{16}{63}$ (b) $\dfrac{56}{33}$
(c) $\dfrac{28}{33}$ (d) None of these

18. At a point on the ground the angle of elevation of a tower is such that its cotangent is $\dfrac{3}{5}$. On walking 32 m towards the tower the cotangent of the angle of elevation is $\dfrac{2}{5}$. The height of the tower is

(a) 160 m (b) 120 m
(c) 64 m (d) None of these

19. The value of $\tan 20° + 2\tan 50° - \tan 70°$ is equal to

(a) 1 (b) 0
(c) $\tan 50°$ (d) $2\tan 20°$

20. The equation of the line passing through the point (1, 2) and perpendicular to the line $x + y + 1 = 0$ is

(a) $y - x + 1 = 0$ (b) $y - x - 1 = 0$
(c) $y - x + 2 = 0$ (d) $y - x - 2 = 0$

21. The coordinates of the foot of the perpendicular from the point (2, 3) on the line $x + y - 11 = 0$ is

(a) $(-6, 5)$ (b) $(5, 6)$

(c) $(-5, 6)$ (d) $(6, 5)$

22. If the two lines $x + (a-1)y = 1$ and $2x + a^2 y = 1$, $(a \in R - \{0, 1\})$ are perpendicular, then the distance of their point of intersection from the origin is

(a) $\frac{2}{5}$ (b) $\frac{\sqrt{2}}{5}$

(c) $\frac{2}{\sqrt{5}}$ (d) $\sqrt{\frac{2}{5}}$

23. The straight line $ax + by + c = 0$, where $abc \neq 0$ will pass through the first quadrant, if

(a) $ac > 0, bc > 0$

(b) $c > 0$ and $bc < 0$

(c) $bc > 0$ and/or $ac > 0$

(d) $ac < 0$ and/or $bc < 0$

24. The middle point of the chord intercepted on the line $lx + my + n = 0$ by the circle $x^2 + y^2 = a^2$ is

(a) $\left(-\frac{nl}{l^2 + m^2}, -\frac{nm}{l^2 + m^2}\right)$

(b) $\left(\frac{nl}{l^2 + m^2}, \frac{nm}{l^2 + m^2}\right)$

(c) $\left(-\frac{l}{l^2 + m^2}, \frac{m}{l^2 + m^2}\right)$

(d) None of the above

25. If the line $y - \sqrt{3}x + 3 = 0$ cuts the parabola $y^2 = x + 2$ at A and B, then $PA \cdot PB$ is equal to [where, $P = (\sqrt{3}, 0)$]

(a) $\frac{4(\sqrt{3} + 2)}{3}$ (b) $\frac{4(2 - \sqrt{3})}{3}$

(c) $\frac{4\sqrt{3}}{3}$ (d) $\frac{2(\sqrt{3} + 2)}{3}$

26. The eccentricity of an ellipse whose latusrectum is equal to distance between foci is

(a) $\frac{-1-\sqrt{5}}{2}$ (b) $\frac{\sqrt{5}-1}{2}$

(c) $\frac{1}{2}$ (d) $\frac{\sqrt{5}}{2}$

27. An ellipse, with foci at (0, 2) and (0, − 2) and minor axis of length 4, passes through which of the following points?

(a) $(\sqrt{2}, 2)$ (b) $(2, \sqrt{2})$

(c) $(2, 2\sqrt{2})$ (d) $(1, 2\sqrt{2})$

28. A hyperbola has its centre at the origin, passes through the point (4, 2) and has transverse axis of length along the X-axis. Then, the eccentricity of the hyperbola is

(a) 2 (b) $\frac{2}{\sqrt{3}}$

(c) $\frac{3}{2}$ (d) $\sqrt{3}$

29. The eccentricity of the hyperbola whose latusrectum is 8 and conjugate axes is equal to half the distance between the foci is

(a) $\frac{4}{3}$ (b) $\frac{4}{\sqrt{3}}$

(c) $\frac{2}{\sqrt{3}}$ (d) None of these

30. The foci of the ellipse $25(x+1)^2 + 9(y+2)^2 = 225$ is

(a) $(-1, 2)$ and $(-1, -6)$

(b) $(-2, 1)$ and $(-2, 6)$

(c) $(-1, -2)$ and $(-2, 1)$

(d) $(-1, -2)$ and $(-1, -6)$

31. If A and B be the points (3, 4, 5) and (− 1, 3, − 7) respectively, find the equation of the set of points P such that $(PA)^2 + (PB)^2 = K^2$, where K is a constant.

(a) $2(x^2+y^2+z^2)+4x+14y+4z$
$+109-K^2=0$

(b) $2(x^2+y^2+z^2)-4x-14y+4z$
$+109-K^2=0$

(c) $x^2+y^2+z^2+4x+14y+4z$
$+109-K^2=0$

(d) None of the above

32. $\lim\limits_{x\to 0}\left(\tan\left(\frac{\pi}{4}+x\right)\right)^{1/x}$ is equal to

(a) e (b) 2 (c) 1 (d) e^2

33. The value of the constants α and β such that $\lim\limits_{x\to\infty}\left(\frac{x^2+1}{x+1}-\alpha x-\beta\right)=0$ are, respectively

(a) $(1,1)$ (b) $(-1,1)$
(c) $(1,-1)$ (d) $(0,1)$

34. If both the mean and the standard deviation of 50 observations $x_1, x_2, \ldots, x_{50}$ are equal to 16, then the mean of $(x_1-4)^2, (x_2-4)^2, \ldots, (x_{50}-4)^2$ is

(a) 480 (b) 400
(c) 380 (d) 525

35. The marks of some students were listed out of 75. The SD of marks was found to be 9. Subsequently the marks were raised to a maximum of 100 and variance of new marks was calculated. The new variance is

(a) 81 (b) 122
(c) 144 (d) None of these

36. The coefficients of a quadratic equation $ax^2+bx+c=0$ $(a\neq b\neq c)$ are chosen from first three prime numbers, the probability that roots of the equation are real is

(a) $\frac{1}{3}$ (b) $\frac{2}{3}$ (c) $\frac{1}{4}$ (d) $\frac{3}{4}$

37. A class consists of 80 students, 25 of them are girls and 55 are boys. If 10 of them are rich and the remaining are poor and also 20 of them are intelligent, then the probability of selecting an intelligent rich girl is

(a) $\frac{5}{128}$ (b) $\frac{25}{128}$
(c) $\frac{5}{512}$ (d) None of these

38. The value of the expression
${}^{47}C_4+\sum\limits_{r-1}^{5}{}^{52-r}C_3$ is equal to

(a) ${}^{47}C_5$ (b) ${}^{52}C_5$
(c) ${}^{52}C_4$ (d) ${}^{52}C_3$

39. If all the words (with or without meaning) having five letters, formed using the letters of the word SMALL and arranged as in a dictionary, then the position of the word SMALL is

(a) 46th (b) 59th (c) 52nd (d) 58th

40. The area of the circle
$(x+1)(x+2)+(y-1)(y+3)=0$ is

(a) $\frac{17\pi}{4}$ (b) $\frac{17\pi}{2}$
(c) $\frac{2\pi}{17}$ (d) None of these

MCQs 2 Marks Questions

41. Let A, B and C be sets such that $\phi\neq A\cap B\subseteq C$. Then, which of the following statements is not true?

(a) $B\cap C\neq\phi$
(b) If $(A-B)\subseteq C$, then $A\subseteq C$
(c) $(C\cup A)\cap(C\cup B)=C$
(d) If $(A-C)\subseteq B$, then $A\subseteq B$

42. If the functions are defined as $f(x) = \sqrt{x}$ and $g(x) = \sqrt{1-x}$, then what is the common domain of the following functions $f+g, f-g, f/g, g/f, g-f$, where $(f \pm g)(x) = f(x) \pm g(x), (f/g)(x) = \dfrac{f(x)}{g(x)}$

(a) $0 \le x \le 1$ (b) $0 \le x < 1$
(c) $0 < x < 1$ (d) $0 < x \le 1$

43. If $(1+x)(1+x^2)(1+x^4)\ldots\ldots(1+x^{128}) = \sum_{r=0}^{n} x^r$, then n is equal to

(a) 256 (b) 255 (c) 254 (d) 128

44. If $a^2 + b^2 = 1$, then $(1+b+ai)(1+b-ai)$ is equal to

(a) 1 (b) 2 (c) $b+ai$ (d) $a+bi$

45. The lines passing through $(3, -2)$ and inclined at angle 60° with $\sqrt{3}\,x + y = 1$ is

(a) $y + 2 = 0$ (b) $x + 2 = 0$
(c) $x + y = 2$ (d) $x - y = \sqrt{3}$

46. The equation of the image of the circle $x^2 + y^2 + 16x - 24y + 183 = 0$ by the line mirror $4x + 7y + 13 = 0$ is

(a) $x^2 + y^2 + 32x - 4y + 235 = 0$
(b) $x^2 + y^2 + 32x + 4y - 235 = 0$
(c) $x^2 + y^2 + 32x - 4y - 235 = 0$
(d) $x^2 + y^2 + 32x + 4y + 235 = 0$

47. The value of $\lim_{x \to 0}\left(\dfrac{e^{x\log(2^x-1)} - (2^x-1)^x \sin x}{e^{x\log x}}\right)^{1/x}$ is

(a) e (b) $\dfrac{1}{e}\log 2$
(c) $e \log 2$ (d) None

48. The probabilities of three events A, B and C are given by $P(A) = 0.6$, $P(B) = 0.4$ and $P(C) = 0.5$. If $P(A \cup B) = 0.8$, $P(A \cap C) = 0.3$, $P(A \cap B \cap C) = 0.2$, $P(B \cap C) = \beta$ and $P(A \cup B \cup C) = \alpha$, where $0.85 \le \alpha \le 0.95$, then β lies in the interval

(a) [0.35, 0.36]
(b) [0.25, 0.35]
(c) [0.20, 0.25]
(d) [0.36, 0.40]

49. If α, β and γ are the roots of the equation $x^3 - 7x + 7 = 0$, then $\dfrac{1}{\alpha^4} + \dfrac{1}{\beta^4} + \dfrac{1}{\gamma^4}$ is

(a) 7/3 (b) 3/7
(c) 4/7 (d) 7/4

50. Let $\bigcup_{i=1}^{50} X_i = \bigcup_{i=1}^{n} Y_i = T$, where each X_i contains 10 elements and each Y_i contains 5 elements. If each element of the set T is an element of exactly 20 of sets X_i's and exactly 6 of sets Y_i's, then n is equal to

(a) 50 (b) 15 (c) 45 (d) 30

Darken your choice with HB Pencil

1.	ⓐ ⓑ ⓒ ⓓ	10.	ⓐ ⓑ ⓒ ⓓ	19.	ⓐ ⓑ ⓒ ⓓ	28.	ⓐ ⓑ ⓒ ⓓ	37.	ⓐ ⓑ ⓒ ⓓ	46.	ⓐ ⓑ ⓒ ⓓ
2.	ⓐ ⓑ ⓒ ⓓ	11.	ⓐ ⓑ ⓒ ⓓ	20.	ⓐ ⓑ ⓒ ⓓ	29.	ⓐ ⓑ ⓒ ⓓ	38.	ⓐ ⓑ ⓒ ⓓ	47.	ⓐ ⓑ ⓒ ⓓ
3.	ⓐ ⓑ ⓒ ⓓ	12.	ⓐ ⓑ ⓒ ⓓ	21.	ⓐ ⓑ ⓒ ⓓ	30.	ⓐ ⓑ ⓒ ⓓ	39.	ⓐ ⓑ ⓒ ⓓ	48.	ⓐ ⓑ ⓒ ⓓ
4.	ⓐ ⓑ ⓒ ⓓ	13.	ⓐ ⓑ ⓒ ⓓ	22.	ⓐ ⓑ ⓒ ⓓ	31.	ⓐ ⓑ ⓒ ⓓ	40.	ⓐ ⓑ ⓒ ⓓ	49.	ⓐ ⓑ ⓒ ⓓ
5.	ⓐ ⓑ ⓒ ⓓ	14.	ⓐ ⓑ ⓒ ⓓ	23.	ⓐ ⓑ ⓒ ⓓ	32.	ⓐ ⓑ ⓒ ⓓ	41.	ⓐ ⓑ ⓒ ⓓ	50.	ⓐ ⓑ ⓒ ⓓ
6.	ⓐ ⓑ ⓒ ⓓ	15.	ⓐ ⓑ ⓒ ⓓ	24.	ⓐ ⓑ ⓒ ⓓ	33.	ⓐ ⓑ ⓒ ⓓ	42.	ⓐ ⓑ ⓒ ⓓ		
7.	ⓐ ⓑ ⓒ ⓓ	16.	ⓐ ⓑ ⓒ ⓓ	25.	ⓐ ⓑ ⓒ ⓓ	34.	ⓐ ⓑ ⓒ ⓓ	43.	ⓐ ⓑ ⓒ ⓓ		
8.	ⓐ ⓑ ⓒ ⓓ	17.	ⓐ ⓑ ⓒ ⓓ	26.	ⓐ ⓑ ⓒ ⓓ	35.	ⓐ ⓑ ⓒ ⓓ	44.	ⓐ ⓑ ⓒ ⓓ		
9.	ⓐ ⓑ ⓒ ⓓ	18.	ⓐ ⓑ ⓒ ⓓ	27.	ⓐ ⓑ ⓒ ⓓ	36.	ⓐ ⓑ ⓒ ⓓ	45.	ⓐ ⓑ ⓒ ⓓ		

Practice Set 03

Time : 60 Mins. Max. Marks : 60

General Instructions

1. This question paper contains 50 questions.
2. All questions are compulsory. There is no negative marking.
3. This question paper is divided into two parts; In first part, there are 40 MCQs of 1 mark each while in second part, there are 10 MCQs of 2 marks each.
4. Use HB pencil / Blue ball point pen to mark your choice of answer by darkening the circles on the OMR Sheet.

MCQs 1 Mark Questions

1. If $0° < \theta < 180°$, then $\sqrt{2+\sqrt{2+\sqrt{2+\ldots+\sqrt{2(1+\cos\theta)}}}}$, then being n number of 2's, is equal to

(a) $2\cos\left(\frac{\theta}{2^n}\right)$ (b) $2\cos\left(\frac{\theta}{2^{n-1}}\right)$

(c) $2\cos\left(\frac{\theta}{2^{n+1}}\right)$ (d) None of these

2. For $x^2-(a+3)|x|+4=0$ to have real solutions, then the range of a is

(a) $(-\infty,-7]\cup[1,\infty)$

(b) $(-3,\infty)$

(c) $(-\infty,-7]$

(d) $[1,\infty)$

3. The value of $0.2^{\log_{\sqrt{5}}\left(\frac{1}{4}+\frac{1}{8}+\frac{1}{16}+\ldots\ldots\right)}$ is

(a) 4 (b) log 4

(c) log 2 (d) None of these

4. If A, B and C are three sets, then

(a) $A\times(B\cup C)=(A\times B)\cup(A\times C)$

(b) $A\times(B-C)=(A\times B)-(A\times C)$

(c) Both (a) and (b)

(d) None of the above

5. If $\cos x=\frac{3}{4}$, then the value of $\sin\frac{x}{2}\sin\frac{5x}{2}$ is

(a) $\frac{1}{32}$ (b) $\frac{11}{32}$ (c) $\frac{11}{8}$ (d) $\frac{11}{16}$

6. If the complex number $z=x+iy$ satisfies the condition $|z+1|=1$, then z lies on

(a) X-axis

(b) circle with centre $(1, 0)$ and radius 1

(c) circle with centre $(-1, 0)$ and radius 1

(d) Y-axis

7. Which of the following is/are true?

I. If $xy<0$, then $x>0$, $y>0$.

II. If $xy>0$, then $x>0$, $y<0$.

III. If $|x|<5$, then $x\in(-5,5)$.

(a) Only I is true (b) Only II is true

(c) Only III is true (d) I and II are true

8. If some or all of n objects are taken at a time, the number of combinations are

(a) 2^n (b) $2^{(n-1)}$

(c) 2^n-1 (d) None of these

9. The number of terms in the expansion of $(x+y+z)^{10}$ is

(a) 11 (b) 33 (c) 66 (d) 1000

10. If A is the arithmetic mean and G_1, G_2 be two geometric means between any two numbers, then which of the following is/are true?

I. $\frac{G_1^2}{G_2} + \frac{G_2^2}{G_1} = A$ II. $\frac{G_1^2}{G_2} + \frac{G_2^2}{G_1} = 2A$

(a) Both I and II are true
(b) Only I is true
(c) Only II is true
(d) Both I and II are false

11. Let $f(x) = \begin{cases} x^2 - 1, 0 < x < 2 \\ 2x + 3, 2 \le x < 3 \end{cases}$

If $\lim_{x \to 2^-} f(x)$ and $\lim_{x \to 2^+} f(x)$ are the roots of a quadratic equation, then the equation is

(a) $x^2 - 10x + 21 = 0$ (b) $x^2 + 10x + 21 = 0$
(c) $x^2 + 4x - 21 = 0$ (d) $x^2 - 4x - 21 = 0$

12. The value of

$$\left(\frac{\cos A + \cos B}{\sin A - \sin B}\right)^n + \left(\frac{\sin A + \sin B}{\cos A - \cos B}\right)^n$$

(where, n is an even) is

(a) $2\tan^n\left(\frac{A-B}{2}\right)$ (b) $2\cot^n\left(\frac{A-B}{2}\right)$
(c) 0 (d) None of these

13. Let $S(5, 12)$ and $S'(-12, 5)$ be the foci of an ellipse passing through the origin. The eccentricity of ellipse is

(a) 1/2 (b) $1/\sqrt{3}$ (c) $1/\sqrt{2}$ (d) 2/3

14. The value of $\lim_{x \to 0} \frac{(1 - \cos 2x)\sin 5x}{x^2 \sin 3x}$ is

(a) $\frac{10}{3}$ (b) $\frac{3}{10}$ (c) $\frac{6}{5}$ (d) $\frac{5}{6}$

15. Let U be the universal set and $A \cup B \cup C = U$ then $[(A - B) \cup (B - C) \cup (C - A)]'$ equals

(a) $A \cup B \cup C$ (b) $A \cup (B \cap C)$
(c) $A \cap (B \cup C)$ (d) $A \cap B \cap C$

16. The domain of the definition of the function $f(x) = \frac{1}{4 - x^2} + \log_{10}(x^3 - x)$ is

(a) $(-1, 0) \cup (1, 2) \cup (3, \infty)$
(b) $(-2, -1) \cup (-1, 0) \cup (2, \infty)$
(c) $(-1, 0) \cup (1, 2) \cup (2, \infty)$
(d) $(1, 2) \cup (2, \infty)$

17. If $[x]^2 - 5[x] + 6 = 0$, where $[\cdot]$ denote the greatest integer function, then

(a) $x \in [3, 4]$ (b) $x \in (2, 3]$
(c) $x \in [2, 3]$ (d) $x \in [2, 4)$

18. If a, b, c, d, are in GP, then $(b - c)^2 + (c - a)^2 + (d - b)^2$ is equal to

(a) $(ad)^2$ (b) $\left(\frac{a}{d}\right)^2$ (c) $(a - d)^2$ (d) $(a + d)^2$

19. For $0 < \theta < \frac{\pi}{2}$, if $x = \sum_{n=0}^{\infty} \cos^{2n}\theta$,

$y = \sum_{n=0}^{\infty} \sin^{2n}\theta$, $z = \sum_{n=0}^{\infty} \cos^{2n}\theta \sin^{2n}\theta$,

then

(a) $xyz = xz + y$ (b) $xyz = xy + z$
(c) $xyz = x + y + z$ (d) $xyz = yz + x$

20. If $z(1 + a) = b + ic$ and $a^2 + b^2 + c^2 = 1$, then $\frac{1 + iz}{1 - iz}$ is equal to

(a) $\frac{a + ib}{1 + c}$ (b) $\frac{b - ic}{1 + a}$
(c) $\frac{a + ic}{1 + b}$ (d) $\frac{b + ic}{1 + a}$

21. If atleast one root of the equation $x^3 + ax^2 + bx + c = 0$ remains unchanged, when a, b and c are decreased by one, then which one of the following is always a root of the given equation ?

(a) 1
(b) −1
(c) ω, an imaginary cube root of unity
(d) i

22. A and B are two sets having 3 and 4 elements respectively and having 2 elements in common. The number of relations which can be defined from A to B is

(a) 2^{10} (b) $2^{10}-1$
(c) $2^{12}-1$ (d) 2^{12}

23. 16 men compete with one another in running, swimming and riding. How many prize lists could be made, if there were altogether 6 prizes of different values, one for running, 2 for swimming and 3 for riding?

(a) $16\times15\times14$ (b) $16^3\times15^2\times14$
(c) $16^3\times15\times14^2$ (d) $16^2\times15\times14$

24. For $2\le r\le n$, ${}^nC_r+2\,{}^nC_{r-1}+{}^nC_{r-2}$ is equal to

(a) ${}^{n+2}C_{r-1}$ (b) $2\,{}^{n+1}C_{r+1}$
(c) ${}^{n+2}C_r$ (d) $2\,{}^{n+2}C_r$

25. The sum of the series $\sum_{r=0}^{10}{}^{20}C_r$ is

(a) 2^{20} (b) 2^{10}
(c) $2^{19}-\frac{1}{2}\,{}^{20}C_{10}$ (d) $2^{19}+\frac{1}{2}\,{}^{20}C_{10}$

26. $\sin47^\circ+\sin61^\circ-\sin11^\circ-\sin25^\circ$ is equal to

(a) $\sin7^\circ$ (b) $\cos7^\circ$
(c) $\sin36^\circ$ (d) $\cos36^\circ$

27. P is a point on either of the two lines $y-\sqrt{3}|x|=2$ at a distance 5 units from their point of intersection. The coordinates of the foot of the perpendicular from P on the bisector of the angle between them are

(a) $\left(0,\frac{4+5\sqrt{3}}{2}\right)$ or $\left(0,\frac{4-5\sqrt{3}}{2}\right)$ depending on which the point P is taken

(b) $\left(0,\frac{4+5\sqrt{3}}{2}\right)$

(c) $\left(0,\frac{4-5\sqrt{3}}{2}\right)$ (d) $\left(\frac{5}{2},\frac{5\sqrt{3}}{2}\right)$

28. The number of integral value of λ for which $x^2+y^2+\lambda x+(1-\lambda)y+5=0$ is the equation of circle whose radius cannot exceed 5 is

(a) 12 (b) 14 (c) 18 (d) 16

29. If P is a point such that the ratio of the squares of the lengths of the tangents from P to the circles $x^2+y^2+2x-4y-20=0$ and $x^2+y^2-4x+2y-44=0$ is 2 : 3, then the locus of P is a circle with centre

(a) $(7,-8)$ (b) $(-7,8)$
(c) $(7,8)$ (d) $(-7,-8)$

30. The area (in sq. units) of an equilateral triangle inscribed in the parabola $y^2=8x$, with one of its vertices on the vertex of this parabola, is

(a) $64\sqrt{3}$ (b) $256\sqrt{3}$ (c) $192\sqrt{3}$ (d) $128\sqrt{3}$

31. The line $x-1=0$ is the direction of parabola $y^2-Kx+8=0$, then one of the value of K is

(a) $\frac{1}{8}$ (b) 8 (c) 4 (d) $\frac{1}{4}$

32. If the ellipse $\frac{(x-h)^2}{M}+\frac{(y-k)^2}{N}=1$ has major axis on the line $y=2$, minor axis on the line $x=-1$. Major axis has length 10 and minor axis has length 4, then the values of h,k,N,M respectively are

(a) $-1,2,5,2$ (b) $-1,2,10,4$
(c) $1,-2,25,4$ (d) $-1,2,25,4$

33. A focus of an ellipse is at the origin. The directrix is the line $x=4$ and the eccentricity is 1/2, then length of semi-major axis is

(a) $\frac{5}{3}$ (b) $\frac{8}{3}$ (c) $\frac{2}{3}$ (d) $\frac{4}{3}$

34. The equation of the hyperbola whose eccentricity is $\sqrt{2}$ and the distance between the foci is 16, taking transverse and conjugate axes of the hyperbola as x and y axes respectively, is

(a) $x^2 - y^2 = 0$ (b) $x^2 - y^2 = 32$

(c) $x^2 - y^2 = 2$ (d) None of the above

35. The mid-points of the sides of a triangle are (5, 7, 11), (0, 8, 5) and (2, 3, – 1). Then, the vertices are

(a) (7, 2, 5), (3, 12, 17), (– 3, 4, – 7)

(b) (7, 2, 5), (3, 12, 17), (3, 4, 7)

(c) (7, 2, 5), (– 3, 12, 17), (– 3, – 4, – 7)

(d) None of the above

36. For each $t \in R$, let $[t]$ be the greatest integer less than or equal to t.

Then, $\lim\limits_{x \to 0^+} x\left(\left[\frac{1}{x}\right] + \left[\frac{2}{x}\right] + \ldots + \left[\frac{15}{x}\right]\right)$

(a) is equal to 0

(b) is equal to 15

(c) is equal to 120

(d) does not exist (in R)

37. The mean of the numbers $a, b, 8, 5$ and 10 is 6 and the variance is 6.80. Then, which one of the following gives possible values of a and b?

(a) $a = 3, b = 4$ (b) $a = 0, b = 7$

(c) $a = 5, b = 2$ (d) $a = 1, b = 6$

38. The mean of 5 observations is 4.4 and their various is 8.24. If three observations are 1, 2 and 6, then other two observation are

(a) 5 and 8 (b) 4 and 9

(c) 7 and 6 (d) None of these

39. Two aeroplanes I and II bomb a target in succession. The probabilities of I and II scoring a hit correctly are 0.3 and 0.2, respectively. The second plane will bomb only, if the first misses the target. The probability that the target is hit by the second plane, is

(a) 0.06 (b) 0.14 (c) 0.32 (d) 0.7

40. If $x = y\cos\frac{2\pi}{3} = z\cos\frac{4\pi}{3}$, then $xy + yz + zx$ is equal to

(a) – 1 (b) 0 (c) 1 (d) 2

MCQs 2 Marks Questions

41. If $z_n = \cos\left(\frac{\pi}{(2n+1)(2n+3)}\right) + i\sin\left(\frac{\pi}{(2n+1)(2n+3)}\right)$, then $\lim\limits_{n \to \infty}(z_1 \cdot z_2 \cdot z_3 \cdots z_n)$ is equal to

(a) $\cos\frac{\pi}{3} + i\sin\frac{\pi}{3}$

(b) $\cos\frac{\pi}{6} + i\sin\frac{\pi}{6}$

(c) $\cos\frac{5\pi}{6} + i\sin\frac{5\pi}{6}$

(d) $\cos\frac{3\pi}{2} + i\sin\frac{3\pi}{2}$

42. If $\cos(\alpha + \beta) = \frac{3}{5}$, $\sin(\alpha - \beta) = \frac{5}{13}$ and $0 < \alpha, \beta < \frac{\pi}{4}$, then $\tan(2\alpha)$ is equal to

(a) $\frac{63}{52}$ (b) $\frac{63}{16}$ (c) $\frac{21}{16}$ (d) $\frac{33}{52}$

43. If $(1 + x)^n = C_0 + C_1x + C_2x^2 + \ldots . C_nx^n$, then the value of $C_0 + 2C_1 + 3C_2 + \ldots\ldots (n+1)C_n$ is

(a) $(n + 1)2^n$ (b) $(n + 1)2^{n-1}$

(c) $(n + 2)2^{n-1}$ (d) $(n + 2)2^n$

44. If $\tan x = \frac{1}{7}$ and $\sin y = \frac{1}{\sqrt{10}}$, then $\tan(x + 2y)$ is equal to

(a) 0 (b) $\frac{1}{2}$

(c) 1 (d) $\frac{3}{4}$

45. Let $A(1, 0)$, $B(6, 2)$ and $C\left(\frac{3}{2}, 6\right)$ be the vertices of a ΔABC. If P is a point inside the ΔABC such that the triangles APC, APB and BPC have equal areas, then the length of the line segment PQ, where Q is the point $\left(-\frac{7}{6}, -\frac{1}{3}\right)$, is

(a) 2 (b) 5

(c) 7 (d) 4

46. If the circles $x^2 + y^2 + 5Kx + 2y + K = 0$ and $2(x^2 + y^2) + 2Kx + 3y - 1 = 0$, $(K \in R)$, intersect at the points P and Q, then the line $4x + 5y - K = 0$ passes through P and Q, for

(a) no values of K

(b) exactly one value of K

(c) exactly two values of K

(d) infinitely many values of K

47. A hyperbola having the transverse axis of length $\sqrt{2}$ has the same foci as that of the ellipse $3x^2 + 4y^2 = 12$, then this hyperbola does not pass through which of the following points?

(a) $\left(\frac{1}{\sqrt{2}}, 0\right)$ (b) $\left(-\sqrt{\frac{3}{2}}, 1\right)$

(c) $\left(1, -\frac{1}{\sqrt{2}}\right)$ (d) $\left(\sqrt{\frac{3}{2}}, \frac{1}{\sqrt{2}}\right)$

48. $\lim_{y \to 0} \frac{\sqrt{1 + \sqrt{1 + y^4}} - \sqrt{2}}{y^4}$

(a) exists and equals $\frac{1}{4\sqrt{2}}$

(b) does not exist

(c) exists and equals $\frac{1}{2\sqrt{2}}$

(d) exists and equals $\frac{1}{2\sqrt{2}(\sqrt{2} + 1)}$

49. Let a_n be nth term of GP of positive number. Let $\sum_{n=1}^{100} a_{2n} = \alpha$ and $\sum_{n=1}^{100} a_{2n-1} = \beta$ such that $\alpha \neq \beta$ then common ratio is

(a) $\frac{\beta}{\alpha}$ (b) $\frac{\alpha}{\beta}$ (c) $\sqrt{\frac{\alpha}{\beta}}$ (d) $\sqrt{\frac{\beta}{\alpha}}$

50. When a missile is fired from a ship, the probability that it is intercepted is $\frac{1}{3}$ and the probability that the missile hits the target, given that it is not intercepted, is $\frac{3}{4}$. If three missilcs are fired independently from the ship, then the probability that all three hit the target, is

(a) $\frac{1}{8}$ (b) $\frac{3}{4}$

(c) $\frac{1}{27}$ (d) $\frac{3}{8}$

Darken your choice with HB Pencil

1.	ⓐ ⓑ ⓒ ⓓ	10.	ⓐ ⓑ ⓒ ⓓ	19.	ⓐ ⓑ ⓒ ⓓ	28.	ⓐ ⓑ ⓒ ⓓ	37.	ⓐ ⓑ ⓒ ⓓ	46.	ⓐ ⓑ ⓒ ⓓ
2.	ⓐ ⓑ ⓒ ⓓ	11.	ⓐ ⓑ ⓒ ⓓ	20.	ⓐ ⓑ ⓒ ⓓ	29.	ⓐ ⓑ ⓒ ⓓ	38.	ⓐ ⓑ ⓒ ⓓ	47.	ⓐ ⓑ ⓒ ⓓ
3.	ⓐ ⓑ ⓒ ⓓ	12.	ⓐ ⓑ ⓒ ⓓ	21.	ⓐ ⓑ ⓒ ⓓ	30.	ⓐ ⓑ ⓒ ⓓ	39.	ⓐ ⓑ ⓒ ⓓ	48.	ⓐ ⓑ ⓒ ⓓ
4.	ⓐ ⓑ ⓒ ⓓ	13.	ⓐ ⓑ ⓒ ⓓ	22.	ⓐ ⓑ ⓒ ⓓ	31.	ⓐ ⓑ ⓒ ⓓ	40.	ⓐ ⓑ ⓒ ⓓ	49.	ⓐ ⓑ ⓒ ⓓ
5.	ⓐ ⓑ ⓒ ⓓ	14.	ⓐ ⓑ ⓒ ⓓ	23.	ⓐ ⓑ ⓒ ⓓ	32.	ⓐ ⓑ ⓒ ⓓ	41.	ⓐ ⓑ ⓒ ⓓ	50.	ⓐ ⓑ ⓒ ⓓ
6.	ⓐ ⓑ ⓒ ⓓ	15.	ⓐ ⓑ ⓒ ⓓ	24.	ⓐ ⓑ ⓒ ⓓ	33.	ⓐ ⓑ ⓒ ⓓ	42.	ⓐ ⓑ ⓒ ⓓ		
7.	ⓐ ⓑ ⓒ ⓓ	16.	ⓐ ⓑ ⓒ ⓓ	25.	ⓐ ⓑ ⓒ ⓓ	34.	ⓐ ⓑ ⓒ ⓓ	43.	ⓐ ⓑ ⓒ ⓓ		
8.	ⓐ ⓑ ⓒ ⓓ	17.	ⓐ ⓑ ⓒ ⓓ	26.	ⓐ ⓑ ⓒ ⓓ	35.	ⓐ ⓑ ⓒ ⓓ	44.	ⓐ ⓑ ⓒ ⓓ		
9.	ⓐ ⓑ ⓒ ⓓ	18.	ⓐ ⓑ ⓒ ⓓ	27.	ⓐ ⓑ ⓒ ⓓ	36.	ⓐ ⓑ ⓒ ⓓ	45.	ⓐ ⓑ ⓒ ⓓ		

Hints and Answers

Chapter 1 Sets

1. *(c)* Given, $2a^2 + 3b^2 = 35$ and $a, b \in Z$

For $b = \pm 1$, $2a^2 + 3(\pm 1)^2 = 35 \Rightarrow a = \pm 4$

For $b = \pm 3$, $2a^2 + 3(\pm 3)^2 = 35 \Rightarrow a = \pm 2$

$\therefore$ (2, 3), (– 2, 3), (2, – 3), (– 2, – 3), (4, 1), (– 4, 1), (4, – 1), (– 4, –1) are 8 elements.

2. *(b)*

3. *(d)* Number of subsets of A containing less than 6 elements is given by

$${}^mC_0 + {}^mC_1 + {}^mC_2 + {}^mC_3 + {}^mC_4 + {}^mC_5 = \sum_{r=0}^{5} {}^mC_r$$

4. *(c)* Number of subsets of $A = 2^{10}$

5. *(d)* $X = \{1, 2, 3, 4, 5, 6, 7, 8, 9\}$

Possible multiples of 3 = 3, 6, 9, 12, 15, 18, 21, 24, 27

Here, 3 and 27 are not possible as they cannot be written in the form $a + b + c$.

$6 \to 1 + 2 + 3$

$9 \to 2 + 3 + 4, 5 + 3 + 1, 6 + 2 + 1$

$12 \to 9 + 2 + 1, 8 + 3 + 1, 7 + 1 + 4, 7 + 2 + 3, 6 + 4 + 2, 6 + 5 + 1, 5 + 4 + 3$

$15 \to 9 + 4 + 2, 9 + 5 + 1, 8 + 6 + 1, 8 + 5 + 2, 8 + 4 + 3, 7 + 6 + 2, 7 + 5 + 3, 6 + 5 + 4$

$18 \to 9 + 8 + 1, 9 + 7 + 2, 9 + 6 + 3, 9 + 5 + 4, 8 + 7 + 3, 8 + 6 + 4, 7 + 6 + 5$

$21 \to 9 + 8 + 4, 9 + 7 + 5, 8 + 7 + 6$

$24 \to 9 + 8 + 7$

Hence, largest possible subsets are 30.

6. *(d)* $X = \{x \in R \mid -4 \le x < 4\} \Rightarrow X = [-4, 4)$

$Y = \{x \in R \mid -5 \le x \le 5\} \Rightarrow Y = [-5, 5]$

$Z = \{x \in R \mid -7 \le x \le 10\} \Rightarrow Z = [-7, 10]$

Clearly, $X \cap Y \cap Z = [-4, 4)$ and $-4 \in (X \cap Y \cap Z)$

7. *(b)* Given, $A \cup B = A \cup C$ and $A \cap B = A \cap C$

Let $x \in A \cup B \Rightarrow x \in A$ or $x \in B$ ...(i)

$\Rightarrow x \in A$ or $x \in C$ $[\because A \cup B = A \cup C]$ ...(ii)

Let $x \in A \cap B \Rightarrow x \in A$ and $x \in B$ ...(iii)

$\Rightarrow x \in A$ and $x \in C$ $[\because A \cap B = A \cap C]$ ...(iv)

From Eqs. (i), (ii), (iii) and (iv), we conclude $B = C$ only

8. *(c)* For $X \cap Y$, $\frac{1}{u} = -u \Rightarrow u^2 = -1$

which is not possible in real number.

$\therefore \quad X \cap Y = \phi$

9. *(a)* $A = \{x^2 : x$ is a natural number$]$

$= \{1^2, 2^2, 3^2, 4^2, 5^2, \ldots\} = \{1, 4, 9, 16, 25, \ldots.\}$

$B = \{x^3 : x$ is a natural number$\}$

$= \{1^3, 2^3, 3^3, 4^3, 5^3, \ldots\}$

$= \{1, 8, 27, 64, 125, \ldots.\}$

$A \cap B = \{1\}$ a finite set

$A \cup B = \{1, 4, 8, 9, 16, 25, 27, \ldots\}$ is an infinite set.

$\therefore \overline{A \cup B}$ is also an infinite set

and $A \cup B \ne$ set of natural numbers.

10. *(b)* All rectangles, rhombus and squares are parallelogram because their opposite sides are equal and parallel.

$\therefore \quad F_2 \subset F_1, F_3 \subset F_1$ and $F_4 \subset F_1$

$\Rightarrow \quad F_1 = F_2 \cup F_3 \cup F_4$

11. *(b)* $X = \{3, 6, 9, 12, 15, 18, \ldots\}$

$Y = \{4, 8, 12, 16, 20, \ldots.\}$

$Z = \{12, 24, 36, 48, \ldots.\}$

$(X - Y) = \{3, 6, 9, 15, 18, 21, 27, \ldots\}$

$(X - Y) \cup Z = X$, which is not a null set.

$(X - Y) \cap Z = \phi$

12. *(d)* $\because$ A is not a subset of B.

$\therefore$ Some point of A will not be a point of B so that point will belong to B^C.

Hence, A and the complement of B are always non-disjoint i.e. $A \cap B^C \ne \phi$.

13. *(c)* $\because \; U - A = \overline{A}$

$\Rightarrow \quad U - (U - A) = A$

$\Rightarrow \quad U - (U - (U - A)) = \overline{A}$

$\Rightarrow \quad U - (U - (U - (U - A))) = A$

$\Rightarrow U - (U - (U - (U - (U - A)))) = \overline{A}$

$= \overline{B \cup C}$

$= \overline{B} \cap \overline{C}$

14. *(a)* $\lambda =$ Universal set and $A \subseteq \lambda$, then

$A - \lambda = \phi, \quad \lambda - A = \overline{A}$

$\therefore (A - \lambda) \cup (\lambda - A) = \phi \cup \overline{A} = \overline{A}$

$\Rightarrow (A - \lambda) \cup (\lambda - A) \cap A = \overline{A} \cap A = \phi$

15. ***(d)*** $\because P, Q, R \neq \phi$ and $P \cup Q = Q \cap R$

i.e. union of P and Q is equal to intersection of Q and R strongest inference is $P \subseteq Q \subseteq R$.

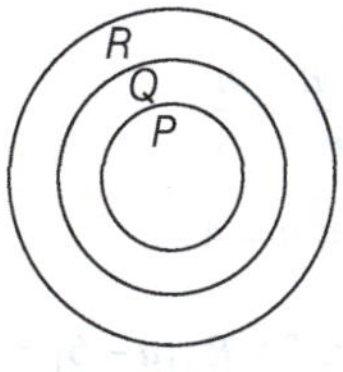

16. ***(c)*** We have, $n^3 + 2n + 1 = 3n^2 + 7$

$\Rightarrow \quad n^3 - 3n^2 + 2n - 6 = 0$

$\Rightarrow \quad (n-3)(n^2+2) = 0$

$\Rightarrow \quad n = 3, n \in N$

$\therefore x = 3(3)^2 + 7 = 34 \in X \cap Y$

17. ***(b)*** For each $x \in X$, we have three choices

1. $x \in Y, x \notin Z$
2. $x \notin Y, x \in Z$
3. $x \notin Y, x \notin Z$

Required ordered pairs $= 3^5$

18. ***(c)*** We have,

$A = \{x \mid x \text{ is a root of } x^2 - 1 = 0\}$

$= \{x \mid x \text{ is a root of } (x+1)(x-1) = 0\}$

$\rightarrow \quad x = \pm 1$

and $B = \{x \mid x \text{ is a root of } x^2 - 2x + 1 = 0\}$

$= \{x \mid x \text{ is a root of } (x-1)^2 = 0\}$

$\Rightarrow \quad x = 1$

$\therefore A \cup B = 1$

19. ***(d)*** **20.** ***(b)*** **21.** ***(a)***

22. ***(c)***

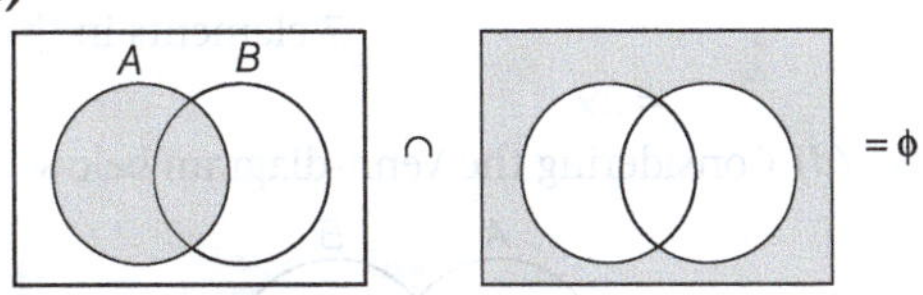

23. ***(b)*** Venn-diagram of $A, B \subseteq X$ is

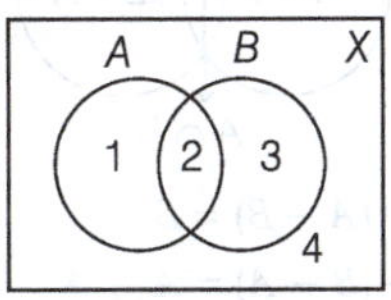

There are four regions

1 : denotes $A - B$, 3 : denotes $B - A$

2 : denotes $A \cap B$

1, 2 and 3 are combined to form $A \cup B$.

Here, $(A - B) \cup (B - A) = A \cup B$

$\Rightarrow$ Region 2 is empty.

$\therefore A \cap B = \phi$ and $(A - B)$,

$(B - A)$ are mutually exclusive as

$(A - B) \cap (B - A) = \phi$.

This means, correct Venn-diagram is

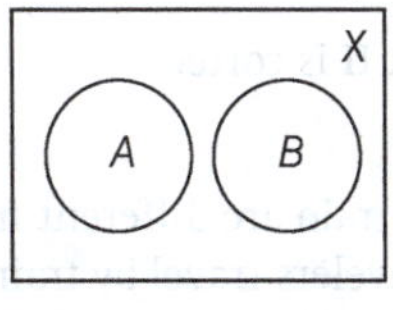

$\therefore A \subset (X - B)$

24. ***(b)*** Venn-diagram of three sets

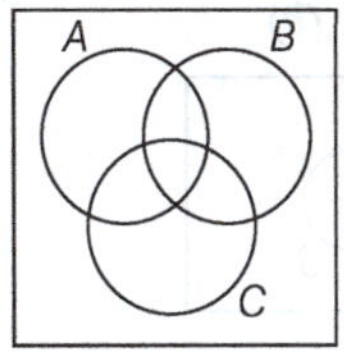

I. $A - (B - C) = (A - B) \cup C$

Venn-diagram of

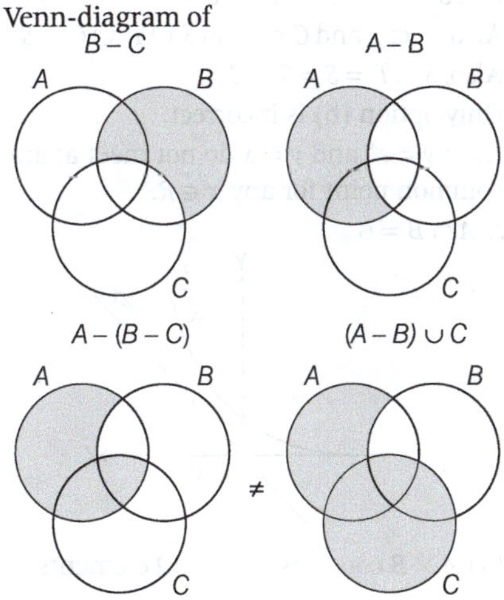

Statement I is not correct.

II. $(A - B) - C = A - (B \cup C)$

Venn-diagram of

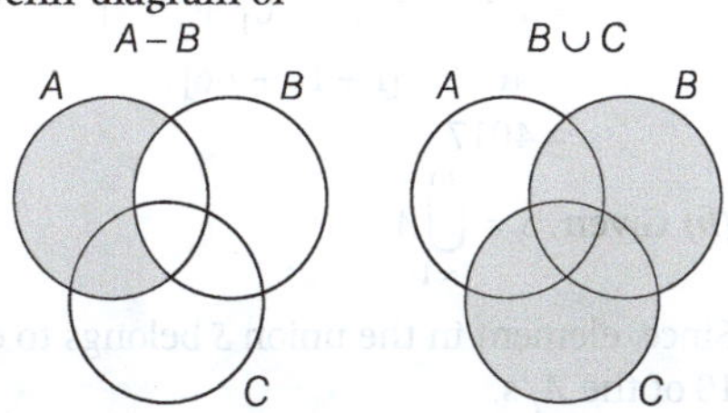

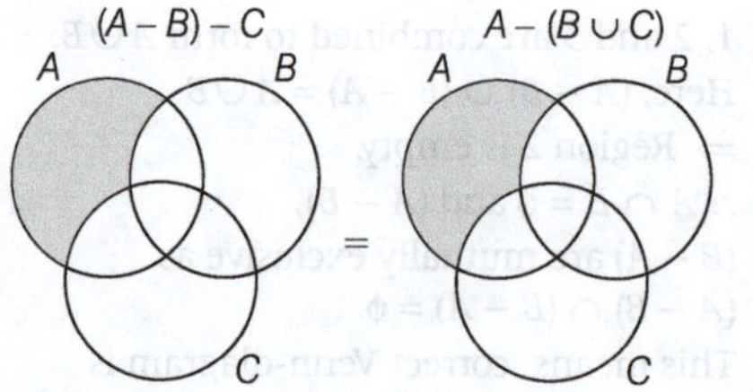

Statement II is correct.

25. *(d)*

26. *(b)* Bus and train are different from each other but some travelers travel by train and some by bus. So, option (b) represents the relationship between travelers, train and bus.

27. *(b)* **28.** *(b)*

29. *(b)*

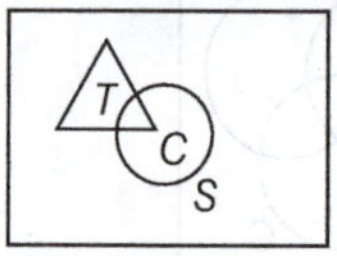

Since, $T \cap C \neq \phi$

and $S \cap T \cap C = T \cap C$

Also, $T \subset S$ and $C \subset S$, so $S \cup T \cup C = S$

Also, $S \cup T = S = S \cup C$

Only option (b) is incorrect.

30. *(c)* $\because y = e^x$ and $y = x$ do not meet at any common point for any $x \in R$.

$\therefore A \cap B = \phi$

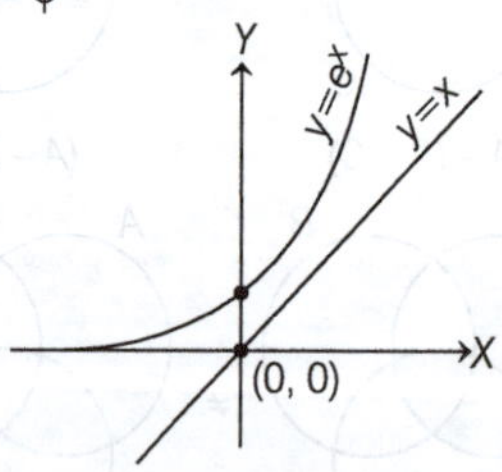

31. *(a)* $A \times B$ contains $3 \times 4 = 12$ elements

Number of subsets of $A \times B$ having 3 or more elements = Number of subsets of $A \times B$ –

(Number of subsets with atmost 2 elements)

$= 2^{12} - [{}^{12}C_0 + {}^{12}C_1 + {}^{12}C_2]$

$= 4096 - [1 + 12 + 66]$

$= 4017$

32. *(b)* Given, $S = \bigcup_{i=1}^{30} A_i$

Since, element in the union S belongs to exactly 10 of the A_i's.

$\Rightarrow n(S) = \frac{1}{10}(5 \times 30) = 15$

Again, $S = \bigcup_{j=1}^{n} B_j$

$\Rightarrow n(S) = \frac{3 \times n}{9} = \frac{n}{3}$

$\Rightarrow 15 = \frac{n}{3} \Rightarrow n = 45$

33. *(a)* $A = \{(a, b) \in R \times R : |a - 5| < 1 \text{ and } |b - 5| < 1\}$

$\Rightarrow \{(a, b) \in R \times R : -1 < (a - 5) < 1$

and $-1 < (b - 5) < 1|\}$

$\Rightarrow \{(a, b) \in R \times R : +4 < a < 6 \text{ and } 4 < b < 6\}$

$\Rightarrow a \in (4, 6)$ and $b \in (4, 6)$

$\therefore A = \{(a, b) : a \in (4, 6) \text{ and } b \in (4, 6)\}$

Now, $B = \{(a, b) \in R \times R : 4(a - 6)^2 + 9(b - 5)^2 \leq 36\}$

From the conditions above for set A, the maximum value of B is

$4(a - 6)^2 + 9(b - 5)^2 = 4(4 - 6)^2 + 9(6 - 5)^2 = 25$

which is less than 36.

Element of A satisfy the conditions of set B.

$\therefore A$ is a subset of B.

34. *(d)* Given, $X = \{n \in N : 1 \leq n \leq 50\}$

Then, $A = \{n \in X : n \text{ is a multiple of } 2\}$

$= \{2, 4, 6, 8, ..., 50\}$

and $B = \{n \in X : n \text{ is multiple of } 7\}$

$= \{7, 14, 21, 28, 35, 42, 49\}$

$\because 14, 28, 42 \in A$

$\therefore$ Smallest subset of X containing both A and B

$= n(A) + n(B) - n(A \cap B) = 25 + 7 - 3$

[$\because$ there are 25 elements in set A and 7 elements in the set B]

$= 29$

35. *(d)* Considering the Venn-diagram below

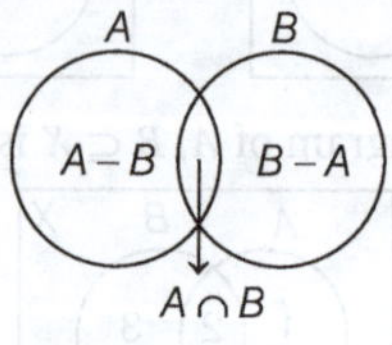

$(A \cup B) - (A - B) = B$

$(A \cup B) - (B - A) = A$

$A \Delta B = (A - B) \cup (B - A)$

$(A \cup B) - (A \Delta B) = A \cap B$ and $(A - B) - A = \phi$

Thus, the required number is 8.

36. ***(b)***

(i) $A \cup B \cup C$

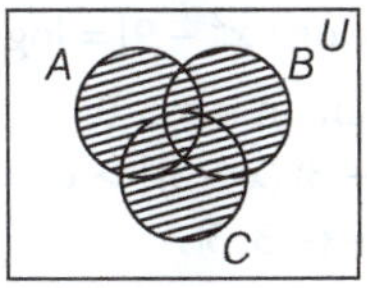

(ii) $(A \cap B^C \cap C^C)$

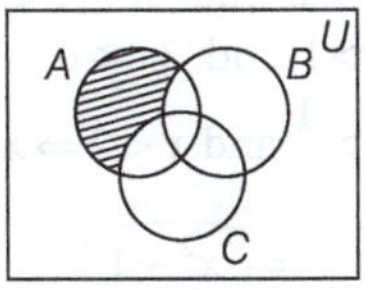

(iii) C^C

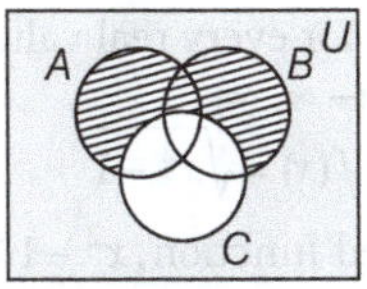

From parts (i), (ii) and (iii), we get

$$(B^C \cap C^C)$$

37. ***(a)*** Some students can be cricket players, some cricket players can be tennis fans and some students can be tennis fans. So, the given items are partly related to each other.

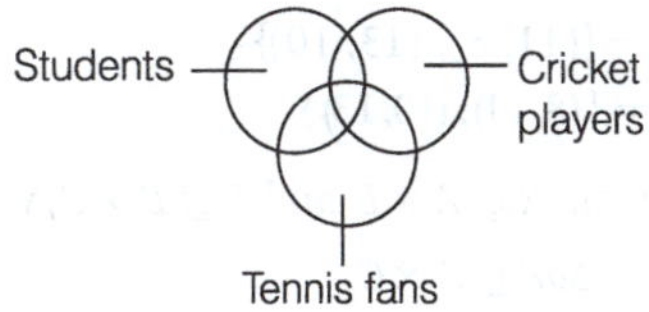

38. ***(a)*** If $X \subseteq A$ and $X \subseteq B$, then necessarily $X \subseteq A$ and hence $X = Y \cup \{d\}$, where Y is any subset of B. The number of subset of B is 2^3 and therefore the required number $= 2^3 = 8$.

39. ***(b)*** Assertion and Reason both are true but Reason is not correct explanation of Assertion.

40. ***(c)*** Assertion is true but Reason is false.

41. ***(c)*** Let the cardinal numbers of set $A = n$ and cardinal numbers of set $B = m$

Given, $n + m = 9$ ....(i)

Also cardinal number of total number of subsets of set $A = 2^n$

and cardinal number of total number of subsets of set $B = 2^m$

Given, $\dfrac{2^n}{2^m} = \dfrac{8}{1} \Rightarrow 2^{n-m} = 8 \Rightarrow 2^{n-m} = 2^3$

$\Rightarrow \quad n - m = 3$ ...(ii)

From Eqs. (i) and (ii), $n = 6$ and $m = 3$

42. ***(a)*** $n(B) = m = 3$

Chapter 2 Relations and Functions

1. ***(c)*** Graphical representation of relations are given as

I.

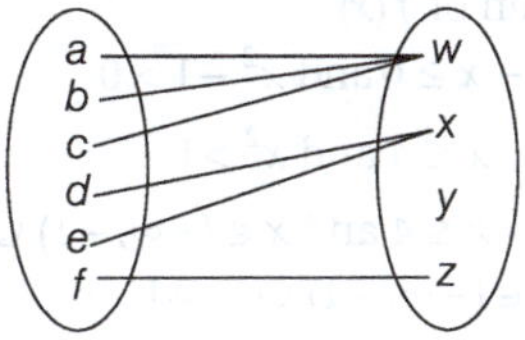

It is a function.

II.

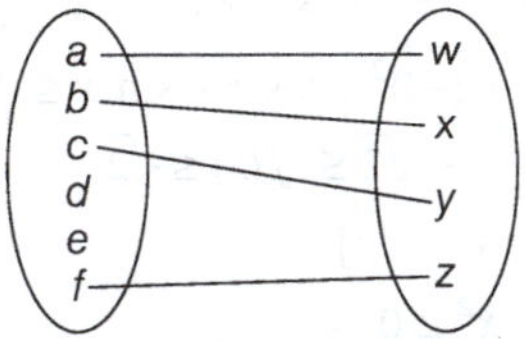

$\because$ d and e are not connected.

So, it is not a function.

III.

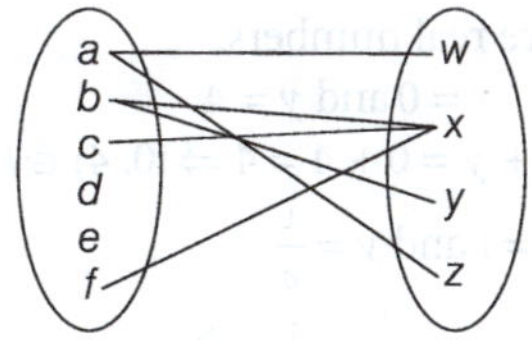

$\because a <^{w}_{z}$, so it is not a function.

IV.

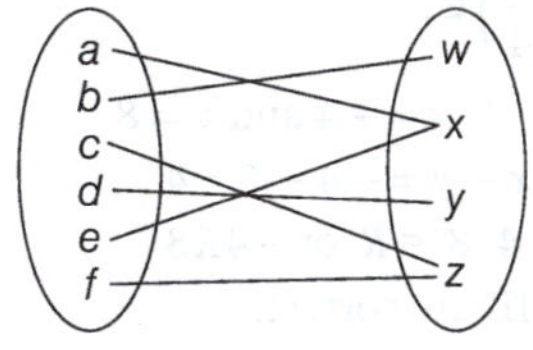

It is a function.

2. ***(c)*** **3.** ***(d)***

4. ***(b)*** Let $A = \{11, 12, 13\}$, $B = \{8, 10, 12\}$

$\therefore \quad R = \{(11, 8), (13, 10)\}$
$R^{-1} = \{(8,11), (10,13)\}$

5. *(b)* Given, $R \subseteq A \times B$ and $S \subseteq B \times C$, we have
$$SoR \subseteq A \times C$$
$\therefore$ SoR is a relation from A to C.

6. *(c)*

7. *(a)* Given, $n(X) = m$
Let R be the relation on X.
Then, $R \subseteq X \times X$
Total number of relations
= Number of subsets of $(X \times X)$
$n(X \times X) = m \cdot m = m^2$
$\therefore$ Number of relations $= 2^{m^2}$

8. *(d)* Given, $P, Q, R \neq \phi$ such that
$$P \cap R = \phi$$
Then, $(P \times Q) \cap (R \times Q) = (P \cap R) \times (Q \cap Q)$
$= \phi \times Q = \phi$

9. *(c)*

10. *(a)* Given, $A = \{2, 5, 8\}$ and $B = \{3, 6, 7\}$
$R = \{x, y\} : x \in A, y \in B$ and $x = y - 1\}$
For $y = 3$, $x = 3 - 1 = 2 \in A$
For $y = 6$, $x = 6 - 1 = 5 \in A$
For $y = 7$, $x = 7 - 1 = 6 \notin A$
$\therefore \quad R = \{(2, 3), (5, 6)\}$
There are two elements only.

11. *(d)*

12. *(b)* We have, $x + y = 4$
x and y are real numbers.
I. $\quad x = 0$ and $y = 4$
$\therefore \quad x + y = 0 + 4 = 4 \Rightarrow (0, 4) \in R$ or $0R4$
II. $\quad x = 1$ and $y = \frac{1}{4}$
$\therefore \quad x + y = 1 + \frac{1}{4} = \frac{5}{4} \neq 4$
$\Rightarrow \left(1, \frac{1}{4}\right) \notin R$
III. $\quad x = -4$ and $y = 8$
$\therefore \quad x + y = -4 + 8 = 4$
$\Rightarrow \quad (-4, 8) \in R$ or $-4R8$
So, I and III are correct.

13. *(a)* **14.** *(d)*

15. *(c)* We have, $0 < a < 1$
$\Rightarrow \quad \log_{10} a = b < 0 \Rightarrow a = 10^b, b < 0 \Rightarrow 0 < 10^b < 1$
Negative power of 10 is between 0 and 1.

16. *(a)* **17.** *(b)*

18. *(c)* Let $f(x) = \log|x^2 - 9| = \log|(x+3)(x-3)|$
For $\log_a x$, domain is $x > 0$.
For $f(x)$, $|(x+3)(x-3)| > 0 \Rightarrow x \neq -3, x \neq 3$
$\therefore$ Domain $R - \{-3, 3\}$.

19. *(b)* We have, $\log_5(3x - 1) < 1$
$\therefore \quad 3x - 1 > 0$ and $3x - 1 < 5$
$\Rightarrow \quad 3x > 1$ and $3x < 6$
$\Rightarrow \quad x > \frac{1}{3}$ and $x < 2 \Rightarrow x \in \left(\frac{1}{3}, 2\right)$

20. *(b)* We have, $f(x) = \sqrt{x^2 + 1}$
For real valued function, $x^2 + 1 \geq 0$
which is true for every real value of x.
$\therefore \quad x \in (-\infty, \infty)$

21. *(d)* We have, $f(x) = \sqrt{x^2 - 1}$
For real valued function, $x^2 - 1 \geq 0 \Rightarrow x^2 \geq 1^2$
$\Rightarrow \quad x \in (-\infty, \infty) - (-1, 1)$

22. *(b)* For domain of $f(x)$, $-1 \leq \log_3 \frac{x}{3} \leq 1$
$\Rightarrow \quad 3^{-1} \leq \frac{x}{3} \leq 3^1 \Rightarrow 1 \leq x \leq 9 \Rightarrow x \in [1, 9]$

23. *(b)* For domain of $f(x)$,
$|x| - x > 0 \Rightarrow |x| > x \Rightarrow x \in (-\infty, 0)$

24. *(c)* For $f(x)$ to be defined $5 - 4x - x^2 \geq 0$ and $x + 4 > 0$
$\Rightarrow \quad -5 \leq x \leq 1$ and $x > -4 \Rightarrow -4 < x \leq 1$

25. *(a)* Given, $f(x) = \sqrt{4 - x} + \frac{1}{\sqrt{x^2 - 1}}$
For domain of $f(x)$,
$4 - x \geq 0$ and $x^2 - 1 > 0$
$\Rightarrow \quad x \leq 4$ and $x^2 > 1$
$\Rightarrow \quad x \leq 4$ and $x \in (-\infty, -1) \cup (1, \infty)$
$\therefore \quad x \in (-\infty, -1) \cup (1, 4]$

26. *(c)* $f(x) = \cos x - \sin x$
$\because -\sqrt{a^2 + b^2} \leq a \cos x + b \sin x \leq \sqrt{a^2 + b^2}$
$\Rightarrow -\sqrt{(1)^2 + (-1)^2} \leq \cos x - \sin x \leq \sqrt{(1)^2 + (-1)^2}$
$\Rightarrow \quad -\sqrt{2} \leq f(x) \leq \sqrt{2}$
Range $= [-\sqrt{2}, \sqrt{2}]$

27. *(a)* $\because \quad x^2 \geq 0$
$\Rightarrow \quad 1 + x^2 \geq 1 \Rightarrow \frac{1}{1 + x^2} \leq 1$

$\Rightarrow \quad 0 \le \frac{x^2}{1+x^2} < 1 \Rightarrow 0 \le f(x) < 1$

$\Rightarrow \quad f(x) \in [0, 1)$

28. *(a)* $f(x) = x - [x]$
gives fractional value it is fraction value function denoted by $\{x\}$ and range of $f(x)$ is $[0, 1)$.

29. *(b)* $f(x) = \frac{x+2}{|x+2|}$

$$= \begin{cases} \frac{x+2}{x+2}, & x \ge -2 \\ \frac{x+2}{-(x+2)}, & x < 2 \end{cases} = \begin{cases} 1, & x \ge 2 \\ -1, & x < 2 \end{cases}$$

Range $(f) = \{1, -1\}$

30. *(b)* Range of $\cos x$ is $[-1, 1]$ for every $x \in R$.

$\Rightarrow$ Range of $\cos\left(\frac{x}{9}\right)$ is $[-1, 1]$

31. *(b)* $\because \quad -1 \le \sin 2x \le 1$

$\Rightarrow \quad -1 \le -\sin 2x \le 1 \Rightarrow 1 \le 2 - \sin 2x \le 3$

$\Rightarrow \quad \frac{1}{3} \le \frac{1}{2 - \sin 2x} \le 1$

$\Rightarrow \quad \frac{1}{3} \le f(x) \le 1$

$\Rightarrow \quad$ Range $\left[\frac{1}{3}, 1\right]$

32. *(b)* We have, $f(x) = \log(x + \sqrt{x^2+1})$

$f(-x) = \log(-x + \sqrt{x^2+1})$

$\therefore \quad f(x) + f(-x) = \log(x + \sqrt{x^2+1}) + \log(-x + \sqrt{x^2+1})$

$= \log[(x + \sqrt{x^2+1})(-x + \sqrt{x^2+1})]$

$= \log 1 = 0$

$\therefore \quad f(x)$ is an odd function.

33. *(c)*

34. *(c)* When $y = f(x)$ is symmetrical about $x = c$, then $f(c+x) = f(c-x)$

$\because \quad y = f(x)$ is symmetrical about the line $x = 3$.

$\therefore \quad f(3+x) = f(3-x)$

35. *(b)* We have, $f(x) = 2x + |x|$

$f(2x) + f(-x) - f(x)$

$= 2(2x) + |2x| + 2(-x) + |-x| - 2x - |x|$

$= 4x + 2|x| - 2x + |x| - 2x - |x|$

$= 2|x|$

36. *(c)* We have, $f(x) = \frac{x}{x-1}$

$$\therefore \quad \frac{f(y)}{f(y+1)} = \frac{\frac{y}{y-1}}{\frac{y+1}{y+1-1}} = \frac{y^2}{y^2-1} = f(y^2)$$

37. *(d)** **38.** *(b)* **39.** *(d)* **40.** *(a)*

41. *(c)* We have, $2f(x) + f\left(\frac{1}{x}\right) = 2x$ ...(i)

On putting $x = 2$, we get

$2f(2) + f\left(\frac{1}{2}\right) = 4$

$\Rightarrow \quad f\left(\frac{1}{2}\right) = 4 - 2f(2)$ ...(ii)

On putting $x = \frac{1}{2}$, we get

$2f\left(\frac{1}{2}\right) + f(2) = 1$

$\Rightarrow 2[4 - 2f(2)] + f(2) = 1$ [from Eq. (i)]

$\Rightarrow \quad 8 - 4f(2) + f(2) = 1$

$\Rightarrow \quad 8 - 3f(2) = 1$

$\Rightarrow \quad f(2) = \frac{7}{3}$

42. *(d)* We have,

$f(x) = 2x^3 + 3x^2 + 3x + 2$

$f\left(\frac{1}{x}\right) = 2\cdot\frac{1}{x^3} + 3\cdot\frac{1}{x^2} + 3\cdot\frac{1}{x} + 2$

$\Rightarrow \quad x^3 f\left(\frac{1}{x}\right) = 2 + 3x + 3x^2 + 2x^3 = f(x)$

43. *(c)* Fractional value function

$f(x) = \{x\} = x - [x]$

is a periodic function with period 1.

44. *(a)* $f(x) = x - [x] = \{x\}$

is fractional part function having period unity.

45. *(a)* Given relation,

$R = \{(x, y) : x, y \in Z, x^2 + 3y^2 \le 8\}$

For $y^2 = 0$, $x^2 = 0, 1, 4$

For $y^2 = 1$, $x^2 = 0, 1, 4$

For $y^2 = 4$, $x^2 \in \phi$

$\therefore$ Range of R is possible values of $y = \{-1, 0, 1\}$

$\therefore$ Domain of R^{-1} = Range of $R = \{-1, 0, 1\}$

46. *(c)* Given, set $A = \{x \in Z : 2^{(x+2)(x^2-5x+6)} = 1\}$

Consider,

$$2^{(x+2)(x^2-5x+6)} = 1 = 2^0$$

$\because \quad (x+2)(x^2-5x+6) = 0$

$\Rightarrow \quad (x+2)(x-2)(x-3) = 0$

$\Rightarrow \quad x = -2, 2, 3$

$\Rightarrow \quad A = \{-2, 2, 3\}$

$\therefore \quad n(A) = 3$

Also, we have set $B = \{x \in Z : -3 < 2x - 1 < 9\}$

$\Rightarrow \quad -3 < 2x - 1 < 9, x \in Z \Rightarrow -2 < 2x < 10, x \in Z$

$\Rightarrow \quad -1 < x < 5, x \in Z \Rightarrow x = 0, 1, 2, 3, 4$

$\because \quad B = \{0, 1, 2, 3, 4\}$

$\therefore \quad n(B) = 5$

So, $n(A \times B) = 3 \times 5 = 15$

Hence, number of relations of set A to set $B = 2^{15}$

47. *(d)* Given, $f(x) = \dfrac{3}{4 - x^2} + \log_{10}(x^3 - x)$

For domain of $f(x)$, $4 - x^2 \neq 0$

$\Rightarrow \quad x^2 \neq 4 \Rightarrow x \neq \pm 2 \quad$ ...(i)

and $\log_{10}(x^3 - x)$, then $x^3 - x > 0$

$$x(x-1)(x+1) > 0$$

$x \in (-1, 0) \cup (1, \infty) \quad$ ...(ii)

From Eqs. (i) and (ii), we get

Domain of $f(x) = (-1, 0) \cup (1, 2) \cup (2, \infty)$

48. *(c)* We have,

$$f(x) = \frac{x^2 - x + 1}{x^2 + x + 1}$$

Let $f(x) = y$

$\therefore \quad y = \dfrac{x^2 - x + 1}{x^2 + x + 1}$

$\Rightarrow \quad x^2y + xy + y = x^2 - x + 1$

$\Rightarrow \quad x^2(y-1) + (y+1)x + y - 1 = 0$

$\because \quad x \in R \Rightarrow D \geq 0$

$\Rightarrow \quad (y+1)^2 - 4(y-1)^2 \geq 0$

$\Rightarrow y^2 + 2y + 1 - 4y^2 + 8y - 4 \geq 0$

$\Rightarrow \quad 3y^2 - 10y + 3 \leq 0$

$\Rightarrow \quad 3y^2 - 9y - y + 3 \leq 0$

$\Rightarrow \quad (3y-1)(y-3) \leq 0$

$\Rightarrow \quad y \in \left[\dfrac{1}{3}, 3\right]$

$\because$ Range of $f(x)$ is $\left[\dfrac{1}{3}, 3\right]$

49. *(a)* We have,

$$f(x) = ax^7 + bx^3 + cx - 5$$

$$f(-7) = a(-7)^7 + b(-7)^3 + c(-7) - 5$$

and $\quad f(7) = a(7)^7 + b(7)^3 + c(7) - 5$

Now, $f(-7) + f(7) = -7^7a - 7^3b - 7c - 5$
$\qquad + 7^7a + 7^3b + 7c - 5$

$\Rightarrow \quad f(-7) + f(7) = -10$

$\Rightarrow \quad 7 + f(7) = -10 \quad [\because f(-7) = 7]$

$\Rightarrow \quad f(7) = -17$

Range of $17\cos x = [-17, 17]$

$\therefore$ Range of $f(7) + 17\cos x$

$$= [-17 - 17, -17 + 17]$$

$$= [-34, 0]$$

50. *(d)* We have, $f(x) = \dfrac{9^x}{9^x + 3}$

$$f(1-x) = \frac{9^{1-x}}{9^{1-x} + 3}$$

$$= \frac{9}{9 + 3 \cdot 9^x} = \frac{9}{3(3 + 9^x)} = \frac{3}{3 + 9^x}$$

$\therefore f(x) + f(1-x) = \dfrac{9^x}{9^x + 3} + \dfrac{3}{3 + 9^x}$

$$= \frac{9^x + 3}{9^x + 3} = 1$$

On putting $x = \dfrac{1}{2022}, \dfrac{2}{2022}, \ldots \dfrac{2021}{2022}$

$f\left(\dfrac{1}{2022}\right) + f\left(\dfrac{2021}{2022}\right) = 1,\ f\left(\dfrac{2}{2022}\right) + f\left(\dfrac{2020}{2022}\right) = 1$

...... $f\left(\dfrac{1010}{2022}\right) + f\left(\dfrac{1012}{2022}\right) = 1,$

$f\left(\dfrac{1011}{2022}\right) + f\left(\dfrac{1011}{2022}\right) = 1,\ f\left(\dfrac{1011}{2022}\right) = \dfrac{1}{2}$

$\therefore f\left(\dfrac{1}{2022}\right) + \left(\dfrac{2}{2022}\right) + \ldots + f\left(\dfrac{2021}{2022}\right)$

$$= (1 + 1 + \ldots + 1010 \text{ times}) + \frac{1}{2}$$

$$= 1010 + 0.05 = 1010.5$$

51. *(b)* (A) $f(x) = \sin 2x - \sqrt{3}\cos 2x$

Period of $\sin 2x$ and

$$\cos 2x = \frac{2\pi}{2} = \pi$$

$\therefore$ Period of $f(x) = \pi$

(B) $f(x) = \text{cosec}^2 \dfrac{3}{4}x + \cot x$

Period of $\text{cosec}^2 \dfrac{3}{4}x = \dfrac{4\pi}{3}$ and period of $\cot x = \pi$

$\therefore$ Period of $f(x)$ is LCM of $\dfrac{4\pi}{3}$ and π i.e. 4π

Hence, period of $f(x) = 4\pi$

(C) $f(x) = 2\sin 3x + 3\sin 2x$

Period of $\sin 3x = \dfrac{2\pi}{3}$ and period of $\sin 2x = \pi$

LCM of $\dfrac{2\pi}{3}$ and $\pi = 2\pi$

$\therefore$ Period of $f(x) = 2\pi$

(D) $f(x) = \sin \dfrac{\pi}{3}x + \sin \dfrac{\pi}{4}x$

Period of $\sin \dfrac{\pi}{3}x = 6\pi$ and period of $\sin \dfrac{\pi}{4}x = 8\pi$

LCM of 6π and $8\pi = 24\pi$

$\therefore$ Period of $f(x) = 24\pi$

52. ***(a)*** Given, $f(x) = |x|$ and $g(x) = f(x+1) + f(x-1)$

So, $g(x) = |x+1| + |x-1|$

$$= \begin{cases} -(x+1)-(x-1), \text{ if } x < -1 \\ x+1-(x-1), \text{ if } -1 \le x < 1 \\ (x+1)+(x-1), \text{ if } x \ge 1 \end{cases}$$

$$= \begin{cases} -2x, \text{ if } x < -1 \\ 2, \text{ if } -1 \le x < 1 \\ 2x, \text{ if } x \ge 1 \end{cases}$$

53. ***(c)*** Domain of $g(x)$ is R.

54. ***(c)*** We have, $g(x) = \begin{cases} -2x, & x < -1 \\ 2, & -1 \le x < 1 \\ 2x, & x \ge 1 \end{cases}$

The graph of $g(x)$ is

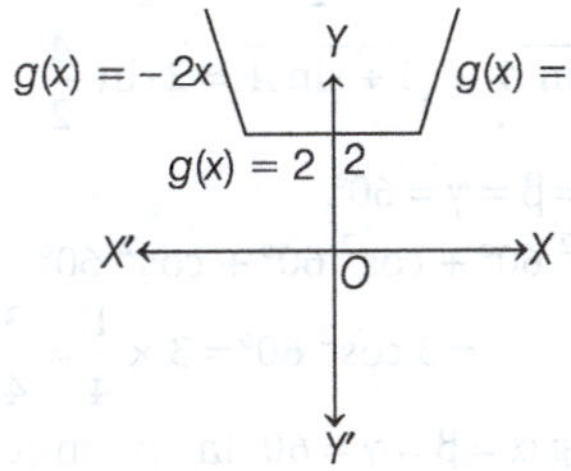

Chapter 3 Trigonometric Functions

1. ***(c)*** $6(\sin^6\theta + \cos^6\theta) - 9(\sin^4\theta + \cos^4\theta) + 4$

$= 6[(\sin^2\theta + \cos^2\theta)^3 - 3\sin^2\theta\cos^2\theta$
$(\sin^2\theta + \cos^2\theta)] - 9[(\sin^2\theta + \cos^2\theta)^2$
$- 2\sin^2\theta\cos^2\theta] + 4$

$= 6[1 - 3\sin^2\theta\cos^2\theta] - 9(1 - 2\sin^2\theta\cos^2\theta) + 4$

$= 6 - 9 + 4 = 1$

2. ***(b)***

3. ***(d)*** $x = 2 + \cot\alpha,\ y = 1 + \tan\alpha$

$\Rightarrow\quad x - 2 = \cot\alpha,\ y - 1 = \tan\alpha$

$\Rightarrow\quad (x-2)(y-1) = 1$

$\Rightarrow\quad xy - x - 2y + 2 = 1$

$\Rightarrow\quad xy + 1 = x + 2y$

4. ***(c)*** Given that

$\sin\theta + \cos\theta = m$ ...(i)

and $\sec\theta + \text{cosec}\theta = n$ ...(ii)

Now, $n(m+1)(m-1) = n(m^2 - 1)$

$= (\sec\theta + \text{cosec}\theta)\, 2\sin\theta\cos\theta$

$[\because m^2 = 1 + 2\sin\theta\cos\theta]$

$= \dfrac{\sin\theta + \cos\theta}{\sin\theta\cos\theta} 2\sin\theta\cos\theta$

$= 2m$ [from Eq. (i)]

5. ***(c)*** **6.** ***(d)***

7. ***(d)*** $x = \sin\alpha + \cos\alpha \Rightarrow x^2 = 1 + 2\sin\alpha\cos\alpha$

$\Rightarrow \dfrac{x^2 - 1}{2} = \sin\alpha\cos\alpha$

Also, $x^3 = \sin^3\alpha + \cos^3\alpha$
$+ 3\sin\alpha\cos\alpha(\sin\alpha + \cos\alpha)$

$\Rightarrow\quad x^3 = y + 3\left(\dfrac{x^2 - 1}{2}\right)x$

$\Rightarrow\quad 2x^3 = 2y + 3x^3 - 3x$

$\Rightarrow\ x^3 - 3x = -2y \Rightarrow x(x^2 - 3) = -2y$

8. ***(b)***

9. ***(b)*** $\sqrt{1 - \sin A} = \left|\cos\dfrac{A}{2} - \sin\dfrac{A}{2}\right|$

$\Rightarrow\quad \sqrt{1 + \sin A} = \left|\cos\dfrac{A}{2} + \sin\dfrac{A}{2}\right|$

$\Rightarrow\quad A = 340° \Rightarrow \dfrac{A}{2} = 170°$

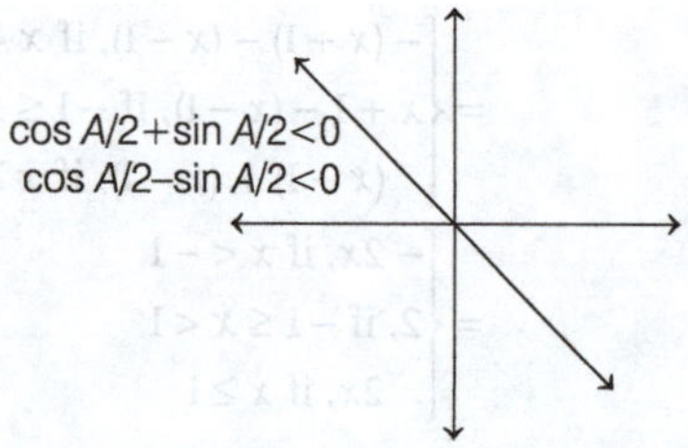

$\therefore\ \sqrt{1-\sin A} = -\left(\cos\frac{A}{2} - \sin\frac{A}{2}\right) = \sin\frac{A}{2} - \cos\frac{A}{2}$

$\Rightarrow\ \sqrt{1+\sin A} = -\left(\cos\frac{A}{2} + \sin\frac{A}{2}\right)$

$= -\sin\frac{A}{2} - \cos\frac{A}{2}$

$\Rightarrow\ \sqrt{1-\sin A} - \sqrt{1+\sin A} = 2\sin\frac{A}{2}$

10. *(c)* Let $\alpha = \beta = \gamma = 60°$

Then, $\cos^2 60° + \cos^2 60° + \cos^2 60°$

$= 3\cos^2 60° = 3 \times \frac{1}{4} = \frac{3}{4}$

On putting $\alpha = \beta = \gamma = 60°$ in option (c), we get

$1 - 2\cos^3\alpha = 1 - 2\cos^3 60° = 1 - 2 \times \frac{1}{8} = \frac{3}{4}$

11. *(d)* Given equation is $\cos\theta = x + \frac{1}{x}$

$\Rightarrow\ x^2 - x\cos\theta + 1 = 0$

For real value of x, $b^2 > 4ac$

$\therefore \cos^2\theta > 4(1)(1) \Rightarrow |\cos\theta| > 2$

which is not possible as $|\cos\theta| \le 1$

$\therefore$ No real value of θ is possible.

12. *(a)* If $A + B = \frac{\pi}{2}$

$\Rightarrow\ \tan(A+B) = \tan\frac{\pi}{2}$

$\Rightarrow\ \frac{\tan A + \tan B}{1 - \tan A \tan B} = \infty \Rightarrow \tan A \tan B = 1$

Here, $\frac{\pi}{24} + \frac{11\pi}{24} = \frac{12\pi}{24} = \frac{\pi}{2}$

$\Rightarrow\ \tan\frac{\pi}{24} \cdot \tan\frac{11\pi}{24} = 1$

$\frac{3\pi}{24} + \frac{9\pi}{24} = \frac{\pi}{2}$ and $\frac{5\pi}{24} + \frac{7\pi}{24} = \frac{\pi}{2}$

$\Rightarrow\ \tan\frac{3\pi}{24} \cdot \tan\frac{9\pi}{24} = 1$ and $\tan\frac{5\pi}{24} \cdot \tan\frac{7\pi}{24} = 1$

$\therefore\ \tan\frac{\pi}{24} \cdot \tan\frac{3\pi}{24} \cdot \tan\frac{5\pi}{24}$

$\cdot \tan\frac{7\pi}{24} \cdot \tan\frac{9\pi}{24} \cdot \tan\frac{11\pi}{24} = 1$

13. *(b)* $\because\ 120° = 80° + 40°$

$\Rightarrow\ \tan 120° = \tan(80° + 40°)$

$\Rightarrow\ -\sqrt{3} = \frac{\tan 80° + \tan 40°}{1 - \tan 80° \tan 40°}$

$\Rightarrow -\sqrt{3} + \sqrt{3}\tan 80° \tan 40°$

$= \tan 80° + \tan 40°$

$\Rightarrow\ \tan 80° + \tan 40° - \sqrt{3}\tan 80° \tan 40°$

$= -\sqrt{3}$

14. *(a)*

15. *(a)* $\because\ 45° = 13° + 32°$

$\Rightarrow\ \tan 45° = \tan(13° + 32°)$

$\Rightarrow\ \tan 13° + \tan 32° + \tan 32° \tan 13° = 1$

$\Rightarrow\ (1 + \tan 13°) + \tan 32°(1 + \tan 13°) = 2$

$\Rightarrow\ (1 + \tan 13°)(1 + \tan 32°) = 2$

Similarly, $(1 + \tan 12°)(1 + \tan 33°) = 2$

$\therefore\ \frac{(1 + \tan 13°)(1 + \tan 32°)}{(1 + \tan 12°)(1 + \tan 33°)} = 1$

16. *(b)* $\because\ A + B = \frac{3\pi}{4}$

$\Rightarrow\ \cot(A+B) = \cot\frac{3\pi}{4}$

$\Rightarrow\ \frac{\cot A \cot B - 1}{\cot B + \cot A} = -1$

$\Rightarrow\ \cot A \cot B - 1 = -\cot B - \cot A$

$\Rightarrow\ \cot A + \cot B + \cot A \cot B = 1$

$\Rightarrow\ (1 + \cot A) + \cot B(1 + \cot A) = 2$

$\Rightarrow\ (1 + \cot A)(1 + \cot B) = 2$

17. *(c)* We have,

$\cos^2(A-B) + \cos^2 B - 2\cos(A-B)\cos A \cos B$

$= \cos^2(A-B) + \cos^2 B - \cos(A-B)$

$\times [\cos(A-B) + \cos(A+B)]$

$= \cos^2 B - \cos(A-B)\cos(A+B)$

$= \cos^2 B - (\cos^2 A - \sin^2 B)$

$= 1 - \cos^2 A = \sin^2 A$

Hence, it depends on A.

18. ***(a)*** $\because A+B+C=\pi$

$\Rightarrow \quad A+C=\dfrac{\pi}{2}$

$\Rightarrow \quad \dfrac{A}{2}+\dfrac{C}{2}=\dfrac{\pi}{4}$

$\Rightarrow \tan\left(\dfrac{A}{2}+\dfrac{C}{2}\right)=1 \Rightarrow \dfrac{\tan\dfrac{A}{2}+\tan\dfrac{C}{2}}{1-\tan\dfrac{A}{2}\tan\dfrac{C}{2}}=1 \quad \ldots(\text{i})$

$\because \tan\dfrac{A}{2}$ and $\tan\dfrac{C}{2}$ are the roots of the equation $ax^2+bx+c=0$.

Then, $\tan\dfrac{A}{2}+\tan\dfrac{C}{2}=-\dfrac{b}{a}$ and $\tan\dfrac{A}{2}\cdot\tan\dfrac{C}{2}=\dfrac{c}{a}$

From Eq. (i), $\dfrac{-\dfrac{b}{a}}{1-\dfrac{c}{a}}=1$

$\Rightarrow \quad -b=a-c \Rightarrow a+b=c$

19. ***(d)*** $\because \cos(A+B)\cos(A-B)=\cos^2 B-\sin^2 A$

$\therefore \cos^2 48°-\sin^2 12°=\cos(48°+12°)\cos(48°-12°)$

$=\cos 60°\cos 36°=\dfrac{1}{2}\cos 36°$

$\because \cos 36°=\dfrac{\sqrt{5}+1}{4}$

$\therefore \cos^2 48°-\sin^2 12°=\dfrac{\sqrt{5}+1}{8}$

20. ***(c)*** $\sin 12°\sin 48°\sin 54°$

$=\dfrac{\sin 12°\sin 48°\sin 54°\sin 72°}{\sin 72°}$

$=\dfrac{\sin 12°\sin(60°-12°)\sin(60+12°)\sin 54°}{\sin 72°}$

$\because \sin\theta\sin(60°-\theta)\sin(60°+\theta)=\dfrac{1}{4}\sin 3\theta$

$=\dfrac{1}{4}\dfrac{\sin 3(12°)\sin 54°}{\sin 72°}=\dfrac{1}{4}\cdot\dfrac{\sin 36°\sin 54°}{\sin 72°}$

$=\dfrac{1}{4}\cdot\dfrac{1}{2}\dfrac{\sin 72°}{\sin 72°}=\dfrac{1}{8}$

21. ***(a)*** Given, $\alpha+\beta-\gamma=\pi \Rightarrow \beta-\gamma=\pi-\alpha$

Now, $\sin^2\alpha+\sin^2\beta-\sin^2\gamma$

$=\sin^2\alpha+\sin(\beta-\gamma)\sin(\beta+\gamma)$

$=\sin^2\alpha+\sin(\pi-\alpha)\sin(\beta+\gamma)$

$=\sin^2\alpha+\sin\alpha\sin(\beta+\gamma)$

$=\sin\alpha[\sin\alpha+\sin(\beta+\gamma)]$

$=\sin\alpha[\sin(\pi-(\beta-\gamma))+\sin(\beta+\gamma)]$ $[\because \alpha+\beta-\gamma=\pi]$

$=\sin\alpha[\sin(\beta-\gamma)+\sin(\beta+\gamma)]$

$=\sin\alpha\cdot 2\sin\beta\cos\gamma$

$=2\sin\alpha\sin\beta\cos\gamma$

22. ***(a)*** Given, $\dfrac{\tan(A+B-C)}{\tan(A-B+C)}=\dfrac{\tan C}{\tan B}$

By componendo and dividendo rule, we get

$\dfrac{\tan(A+B-C)+\tan(A-B+C)}{\tan(A+B-C)-\tan(A-B+C)}$

$=\dfrac{\tan C+\tan B}{\tan C-\tan B}$

$\Rightarrow \quad \dfrac{\sin 2A}{\sin(2B-2C)}=\dfrac{\sin(C+B)}{\sin(C-B)}$

$\Rightarrow \quad \dfrac{\sin 2A}{2\sin(B-C)\cos(B-C)}=\dfrac{\sin(B+C)}{-\sin(B-C)}$

$\Rightarrow \quad \sin 2A=-2\sin(B+C)\cos(B-C)$

$\Rightarrow \quad \sin 2A=-(\sin 2B+\sin 2C)$

$\Rightarrow \quad \sin 2A+\sin 2B+\sin 2C=0$

23. ***(d)*** Given, $x\sin\dfrac{A}{8}\cos\dfrac{A}{8}\cos\dfrac{A}{4}\cos\dfrac{A}{2}=\sin A$

$=2\sin\dfrac{A}{2}\cos\dfrac{A}{2}=2\cdot 2\sin\dfrac{A}{4}\cos\dfrac{A}{4}\cos\dfrac{A}{2}$

$=4\cdot 2\sin\dfrac{A}{8}\cos\dfrac{A}{8}\cos\dfrac{A}{4}\cos\dfrac{A}{2}$

Comparing both sides, we get $x=8$

24. ***(a)*** $\sqrt{4\sin^4 x+\sin^2 2x+4\cos^2\left(\dfrac{\pi}{4}-\dfrac{x}{2}\right)}$

$=\sqrt{4\sin^4 x+4\sin^2 x\cos^2 x}+2\cdot 2\cos^2\left(\dfrac{\pi}{4}-\dfrac{x}{2}\right)$

$=\sqrt{(2\sin x)^2(\sin^2 x+\cos^2 x)}+2\left[1+\cos\left(\dfrac{\pi}{2}-x\right)\right]$

$=|2\sin x|+2(1+\sin x)$

$=-2\sin x+2+2\sin x \quad \left[\because \pi\le x\le\dfrac{3\pi}{2}\right]$

$=2$

25. ***(d)*** Given, $\cos\alpha=\dfrac{2\cos\beta-1}{2-\cos\beta}$ and $\alpha+\beta=\pi$

Since, $\tan^2\dfrac{\alpha}{2}=\dfrac{1-\cos\alpha}{1+\cos\alpha}=\dfrac{1-\dfrac{2\cos\beta-1}{2-\cos\beta}}{1+\dfrac{2\cos\beta-1}{2-\cos\beta}}$

$$= 3\left(\frac{1-\cos\beta}{1+\cos\beta}\right)$$

$$= 3\tan^2\frac{\beta}{2}$$

$$\Rightarrow \tan^2\frac{\alpha}{2} = 3\tan^2\left(\frac{\pi}{2}-\frac{\alpha}{2}\right) \quad [\because \beta = \pi - \alpha]$$

$$\Rightarrow \tan^2\frac{\alpha}{2} = 3\cot^2\frac{\alpha}{2} \Rightarrow \tan^4\frac{\alpha}{2} = 3$$

$$\Rightarrow \tan\frac{\alpha}{2} = 3^{\frac{1}{4}}$$

26. *(b)* $\tan\left(\frac{\theta+A}{2}\right)\tan\left(\frac{\theta-A}{2}\right)$

$$= \frac{\left(\tan\frac{\theta}{2}+\tan\frac{A}{2}\right)}{\left(1-\tan\frac{\theta}{2}\tan\frac{A}{2}\right)} \cdot \frac{\left(\tan\frac{\theta}{2}-\tan\frac{A}{2}\right)}{\left(1+\tan\frac{\theta}{2}\tan\frac{A}{2}\right)}$$

$$= \frac{\tan^2\frac{\theta}{2}-\tan^2\frac{A}{2}}{1-\tan^2\frac{\theta}{2}\tan^2\frac{A}{2}}$$

$$= \frac{\frac{1-\cos\theta}{1+\cos\theta}-\frac{1-\cos A}{1+\cos A}}{1-\left(\frac{1-\cos\theta}{1+\cos\theta}\right)\left(\frac{1-\cos A}{1+\cos A}\right)}$$

$$= \frac{\cos A-\cos\theta}{\cos A+\cos\theta}$$

$$= \frac{\cos A(1-\cos B)}{\cos A(1+\cos B)} \quad [\because \cos\theta = \cos A\cos B]$$

$$= \frac{1-\cos B}{1+\cos B} = \tan^2\frac{B}{2}$$

27. *(b)* We have, $\cos(\alpha+\beta) = \frac{4}{5}$

and $\sin(\alpha-\beta) = \frac{5}{13}$

$$\Rightarrow \sin(\alpha+\beta) = \frac{3}{5} \text{ and } \cos(\alpha-\beta) = \frac{12}{13}$$

$$\Rightarrow \text{Now, } \tan(\alpha+\beta) = \frac{3}{4} \text{ and } \tan(\alpha-\beta) = \frac{5}{12}$$

$$\tan 2\alpha = \tan(\alpha+\beta+\alpha-\beta)$$

$$= \frac{\tan(\alpha+\beta)+\tan(\alpha-\beta)}{1-\tan(\alpha+\beta)\tan(\alpha-\beta)}$$

$$= \frac{\frac{3}{4}+\frac{5}{12}}{1-\frac{3}{4}\times\frac{5}{12}} = \frac{56}{33}$$

$$\because \quad \tan 2\alpha = \frac{56}{33}$$

28. *(b)* Given, $\cos\alpha+\cos\beta = 0$ and $\sin\alpha+\sin\beta = 0$

On squaring and subtracting both the equations, we get

$$(\cos\alpha+\cos\beta)^2-(\sin\alpha+\sin\beta)^2 = 0$$

$$\Rightarrow (\cos^2\alpha+\cos^2\beta+2\cos\alpha\cos\beta) - (\sin^2\alpha+\sin^2\beta+2\sin\alpha\sin\beta) = 0$$

$$\Rightarrow (\cos^2\alpha-\sin^2\alpha)+(\cos^2\beta-\sin^2\beta) + 2[\cos\alpha\cos\beta-\sin\alpha\sin\beta] = 0$$

$$\Rightarrow \cos 2\alpha+\cos 2\beta+2\cos(\alpha+\beta) = 0$$

$$\Rightarrow \cos 2\alpha+\cos 2\beta = -2\cos(\alpha+\beta)$$

29. *(c)* $\sin 20^\circ\sin 40^\circ\sin 60^\circ\sin 80^\circ$

$$= \frac{1}{2}\sin 20^\circ\sin 60^\circ(2\sin 40^\circ\sin 80^\circ)$$

$$= \frac{1}{2}\sin 20^\circ\sin 60^\circ(\cos 40^\circ-\cos 120^\circ)$$

$$= \frac{1}{2}\cdot\frac{\sqrt{3}}{2}\sin 20^\circ\left(1-2\sin^2 20^\circ+\frac{1}{2}\right)$$

$$= \frac{\sqrt{3}}{4}\sin 20^\circ\left(\frac{3}{2}-2\sin^2 20^\circ\right)$$

$$= \frac{\sqrt{3}}{8}(3\sin 20^\circ-4\sin^3 20^\circ)$$

$$= \frac{\sqrt{3}}{8}\sin 60^\circ = \frac{\sqrt{3}}{8}\cdot\frac{\sqrt{3}}{2} = \frac{3}{16}$$

30. *(b)* Since, $A+B+C = \pi$

$$\Rightarrow A = \pi-(B+C)$$

We have, $\cos A = \cos B\cos C$

$$\Rightarrow \cos[\pi-(B+C)] = \cos B\cos C$$

$$\Rightarrow -\cos(B+C) = \cos B\cos C$$

$$\Rightarrow -[\cos B\cos C-\sin B\sin C] = \cos B\cos C$$

$$\Rightarrow \sin B\sin C = 2\cos B\cos C$$

$$\Rightarrow \tan B\tan C = 2$$

31. *(a)* We have, $\alpha+\beta-\gamma = \pi$

Now, $\sin^2\alpha+\sin^2\beta-\sin^2\gamma$

$$= \sin^2\alpha+\sin(\beta-\gamma)\sin(\beta+\gamma)$$

$$= \sin^2\alpha+\sin(\pi-\alpha)\sin(\beta+\gamma) \quad [\because \alpha+\beta-\gamma = \pi]$$

$$= \sin^2\alpha+\sin\alpha\sin(\beta+\gamma)$$

$$= \sin\alpha[\sin\alpha+\sin(\beta+\gamma)]$$

$$= \sin\alpha[\sin(\pi-(\beta-\gamma))+\sin(\beta+\gamma)]$$

$= \sin\alpha[\sin(\beta-\gamma)+\sin(\beta+\gamma)]$
$= \sin\alpha[2\sin\beta\cos\gamma]$
$= 2\sin\alpha\sin\beta\cos\gamma$

32. ***(c)*** $\dfrac{\cos 12^\circ - \sin 12^\circ}{\cos 12^\circ + \sin 12^\circ} + \dfrac{\sin 147^\circ}{\cos 147^\circ}$

$$= \frac{1-\tan 12^\circ}{1+\tan 12^\circ} + \tan 147^\circ$$
$$= \tan(45^\circ - 12^\circ) + \tan(180^\circ - 33^\circ)$$
$$= \tan 33^\circ - \tan 33^\circ = 0$$

33. ***(b)*** We have, $x = y\cos\dfrac{2\pi}{3} = z\cos\dfrac{4\pi}{3}$

$$x = y\left(-\frac{1}{2}\right) = z\left(-\frac{1}{2}\right)$$
$$\Rightarrow \quad x = -\frac{y}{2} = -\frac{z}{2} = \lambda$$
$$x = \lambda,\ y = -2\lambda,\ z = -2\lambda$$
$$\therefore\ xy + yz + zx = \lambda(-2\lambda) + (-2\lambda)(-2\lambda) + (-2\lambda)(\lambda)$$
$$= -2\lambda^2 + 4\lambda^2 - 2\lambda^2$$
$$= 0$$

34. ***(b)*** We have, $(\cos x + \sin x)^2 + k\sin x\cos x - 1 = 0$ is an identity.

$\therefore \quad \cos^2 x + \sin^2 x + 2\sin x\cos x + k\sin x\cos x - 1 = 0$
$\Rightarrow \quad 1 + \sin x\cos x(2+k) - 1 = 0$
$\Rightarrow \quad (k+2)(\sin x\cos x) = 0$
$\therefore \quad k + 2 = 0 \Rightarrow k = -2$

35. ***(d)***

36. ***(d)*** Given, $\dfrac{\sin x}{\sin y} = \dfrac{1}{2},\quad \dfrac{\cos x}{\cos y} = \dfrac{3}{2}$

$$\Rightarrow \quad \frac{\tan x}{\tan y} = \frac{1}{3}$$
$$\tan(x+y) = \frac{\tan x + \tan y}{1 - \tan x\tan y} = \frac{4\tan x}{1 - 3\tan^2 x}$$

Also, $\quad \sin y = 2\sin x,\quad \cos y = \dfrac{2}{3}\cos x$

$$\Rightarrow \sin^2 y + \cos^2 y = 4\sin^2 x + \frac{4\cos^2 x}{9} = 1$$
$$\Rightarrow\ 36\tan^2 x + 4 = 9\sec^2 x = 9(1 + \tan^2 x)$$
$$\Rightarrow \quad 27\tan^2 x = 5$$
$$\Rightarrow \quad \tan x = \frac{\sqrt{5}}{3\sqrt{3}}$$
$$\Rightarrow \quad \tan(x+y) = \frac{\dfrac{4\sqrt{5}}{3\sqrt{3}}}{1 - \dfrac{15}{27}} = \sqrt{15}$$

37. ***(d)*** Given, $\tan(A+B) = p$ and $\tan(A-B) = q$

Now, $\tan 2A = \tan(A + B + A - B)$
$$= \frac{\tan(A+B) + \tan(A-B)}{1 - \tan(A+B)\tan(A-B)} = \frac{p+q}{1-pq}$$

38. ***(d)*** We have,

$(\sin 47^\circ + \sin 61^\circ) - (\sin 11^\circ + \sin 25^\circ)$
$$= 2\sin 54^\circ\cos 7^\circ - 2\sin 18^\circ\cos 7^\circ$$
$$= 2\cos 7^\circ(\sin 54^\circ - \sin 18^\circ)$$
$$= 2\cos 7^\circ(2\cos 36^\circ\sin 18^\circ)$$
$$= 4\cos 7^\circ\left(\frac{\sqrt{5}+1}{4}\right)\left(\frac{\sqrt{5}-1}{4}\right)$$
$$= 4\cos 7^\circ\left(\frac{5-1}{16}\right) = 4\cos 7^\circ\left(\frac{1}{4}\right) = \cos 7^\circ$$

39. ***(b)*** We have, $b\cos 2x + a\sin 2x$

$$= b\left(\frac{1-\tan^2 x}{1+\tan^2 x}\right) + a\left(\frac{2\tan x}{1+\tan^2 x}\right)$$
$$= \frac{b - b\tan^2 x + 2a\tan x}{1 + \tan^2 x}$$
$$= \frac{b - b\left(\dfrac{a^2}{b^2}\right) + 2a\left(\dfrac{a}{b}\right)}{1 + \dfrac{a^2}{b^2}}$$
$$= \frac{b^3 - a^2 b + 2a^2 b}{a^2 + b^2} = \frac{b(a^2+b^2)}{a^2+b^2} = b$$

40. ***(a)*** $\sqrt{\dfrac{a+b}{a-b}} + \sqrt{\dfrac{a-b}{a+b}}$

$$= \sqrt{\frac{1+\dfrac{b}{a}}{1-\dfrac{b}{a}}} + \sqrt{\frac{1-\dfrac{b}{a}}{1+\dfrac{b}{a}}} = \frac{1+\dfrac{b}{a}+1-\dfrac{b}{a}}{\sqrt{\left(1-\dfrac{b}{a}\right)\left(1+\dfrac{b}{a}\right)}}$$

[dividing by a in numerator and denominator of both the terms]

$$= \frac{2}{\sqrt{1-\dfrac{b^2}{a^2}}} = \frac{2}{\sqrt{1-\tan^2 x}} = \frac{2}{\sqrt{1-\dfrac{\sin^2 x}{\cos^2 x}}}$$

$$\left[\because \tan x = \frac{b}{a}\right]$$

$$= \frac{2\cos x}{\sqrt{\cos^2 x - \sin^2 x}} = \frac{2\cos x}{\sqrt{\cos 2x}}$$

$[\because \cos^2 x - \sin^2 x = \cos 2x]$

41. ***(b)*** Since, $(a-b)\sin(\theta+\phi) = (a+b)\sin(\theta-\phi)$

$$\Rightarrow a\{\sin(\theta+\phi) - \sin(\theta-\phi)\} = b\{\sin(\theta-\phi) + \sin(\theta+\phi)\}$$

$$\Rightarrow 2a\sin\phi\cos\theta = 2b\sin\theta\cos\phi$$

$$\Rightarrow a\tan\phi = b\tan\theta$$

$$\Rightarrow \frac{2a\tan\frac{\phi}{2}}{1-\tan^2\frac{\phi}{2}} = \frac{2b\tan\frac{\theta}{2}}{1-\tan^2\frac{\theta}{2}} \quad \ldots\text{(i)}$$

Since, $a\tan\frac{\theta}{2} - b\tan\frac{\phi}{2} = c$ [given]

$$\Rightarrow \tan\frac{\theta}{2} = \frac{b\tan\frac{\phi}{2}+c}{a} \quad \ldots\text{(ii)}$$

From Eqs. (i) and (ii), we get

$$\frac{a\tan\frac{\phi}{2}}{1-\tan^2\frac{\phi}{2}} = \frac{b\frac{\left(b\tan\frac{\phi}{2}+c\right)}{a}}{1-\frac{\left(b\tan\frac{\phi}{2}+c\right)^2}{a^2}}$$

$$\Rightarrow \tan\frac{\phi}{2}(a^2-b^2-c^2) = bc\left(1+\tan^2\frac{\phi}{2}\right)$$

Now, $$\sin\phi = \frac{2\tan\frac{\phi}{2}}{1+\tan^2\frac{\phi}{2}} = \frac{2bc}{a^2-b^2-c^2}$$

42. ***(d)*** Reason is true.

The maximum value of $\sin\theta$ is 1 and that of $\cos\theta$ is 1.

$$\sin\theta + \cos\theta = \sqrt{2}\left(\frac{1}{\sqrt{2}}\cos\theta + \frac{1}{\sqrt{2}}\sin\theta\right)$$

$$= \sqrt{2}\left(\sin\frac{\pi}{4}\cos\theta + \cos\frac{\pi}{4}\sin\theta\right)$$

$$= \sqrt{2}\left(\sin\left(\frac{\pi}{4}+\theta\right)\right)$$

Maximum value of $\sin\theta + \cos\theta = \sqrt{2}$.

Assertion is false.

43. ***(a)*** $\tan\theta\tan(60^\circ-\theta)\tan(60^\circ+\theta) = \tan 3\theta$

$\therefore$ Reason is true.

Assertion $\tan 6^\circ \tan 42^\circ \tan 66^\circ \tan 78^\circ$

$$= \frac{\tan 6^\circ \tan 54^\circ \tan 66^\circ \tan 42^\circ \tan 78^\circ}{\tan 54^\circ}$$

$$= \frac{\tan 6^\circ \tan(60^\circ-6^\circ)\tan(60^\circ+6^\circ)\tan 42^\circ \tan 78^\circ}{\tan 54^\circ}$$

$$= \frac{\tan 3(6^\circ)\tan 42^\circ \tan 78^\circ}{\tan 54^\circ}$$

$$= \frac{\tan 18^\circ \tan(60^\circ-18^\circ)\tan(60^\circ+18^\circ)}{\tan 54^\circ}$$

$$= \frac{\tan(3)(18^\circ)}{\tan 54^\circ} = \frac{\tan 54^\circ}{\tan 54^\circ} = 1$$

Hence, Assertion and Reason both are true and Reason is correct explanation of Assertion.

44. ***(a)*** $$\left(1+\cos\frac{\pi}{8}\right)\left(1+\cos\frac{3\pi}{8}\right)\left(1+\cos\frac{5\pi}{8}\right)\left(1+\cos\frac{7\pi}{8}\right)$$

$$= \left(1+\cos\frac{\pi}{8}\right)\left(1+\cos\frac{3\pi}{8}\right)\left(1+\cos\left(\pi-\frac{3\pi}{8}\right)\right)\left(1+\cos\left(\pi-\frac{\pi}{8}\right)\right)$$

$$= \left(1-\cos^2\frac{\pi}{8}\right)\left(1-\cos^2\frac{3\pi}{8}\right)$$

$\left[\because 1+\cos\left(\pi-\frac{3\pi}{8}\right) = 1-\cos\frac{3\pi}{8} \text{ and } 1+\cos\left(\pi-\frac{\pi}{8}\right) = 1-\cos\frac{\pi}{8}\right]$

$$= \sin^2\frac{\pi}{8}\sin^2\frac{3\pi}{8} = \frac{1}{4}\left(1-\cos\frac{\pi}{4}\right)\left(1-\cos\frac{3\pi}{4}\right)$$

$\left[\because \sin^2\theta = \frac{1}{2}(1-\cos 2\theta)\right]$

$$= \frac{1}{4}\left(1-\cos\frac{\pi}{4}\right)\left(1+\cos\frac{\pi}{4}\right)$$

$$= \frac{1}{4}\left(1-\cos^2\frac{\pi}{4}\right) = \frac{1}{4}\left(1-\frac{1}{2}\right) = \frac{1}{8}$$

$[\because (a-b)(a+b) = a^2-b^2]$

Hence, Assertion and Reason both are true and Reason is correct explanation of Assertion.

Solutions (Q.Nos. 45-47)

$A = x\cos\theta - y\sin\theta;\ B = x\sin\theta + y\cos\theta$

$$A^2 + B^2 = (x\cos\theta - y\sin\theta)^2 + (x\sin\theta + y\cos\theta)^2$$

$$= x^2 + y^2$$

and $AB = (x\cos\theta - y\sin\theta)(x\sin\theta + y\cos\theta)$

$$= x^2\cos\theta\sin\theta + xy\cos^2\theta - xy\sin^2\theta - y^2\sin\theta\cos\theta$$

$$= (x^2 - y^2)\sin\theta\cos\theta + xy\cos 2\theta$$

Now, $A^2 + 4AB + B^2 = x^2 + y^2 + 4(x^2 - y^2)\sin\theta\cos\theta + 4xy\cos 2\theta$

$A^2 + 4AB + B^2$

$$= x^2 + y^2 + 2(x^2 - y^2)\sin 2\theta + 4xy\cos 2\theta$$

Given, $A^2 + 4AB + B^2 = px^2 + qy^2$

$$\Rightarrow px^2 + qy^2 = x^2(1 + 2\sin 2\theta) + y^2(1 - 2\sin 2\theta) + xy(4\cos 2\theta) \quad \text{...(i)}$$

45. *(c)* Comparing coefficient of xy from both sides of Eq. (i), we get

$$4\cos 2\theta = 0$$

$$\Rightarrow \cos 2\theta = 0$$

46. *(b)* Putting $\theta = \frac{\pi}{4}$ in Eq. (i), we get

$$px^2 + qy^2 = 3x^2 - y^2 \quad \text{...(ii)}$$

Comparing coefficient of x^2 from both sides of Eq. (ii), we get

$$p = 3$$

47. *(a)* Comparing coefficient of y^2 from both sides of Eq. (ii), we get

$$q = -1$$

Chapter 4 Complex Number

1. *(c)* $(n + i)^4 = (n^2 - 1 + 2ni)^2$

$$= (n^2 - 1)^2 - 4n^2 + 4n(n^2 - 1)i$$

For integral solution, imaginary part must be zero.

$$\therefore \quad 4n(n^2 - 1) = 0$$

$$n = 0 \text{ or } n = \pm 1$$

Hence, number of integral solution is 3.

2. *(d)* $\dfrac{1 + a + ib}{1 + a - ib} = \dfrac{(1 + a + ib)(1 + a + ib)}{(1 + a - ib)(1 + a + ib)}$

$$= \frac{1 - b^2 + a^2 + 2a + 2iab + 2ib}{(1 + a)^2 + b^2}$$

$$[\because 1 - b^2 = a^2]$$

$$= \frac{2a^2 + 2a + 2ib(a + 1)}{1 + a^2 + 2a + b^2}$$

$$= \frac{2a(a + 1) + 2ib(a + 1)}{2(a + 1)}$$

$$= \frac{2(a + 1)(a + ib)}{2(a + 1)} = a + ib$$

3. *(d)* Let $z = \dfrac{1}{i - 1}$

Then, $\bar{z} = \overline{\left(\dfrac{1}{i - 1}\right)} = \dfrac{1}{-i - 1} = \dfrac{-1}{i + 1}$

4. *(c)*

5. *(a)* $|z - 1| = |z + 1| \Rightarrow |z - 1|^2 = |z + 1|^2$

$$\Rightarrow \quad |(x - 1) + iy|^2 = |(x + 1) + iy|^2$$

$$\Rightarrow \quad (x - 1)^2 + y^2 = (x + 1)^2 + y^2$$

$$\Rightarrow \quad (x - 1)^2 - (x + 1)^2 = 0$$

$$\Rightarrow \quad x = 0$$

6. *(a)*

7. *(c)* Here, $\dfrac{2^n}{(1 + i)^{2n}} + \dfrac{(1 + i)^{2n}}{2^n}$

$$= \frac{2^n}{(1 + i^2 + 2i)^n} + \frac{(1 + i^2 + 2i)^n}{2^n}$$

$$= \frac{2^n}{(2i)^n} + \frac{(2i)^n}{2^n} = \frac{1}{i^n} + i^n = \frac{i^n}{i^{2n}} + i^n$$

$$= \frac{i^n}{(-1)^n} + i^n$$

$$= i^n\left\{\frac{1}{(-1)^n} + 1\right\} \text{ or } i^n\{(-1)^n + 1\}$$

8. *(b)* Given, $(3 + 2\sqrt{-54})^{1/2} - (3 - 2\sqrt{-54})^{1/2}$

$$= (3 + 2 \times 3\sqrt{6}i)^{1/2} - (3 - 2 \times 3\sqrt{6}i)^{1/2}$$

$$= (9 - 6 + 2 \times 3\sqrt{6}i)^{1/2} - (9 - 6 - 2 \times 3\sqrt{6}i)^{1/2}$$

$$= \{3^2 + (\sqrt{6}i)^2 + 2 \times 3 \times \sqrt{6}i\}^{1/2} - \{3^2 + (\sqrt{6}i)^2 - 2 \times 3 \times \sqrt{6}i\}^{1/2}$$

$$= [(3 + \sqrt{6}i)^2]^{1/2} - [(3 - \sqrt{6}i)^2]^{1/2}$$

$$= \pm(3 + \sqrt{6}i) \mp (3 - \sqrt{6}i) = \pm 2\sqrt{6}\,i$$

$\therefore$ Imaginary part of $(3 + 2\sqrt{-54})^{1/2} - (3 - 2\sqrt{-54})^{1/2}$

$$= I_m(\pm 2\sqrt{6}i) = \pm 2\sqrt{6}$$

So, from the option $-2\sqrt{6}$ is correct.

9. *(b)* Let $z = \dfrac{1}{1 - \cos\theta + i\sin\theta}$

$$= \frac{1}{2\sin^2(\theta/2) + 2i\sin(\theta/2)\cos(\theta/2)}$$

$$= \frac{1}{2i\sin(\theta/2)}\frac{1}{[\cos(\theta/2) - i\sin(\theta/2)]}$$

$$= \frac{\cos(\theta/2) + i\sin(\theta/2)}{2i\sin(\theta/2)} = \frac{1}{2} + \frac{1}{2i}\cot(\theta/2)$$

$$= \frac{1}{2} - i\cdot\frac{1}{2}\cot\frac{\theta}{2}$$

$\therefore$ Real part of z is $\frac{1}{2}$.

10. *(a)* $\frac{1+iz}{1-iz} = \frac{1 + i\frac{(b+ic)}{1+a}}{1 - i\frac{(b+ic)}{1+a}} = \frac{1+a-c+ib}{1+a+c-ib}$

$$= \frac{(1+a-c+ib)(1+a+c+ib)}{(1+a+c)^2+b^2}$$

$$= \frac{a^2+a+iab+ib}{1+a+ac+c}$$

$$= \frac{(a+1)(a+ib)}{(a+1)(1+c)} = \frac{a+ib}{1+c}$$

11. *(a)* We have, $z = \frac{q+ir}{1+p}$

$\therefore \quad iz = \frac{-r+iq}{1+p}$

By componendo and dividendo, we get

$$\frac{1+iz}{1-iz} = \frac{1+p-r+iq}{1+p+r-iq}$$

$\therefore \quad \frac{p+iq}{1+r} = \frac{1+iz}{1-iz},$

if $\quad \frac{p+iq}{1+r} = \frac{1+p-r+iq}{1+p+r-iq}$

$\Rightarrow \quad p(1+p+r) + q^2 + i\{q(1+p+r) - pq\}$

$$= (1+r)(1+p-r) + iq(1+r)$$

$\Rightarrow \quad p(1+p+r) + q^2 = (1+r)(1+p-r)$

and $\quad q(1+p+r) - pq = q(1+r)$

[this is obviously true]

$\therefore$ The condition is

$$p(1+p+r) + q^2 = (1+r)(1+p-r)$$

$\Rightarrow \quad p + p^2 + pr + q^2 = 1 + p - r + r + pr - r^2$

$\Rightarrow \quad p^2 + q^2 + r^2 = 1$

12. *(c)* If $z = 1 + i$ is rotated counter clockwise by angle $\frac{\pi}{2}$, then new number is

$$iz = (1+i)i = i - 1 = -\bar{z}$$

13. *(c)* $a + ib = \frac{3}{2+\cos\theta + i\sin\theta} \times \frac{2+\cos\theta - i\sin\theta}{2+\cos\theta - i\sin\theta}$

$$= \frac{6+3\cos\theta - 3i\sin\theta}{(2+\cos\theta)^2 + \sin^2\theta}$$

$$= \frac{6+3\cos\theta}{5+4\cos\theta} - \frac{3i\sin\theta}{5+4\cos\theta}$$

Equating real and imaginary parts, we get

$$a = \frac{6+3\cos\theta}{5+4\cos\theta} \text{ and } b = \frac{-3\sin\theta}{5+4\cos\theta}$$

$\therefore \quad (a-3)(a-1) = \frac{-9\sin^2\theta}{(5+4\cos\theta)^2}$

$$(a-3)(a-1) + b^2 = -\frac{9\sin^2\theta}{(5+4\cos\theta)^2} + \frac{9\sin^2\theta}{(5+4\cos\theta)^2}$$

$$= 0$$

14. *(d)* Given, $\left|\frac{z-2i}{z+i}\right| = 2$

$|z-2i| = 2|z+i|$, put $z = x+iy$, we get

$|x + (yi - 2i)| = 2|x + (yi + i)|$

$\Rightarrow \quad x^2 + (y-2)^2 = 4(x^2 + (y+1)^2)$

$\Rightarrow \quad 3x^2 + 3y^2 + 12y = 0$

$\Rightarrow \quad x^2 + y^2 + 4y = 0$

$\therefore$ Centre $(0, -2)$.

15. *(b)* $|z| = \left|\left(z - \frac{4}{z}\right) + \frac{4}{z}\right|$

$\Rightarrow |z| < \left|z - \frac{4}{z}\right| + \frac{4}{|z|}$

$\Rightarrow |z| \leq 2 + \frac{4}{|z|}$

$\Rightarrow \quad \frac{|z|^2 - 2|z| - 4}{|z|} \leq 0$

Since, $|z| > 0 \Rightarrow |z|^2 - 2|z| - 4 \leq 0$

$\Rightarrow [|z| - (\sqrt{5}+1)][|z| - (1-\sqrt{5})] \leq 0$

$\Rightarrow \quad 1 - \sqrt{5} \leq |z| \leq \sqrt{5} + 1$

16. *(c)*

17. *(d)* $xyz = (p+q)(p\omega + q\omega^2)(p\omega^2 + q\omega)$

So, $xyz = (p+q)(p^2\omega^3 + qp\omega^2 + pq\omega^4 + q^2\omega^3)$

$= (p+q)[p^2 + pq(\omega^2 + \omega) + q^2]$

$= (p+q)[p^2 - pq + q^2] \Rightarrow xyz = p^3 + q^3$

18. ***(b)*** Let $z = x + iy$

$$\frac{z-1}{z+1} = \frac{x+iy-1}{x+iy+1} = \frac{(x-1)+iy}{(x+1)+iy} \times \frac{(x+1)-iy}{(x+1)-iy}$$

$$= \frac{(x-1)(x+1) - iy(x-1) + iy(x+1) - i^2y^2}{(x+1)^2 - i^2y^2}$$

$$= \frac{x^2 - 1 + iy(x+1-x+1) + y^2}{(x+1)^2 + y^2}$$

$$\Rightarrow \frac{z-1}{z+1} = \frac{(x^2+y^2-1)}{(x+1)^2+y^2} + \frac{i(2y)}{(x+1)^2+y^2}$$

$\because \frac{z-1}{z+1}$ is purely imaginary.

$$\therefore \quad \text{Re}\left(\frac{z-1}{z+1}\right) = 0$$

$$\Rightarrow \quad \frac{x^2+y^2-1}{(x+1)^2+y^2} = 0$$

$$\Rightarrow \quad x^2 + y^2 - 1 = 0$$

$$\Rightarrow \quad x^2 + y^2 = 1$$

$$\Rightarrow \quad |z^2| = 1 \Rightarrow |z| = 1$$

19. ***(d)*** $(\sin x + i\cos 2x) = \overline{(\cos x - i\sin 2x)}$

$\Rightarrow \sin x + i\cos 2x = \cos x + i\sin 2x$

On comparing real and imaginary parts, we get

$$\sin x = \cos x \quad \text{and} \quad \cos 2x = \sin 2x$$

$$\Rightarrow \quad \tan x = 1 \quad \text{and} \quad \tan 2x = 1$$

$$\Rightarrow \quad x = \frac{\pi}{4} \quad \text{and} \quad 2x = \frac{\pi}{4}$$

$$\therefore \quad x = \frac{\pi}{4} \quad \text{and} \quad x = \frac{\pi}{8}$$

$\because$ We got two different values of x, hence conjugate $\sin x + i\cos 2x$ is not conjugate of $(\cos x - i\sin 2x)$.

$\Rightarrow$ No value of x.

20. ***(d)*** $$z + \sqrt{2}|z+1| + i = 0$$

$$\Rightarrow \quad (x+iy) + \sqrt{2}|x+iy+1| + i = 0$$

$$\Rightarrow \quad (x+iy) + \sqrt{2}|(x+1)+iy| + i = 0$$

$$\Rightarrow \quad (x+iy) + \sqrt{2}\sqrt{(x+1)^2+y^2} + i = 0$$

$$\Rightarrow \quad x + \sqrt{2(x+1)^2 + 2y^2} + i(y+1) = 0$$

On comparing real and imaginary parts, we get

$$x + \sqrt{2(x+1)^2 + 2y^2} = 0 \text{ and } y + 1 = 0$$

$$\Rightarrow \quad x^2 = 2x^2 + 2 + 4x + 2y^2 \text{ and } y = -1$$

$$\because \quad x^2 = 2x^2 + 4x + 2(-1)^2 + 2$$

$$\Rightarrow \quad x^2 + 2 + 4x + 2 = 0$$

$$\Rightarrow \quad x^2 + 4x + 4 = 0$$

$$\therefore \quad (x+2)^2 = 0 \Rightarrow x = -2$$

Hence, $x = -2$ and $y = -1$

$$\therefore \quad z = -2 - i$$

21. ***(d)*** $|z_1| = |z_2|$

$\text{Re}(z_1) > 0, \text{Im}(z_2) < 0$

$$\text{Re}\left(\frac{z_1+z_2}{z_1-z_2}\right) = \frac{1}{2}\left(\frac{z_1+z_2}{z_1-z_2} + \frac{\bar{z}_1+\bar{z}_2}{\bar{z}_1-\bar{z}_2}\right)$$

$$= \frac{1}{2}\left(\frac{(z_1+z_2)(\overline{z_1}-\overline{z_2}) + (\overline{z_1}+\overline{z_2})(\overline{z_1}-\overline{z_2})}{(z_1-z_2)(\overline{z_1}-\overline{z_2})}\right)$$

$$= \frac{1}{2}\left(\frac{z_1\bar{z}_1 - z_1\bar{z}_2 + z_2\bar{z}_1 - z_2\bar{z}_2 + z_1\bar{z}_1 + z_1\bar{z}_2 - z_2\bar{z}_1 - z_2\bar{z}_2}{|(z_1-z_2)|^2}\right)$$

$$= \frac{1}{2}\left(\frac{2|z_1|^2 - 2|z_2|^2}{|z_1-z_2|^2}\right) = 0$$

$$\Rightarrow \left(\frac{z_1+z_2}{z_1-z_2}\right) \text{ is purely imaginary.}$$

22. ***(b)*** $\log_{\frac{1}{\sqrt{2}}}\left(\frac{|z|+11}{(|z|-1)^2}\right) \le 2$

$$\Rightarrow \quad \frac{|z|+11}{(|z|-1)^2} \ge \frac{1}{2}$$

$$\Rightarrow \quad 2|z| + 22 \ge (|z|-1)^2$$

$$\Rightarrow \quad 2|z| + 22 \ge |z|^2 + 1 - 2|z|$$

$$\Rightarrow \quad |z|^2 - 4|z| - 21 \le 0$$

$$\Rightarrow \quad |z| \le 7$$

$\therefore$ Largest value of $|z|$ is 7.

23. ***(b)*** $|z-2| = \min\{|z-1|, |z-5|\}$

i.e. $|z-2| = |z-1|$, where $|z-1| < |z-5|$

$\Rightarrow$ Re $(z) = \frac{3}{2}$, which satisfy $|z-1| < |z-5|$

Also, $\quad |z-2| = |z-5|$, where $|z-5| < |z-1|$

$\Rightarrow$ Re $(z) = \frac{7}{2}$, which satisfy $|z-5| < |z-1|$

24. *(a)* We have, $|1-\bar{z}_1 z_2|^2 - |z_1 - z_2|^2$

$= (1-\bar{z}_1 z_2)\overline{(1-\bar{z}_1 z_2)} - (z_1 - z_2)\overline{(z_1 - z_2)}$ $[\because z\bar{z} = |z^2|]$

$= (1-\bar{z}_1 z_2)(1-\overline{\bar{z}_1 z_2}) - (z_1 - z_2)(\bar{z}_1 - \bar{z}_2)$ $[\because \overline{z_1 - z_2} = \bar{z}_1 - \bar{z}_2 \text{ and } \bar{1} = 1]$

$= (1-\bar{z}_1 z_2)(1 - z_1\bar{z}_2) - (z_1 - z_2)(\bar{z}_1 - \bar{z}_2)$ $[\because \overline{(\bar{z}_1)} = z_1]$

$= 1 - z_1\bar{z}_2 - \bar{z}_1 z_2 + z_1\bar{z}_1 z_2\bar{z}_2 - z_1\bar{z}_1 + z_1\bar{z}_2 + \bar{z}_1 z_2 - z_2\bar{z}_2$

$= 1 + |z_1|^2|z_2|^2 - |z_1|^2 - |z_2|^2$

$= (1-|z_1|^2)(1-|z_2^2|)$

$\therefore \quad k = 1$

25. *(b)* We have, $\left|\frac{z-a}{z+\bar{a}}\right| = 1$

$\Rightarrow |z-a| = |z+\bar{a}|$

$\Rightarrow |z-a|^2 = |z+\bar{a}|^2$

$\Rightarrow (z-a)\overline{(z-a)} = (z+\bar{a})\overline{(z+\bar{a})}$

$\Rightarrow (z-a)(\bar{z}-\bar{a}) = (z+\bar{a})(\bar{z}+a)$ $[\because \overline{(\bar{a})} = a]$

$\Rightarrow z\bar{z} - z\bar{a} - a\bar{z} + a\bar{a} = z\bar{z} + za + \bar{a}\bar{z} + \bar{a}a$

$\Rightarrow za + z\bar{a} + \bar{a}\bar{z} + a\bar{z} = 0$

$\Rightarrow (a+\bar{a})(z+\bar{z}) = 0$

$\Rightarrow z + \bar{z} = 0$ $[\because a + \bar{a} = 2\,\text{Re}(a) \neq 0]$

$\Rightarrow 2\text{Re}(z) = 0$

$\Rightarrow 2x = 0$

$\Rightarrow x = 0$

$\Rightarrow$ *Y*-axis

26. *(a)*

27. *(a)* We have, $\tan^{-1}(\alpha + i\beta) = x + iy$

$\Rightarrow \alpha + i\beta = \tan(x+iy)$ ...(i)

Taking conjugate, we get

$(\alpha - i\beta) = \tan(x - iy)$ ...(ii)

$\therefore \tan 2x = \tan[(x+iy)+(x-iy)]$

$\Rightarrow \tan 2x = \frac{(\alpha+i\beta)+(\alpha-i\beta)}{1-(\alpha+i\beta)(\alpha-i\beta)}$

$= \frac{2\alpha}{1-(\alpha^2+\beta^2)}$

$\therefore \quad x = \frac{1}{2}\tan^{-1}\left(\frac{2\alpha}{1-\alpha^2-\beta^2}\right)$

28. *(a)* $|z_1| = |z_2| = |z_3| = 1$

Now, $|z_1| = 1 \Rightarrow |z_1|^2 = 1$

$\Rightarrow z_1\bar{z}_1 = 1$

Similarly, $z_2\bar{z}_2 = 1$ and $z_3\bar{z}_3 = 1$

Again, $\left|\frac{1}{z_1} + \frac{1}{z_2} + \frac{1}{z_3}\right| = 1$

$\Rightarrow |\bar{z}_1 + \bar{z}_2 + \bar{z}_3| = 1$

$\Rightarrow |\overline{z_1 + z_2 + z_3}| = 1$

$\Rightarrow |z_1 + z_2 + z_3| = 1$ $[\because |z| = |\bar{z}|]$

29. *(c)* $|z - i\,\text{Re}(z)| = |z - \text{Im}(z)|$

If $z = x + iy$,

then $|x + iy - ix| = |x + iy - y|$

$\sqrt{x^2 + (y-x)^2} = \sqrt{(x-y)^2 + y^2}$

$\Rightarrow x^2 = y^2$

$\therefore x = \pm y$

$\Rightarrow \text{Re}(z) = \pm\,\text{Im}(z)$

$\Rightarrow \text{Re}(z) + \text{Im}(z) = 0$

and $\text{Re}(z) - \text{Im}(z) = 0$

30. *(b)* We have, $|z| + z = 3 + i$

By inspection it is clearly that imaginary part is 1.

$\therefore z = x + i$ for some $x \in R$

$\Rightarrow |x + i| + x + i = 3 + i$

$\Rightarrow \sqrt{x^2+1} = 3 - x$

$\Rightarrow x^2 + 1 = 9 - 6x + x^2$

$\Rightarrow 6x = 8 \Rightarrow x = \frac{4}{3}$

$\Rightarrow z = \frac{4}{3} + i$

$\Rightarrow |z| = \sqrt{\frac{16}{9} + 1} = \sqrt{\frac{25}{9}} \Rightarrow |z| = \frac{5}{3}$

31. *(c)* For $z = x + iy$, $z^2 = i|z|^2$

$\Rightarrow x^2 - y^2 + 2i\,xy = ix^2 + iy^2$

$\Rightarrow x^2 - y^2 = i(x-y)^2$

$\Rightarrow (x-y)(x+y) = i(x-y)^2$

$\Rightarrow x = y$ or $x + y = i(x-y)$

So, the z lies on the line, $y = x$.

32. ***(c)*** Let $\frac{p}{a}=A, \frac{q}{b}=B, \frac{r}{c}=C$

$\therefore \quad A+B+C=1+i, \frac{1}{A}+\frac{1}{B}+\frac{1}{C}=0$

or $\quad AB+BC+CA=0$

$\Rightarrow \quad (A+B+c)^2=(1+i)^2$

$\Rightarrow \quad A^2+B^2+C^2+2(AB+BC+CA)$

$=1+i^2+2i=1-1+2i$

$\Rightarrow \quad A^2+B^2+C^2+0=2i$

$\Rightarrow \quad \frac{p^2}{a^2}+\frac{q^2}{b^2}+\frac{r^2}{c^2}=2i.$

33. ***(a)*** $\frac{1+z}{1+\bar{z}}=\frac{z(1+z)}{z+z\bar{z}}=\frac{z(1+z)}{z+|z|^2}=\frac{z(1+z)}{(z+1)}=z$

$[\because |z|=1]$

34. ***(d)*** Since, $x_1<x_2 \Rightarrow \sqrt{x_1^2+y_1^2}<\sqrt{x_2^2+y_2^2}$

$[\because y_1=y_2]$

$\therefore \quad |z_1|<|z_2| \quad \ldots(i)$

$|z_3|=\frac{1}{2}|z_1+z_2|<\frac{1}{2}|z_1|+\frac{1}{2}|z_2|<\frac{1}{2}|z_2|+\frac{1}{2}|z_2|$

$\Rightarrow \quad |z_3|<|z_2| \quad \ldots(ii)$

From Eqs. (i) and (ii),

$|z_1|<|z_3|<|z_2|$

35. ***(a)*** Since, $\frac{z(\sqrt{3}+4i)}{19}=1$

$\Rightarrow \quad z=\frac{19}{(\sqrt{3}+4i)}\times\frac{\sqrt{3}-4i}{\sqrt{3}-4i}=\sqrt{3}-4i$

36. ***(d)*** $\because \quad z^{1/3}=p+iq$

$\therefore \quad z=(p+iq)^3$

$=p^3-iq^3+3ip^2q-3pq^2$

Given that $z=x-iy$

$\therefore \quad x-iy=p^3-3pq^2+i(3p^2q-q^3)$

$\Rightarrow \quad x=p^3-3pq^2$

and $\quad -y=3p^2q-q^3$

$\Rightarrow \quad \frac{x}{p}=p^2-3q^2$

and $\quad \frac{y}{q}=-3p^2+q^2$

$\therefore \quad \frac{x}{p}+\frac{y}{q}=-2p^2-2q^2$

$\Rightarrow \quad \frac{1}{(p^2+q^2)}\left(\frac{x}{p}+\frac{y}{q}\right)=-2$

37. ***(a)*** Now, $\left(\frac{1+i}{1-i}\right)^x=\left[\frac{(1+i)(1+i)}{(1-i)(1+i)}\right]^x$

$=\left[\frac{(1+i)^2}{1-i^2}\right]^x=\left[\frac{1-1+2i}{2}\right]^x$

$\Rightarrow \quad \left(\frac{1+i}{1-i}\right)^x=(i)^x=1 \quad$ [given]

$\Rightarrow \quad (i)^x=(i)^{4n}$

where, n is any positive integer.

$\therefore \quad x=4n$

38. ***(c)***

39. ***(a)*** Given, $\frac{x+iy}{27}=\left(-2-\frac{1}{3}i\right)^3$

$=\left(-\frac{1}{3}\right)^3(6+i)^3$

$=\frac{-1}{27}(216+108i+18i^2+i^3)$

$=-\frac{1}{27}(198+107i)$

Equating real and imaginary parts, we get

$x=-198$ and $y=-107$

$\Rightarrow y-x=-107+198=91$

40. ***(b)*** Given, complex number

$z=\frac{(1+i)^2}{a-i}=\frac{1-1+2i}{a-i}=\frac{2i(a+i)}{(a-i)(a+i)}=\frac{2ai-2}{a^2+1}$

$|z|=\sqrt{\frac{4+4a^2}{(a^2+1)^2}}=\frac{\sqrt{2}}{\sqrt{5}} \quad \left[\because |z|=\sqrt{\frac{2}{5}}\right]$

$\Rightarrow \quad \frac{4(1+a^2)}{(a^2+1)^2}=\frac{2}{5}\Rightarrow\frac{4}{a^2+1}=\frac{2}{5}\Rightarrow a^2+1=10$

$\Rightarrow \quad a^2=9\Rightarrow a=3 \quad [\because a>0]$

So, $z=\frac{6i-2}{10}=\frac{-1}{5}+\frac{3}{5}i \Rightarrow \bar{z}=-\frac{1}{5}-\frac{3}{5}i$

41. ***(d)*** Given, $\frac{z-\alpha}{z+\alpha}$ $(\alpha\in R)$ is purely imaginary number. Then,

$\frac{z-\alpha}{z+\alpha}+\overline{\left(\frac{z-\alpha}{z+\alpha}\right)}=0\Rightarrow\frac{z-\alpha}{z+\alpha}+\frac{\bar{z}-\alpha}{\bar{z}+\alpha}=0$

$\Rightarrow z\bar{z}-\alpha\bar{z}+\alpha z-\alpha^2+z\bar{z}-\alpha z+\alpha\bar{z}-\alpha^2=0$

$2z\bar{z}-2\alpha^2=0\Rightarrow 2|z|^2-2|\alpha|^2=0$

$\Rightarrow \quad |z|^2=|\alpha|^2\Rightarrow|\alpha|^2=4\ [\because |z|=2]$

$\Rightarrow \quad |\alpha|=2\Rightarrow\alpha=2$

42. **(b)** $\dfrac{1+i\cos x}{1-2i\cos x}=\dfrac{(1+i\cos x)(1+2i\cos x)}{(1-2i\cos x)(1+2i\cos x)}$

$=\dfrac{(1-2\cos^2 x)+i(3\cos x)}{1+4\cos^2 x}$ is real

and imaginary part = 0

$\Rightarrow \quad 3\cos x = 0$

$\Rightarrow \quad \cos x = 0$

$\Rightarrow \quad x = 2n\pi \pm \dfrac{\pi}{2}, n \in Z$

43. **(b)** $f(z)=|z|+|z-2|$

Critical points, $z=0, 2$

$\therefore$Minimum value of $f(z)=\min\{f(0), f(2)\}$

$=\min\{2, 2\}=2$

44. **(a)** By triangle inequality, we have

$$|z|-\frac{2}{|z|}\le\left|z+\frac{2}{z}\right|\le|z|+\frac{2}{|z|}$$

$$\Rightarrow \quad \left|z+\frac{2}{z}\right|\ge|z|-\frac{2}{|z|}\ge 5-\frac{2}{5}\ge\frac{23}{5}$$

45. **(a)** Let $z=x+iy$

$\Rightarrow z^2=(x+iy)^2$

$\Rightarrow z^2=x^2+i^2y^2+2ixy$

$\Rightarrow z^2=(x^2-y^2)+i(2xy)$

$\Rightarrow$ Re $(z^2)=x^2-y^2$

Given, $(z^2)=0$

$\Rightarrow x^2-y^2=0$

$\Rightarrow \quad x=\pm y$

$\Rightarrow \quad x=y$ ...(i)

and $\quad x=-y$ ...(ii)

Again, $\quad |z|=2$

$\Rightarrow \quad |z|^2=4$

$\Rightarrow \quad x^2+y^2=4$ ...(iii)

From Eqs. (i) and (iii), we get

$y^2+y^2=4$

$\Rightarrow \quad 2y^2=4$

$\Rightarrow \quad y^2=2 \Rightarrow y=\pm\sqrt{2}$

Therefore, from Eq. (i), we get

$x=\pm\sqrt{2}$

$\therefore \quad z=\pm\sqrt{2}\pm i\sqrt{2}$

On putting the value of x from Eq. (ii) in Eq. (iii), we get

$(-y)^2+y^2=4 \Rightarrow 2y^2=4$

$\Rightarrow \quad y^2=2 \Rightarrow y=\pm\sqrt{2}$

From Eq. (ii), $x=\mp\sqrt{2}$

$\therefore \quad z=x+iy, z=\mp\sqrt{2}\pm i\sqrt{2}$

46. **(b)** Given, $x=a+ib$

On squaring both sides,

$x^2=(a^2-b^2+2iab)$

$\Rightarrow \quad 3+4i=a^2-b^2+2iab$

On comparing,

$a^2-b^2=3$ and $2ab=4$

$\Rightarrow \quad a^2-b^2=3$ and $ab=2$

Now, $\quad a^2-\dfrac{4}{a^2}=3$

$\Rightarrow \quad a^4-3a^2-4=0$

$\Rightarrow \quad (a^2-4)(a^2+1)=0$

$\Rightarrow \quad a^2=4$ or $a^2=-1$ [rejected]

$\therefore \quad a=\pm 2$

If $a=2$, then $b=1$

If $a=-2$, then $b=-1$

$x^3=a^3-ib^3+3iab(a+ib)$

When, $\quad a=2, b=1$

Then, $\quad x^3=8-i+6i(2+i)$

$\Rightarrow \quad x^3=8-i+12i-6$

$\therefore \quad x^3=2+11i$

Hence, $a=2, b=1$ satisfy it.

$\therefore \quad a+b=2+1=3$

47. **(b)** Given, $\quad |z_1|=12$ ...(i)

and $\quad |z_2-3-4i|=5$

$\Rightarrow \quad |z_2-(3+4i)|=5$

Now, $|z_2-(3+4i)|\ge|z_2|-|3+4i|$

$[\because |z_1-z_2|\ge|z_1|-|z_2|]$

$\Rightarrow \quad 5\ge|z_2|-\sqrt{3^2+4^2}$

$\Rightarrow \quad 5\ge|z_2|-\sqrt{25}$

$\Rightarrow \quad 5\ge|z_2|-5$

$\Rightarrow \quad 10\ge|z_2|$ ...(ii)

Now, $|z_1 - z_2| \geq |z_1| - |z_2|$
$[\because |z_1 - z_2| \geq |z_1| - |z_2|]$
$\geq 12 - 10$
[using Eqs. (i) and (ii)]
$|z_1 - z_2| \geq 2$

Hence, the minimum value of $|z_1 - z_2|$ is 2.

48. *(c)* Let $z = x + 10i$, as $\text{Im}(z) = 10$ (given).

Since z satisfies,

$$\frac{2z - n}{2z + n} = 2i - 1, n \in N,$$

$\therefore \quad (2x + 20i - n) = (2i - 1)(2x + 20i + n)$

$\Rightarrow (2x - n) + 20i = (-2x - n - 40) + (4x + 2n - 20)i$

On comparing real and imaginary parts, we get

$2x - n = -2x - n - 40$ and $20 = 4x + 2n - 20$

$\Rightarrow \quad 4x = -40$ and $4x + 2n = 40$

$\Rightarrow \quad x = -10$ and $-40 + 2n = 40 \Rightarrow n = 40$

So, $\quad n = 40$ and $x = \text{Re}(z) = -10$

49. *(a)* We have, $|z_1| = |z_2| = \ldots = |z_n| = 1$

$\Rightarrow \quad |z_1|^2 = |z_2|^2 = \ldots = |z_n|^2 = 1$

$\Rightarrow \quad z_1\bar{z}_1 = z_2\bar{z}_2 = \ldots = z_n\bar{z}_n = 1$

$\Rightarrow \quad \bar{z}_1 = \frac{1}{z_1}, \bar{z}_2 = \frac{1}{z_2}, \ldots. \bar{z}_n = \frac{1}{z_n}$

Now, $|z_1 + z_2 + z_3 + \ldots z_n|$

$= |\overline{z_1 + z_2 + z_3 \ldots + z_n}| \quad [\because |z| = |\bar{z}|]$

$= |\bar{z}_1 + \bar{z}_2 + \bar{z}_3 + \ldots \bar{z}_n|$

$= \left|\frac{1}{z_1} + \frac{1}{z_2} + \frac{1}{z_3} + \ldots \frac{1}{z_n}\right|$

Hence, Assertion and Reason both are true and Reason is correct explanation of Assertion.

50. *(a)* Let $\frac{5z_2}{11z_1} = i\lambda \ (\lambda \neq 0)$

$\Rightarrow \quad \frac{z_2}{z_1} = \frac{11i\lambda}{5}$

$$\left|\frac{2z_1 + 3z_2}{2z_1 - 3z_2}\right| = \left|\frac{2 + 3\frac{z_2}{z_1}}{2 - 3\frac{z_2}{z_1}}\right| = \left|\frac{2 + \frac{33i\lambda}{5}}{2 - \frac{33i\lambda}{5}}\right|$$

$$= \left|\frac{10 + 33i\lambda}{10 - 33i\lambda}\right| = 1$$

51. *(c)* We have, $\alpha^2 + \beta^2 + \gamma^2 - \gamma = 0$

$\Rightarrow \quad \alpha^2 + \beta^2 = \gamma - \gamma^2$ and $z = \frac{\alpha + i\beta}{1 - \gamma}$

$$|z| = \frac{\sqrt{\alpha^2 + \beta^2}}{1 - \gamma}$$

$$\Rightarrow \quad |z|^2 = \frac{\alpha^2 + \beta^2}{(1 - \gamma)^2} = \frac{\gamma - \gamma^2}{(1 - \gamma)^2} = \frac{\gamma(1 - \gamma)}{(1 - \gamma)^2} = \frac{\gamma}{1 - \gamma}$$

52. *(b)* $|z|^2 = \frac{\gamma}{1 - \gamma} = -1 + \frac{1}{1 - \gamma}$

$1 + |z|^2 = \frac{1}{1 - \gamma}$

$\Rightarrow \quad \gamma = \frac{|z|}{1 + |z|^2}$

Now, $z + \bar{z} = \frac{\alpha + i\beta}{1 - \gamma} + \frac{\alpha - i\beta}{1 - \gamma} = \frac{2\alpha}{1 - \gamma}$

$2\alpha = (z + \bar{z})(1 - \gamma)$

$\Rightarrow \quad 2\alpha = (z + \bar{z})\left(1 - \frac{|z|^2}{1 + |z|^2}\right)$

$\Rightarrow \quad 2\alpha = \frac{z + \bar{z}}{1 + |z|^2}$

$\Rightarrow \quad \alpha = \frac{z + \bar{z}}{2(1 + |z|^2)}$

53. *(b)* $z - \bar{z} = \left(\frac{\alpha + i\beta}{1 - \gamma}\right) - \left(\frac{\alpha - i\beta}{1 - \gamma}\right) = \frac{2i\beta}{1 - \gamma}$

$\Rightarrow \quad 2i\beta = (z - \bar{z})(1 - \gamma)$

$\Rightarrow \quad 2i\beta = (z - \bar{z})\left(1 - \frac{|z|^2}{1 + |z|^2}\right)$

$= \frac{(z - \bar{z})}{1 + |z|^2}$

$\Rightarrow \quad \beta = \frac{-(z - \bar{z})i}{2(1 + |z|^2)} = \frac{(\bar{z} - z)i}{2(1 + |z|^2)}$

Chapter 5 Linear Inequalities

1. *(c)* The inequality $\log_{0.5}\frac{x+2}{x} \le 1$ is true for

$$\frac{x+2}{x} > 0$$

Multiplying the numerator and denominator by x, we get

$$\frac{x(x+2)}{x^2} > 0$$

$\Rightarrow \quad x(x+2) > 0$

$\Rightarrow \quad x < -2$ or $x > 0$ ...(i)

Also, $\log_{0.5}\frac{x+2}{x} \le 1$

$\Rightarrow \quad \frac{x+2}{x} \ge 0.5$

$\Rightarrow \quad \frac{x+2}{x} - \frac{1}{2} \ge 0$

$\Rightarrow \quad \frac{x+4}{2x} \ge 0 \Rightarrow 2x(x+4) \ge 0$

$\Rightarrow \quad x \le -4$ or $x \ge 0$ ...(ii)

From Eqs. (i) and (ii), we get

$\Rightarrow \quad x \in (-\infty, -2) \cup (0, \infty)$

2. *(b)* $\frac{2p+x}{3} \le \frac{4px-1}{2}$

$\Rightarrow \quad 4p + 2x \le 12px - 3$

$\Rightarrow \quad 2(6p-1)x \ge 4p + 3$

$\because \quad x \ge \frac{3}{4} \Rightarrow 6p - 1 > 0$

and $\quad \frac{4p+3}{2(6p-1)} = \frac{3}{4}$

$\therefore \quad 2(4p+3) = 3(6p-1)$

$\Rightarrow \quad 8p + 6 = 18p - 3$

$\Rightarrow \quad 9 = 18p - 8p \Rightarrow 9 = 10p$

$\Rightarrow \quad p = \frac{9}{10}$

3. *(c)*

4. *(a)* $|2x+3| < |x+6|$

$\Rightarrow |2x+3| - |x+6| < 0$

Case I If $x < -6$

$$-(2x+3) + (x+6) < 0$$

$\Rightarrow \quad x > 3$

But $\quad -6 < 3$

So, no common solution.

$\therefore \quad x \in \phi$

Case II $-6 \le x < \frac{-3}{2}$

$$-(2x+3) - (x+6) < 0$$

$\Rightarrow \quad -2x - 3 - x - 6 < 0$

$\Rightarrow \quad -3x - 9 < 0$

$\Rightarrow \quad -3x < 9$

$\Rightarrow \quad -x < 3$

$\Rightarrow \quad x > -3$

$\Rightarrow \quad x \in \left(-3, -\frac{3}{2}\right)$

Case III $x \ge \frac{-3}{2}$

$$(2x+3) - (x+6) < 0$$

$\Rightarrow \quad x < 3 \Rightarrow \frac{-3}{2} \le x < 3$

$\therefore$ Solution set $x \in (-3, 3)$.

5. *(d)*

6. *(b)* $\frac{|x+1| + x}{x-1} > 1$

$\Rightarrow \quad \frac{|x+1| + x}{x-1} - 1 > 0$

$\Rightarrow \quad \frac{|x+1| + x - x + 1}{x-1} > 0$

$\Rightarrow \quad \frac{|x+1| + 1}{x-1} > 0$

Case I If $\quad x + 1 \ge 0$

$\Rightarrow \quad x \ge -1$

Then, $\quad \frac{|x+1|+1}{x-1} > 0 \Rightarrow \frac{x+2}{x-1} > 0$

$\Rightarrow \quad \{x + 2 > 0 \text{ and } x - 1 > 0\}$

or $\quad \{x + 2 < 0 \text{ and } x - 1 < 0\}$

$\Rightarrow \quad \{x > -2 \text{ and } x > 1\}$

or $\quad \{x < -2 \text{ and } x < 1\}$

$\Rightarrow \quad x > 1$ or $x < -2$

$\Rightarrow \quad x \in (1, \infty)$ or $x \in (-\infty, -2)$

But $x \ge -1 \Rightarrow x \in (1, \infty)$

Case II If $x + 1 < 0 \Rightarrow x < -1$

Then, $\quad \frac{-(x+1)+1}{x-1} > 0$

$\Rightarrow \quad \frac{-x}{x-1} > 0 \Rightarrow \frac{x}{x-1} < 0$

Multiplying numerator and denominator by $(x-1)$, we get

$$\frac{x(x-1)}{(x-1)} < 0$$

$\Rightarrow \quad x(x-1) < 0$

$\Rightarrow \quad 0 < x < 1$

But $\quad x < -1$

$\Rightarrow \quad x = \phi$

$\therefore$ Solution set is $(1, \infty)$.

7. *(b)* $|9^x - 3^{x+1} - 15| < 2 \cdot 9^x - 3^x$

Let $3^x = t$, then

$$|t^2 - 3t - 15| < 2t^2 - t$$

Inequality is true, if

$$2t^2 - t > 0$$

$\Rightarrow \quad t(2t-1) > 0 \Rightarrow t < 0 \text{ or } t > \frac{1}{2}$

But $t \nless 0 \quad [\because 3^x = t, t > 0]$

$\Rightarrow \quad t > \frac{1}{2}$

On solving the inequality, we get

$$-(2t^2 - t) < t^2 - 3t - 15 < 2t^2 - t$$

$\Rightarrow \quad 3t^2 - 4t - 15 > 0 \text{ and } t^2 + 2t + 15 > 0$

$\Rightarrow \quad t < \frac{-5}{3} \text{ or } t > 3 \text{ and } t \in R$

$\Rightarrow \quad t > 3$

$\Rightarrow \quad 3^x > 3$

$\Rightarrow \quad x > 1$

$\Rightarrow \quad x \in (1, \infty)$

8. *(c)* $\text{IQ} = \frac{\text{MA}}{\text{CA}} \times 100$

$\because \quad \text{CA} = 15$

$\therefore \quad \text{IQ} = \frac{\text{MA}}{15} \times 100$

$\quad \text{IQ} = \frac{100}{15}\text{MA}$

$\because \quad 100 \le \text{IQ} \le 160$

$\Rightarrow \quad 100 \le \frac{100}{15}\text{MA} \le 160$

$\Rightarrow \quad \frac{15 \times 100}{100} \le \text{MA} \le \frac{15 \times 160}{100}$

$\Rightarrow \quad 15 \le \text{MA} \le 24$

9. *(a)* **Statement I** We have, $\frac{|x-2|}{x-2} \ge 0$

Case I If $x < 2$

$$\frac{|x-2|}{x-2} \ge 0$$

$\Rightarrow \quad \frac{-(x-2)}{x-2} \ge 0 \quad [\because |x-2| = -(x-2), \text{ if } x < 2]$

$\Rightarrow \quad -1 \ge 0$, which is not true.

Case II If $x > 2$

$$\frac{|x-2|}{x-2} \ge 0$$

$\Rightarrow \quad \frac{x-2}{x-2} \ge 0 \quad [\because |x-2| = (x-2), \text{ if } x > 2]$

$\Rightarrow \quad 1 \ge 0$, which is true

Also, given expression is not defined at $x = 2$.

Hence, $x > 2$ i.e. $x \in (2, \infty)$ is the required solution.

Statement II We have,

$$|x| > b, b > 0$$

$\Rightarrow \quad x < -b \text{ and } x > b$

$\Rightarrow \quad x \in (-\infty, -b) \cup (b, \infty)$

Hence, Statement I is true but Statement II is false.

10. *(a)* 11. *(a)* 12. *(a)*

13. *(a)* 14. *(a)* 15. *(d)* 16. *(a)*

17. *(c)* We have,

$$\frac{5-2x}{3} \le \frac{x}{6} - 5$$

or $\quad 2(5-2x) \le x - 30$

or $\quad 10 - 4x \le x - 30$

or $\quad -5x \le -40$, i.e. $x \ge 8$

Thus, all real numbers x which are greater than or equal to 8 are the solutions of the given inequality, i.e. $x \in [8, \infty)$.

18. *(a)* We have, $\frac{x}{4} < \frac{(5x-2)}{3} - \frac{(7x-3)}{5}$

$$\frac{x}{4} < \frac{5(5x-2) - 3(7x-3)}{15}$$

$\Rightarrow \quad 15x < 4[(25x-10) - (21x-9)]$

$\Rightarrow \quad 15x < 4[25x - 10 - 21x + 9]$

$\Rightarrow \quad 15x < 4[4x - 1]$

$\Rightarrow \quad 15x < 16x - 4$

Transferring the term $16x$ to LHS.

$$15x - 16x < -4 \Rightarrow -x < -4$$

Multiplying by -1 both sides, we get

$$x > 4$$

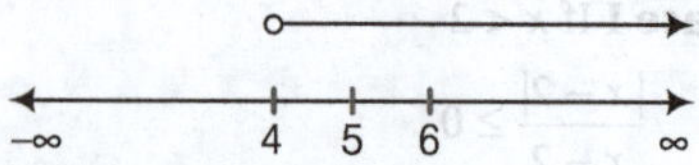

$\therefore$ Solution set is $(4, \infty)$.

19. *(b)* We have, $5(2x - 7) - 3(2x + 3) \le 0$

$$10x - 35 - 6x - 9 \le 0$$
$$4x - 44 \le 0$$

Adding 44 on both sides,

$$4x - 44 + 44 \le 0 + 44$$
$$\Rightarrow \quad 4x \le 44 \Rightarrow x \le \frac{44}{4}$$
$$\Rightarrow \quad x \le 11 \quad \ldots\text{(i)}$$

Now, $\quad 2x + 19 \le 6x + 47$

Transferring the term $6x$ to LHS and the term 19 to RHS,

$$2x - 6x \le 47 - 19 \Rightarrow -4x \le 28$$

Dividing both sides by 4,

$$\frac{-4x}{4} \le \frac{28}{4} \Rightarrow -x \le 7$$
$$\Rightarrow \quad x \ge -7 \quad \ldots\text{(ii)}$$

Draw the graph of inequalities (i) and (ii) on the number line,

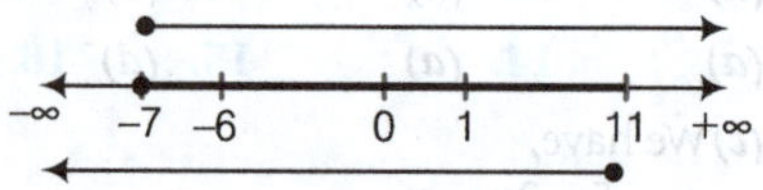

Hence, solution set of the inequalities are real numbers x lying between -7 and 11, including -7 and 11

i.e. $\quad -7 \le x \le 11$

$\therefore$ Solutions set is $[-7, 11]$.

20. *(b)*

21. *(d)* **Case I** $|x - 3| - 4 > 3$

$\Rightarrow \quad |x - 3| > 7$

$\Rightarrow \; x - 3 > 7$ or $x - 3 < -7$

$\Rightarrow \quad x > 10$ or $x < -4$

$\Rightarrow \quad x \in (-\infty, -4) \cup (10, \infty)$

Case II $|x - 3| - 4 < -3$

$\Rightarrow \quad |x - 3| < 1$

$\Rightarrow \; x - 3 < 1$ or $x - 3 > -1$

$\Rightarrow \quad -1 < x - 3 < 1 \Rightarrow \quad 2 < x < 4$

So, from Case I and Case II, we get

$$x \in (-\infty, -4) \cup (2, 4) \cup (10, \infty)$$

22. *(d)* Given, $\dfrac{x}{x+2} \le \dfrac{1}{|x|}$

$$\Rightarrow \quad \frac{|x|\,x}{x+2} \le 1 \Rightarrow \frac{x|x| - x - 2}{x+2} \le 0$$

Case I If $x \in [0, \infty)$

$\Rightarrow \quad |x| = x$

$$\frac{x^2 - x - 2}{x+2} \le 0 \Rightarrow \frac{(x-2)(x+1)}{x+2} \le 0$$

$\Rightarrow \quad x \le 2 \qquad [\because x \in [0, \infty)]$

i.e. integral values of x are 0, 1, 2.

Case II If $x \in (-\infty, 0) \Rightarrow \quad |x| = -x$

$$\frac{-x^2 - x - 2}{x+2} \le 0$$

$\Rightarrow \quad -2 < x < 0 \qquad [\because x \in (-\infty, 0)]$

i.e. integral value of x is -1.

So, there are 4 integral values of x satisfying the inequation.

23. *(b)* Given, $\dfrac{|x+3| + x}{x+2} > 1$

Clearly, LHS of the inequation is meaningful for $x \ne -2$.

$$\frac{|x+3| + x}{x+2} > 1 \Rightarrow \frac{|x+3| + x}{x+2} - 1 > 0$$
$$\Rightarrow \quad \frac{|x+3| + x - x - 2}{x+2} > 0 \Rightarrow \frac{|x+3| - 2}{x+2} > 0$$

If $|x+3| - 2 = 0 \Rightarrow x + 3 = \pm 2 \Rightarrow x = -5, -1$

Sign scheme of the expression $\dfrac{|x+3| - 2}{x+2}$ is as

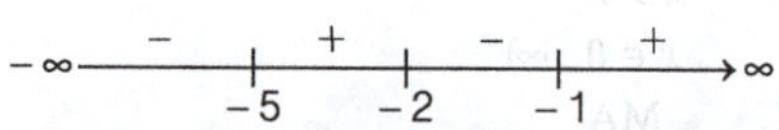

$$x \in (-5, -2) \cup (-1, \infty)$$

24. *(a)* Given, $0 < |3x + 1| < \dfrac{1}{3}$

$$\Rightarrow \quad -\frac{1}{3} < (3x + 1) < \frac{1}{3} \Rightarrow -1 - \frac{1}{3} < (3x) < \frac{1}{3} - 1$$
$$\Rightarrow \quad -\frac{4}{3} < (3x) < -\frac{2}{3} \Rightarrow \frac{-4}{9} < x < \frac{-2}{9}$$

Also, $|3x + 1| > 0$ is satisfied by each x except when $3x + 1 = 0$ i.e. $x = -\dfrac{1}{3}$

$$\therefore \text{ Solution is } \left(-\frac{4}{9}, -\frac{2}{9}\right) - \left\{-\frac{1}{3}\right\}.$$

So, by comparing, we get

$$K_1 = -\frac{4}{9}\; K_2 = \frac{-2}{9} \text{ and } K_3 = -\frac{1}{3}$$

$$\Rightarrow K_1 + K_2 - K_3 = -\frac{4}{9} - \frac{2}{9} + \frac{1}{3}$$
$$= \frac{-6+3}{9} = \frac{-3}{9} = \frac{-1}{3}$$

25. ***(d)*** Given, $\log_2\{\log_3(4x+1)\} > \log_2\{\log_3(2x+3)\}$

$\because$ The base is $2 > 1$, we get
$\log_3(4x+1) > \log_3(2x+3)$
$\Rightarrow \quad 4x+1 > 2x+3 \quad [\because \text{ base is } 3 > 1]$
$\Rightarrow \quad 2x > 2 \Rightarrow x > 1$
Also, $4x+1>0 \Rightarrow x > -1/4$
and $2x+3>0 \Rightarrow x > -3/2$
$\therefore$ The solution set is $x \in (1, \infty)$.

26. ***(b)*** The possible error of $\pm$ 0.02 A means that the difference between the actual current and the value of 0.036 A cannot be more than 0.002 A.
So, the values of i can be expressed as
$$0.034 \le i \le 0.038$$
which can be written as $|i - 0.036| \le 0.002$

27. ***(d)*** Given, $\log_{\frac{x+4}{2}}\left(\log_2 \frac{2x-1}{3+x}\right) < 0$

First the base must be positive and not equal to 1.
$$\Rightarrow \quad \frac{x+4}{2} > 0 \text{ and } x \ne -2$$
$$\Rightarrow \quad x > -4 \text{ and } x \ne -2$$
Similarly, $\log_2 \frac{2x-1}{3+x} > 0$
$$\Rightarrow \quad \frac{2x-1}{x+3} > 0 \Rightarrow x > \frac{1}{2} \text{ or } x < -3$$
$\therefore$ The only possible values of x are
$$x > \frac{1}{2} \text{ or } -4 < x < -3$$

Case I $0 < \frac{x+4}{2} < 1 \Rightarrow -4 < x < -2$

It is necessary that $\log_2 \frac{2x-1}{3+x} > 1$
$$\Rightarrow \quad \frac{2x-1}{3+x} > 2$$
$$\Rightarrow \quad \frac{2x-1}{3+x} - 2 > 0$$
$$\Rightarrow \quad \frac{-7}{3+x} > 0$$
$$\Rightarrow \quad x+3 < 0 \Rightarrow x < -3$$
$$\therefore \quad x \in (-4, -3)$$

Case II $\frac{x+4}{2} > 1 \Rightarrow x > -2$

It is necessary that $\log_2 \frac{2x-1}{3+x} < 1$
$$\Rightarrow \quad \frac{2x-1}{3+x} < 2$$
$$\Rightarrow \quad \frac{2x-1}{3+x} - 2 < 0$$
$$\Rightarrow \quad \frac{-7}{3+x} < 0$$
which is always true as $x > -2$.
Therefore, the solution set is
$$x > \frac{1}{2}, -4 < x < -3$$
$$x \in (-4, -3) \cup \left(\frac{1}{2}, \infty\right)$$

28. ***(d)***

29. ***(b)*** Using AM $\ge$ GM.
$$\frac{\frac{a}{b+c} + \frac{b}{c+a} + \frac{c}{a+b}}{3} \ge \sqrt[3]{\frac{abc}{(a+b)(b+c)(c+a)}} \quad \ldots\text{(i)}$$
Again, using AM $\ge$ GM
$$\frac{a+b}{2} \ge \sqrt{ab}, \frac{b+c}{2} \ge \sqrt{bc},$$
$$\frac{c+a}{2} \ge \sqrt{ca}$$
$$\Rightarrow \quad (a+b)(b+c)(c+a) \ge 8abc$$
$$\Rightarrow \quad \sqrt[3]{\frac{abc}{(a+b)(b+c)(c+a)}} \le \frac{1}{2}$$
From Eq. (i),
$$\frac{a}{b+c} + \frac{b}{c+a} + \frac{c}{a+b} \ge \frac{3}{2}$$

30. ***(b)*** Given, ${}^{n+1}C_{n-2} - {}^{n+1}C_{n-1} \le 50$
$$\Rightarrow \quad \frac{(n+1)!}{3!(n-2)!} - \frac{(n+1)!}{2!(n-1)!} \le 50$$
$$\Rightarrow \quad \frac{(n+1)!}{3!}\left[\frac{1}{(n-2)!} - \frac{3}{(n-1)!}\right] \le 50$$
$$\Rightarrow \quad (n+1)!\left(\frac{n-1-3}{(n-1)!}\right) \le 300$$
$$\Rightarrow \quad (n+1)\,n\,(n-4) \le 300$$
For $n = 8$, satisfy the above inequality.
But $n = 1$, it does not satisfy the above inequality.

Chapter 6 Permutation & Combination

1. (a)

2. (b) $1\cdot3\cdot5.....(2n-1)2^n$

$$= \frac{1\cdot3\cdot5....(2n-1)2^n\cdot(1\cdot2\cdot3....n)}{1\cdot2\cdot3....n}$$

$$= \frac{1\cdot3\cdot5....(2n-1)(2\cdot4\cdot6....(2n))}{n!}$$

$$= \frac{1\cdot2\cdot3\cdot4\cdot5....(2n-1)(2n)}{n!} = \frac{(2n)!}{n!}$$

3. (c) $\because n\cdot n! = (n+1-1)\cdot n!$

$= (n+1)\,n! - n! = (n+1)! - n!$

$\therefore \quad r\cdot r! = (r+1)! - r!$

$$\sum_{r=1}^{n} r\cdot r! = \sum_{r=1}^{n}[(r+1)! - r!]$$

$= 2! - 1! + 3! - 2! + (n+1)! - n!$

$= -1! + (n+1)! = (n+1)! - 1$

4. (b)

5. (c) We know that ${}^nP_r + r\cdot{}^nP_{r-1} = {}^{n+1}P_r$

$\therefore \quad {}^9P_5 + 5\cdot{}^9P_4 = {}^{10}P_5 = {}^{10}P_r \Rightarrow r = 5$

6. (c)

7. (d) Given, word –'KANPUR'

Vowels –A, U and Consonants –K, N, P, R

Total number of letters = 6

∴ Three even places to be occupied by two vowels and four consonants will occupy remaining 4 places.

Number of vowels can be formed

$= {}^3P_2 \times {}^4P_4 = 3\times2\times4!$

$= 6\times24 = 144$

8. (d) Given, letters = 6

Letters to be selected = 4

Out of 4 places every word starts with 'K' and ends with 'R'

∴ 2 letters are already selected.

Number of required arrangements

= Permutation of 2 letters out of 4 remaining letters

$= {}^4P_2 = 4\times3 = 12$

9. (b) Any number divisible by 5, if either 0 or 5 in unit place.

6			0 or 5
Th	H	T	U

In unit's place, the number of ways $= {}^2C_1 = 2$

In thousand place number 6 is fixed.

In ten and hundred place, the number of ways of selection $= 8\times7$

∴ Required number of ways $= 2\times8\times7 = 112$

10. (a) 11. (b)

12. (c) 4 men, 3 boys, 2 girls (Three objects)

are arranged so that they remains together is $(4!)\,(3!)\,(2!)\times3! = (4!)\,(3!)^2(2!)$.

13. (c)

14. (b) We have,

$a = {}^{x+2}P_{x+2} = (x+2)!$

$b = {}^xP_{11} = \frac{x!}{(x-11)!}$

and $\quad c = {}^{x-11}P_{x-11} = (x-11)!$

$$(x+2)! = 182\times\frac{x!}{(x-11)!}\times(x-11)!$$

$\Rightarrow \quad (x+2)! = 182x!$

$\Rightarrow \quad (x+2)(x+1) = 182$

$\Rightarrow \quad x^2 + 3x + 2 = 182$

$\Rightarrow \quad x^2 + 3x - 180 = 0$

$\Rightarrow \quad (x+15)(x-12) = 0$

$\Rightarrow \quad x = +12, -15$

15. (d) Number of ways white balls can be arranged $= 5!$

Number of ways black balls can be arranged $= 5!$

Neighbouring balls are of different colours it means balls are to be arranged alternatively we have two options either start arrange with black or start with white

i.e. $B_1W_1, B_2W_2, B_3W_3, B_4W_4, B_5W_5$

or $\quad W_1B_1, W_2B_2, W_3B_3, W_4B_4, W_5B_5$

∴ Number of required arrangements

$= 5!\times5!\times2! = 2\cdot(5!)^2$

16. (d)

17. (a) Total number of digits = 9

Out of 9 digits 5 are odd.

Four-digit number (odd) (ending with odd digit)

$= {}^8P_3\times{}^5P_1$

$= 8\times7\times6\times5 = 1680$

18. ***(b)*** Total number of letters = 6
R and D can be arranged in 2! ways between R and D two letters to be arranged, so ${}^4P_2$ ways and they can be considered as one unit with R and D and remaining two letters makes total 3 units.

$\therefore$ Total number of arrangements $= 2! \times {}^4P_2 \times 3!$
$= 2 \times 4 \times 3 \times 6$
$= 144$

19. ***(a)*** Odd digits 1, 3, 5, 7, 9
Numbers which are divisible by 5 ends by 5.
Such number of arrangements $= 4 \times 3 \times 2 = 24$
Total number of possible arrangements $= {}^5P_4$
$= 120$
Number of required arrangements $= 120 - 24 = 96$

20. ***(c)*** The number divisible by 6, if it is divisible by both 2 and 3.
Given, digits 0, 1, 2, 3, 4, 5

	Delete 0	**Number of arrangements**
Case I	(a) Fix 2 in units place	$4! = 24$
	(b) Fix 4 in units place	$4! = 24$

	Delete 3	**Number of arrangements**
Case II	(a) Fix 0 in units place	$4! = 24$
	(b) Fix 2 in units place	$4! - 3! = 24 - 6 = 18$
	(c) Fix 4 in units place	$4! - 3! = 24 - 6 = 18$

Total number of arrangements = 108

21. ***(d)*** Given, word – 'ENGINEERING'
Letters – EEE, NNN, GG, II, R
NNN are together = 1 unit
Remaining 8 letters
Total number of units = 9

$$\underbrace{\text{NNN,}}_{\text{1 unit}}\ \underbrace{\text{E, E, E, G, G, I, I, R}}_{\text{8 units}}$$

Total arrangements $= \dfrac{9!}{3!2!2!}$

When EEE are together, then

$$\underbrace{\text{NNN, EEE, G, G, I, I, R}}_{\text{7 units}}$$

Total number of arrangements (E's together)
$= \dfrac{7!}{2!\,2!}$

$\therefore$ Required permutation $= \dfrac{9!}{3!2!\,2!} - \dfrac{7!}{2!\,2!}$

22. ***(a)*** 2 particular persons are on the either sides this can be done in 2! ways, remaining 18 persons + 1 host = 19 persons
Then, 19 persons can be seated on circular table in $(19-1)!$ i.e. $18!$ ways
$\therefore$ Required number of arrangements $= 2! \times 18!$

23. ***(d)***

24. ***(b)*** $\therefore$ Required number of ways
$= {}^{10}C_1 + {}^{10}C_2 + {}^{10}C_3 + \ldots + {}^{10}C_{10}$
$= 2^{10} - 1 = 1024 - 1 = 1023$

25. ***(d)***

26. ***(c)*** Given, $n(A) = 2$ and $n(B) = 4$
$\therefore \quad n(A \times B) = 8$
Required subsets $= {}^8C_3 + {}^8C_4 + \ldots + {}^8C_8$
$= ({}^8C_0 + {}^8C_1 + \ldots + {}^8C_8)$
$- ({}^8C_0 + {}^8C_1 + {}^8C_2)$
$= 2^8 - {}^8C_0 - {}^8C_1 - {}^8C_2$
$[\because 2^n = {}^nC_0 + {}^nC_1 + \ldots + {}^nC_n]$
$= 256 - 1 - 8 - 28 = 219$

27. ***(b)*** The total number of ways of dividing identical falls in r different boxes so that none of the box is empty $= {}^{n-1}C_{r-1}$
Here, we have to distribute 12 identical falls in 3 distinct boxes.
This can be done in ${}^{12-1}C_{3-1} = {}^{11}C_2 = 55$

28. ***(c)*** **29.** ***(a)***

30. ***(c)*** Parallelogram having opposite pair of side parallel.
So, number of parallelogram formed
$= {}^mC_2 \times {}^nC_2 = \dfrac{m!}{2!(m-2)!} \times \dfrac{n!}{2!\,(n-2)!}$

31. ***(a)*** The number of ways of selecting four numbers from 1 to 30 without any restriction
$= {}^{30}C_4$
The number of ways of selecting four consecutive [i.e. (1, 2, 3, 4), (2, 3, 4, 5), ... (27, 28, 29, 30)] number is 27.
Hence, required number of ways
$= {}^{30}C_4 - 27 = \dfrac{30 \times 29 \times 28 \times 27}{24} - 27 = 27378$

32. *(c)* Number of required committees

= Total number of committees

– Number of committees in two particular women are together

$= {}^7C_5 \times {}^6C_3 - {}^7C_5 \times {}^4C_1$

$= {}^7C_2 \times {}^6C_3 - {}^7C_2 \times 4$ [using ${}^nC_r = {}^nC_{n-r}$]

$= 21 \times 20 - 21 \times 4 = 336$

33. *(d)*

Groups		Number of ways
A (6)	**B (8)**	
4	5	${}^6C_4 \times {}^8C_5 = 840$
5	4	${}^6C_5 \times {}^8C_4 = 420$
6	3	${}^6C_6 \times {}^8C_3 = 56$
Total		1316

34. *(c)*

	Groups		Number of ways
	Men (7)	**Women (4)**	
I	3	2	${}^7C_3 \times {}^4C_2 = 35 \times 6 = 210$ (True)
II	(i) 3 (ii) 2 (iii) 1	2 3 4	${}^7C_3 \times {}^4C_2 + {}^7C_2 \times {}^4C_3 + {}^7C_1 \times {}^4C_4$ $= 210 + 84 + 7 = 301$ (True)

35. *(d)* When the first place digit is 1, we have $7 \times 6 \times 5 = 210$ number of choices.

When the hundred place digit is 1, 0 cannot be the first digit then, we have $6 \times 6 \times 5 = 180$ number of choice.

Similarly for tens place and unit place, digit is 1. We have 180 number of choices.

∴Total numbers of choice

$= 210 + 180 + 180 + 180 = 750$

36. *(c)*

37. *(b)* Arrange the letters of the word 'KRISHNA' in alphabetical order

A H I K N R S

Write the factorial beginning with one less than number of boxes 6! 5! 4! 3! 2! 1! 0!

In 'KRISHNA' first letter is K. Then, multiply first factorial with number of letters before K in arrangement and then process will continue till end.

On adding them, we get the rank

$\therefore$ Rank $= 3 \times 6! + 4 \times 5! + 2 \times 4! + 3 \times 3! + 1 \times 2! + 1 \times 1! + 0!$

$= 2710$

38. *(b)* At first, we have to accomodate those 5 animals which cannot enter in 4 cages, therefore number of ways are ${}^6P_5$ and rest of the 5 animals are arranged in 5! ways.

$\therefore$ Total number of ways $= 5! \times {}^6P_5$

$= 120 \times 720 = 86400$

39. *(a)* Given word is 'MISSISSIPPI'

I = 4 times, S = 4 times

P = 2 times, M = 1 time

_M_I_I_I_I_P_P_

Required number of words $= {}^8C_4 \times \dfrac{7!}{4! \times 2!}$

$= {}^8C_4 \times \dfrac{7 \times 6 \times 5}{2}$

$= 7 \cdot {}^8C_4 \cdot {}^6C_4$

40. *(d)* As each section has 5 questions, so number of ways to select 5 questions are

S_1	S_2	S_3
1	1	3
1	3	1
3	1	1

and

1	2	2
2	1	2
2	2	1

$\therefore$ Total number of selection of 5 questions

$= 3 \times ({}^5C_1 \times {}^5C_1 \times {}^5C_3) + 3 \times ({}^5C_1 \times {}^5C_2 \times {}^5C_2)$

$= 3 \times (5 \times 5 \times 10) + 3\,(5 \times 10 \times 10)$

$= 2250$

41. *(a)* Let total number of players be n.

Number of games $= {}^{n-2}C_2$

Two players play 3 games each they played in total 6 games.

$\therefore \quad {}^{n-2}C_2 + 6 = 84$

$\Rightarrow \quad \dfrac{(n-2)(n-3)}{2} = 78$

$\Rightarrow \quad (n-2)(n-3) = 156$

$\Rightarrow \quad (n-2)(n-3) = 13 \times 12$

$\Rightarrow \quad n = 15$

42. ***(a)*** If a, b and c are sides of a triangle, then $a+b>c, b+c>a, a+c>b$.

$\therefore$ Number of triangles not formed by given sides $=7$

i.e. (2, 3, 5), (2, 3, 6), (2, 3, 7), (2, 4, 6), (2, 4, 7), (2, 5, 7), (3, 4, 7)

$\therefore$ Number of triangles formed $= {}^6C_3 - 7 = 13$

43. ***(a)*** Number of new lines formed

$$= \frac{n(n-1)(n-2)(n-3)}{8} = \frac{10\times 9\times 8\times 7}{8} = 630$$

44. ***(d)*** I. The number of ways of dividing 12 objects in 3 equal groups $= \dfrac{12!}{(4!)^3\times 3!}$

So, Statement I is false.

II. The number of ways in which 52 cards distributed among 4 players $= \dfrac{(52)!}{(13!)^4}$

So, Statement II is false.

45. ***(c)*** Given, ${}^nC_4$, ${}^nC_5$ and ${}^nC_6$ are in AP.

$\because \quad 2b = a + c \quad [\therefore 2\times {}^nC_5 = {}^nC_4 + {}^nC_6]$

$$\Rightarrow \frac{2(n!)}{5!(n-5)!} = \frac{n!}{4!(n-4)!} + \frac{n!}{6!(n-6)!}$$

$$\Rightarrow \frac{2n!}{5\cdot 4!(n-5)(n-6)!} = \frac{n!}{4!(n-6)!}\cdot\left[\frac{1}{(n-4)(n-5)} + \frac{1}{6\times 5}\right]$$

$$\Rightarrow \frac{2}{5(n-5)} = \frac{30+n^2-9n+20}{6\times 5(n-4)(n-5)}$$

$$\Rightarrow 12(n-4) = n^2 - 9n + 50$$

$$\Rightarrow n^2 - 21n + 98 = 0 \Rightarrow (n-7)(n-14) = 0$$

$$\Rightarrow n = 7, 14$$

46. ***(d)*** We have, $n = {}^mC_2 = \dfrac{m(m-1)}{2}$

$$\therefore {}^nC_2 = \frac{n(n-1)}{2} = \frac{m(m-1)}{4}\left(\frac{m(m-1)}{2} - 1\right)$$

$$= \frac{m(m-1)}{8}(m^2-m-2) = \frac{m(m-1)(m+1)(m-2)}{8}$$

$$= \frac{(m+1)(m)(m-1)(m-2)}{8}$$

$$= 3\frac{(m+1)(m)(m-1)(m-2)}{24}$$

$$= \frac{3(m+1)(m)(m-1)(m-2)(m-3)!}{(m-3)!\,4!} \quad [\because 4! = 24]$$

$$= 3\,{}^{m+1}C_4$$

47. ***(d)*** **Assertion** There are 11 letters in word 'ASSOCIATION' in which 2 S's, 2 O's, 2 A's and 2 I's occur.

Now, the arrangement of 2A, 2 O, T, N, C and 2S's can be done in $\dfrac{8!}{2!2!}$ ways.

Now, there are 9 places in which we can arrange 2 I's.

$\therefore$ Arrangement of 2I's is at 9 places in ${}^9C_2$.

$\therefore$ Total arrangement of letters when, 2S's come together and 2 I's is are not come together is $\dfrac{8!}{2!\,2!}\times {}^9C_2$.

Hence, Assertion is false.

48. ***(a)*** Reason is true, ${}^nC_{r-1} + {}^nC_r = {}^{n+1}C_r$

Assertion We have, ${}^{47}C_4 + \sum_{i=1}^{5} {}^{52-i}C_3$

$$= {}^{47}C_4 + {}^{51}C_3 + {}^{50}C_3 + {}^{49}C_3 + {}^{48}C_3 + {}^{47}C_3$$

$$= {}^{47}C_3 + {}^{47}C_4 + {}^{48}C_3 + {}^{49}C_3 + {}^{50}C_3 + {}^{51}C_3$$

$${}^{48}C_4 + {}^{48}C_3 + {}^{49}C_3 + {}^{50}C_3 + {}^{51}C_3$$

$$= {}^{49}C_4 + {}^{49}C_3 + {}^{50}C_3 + {}^{51}C_3$$

$$= {}^{50}C_4 + {}^{50}C_3 + {}^{51}C_3 = {}^{51}C_4 + {}^{51}C_3 = {}^{52}C_4$$

$\therefore$ Assertion and Reason both are true and Reason is correct explanation of Assertion.

49. ***(b)*** When there is no restriction, we can use all 10 digits. So, the number of different telephone number in each zone

$$= 10\times 10\times 10\times 10\times 10\times 10 = 10^6$$

As the city is divided into 6 zones, so the number of different telephone numbers in the city

$$= 6\times 10^6$$

50. ***(a)*** Since, first two digits of different zone are already fixed.

So, the remaining 5 places can be filled in

$= 10\times 10\times 10\times 10\times 10 = 10^5$ ways

$\therefore$ The number of different telephone number in the city $= 6\times 10^5$

51. ***(d)*** First place is already filled will a specific non-zero digit.

So, we are left with 9 different digits.

Remaining 6 places with different digits can be filled in ${}^9P_6$ ways.

So, the number different telephone number in each zone $= {}^9P_6$

Chapter 7 Binomial Theorem

1. *(c)* The number of terms in the expansion $(2x + 3y - 4z)^n$ is

$${}^{n+3-1}C_{3-1} = {}^{n+2}C_2 = \frac{(n+2)(n+1)}{2}$$

2. *(c)*

3. *(a)*

4. *(d)* $(\sqrt{2}+1)^{2n} = {}^{2n}C_0(\sqrt{2})^{2n} + {}^{2n}C_1(\sqrt{2})^{2n-1} + {}^{2n}C_2(\sqrt{2})^{2n-2} + \ldots + {}^{2n}C_{2n}(1)^{2n} \quad \ldots(i)$

$(\sqrt{2}-1)^{2n} = {}^{2n}C_0(\sqrt{2})^{2n} - {}^{2n}C_1(\sqrt{2})^{2n-1} + {}^{2n}C_2(\sqrt{2})^{2n-2} - \ldots + {}^{2n}C_{2n}(-1)^{2n} \quad \ldots(ii)$

On subtracting Eq. (ii) from Eq. (i), we get

$$(\sqrt{2}+1)^{2n} - (\sqrt{2}-1)^{2n} = 2[{}^{2n}C_1(\sqrt{2})^{2n-1} + {}^{2n}C_3(\sqrt{2})^{2n-3} + {}^{2n}C_5(\sqrt{2})^{2n-5} + \ldots]$$

All the powers of $\sqrt{2}$ are odd, so it is irrational number.

5. *(c)* $(x+a)^n = {}^nC_0 x^n + {}^nC_1 x^{n-1}a + {}^nC_2 x^{n-2}a^2 + \ldots + {}^nC_n a^n$

$A = {}^nC_0 x^n + {}^nC_2 x^{n-2}a^2 + {}^nC_4 x^{n-4}a^4 + \ldots$

$B = {}^nC_1 x^{n-1}a + {}^nC_3 x^{n-3}a^3 + {}^nC_5 x^{n-5}a^5 + \ldots$

$\therefore 4AB = (A+B)^2 - (A-B)^2$

$= [(x+a)^n]^2 - [(x-a)^n]^2$

$= (x+a)^{2n} - (x-a)^{2n}$

6. *(c)*

7. *(c)* $\frac{1}{(1!)(n-1)!} + \frac{1}{(3!)(n-3)!} + \frac{1}{(5!)(n-5)!} + \ldots$

$$= \frac{1}{n!}\left[\frac{n!}{(1!)(n-1)!} + \frac{n!}{(3!)(n-3)!} + \frac{n!}{(5!)(n-5)!} + \ldots\right]$$

$$= \frac{1}{n!}[{}^nC_1 + {}^nC_3 + {}^nC_5 + \ldots] = \frac{1}{n!}(2^{n-1}) = \frac{2^{n-1}}{n!}$$

8. *(b)*

9. *(b)* $(1+x)^n = \sum_{r=0}^{n} {}^nC_r \cdot x^r$

Put $x = -1$ both sides, we get

$$(1-1)^n = \sum_{r=0}^{n} {}^nC_r(-1)^r$$

$$\therefore \sum_{r=0}^{n} {}^nC_r(-1)^r = 0$$

10. *(b)* We know, $(1+x)^{13} = {}^{13}C_0 + {}^{13}C_1 x + {}^{13}C_2 x^2 + {}^{13}C_3 x^3 \ldots + {}^{13}C_{13}x^{13}$

Put $x = 1$ both sides, we get

$$2^{13} = 1 + {}^{13}C_1 + {}^{13}C_2 + {}^{13}C_3 + {}^{13}C_4 + \ldots\ldots {}^{13}C_{13}$$

$$\Rightarrow {}^{13}C_2 + {}^{13}C_3 + {}^{13}C_4 \ldots\ldots + {}^{13}C_{13} = 2^{13} - 1 - 13 = 2^{13} - 14$$

11. *(c)* $\sum_{r=1}^{n} r \cdot {}^nC_r = \sum_{r=1}^{n} r\frac{n}{r}\,{}^{n-1}C_{r-1}$ $\quad\left[\because {}^nC_r = \frac{n}{r}\,{}^{n-1}C_{r-1}\right]$

$= \sum_{r=1}^{n} n\,{}^{n-1}C_{r-1}$

$= n\sum_{r=1}^{n} {}^{n-1}C_{r-1}$

$= n \cdot 2^{n-1}$ $\quad\left[\because \sum_{r=1}^{n} {}^{n-1}C_{r-1} = 2^{n-1}\right]$

12. *(a)*

13. *(d)* We have, $7^{103} = 7(7)^{102} = 7(49)^{51}$

$= 7(50-1)^{51}$

$= 7(50K - 1)$, where K is positive integer.

$= 7 \times 25 \times 2K - 7$

$= 25m - 7 - 18 + 18$, where m is positive integer.

$= 25m - 25 + 18 = 25(m-1) + 18$

$\therefore 7^{103}$ is divided by 25 remainder is 18.

14. *(a)* $8^{2n} - (62)^{2n+1} = (9-1)^{2n} - (63-1)^{2n+1}$

$= [({}^{2n}C_0 9^{2n} + {}^{2n}C_1 9^{2n-1}(-1) + \ldots + {}^{2n}C_{2n-1} 9(-1)^{2n-1} + 1) - ({}^{2n+1}C_0(63)^{2n+1} - {}^{2n+1}C_1(63)^{2n} + \ldots + {}^{2n+1}C_{2n}(63) - 1)]$

All the terms are divisible by 9 except last term in both expansions.

$\therefore$ Remainder $= 1 - (-1) = 2$

15. *(c)** **16.** *(c)* **17.** *(c)*

18. *(c)* $\left(x^2+\frac{3}{x}\right)^4 = x^8 + 4\times(x^2)^3\left(\frac{3}{x}\right)$

$$+ 6(x^2)^2\left(\frac{3}{x}\right)^2 + 4x^2\left(\frac{3}{x}\right)^3 + \left(\frac{3}{x}\right)^4$$

$$= x^8 + 12x^5 + 54x^2 + \frac{108}{x} + \frac{81}{x^4}$$

19. *(c)* $(101)^{50} = (100+1)^{50} = 100^{50} + {}^{50}C_1 100^{49}$

$$+ {}^{50}C_2 100^{48} + \ldots + 1 \quad \ldots \text{(i)}$$

and $(99)^{50} = (100-1)^{50}$

$$= 100^{50} - {}^{50}C_1 100^{49} + {}^{50}C_2\, 100^{48} \ldots + 1 \ldots \text{(ii)}$$

Subtracting Eq. (ii) from Eq. (i), we get

$(101)^{50} - (99)^{50} = 2({}^{50}C_1 100^{49} + {}^{50}C_3 100^{47} \ldots\ldots)$

$$= 10\times 100^{49} + \text{ a positive number}$$

$$= 100^{50} + \text{a positive number} > 100^{50}$$

$\therefore (101)^{50} - (99)^{50} > (100)^{50}$

$\Rightarrow (101)^{50} > (100)^{50} + (99)^{50}$

$\Rightarrow (100)^{50} + (99)^{50} < (101)^{50}$

20. *(b)*

21. *(d)* $(27)^{999} = (28-1)^{999}$

$$= 28^{999} - {}^{999}C_1 28^{998} \ldots\ldots + (-1)^{999}$$

$$= 28 \text{ (integer)} - 1$$

$$= 7\lambda - 7 + 6 = 7(\lambda - 1) + 6$$

$\therefore$ Remainder $= 6$

22. *(d)* **23.** *(b)*

24. *(c)* $\sum_{k=1}^{12} {}^{24}C_k = {}^{24}C_1 + {}^{24}C_2 + {}^{24}C_3 + \ldots + {}^{24}C_{12}$

$\because (1+x)^{24} = {}^{24}C_0 + {}^{24}C_1 x + {}^{24}C_2 x^2 + \ldots + {}^{24}C_{24} x^{24}$

On putting $x = 1$, we get

$$2^{24} = {}^{24}C_0 + {}^{24}C_1 + {}^{24}C_2 + \ldots + {}^{24}C_{11} + {}^{24}C_{12} + \ldots + {}^{24}C_{24}$$

$\Rightarrow 2^{24} = 2({}^{24}C_0 + {}^{24}C_1 + {}^{24}C_2 + \ldots + {}^{24}C_{12}) - {}^{24}C_{12}$

$\Rightarrow {}^{24}C_0 + {}^{24}C_1 + {}^{24}C_2 + \ldots + {}^{24}C_{12} = \frac{2^{24}}{2} + \frac{1}{2}\,{}^{24}C_{12}$

$\Rightarrow {}^{24}C_1 + {}^{24}C_2 + \ldots + {}^{24}C_{12} = 2^{23} + \frac{1}{2}\cdot {}^{24}C_{12} - 1$

25. *(b)* $\because {}^nC_0 x + {}^nC_1 \frac{x^2}{2} + {}^nC_2 \frac{x^3}{3} + \ldots + {}^nC_n \frac{x^{n+1}}{n+1}$

$$= \frac{(1+x)^{n+1}}{n+1}$$

On putting $x = 2$, we get

$$2^1\cdot {}^nC_0 + 2^2\cdot\frac{{}^nC_1}{2} + 2^3\cdot\frac{{}^nC_2}{3} + \ldots + 2^{n+1}\cdot\frac{{}^nC_n}{n+1} = \frac{3^{n+1}}{n+1}$$

26. *(c)* Given, $1 + a_1 x + a_2 x^2 + \ldots + a_{12} x^{12}$

$$= (1 + x - 2x^2)^6 \quad \ldots\text{(i)}$$

On putting $x = 1$ in Eq. (i), we get

$$1 + a_1 + a_2 + a_3 + \ldots + a_{12} = 0$$

$\Rightarrow \quad a_1 + a_2 + a_3 + \ldots + a_{12} = -1 \quad \ldots$(ii)

On putting $x = -1$ in Eq. (i), we get

$$1 - a_1 + a_2 - a_3 + \ldots + a_{12} = 64$$

$\Rightarrow \quad -a_1 + a_2 - a_3 + \ldots + a_{12} = 63 \quad \ldots$(iii)

On adding Eqs. (ii) and (iii), we get

$$2(a_2 + a_4 + a_6 + \ldots + a_{12}) = 62$$

$\Rightarrow \quad a_2 + a_4 + a_6 + \ldots + a_{12} = 31$

27. *(b)* We have,

$(1 + x + x^2)^n = a_0 + a_1 x + a_2 x^2 + \ldots + a_{2n} x^{2n} \quad \ldots$(i)

On putting $x = 1$, we get

$$3^n = a_0 + a_1 + a_2 + a_3 + \ldots + a_{2n}$$

$$3^n = (a_0 + a_{2n} + a_1 + a_{2n-1} + a_2 + a_{2n-2} + a_{n-1} + a_{n+1} \ldots) + a_n$$

$\Rightarrow 3^n = 2(a_0 + a_1 + a_2 + \ldots + a_{n-1}) + a_n$

$[\because a_0 = a_{2n} \text{ and } a_1 = a_{2n-1}]$

Hence, $2(a_0 + a_1 + a_2 \ldots + a_{n-1}) + a_n = 3^n$

28. *(a)* On putting $x = -\frac{1}{x}$ in place of x in Eq. (i), we get

$$\left(1 - \frac{1}{x} + \frac{1}{x^2}\right)^n = a_0 - \frac{a_1}{x} + \frac{a_2}{x^2} - \frac{a_3}{x^3} \ldots + \frac{a_{2n}}{x^{2n}}$$

$\Rightarrow (x^2 - x + 1)^n = a_0 x^{2n} - a_1 x^{2n-1} + \ldots + a_{2n} \ldots$ (ii)

On multiplying Eqs. (i) and (ii), we get

$(1 + x^2 + x^4)^n = (a_0 + a_1 x + a_2 x^2 + \ldots + a_{2n} x^{2n})(a_0 x^{2n} - a_1 x^{2n-1} \ldots + a_{2n})$

Coefficient of $x^{2n} = a_0^2 - a_1^2 + a_2^2 \ldots + a_{2n}^2$

On putting x^2 in place of x in Eq. (i), we get

$(1 + x^2 + x^4)^n = a_0 + a_1 x^2 + a_2 x^4 + \ldots a_{2n} x^{4n}$

Coefficient of x^{2n} in $(1 + x^2 + x^4)^n$ is a_n.

On equating the coefficient of x^{2n}, we get

$a_0^2 - a_1^2 + a_2^2 - a_3^2 \ldots + a_{2n}^2 = a_n$

Hence, $K = 1$

Chapter 8 Sequence and Series

1. *(c)* We have, $(\alpha^2+\beta^2)^2=(\alpha+\beta)(\alpha^3+\beta^3)$

$$\Rightarrow \alpha^4+\beta^4+2\alpha^2\beta^2=\alpha^4+\alpha\beta^3+\beta\alpha^3+\beta^4$$

$$\Rightarrow \alpha\beta(\alpha^2+\beta^2-2\alpha\beta)=0$$

$$\Rightarrow \alpha\beta\{(\alpha+\beta)^2-4\alpha\beta\}=0$$

$$\Rightarrow \frac{c}{a}\left\{\frac{b^2}{a^2}-\frac{4c}{a}\right\}=0$$

$$\Rightarrow c(b^2-4ac)=0\Rightarrow c\Delta=0$$

2. *(d)* Since $x, 2x+2, 3x+3, \ldots$ are in GP

$$\therefore \frac{2x+2}{x}=\frac{3x+3}{2x+2}=r(x\neq-1)$$

$$\therefore r=3/2$$

and $\frac{2x+2}{x}=\frac{3}{2}$

$$\therefore x=-4$$

Then next term $=r(3x+3)$

$$=\frac{3}{2}(-12+3)$$

$$=-13.5$$

3. *(b)* Let first term be A and common ratio be R.

Given, pth term, $T_p=q$ and qth term, $T_q=p$

$$AR^{p-1}=q \text{ and } AR^{q-1}=p \quad \ldots(i)$$

$$\therefore \frac{AR^{p-1}}{AR^{q-1}}=\frac{q}{p}$$

$$\Rightarrow R^{p-q}=\frac{q}{p}\Rightarrow R=\left(\frac{q}{p}\right)^{\frac{1}{p-q}}$$

On putting the value of R in Eq. (i), we get

$$A\cdot\left(\frac{q}{p}\right)^{\frac{p-1}{p-q}}=q\Rightarrow A=q\cdot\left(\frac{p}{q}\right)^{\frac{p-1}{p-q}}$$

Now, $(p+q)$th term, $T_{p+q}=AR^{p+q-1}$

$$=q\cdot\left(\frac{p}{q}\right)^{\frac{p-1}{p-q}}\times\left(\frac{q}{p}\right)^{\frac{p+q-1}{p-q}}$$

$$=\frac{q^{1-\frac{p-1}{p-q}+\frac{p+q-1}{p-q}}}{p^{\frac{p+q-1}{p-q}-\frac{p-1}{p-q}}}$$

$$=\frac{q^{\frac{p-q-p+1+p+q-1}{p-q}}}{p^{\frac{p+q-1-p+1}{p-q}}}$$

$$=\frac{q^{\frac{p}{p-q}}}{p^{\frac{q}{p-q}}}=\left(\frac{q^p}{p^q}\right)^{\frac{1}{p-q}}$$

4. *(b)* We have,

$$(a^2+b^2+c^2)p^2-2(ab+bc+cd)p+(b^2+c^2+d^2)\le 0 \quad \ldots(i)$$

$$\text{LHS}=(a^2p^2-2abp+b^2)+(b^2p^2-2bcp+c^2)+(c^2p^2-2cdp+d^2)$$

$$=(ap-b)^2+(bp-c)^2+(cp-d)^2\ge 0 \quad \ldots(ii)$$

Since, the sum of squares of real number is non-negative.

From Eqs. (i) and (ii), we get

$$(ap-b)^2+(bp-c)^2+(cp-d)^2=0$$

$$\Rightarrow ap-b=0=bp-c=cp-d$$

$$\Rightarrow \frac{b}{a}=\frac{c}{b}=\frac{d}{c}=p$$

$\therefore a, b, c$ and d are in GP.

5. *(a)* Let a be the first term and r be the common ratio of GP.

$$\Rightarrow ar+ar^5=\frac{25}{2}$$

$$\Rightarrow ar^2\times ar^4=25$$

$$\Rightarrow a^2r^6=25$$

$$\Rightarrow ar^3=5$$

$$\Rightarrow a=\frac{5}{r^3}$$

$$\Rightarrow \frac{5r}{r^3}+\frac{5r^5}{r^3}=\frac{25}{2}$$

$$\Rightarrow \frac{1}{r^2}+r^2=\frac{5}{2}$$

Put $r^2=t$

$$\Rightarrow \quad \frac{t^2+1}{t} = \frac{5}{2}$$

$$\Rightarrow \quad 2t^2 - 5t + 2 = 0$$

$$\Rightarrow \quad 2t^2 - 4t - t + 2 = 0$$

$$\Rightarrow \quad (2t-1)(t-2) = 0$$

$$\Rightarrow \quad t = \frac{1}{2}, 2 \Rightarrow r^2 = \frac{1}{2}, 2$$

$$\Rightarrow \quad r = \sqrt{2}$$

$$= ar^3 + ar^5 + ar^7$$

$$= ar^3(1 + r^2 + r^4)$$

$$= 5[1 + 2 + 4] = 35$$

6. *(b)* Let the first term and common ratio of the GP be a and r respectively, so according to the given information

$$ar + ar^2 + ar^3 = 3 \quad \ldots\text{(i)}$$

and $$ar^5 + ar^6 + ar^7 = 243 \quad \ldots\text{(ii)}$$

From Eqs. (i) and (ii), we get

$$\therefore \quad r^4 = 81 \Rightarrow r = 3$$

[$\because$ terms are positive]

$$\therefore \ 3a + 9a + 27a = 3$$

$$\Rightarrow \quad a + 3a + 9a = 1 \Rightarrow a = \frac{1}{13}$$

$\therefore$ Sum of first 50 terms of the GP be

$$S_{50} = \frac{1}{13}\frac{(3^{50}-1)}{3-1} = \frac{1}{26}(3^{50}-1)$$

7. *(c)* $$s = 1 + \frac{2}{3} + \frac{7}{3^2} + \frac{12}{3^3} + \frac{17}{3^4} + \frac{22}{3^5} + \ldots \infty$$

$$\frac{s}{3} = \frac{1}{3} + \frac{2}{3^2} + \frac{7}{3^3} + \ldots\ldots \infty$$

$$\frac{2s}{3} = 1 + \frac{1}{3} + \frac{5}{3^2} + \frac{5}{3^3} + \ldots\ldots \infty$$

$$\frac{2s}{3} = \frac{4}{3} + \frac{5}{3}\left[\frac{1/3}{1-\frac{1}{3}}\right] = \frac{5}{6} + \frac{4}{3} = \frac{13}{6}$$

$$s = \frac{13}{4}$$

8. *(c)* As we know, sum of infinite terms of GP,

$$S_\infty = \begin{cases} \dfrac{a}{1-r}, & |r|<1 \\ \infty, & |r|\geq 1 \end{cases}$$

$$\therefore \quad S_\infty = \frac{x}{1-r} = 5 \quad [\text{thus } |r|<1]$$

$$\Rightarrow \quad 1 - r = \frac{x}{5}$$

$$\Rightarrow \quad r = \frac{5-x}{5} \text{ exists only when } |r|<1$$

$$\Rightarrow \quad -1 < \frac{5-x}{5} < 1$$

$$\therefore \quad -10 < -x < 0 \Rightarrow 0 < x < 10$$

9. *(d)* Given, $\sum_{n=0}^{\infty} r^n = S$

$$\Rightarrow \quad 1 + r + r^2 + \ldots\infty = S \Rightarrow \frac{1}{1-r} = S$$

$$\Rightarrow \quad 1 = S - rS \Rightarrow r = \frac{S-1}{S}$$

Now, $$\sum_{n=0}^{\infty} r^{2n} = 1 + r^2 + r^4 + \ldots\infty$$

$$= \frac{1}{1-r^2} = \frac{1}{1-\left(\frac{S-1}{S}\right)^2}$$

$$= \frac{S^2}{S^2-(S-1)^2}$$

$$= \frac{S^2}{(S-S+1)(S+S-1)}$$

$$= \frac{S^2}{(2S-1)}$$

10. *(c)* Given, sum

$$= (x+2)^{n-1}\left\{1 + \left(\frac{x+1}{x+2}\right) + \left(\frac{x+1}{x+2}\right)^2 + \ldots + \left(\frac{x+1}{x+2}\right)^{n-1}\right\}$$

$$= (x+2)^{n-1}\left\{\frac{1-\left(\frac{x+1}{x+2}\right)^n}{1-\left(\frac{x+1}{x+2}\right)}\right\}$$

$$= \frac{(x+2)^{n-1}\{(x+2)^n - (x+1)^n\}\cdot(x+2)}{(x+2)^n}$$

$$= (x+2)^n - (x+1)^n$$

11. ***(b)*** $\underbrace{(666\ldots6)}_{n \text{ digits}}$

$$= 6 + 6\times10 + 6\times10^2 + \ldots + 6\times10^{n-1}$$

$$= 6(1 + 10 + 10^2 + \ldots + 10^{n-1})$$

$$= \frac{6}{9}(10^n - 1) = \frac{2}{3}(10^n - 1)$$

Similarly, $\underbrace{(888\ldots8)}_{n \text{ digits}} = \frac{8}{9}(10^n - 1)$

Hence, required sum $= \frac{4}{9}(10^n - 1)^2 + \frac{8}{9}(10^n - 1)$

$$= \frac{4}{9}(10^{2n} - 2\cdot10^n + 1 + 2\cdot10^n - 2)$$

$$= \frac{4}{9}(10^{2n} - 1)$$

12. ***(d)*** Since, each term is equal to the sum of two preceding terms.

$\therefore \quad ar^{n-1} = ar^n + ar^{n+1}$

$\Rightarrow \quad \frac{1}{r} = 1 + r \Rightarrow r^2 + r - 1 = 0$

$\therefore \quad r = \frac{\sqrt{5}-1}{2} \quad \left[\because r \neq \frac{-\sqrt{5}-1}{2}\right]$

13. ***(a)*** Let $\frac{A}{R}$, A, AR be the roots of the equation $px^3 + qx^2 + rx + s = 0$.

$\therefore \quad \left(\frac{A}{R}\right)\cdot(A)(AR) = -\frac{s}{p}$

$$A^3 = \frac{-s}{p}$$

$\Rightarrow \quad A = \left(-\frac{s}{p}\right)^{\frac{1}{3}}$

$\because$ A is a root.

$\Rightarrow \quad p\left(-\frac{s}{p}\right) + q\left(-\frac{s}{p}\right)^{\frac{2}{3}} + r\left(-\frac{s}{p}\right)^{\frac{1}{3}} + s = 0$

$\Rightarrow \quad q\left(-\frac{s}{p}\right)^{\frac{2}{3}} = r\left(\frac{s}{p}\right)^{\frac{1}{3}}$

Taking cube both sides,

$$q^3\frac{s^2}{p^2} = r^3\frac{s}{p}$$

$\Rightarrow \quad q^3 s = r^3 p$

14. ***(b)*** Given, $a_1 < 0$,

$$a_1 + a_2 = 4 \text{ and } a_3 + a_4 = 16$$

Let first term $= a$ and common ratio $= r$

Then $\quad a + ar = 4$ and $ar^2 + ar^3 = 16$

$\Rightarrow \quad a(1 + r) = 4$ and $ar^2(1 + r) = 16$

$\Rightarrow \quad r^2 = 4$

$\Rightarrow \quad r = \pm 2$

If $\quad r = 2$, then

$$a(1 + r) = 4 \Rightarrow a = \frac{4}{3} > 0$$

$\therefore \quad r \neq 2$

If $\quad r = -2$, then

$$a(1 + r) = 4 \Rightarrow a = -4 < 0$$

Sum of first nine terms $= 4k$

$\Rightarrow \quad \frac{(-4)[(-2)^9 - 1]}{-2-1} = 4k$

$\Rightarrow \quad 4\left(-\frac{513}{3}\right) = 4k \Rightarrow k = -171$

15. ***(d)*** $\sum_{n=1}^{100} T_{2n+1} = 200$

$\Rightarrow T_3 + T_5 + T_7 + \ldots + T_{201} = 200$

$\Rightarrow \quad ar^2\left(\frac{r^{200}-1}{r^2-1}\right) = 200 \quad \ldots\text{(i)}$

and $\quad \sum_{n=1}^{100} T_{2n} = 100$

$\Rightarrow T_2 + T_4 + T_6 + \ldots + T_{200} = 100$

$\Rightarrow \quad ar\frac{(r^{200}-1)}{r^2-1} = 100 \quad \ldots\text{(ii)}$

On dividing Eq. (i) by Eq. (ii), we get

$$r = 2$$

On adding both given series, we get

$$T_2 + T_3 + T_4 + \ldots + T_{200} + T_{201} = 300$$

$\Rightarrow \quad r(T_1 + T_2 + T_3 + \ldots + T_{200}) = 300$

$\Rightarrow \quad \sum_{n=1}^{200} T_n = \frac{300}{2} = 150$

16. ***(c)*** Let $a =$ first term, $r =$ common ratio

Given, $T_n = T_{n+1} + T_{n+2}$

$\Rightarrow \quad ar^{n-1} = ar^n + ar^{n+1}$

$\Rightarrow \quad r^{n-1} - r^n - r^{n+1} = 0$

$\Rightarrow \quad r^{n-1}(1 - r - r^2) = 0$

$\Rightarrow \quad r^2 + r - 1 = 0$

$$\Rightarrow \quad r = \frac{\sqrt{5}-1}{2} = 2\sin 18°$$

$$\left[\text{neglecting, } r = \frac{1-\sqrt{5}}{2}\right]$$

17. *(c)* We have, $\frac{a}{1-r} = p$

[sum of infinite series of GP]

and $\frac{a^2}{1-r^2} = \frac{a}{1-r} \cdot \frac{a}{1+r} = q$

$$\Rightarrow \quad q = p \cdot \frac{a}{1+r} = p \cdot \frac{p(1-r)}{1+r}$$

$$\Rightarrow \quad \frac{q}{p^2} = \frac{1-r}{1+r}$$

$$\Rightarrow \quad \frac{p^2}{q} = \frac{1+r}{1-r} \Rightarrow \frac{p^2}{q}(1-r) = 1+r$$

$$\Rightarrow r\left[1 + \frac{p^2}{q}\right] = -1 + \frac{p^2}{q} \Rightarrow r = \frac{p^2-q}{p^2+q}$$

18. *(c)* $\because \alpha, \beta, \gamma, \delta$ are in GP.

Let $\alpha = A, \beta = Ar, \gamma = Ar^2, \delta = Ar^3$

$\because$ α and β are the roots of the equation $x^2 - 3x + a = 0$, then

$$\alpha + \beta = 3 \Rightarrow A(1+r) = 3 \quad \text{... (i)}$$

γ and δ are the roots of the equation $x^2 - 12x + b = 0$, then

$$\gamma + \delta = 12$$

$$\Rightarrow \quad Ar^2(1+r) = 12 \quad \text{... (ii)}$$

On solving Eqs. (i) and (ii), we get

$$A = 1, r = 2$$

$$\Rightarrow \quad \alpha = 1, \beta = 2, \gamma = 4, \delta = 8$$

$$\therefore \quad a = \alpha\beta = 1 \times 2 = 2$$

and $b = \gamma\delta = 4 \times 8 = 32$

19. *(c)* Given equation,

$$(a^2 + b^2 + c^2)p^2 - 2(ab + bc + cd)p + (b^2 + c^2 + d^2) = 0$$

$$\Rightarrow (a^2p^2 - 2apb + b^2) + (b^2p^2 - 2bpc + c^2) + (c^2p^2 - 2cpd + d^2) = 0$$

$$\Rightarrow \quad (ap-b)^2 + (bp-c)^2 + (cp-d)^2 = 0$$

$$\Rightarrow \quad ap - b = 0 = bp - c = cp - d$$

$$\Rightarrow \quad p = \frac{b}{a} = \frac{c}{b} = \frac{d}{c}$$

$\Rightarrow$ a, b, c, d are in GP.

20. *(d)* Let r be the common ratio of given GP, then we have the following sequence

$$a_1, a_2 = a_1r, a_3 = a_1r^2, \ldots, a_{10} = a_1r^9$$

Now, $a_3 = 25\, a_1$

$$\Rightarrow \quad a_1r^2 = 25a_1 \Rightarrow r^2 = 25$$

Consider, $\frac{a_9}{a_5} = \frac{a_1r^8}{a_1r^4} = r^4 = (25)^2 = 5^4$

21. *(a)* Let r be the common ratio.

$$\therefore \quad \frac{\sum_{n=1}^{100} a_{2n}}{\sum_{n=1}^{100} a_{2n-1}} = \frac{a_2 + a_4 + a_6 + \ldots + a_{200}}{a_1 + a_3 + a_5 + \ldots + a_{199}}$$

$$= \frac{a_1(r + r^3 + r^5 + \ldots + r^{199})}{a_1(1 + r^2 + r^4 + \ldots + r^{198})} = r$$

$$\Rightarrow \quad \frac{\alpha}{\beta} = r$$

22. *(c)* LHS $= \frac{1(1-\lambda^{n+1})}{1-\lambda} = \frac{1-\lambda^{n+1}}{1-\lambda}$

and RHS $= (1+\lambda)(1+\lambda^2)(1+\lambda^4)(1+\lambda^8)(1+\lambda^{16})$

$$= \frac{(1-\lambda)(1+\lambda)(1+\lambda^2)(1+\lambda^4)(1+\lambda^8)(1+\lambda^{16})}{(1-\lambda)}$$

$$= \frac{(1-\lambda^2)(1+\lambda^2)(1+\lambda^4)(1+\lambda^8)(1+\lambda^{16})}{1-\lambda}$$

$$= \frac{(1-\lambda^{32})}{1-\lambda}$$

$$\therefore \quad \frac{1-\lambda^{n+1}}{1-\lambda} = \frac{1-\lambda^{32}}{1-\lambda}$$

$$\Rightarrow \quad 1-\lambda^{n+1} = 1-\lambda^{32}$$

$$\therefore \quad n+1 = 32$$

$$\Rightarrow \quad n = 31$$

23. *(c)* $S_{10} = 0.7 + 0.77 + 0.777 + \ldots + 10 \text{ terms}$

$$= \frac{7}{9}[0.9 + 0.99 + 0.999 + \ldots + 10 \text{ terms}]$$

$$= \frac{7}{9}[(1 + 1 + 1 + \ldots 10 \text{ terms}) - (0.1 + 0.01 + 0.001 + \ldots + 10 \text{ terms})]$$

$$= \frac{7}{9}\left[10 - \left(\frac{1}{10} + \frac{1}{10^2} + \ldots + \frac{1}{10^{10}}\right)\right]$$

$$= \frac{7}{9}\left[10 - \frac{\frac{1}{10}\left(\left(\frac{1}{10}\right)^{10} - 1\right)}{\frac{1}{10} - 1}\right]$$

$$= \frac{7}{9}\left[10 + \frac{1}{9}(10^{-10} - 1)\right]$$

$$= \frac{7}{81}(90 + 10^{-10} - 1) = \frac{7}{81}(89 + 10^{-10})$$

24. *(a)* $S_{20} = 1 + \frac{3}{2} + \frac{7}{4} + \frac{15}{8} + \frac{31}{16} + \ldots$ 20 terms

$$= (2-1) + \left(2 - \frac{1}{2}\right) + \left(2 - \frac{1}{2^2}\right) + \left(2 - \frac{1}{2^3}\right) + \left(2 - \frac{1}{2^4}\right) + \ldots \text{ 20 terms}$$

$$= (2 + 2 + 2 + \ldots + 20 \text{ terms}) - \left(1 + \frac{1}{2} + \frac{1}{2^2} + \frac{1}{2^3} + \ldots + 20 \text{ terms}\right)$$

$$= 40 - \left(\frac{1 - \left(\frac{1}{2}\right)^{20}}{1 - \frac{1}{2}}\right)$$

$$= 40 - 2 + \frac{1}{2^{19}}$$

$$= 38 + \frac{1}{2^{19}}$$

25. *(a)* $2 + \frac{3}{x} + \frac{9}{x^2} + \frac{27}{x^3} + \ldots \infty$

$= 1 + \left(1 + \frac{3}{x} + \frac{9}{x^2} + \frac{27}{x^3} + \ldots \infty\right)$ is finite when common ratio $|r| < 1$

$$\Rightarrow \left|\frac{3}{x}\right| < 1 \Rightarrow |x| > 3$$

26. *(c)* $\frac{1}{3} + \frac{1}{3^2} + \frac{1}{3^3} + \ldots$ upto $\infty = \frac{\frac{1}{3}}{1 - \frac{1}{3}} = \frac{1}{2} = 0.5$

$\therefore \quad x = (0.36)^{\log_{0.25} 0.5}$

$= (0.6)^{2\log_{0.25} 0.5}$

$= (0.6)\log_{0.25}{}^{(0.25)}$

$= 0.6$

27. *(a)*

28. *(c)* $x = 1 - \tan^2\theta + \tan^4\theta \ldots = \frac{1}{1 + \tan^2\theta}$

$x = \cos^2\theta$

$$y = 1 + \cos^2\theta + \cos^4\theta + \ldots = \frac{1}{1 - \cos^2\theta} = \frac{1}{1-x}$$

$\Rightarrow y(1 - x) = 1$

29. *(d)* We have, $1 + \cos\alpha + \cos^2\alpha + \ldots \infty = 2 - \sqrt{2}$

$$\Rightarrow \frac{1}{1 - \cos\alpha} = 2 - \sqrt{2}$$

$$\Rightarrow 1 - \cos\alpha = \frac{1}{2 - \sqrt{2}} = 1 + \frac{1}{\sqrt{2}}$$

$$\Rightarrow \cos\alpha = -\frac{1}{\sqrt{2}} \Rightarrow \alpha = \frac{3\pi}{4}$$

30. *(d)* Let the three terms of GP are $\frac{a}{r}, a, ar$.

As, it is given that $\frac{a}{r} \times a \times ar = 27 \Rightarrow a = 3$

and $S = \frac{a}{r} + a + ar \Rightarrow S = 3\left(\frac{1 + r + r^2}{r}\right)$

$\Rightarrow \quad 3r^2 + (3 - S)r + 3 = 0 \qquad [\because r \neq 0]$

$\because \quad r \in R$

$\therefore \quad D \geq 0 \Rightarrow (3 - S)^2 - 4(3)(3) \geq 0$

$\Rightarrow \quad (3 - S - 6)(3 - S + 6) \geq 0$

$\Rightarrow \quad (S + 3)(S - 9) \geq 0 \Rightarrow S \in (-\infty, -3] \cup [9, \infty)$

31. *(c)* Since, $\quad a + ar = a(1 + r) = 12 \qquad \ldots$(i)

and $\quad ar^2 + ar^3 = ar^2(1 + r) = 48 \qquad \ldots$(ii)

From Eqs. (i) and (ii), we get

$r^2 = 4$

$\Rightarrow \quad r = -2$

[since, the series is alternately sign, so we take negative values]

On putting the value of r in Eq. (i), we get

$a = -12$

32. *(b)* $\sum_{r=1}^{n}\sum_{s=1}^{n} S_{rs} 2^r 3^s = 2 \cdot 3 + 2^2 \cdot 3^2 + 2^3 \cdot 3^3 + \ldots + 2^n \cdot 3^n$

[as $S_{rs} = 0$, if $r \neq s$ and $S_{rs} = 1$, if $r = s$)]

$$= \frac{6(6^n - 1)}{6 - 1} = \frac{6}{5}(6^n - 1)$$

33. *(c)* Since, $n^m + 1$ divides $1 + n + n^2 + \dots + n^{127}$

Therefore, $\dfrac{1 + n + n^2 + \dots + n^{127}}{n^m + 1}$ is an integer.

$\Rightarrow \dfrac{1 - n^{128}}{1 - n} \times \dfrac{1}{n^m + 1}$ is an integer.

$\Rightarrow \dfrac{(1 - n^{64})(1 + n^{64})}{(1 - n)(n^m + 1)}$ is an integer when largest

$m = 64$

34. *(b)* Given, x, y, z are in GP and $a^x = b^y = c^z$

Since, x, y, z are in GP.

$$\Rightarrow \quad y^2 = xz \quad \dots\text{(i)}$$

We have,

$$a^x = b^y = c^z = k \text{ (say)}; k > 0$$

On taking log both sides, we get

$$x \log a = y \log b = z \log c = \log k$$

$$\Rightarrow \quad x = \frac{\log k}{\log a}, y = \frac{\log k}{\log b}, z = \frac{\log k}{\log c}$$

On substituting the values of x, y and z in Eq. (i), we get

$$\left(\frac{\log k}{\log b}\right)^2 = \frac{\log k}{\log a} \cdot \frac{\log k}{\log c}$$

$$\Rightarrow \quad \frac{(\log k)^2}{(\log b)^2} = \frac{(\log k)^2}{\log a \cdot \log c}$$

$$\Rightarrow \quad (\log b)^2 = \log a \cdot \log c$$

$$\Rightarrow \quad \frac{\log a}{\log b} = \frac{\log b}{\log c}$$

$$\therefore \quad \log_b a = \log_c b \quad \left[\because \frac{\log_e x}{\log_e y} = \log_y x\right]$$

35. *(c)* Let r be the common ratio.

If $r \geq 1$, then ar^2 is the greatest term.

$$\therefore \quad ar^2 < a + ar$$

$$\Rightarrow \quad r^2 - r - 1 < 0$$

$$\Rightarrow \quad r = \frac{1 \pm \sqrt{1 + 4}}{2}$$

$$\Rightarrow \quad r = \frac{1 \pm \sqrt{5}}{2}$$

$$\Rightarrow \quad r \in \left(\frac{1 - \sqrt{5}}{2}, \frac{1 + \sqrt{5}}{2}\right)$$

As, $\quad r \geq 1, 1 \leq r < \frac{1}{2}(\sqrt{5} + 1)$

In case, $\quad 0 < r < 1$

$$a < ar + ar^2$$

$$\Rightarrow \quad r^2 + r - 1 > 0$$

$$\Rightarrow \quad r = \frac{-1 \pm \sqrt{5}}{2} \Rightarrow r < -\frac{1}{2}(\sqrt{5} + 1)$$

or $\quad r > \frac{1}{2}(\sqrt{5} - 1)$

As $\quad 0 < r < 1 \Rightarrow \dfrac{\sqrt{5} - 1}{2} < r < 1$

$$\therefore \quad r \in \left(\frac{\sqrt{5} - 1}{2}, \frac{\sqrt{5} + 1}{2}\right)$$

36. *(c)* Given, α_1, β_1 are the roots of the equation

$$x^2 - 6x + p = 0$$

$$\Rightarrow \quad \alpha_1 + \beta_1 = 6 \quad \dots\text{(i)}$$

$$\Rightarrow \quad \alpha_1 \cdot \beta_1 = p \quad \dots\text{(ii)}$$

and α_2, β_2 are the roots of the equation

$$x^2 - 54x + q = 0$$

$$\Rightarrow \quad \alpha_2 + \beta_2 = 54 \quad \dots\text{(iii)}$$

$$\Rightarrow \quad \alpha_2 \cdot \beta_2 = q \quad \dots\text{(iv)}$$

Since, $\alpha_1, \beta_1, \alpha_2, \beta_2$ are in GP.

$$\therefore \quad \alpha_1 = a, \beta_1 = ar, \alpha_2 = ar^2, \beta_2 = ar^3$$

Now, $\quad \alpha_1 + \beta_1 = 6$

$$\therefore \quad a + ar = 6 \quad \dots\text{(v)}$$

and $\quad \alpha_2 + \beta_2 = 54$

$$ar^2 + ar^3 = 54 \quad \dots\text{(vi)}$$

From Eqs. (v) and (vi), we get

$$r^2 = 9 \Rightarrow r = \pm 3$$

$$\because \quad a(1 + r) = 6 \Rightarrow a(1 \pm 3) = 6$$

$$a = -3, 3/2$$

$$q - p = a^2r^5 - a^2r = a^2r(r^4 - 1)$$

$$= \left(\frac{3}{2}\right)^2 (3)(81 - 1)$$

$$= \frac{9}{4} \times 3 \times 80 = 540$$

37. *(c)* $\frac{1}{1^2}+\frac{1}{2^2}+\frac{1}{3^2}+\ldots \text{ upto } \infty=\frac{\pi^2}{6}$

Let $\frac{1}{1^2}+\frac{1}{3^2}+\frac{1}{5^2}+\ldots \text{ upto } \infty = x$

$$\Rightarrow \left(\frac{1}{1^2}+\frac{1}{3^2}+\frac{1}{5^2}+\ldots\right)+\left(\frac{1}{2^2}+\frac{1}{4^2}+\frac{1}{6^2}+\ldots\right)=\frac{\pi^2}{6}$$

$$\Rightarrow x+\frac{1}{2^2}\left(\frac{1}{1^2}+\frac{1}{2^2}+\frac{1}{3^2}+\ldots\right)=\frac{\pi^2}{6}$$

$$\Rightarrow \quad x+\frac{1}{4}\cdot\frac{\pi^2}{6}=\frac{\pi^2}{6}$$

$$\therefore \quad x=\frac{\pi^2}{8}$$

38. *(d)* Given series $=1+\frac{1}{2}+\frac{1}{4}+\frac{1}{8}+\cdots$

Here, $a=1, r=\frac{1}{2}$

$$\therefore \quad S=\frac{1}{1-\frac{1}{2}}=2 \qquad \left[S_\infty=\frac{a}{1-r}\right] \ldots\text{(i)}$$

and $$S_n=\frac{1\left[1-\left(\frac{1}{2}\right)^n\right]}{1-\frac{1}{2}}$$

$$\left[\because S_n=\frac{a(1-r^n)}{1-r}, r<1\right]$$

$$=2\left(1-\frac{1}{2^n}\right) \qquad \ldots\text{(ii)}$$

It is given that $S-S_n<\frac{1}{1000}$

$$\Rightarrow \quad 2-2\left(1-\frac{1}{2^n}\right)<\frac{1}{1000}$$

[from Eqs. (i) and (ii)]

$$\Rightarrow \quad 2-2+\frac{2}{2^n}<\frac{1}{1000}$$

$$\frac{1}{2^{n-1}}<\frac{1}{1000}$$

$$\Rightarrow \quad 2^{n-1}>1000 \quad \left[\because \frac{1}{a}<\frac{1}{b}\Rightarrow a>b\right]$$

$$\Rightarrow \quad n-1\geq 10$$

$$\Rightarrow \quad n\geq 11$$

So, the least value of n is 11.

39. *(a)* Let $S=1+\frac{2}{3}+\frac{6}{3^2}+\frac{10}{3^3}+\frac{14}{3^4}+\ldots$

$$\Rightarrow \quad S-1=\frac{2}{3}+\frac{6}{3^2}+\frac{10}{3^3}+\frac{14}{3^4}+\ldots \qquad \ldots\text{(i)}$$

$$\Rightarrow \quad \frac{S-1}{3}=\frac{2}{3^2}+\frac{6}{3^3}+\frac{10}{3^4}+\frac{14}{3^5}+\ldots \qquad \ldots\text{(ii)}$$

On subtracting Eq. (ii) from Eq. (i), we get

$$\frac{2}{3}(S-1)=\frac{2}{3}+\frac{4}{3^2}+\frac{4}{3^3}+\frac{4}{3^4}+\ldots$$

$$\Rightarrow \quad S-1=1+\frac{2}{3}+\frac{2}{3^2}+\frac{2}{3^3}+\ldots$$

$$\Rightarrow \quad S=2+\frac{\frac{2}{3}}{1-\frac{1}{3}}=2+1=3$$

40. *(b)* Since, 5th term of a GP = 2

$$\therefore \quad ar^4=2 \qquad \ldots\text{(i)}$$

where, a and r are the first term and common ratio of a GP.

Now, required product

$=a\times ar\times ar^2\times ar^3\times ar^4\times ar^5\times ar^6\times ar^7\times ar^8$

$=a^9r^{36}=(ar^4)^9$

$=2^9=512$ [from Eq. (i)]

41. *(a)* $\because$ $\{a_n\}$ be a GP

$\therefore \quad a_1, a_2, a_3, a_4, \ldots, a_n$ are in GP

$$\because \quad \frac{a_4}{a_6}=\frac{1}{4}\Rightarrow\frac{a_1r^3}{a_1r^5}=\frac{1}{4}$$

$$\Rightarrow \quad r^2=4$$

$$\therefore \quad r=\pm 2$$

and $a_2+a_5=216$

$$a_1r+a_1r^4=216$$

$$a_1(r+r^4)=216$$

For $r=2, a_1(2+16)=216$

$\therefore \quad a_1=12$

and for $r=-2, a_1(-2+16)=216$

$$\therefore \quad a_1=\frac{216}{14}=\frac{108}{7}$$

42. *(c)* Since $\sin\theta, \sqrt{2}(\sin\theta+1), 6\sin\theta+6$ are in GP.

$$\therefore \quad 2(\sin\theta+1)^2 = \sin\theta(6\sin\theta+6)$$

$$\Rightarrow \quad 2\sin^2\theta + 4\sin\theta + 2 = 6\sin^2\theta + 6\sin\theta$$

$$\Rightarrow \quad 4\sin^2\theta + 2\sin\theta - 2 = 0$$

$$\Rightarrow \quad 2\sin^2\theta + \sin\theta - 1 = 0$$

$$(\sin\theta+1)(2\sin\theta-1) = 0$$

$$\sin\theta \neq -1,$$

$$\therefore \quad \sin\theta = \frac{1}{2}$$

Then $\frac{1}{2}, \frac{3\sqrt{2}}{2}, 9, \ldots$ are in GP

$$\text{Common ratio} = \frac{\frac{3\sqrt{2}}{2}}{\frac{1}{2}} = 3\sqrt{2}$$

$$\therefore \text{ Fifth term} = \frac{1}{2}(3\sqrt{2})^4 = \frac{324}{2} = 162.$$

43. *(a)* Since, $(0.16)^{\log_{2.5}\left(\frac{1}{3}+\frac{1}{3^2}+\frac{1}{3^3}+\ldots\text{ to }\infty\right)}$

$$= (0.16)^{\log_{2.5}\left(\frac{1/3}{1-1/3}\right)}$$

$$= (0.16)^{\log_{2.5}\left(\frac{1}{2}\right)}$$

$$= \frac{16}{100}^{\log_{2.5}(2)^{-1}}$$

$$= \left(\frac{100}{16}\right)^{\log_{2.5}2}$$

$$= \left(\frac{10}{4}\right)^{2\log_{2.5}2}$$

$$= (2.5)^{\log_{2.5}2^2}$$

$$= 2^2 = 4$$

Hence, answer is 4.

44. *(a)* Let first term and common ratio of given GP. $a_1, a_2, a_3, \ldots$ are $a_1 = a < 0$ and r respectively.

Now, $\quad a_1 + a_2 = 4 \quad$ [given]

$$\Rightarrow \quad a + ar = 4$$

$$\Rightarrow \quad a(1+r) = 4 \quad \ldots(i)$$

$$a_3 + a_4 = 16 \quad \text{[given]}$$

$$\Rightarrow \quad ar^2 + ar^3 = 16$$

$$\Rightarrow \quad ar^2(1+r) = 16 \quad \ldots(ii)$$

From Eqs. (i) and (ii), we get

$$r^2 = 4$$

$$\Rightarrow \quad r = \pm 2 \quad \ldots(iii)$$

From Eqs. (i) and (iii), we get

$a = \frac{4}{3} > 0$ (rejected),

if $r = 2$ and $a = -4 < 0$,

if $r = -2$

$$\text{Now,} \quad \sum_{i=1}^{9} a_i = a_1 + a_2 + a_3 + \ldots\ldots + a_9$$

$$= \frac{-4((-2)^9 - 1)}{-2-1}$$

$$= -\frac{4}{3}(512+1)$$

$$= -\frac{4}{3}(513) = 4\lambda \quad \text{[given]}$$

$$\Rightarrow \quad \lambda = -171$$

45. *(c)* Given product

$$2^{\frac{1}{4}} \cdot 4^{\frac{1}{16}} \cdot 8^{\frac{1}{48}} \cdot 16^{\frac{1}{128}} \ldots \text{ to } \infty$$

$$2^{\frac{1}{4}} \cdot 2^{\frac{2}{16}} \cdot 2^{\frac{3}{48}} \cdot 2^{\frac{4}{128}} \ldots \text{ to } \infty$$

$$= 2^{\left(\frac{1}{4}+\frac{1}{8}+\frac{1}{16}+\frac{1}{32}+\ldots\text{to }\infty\right)}$$

$\because \frac{1}{4}+\frac{1}{8}+\frac{1}{16}+\frac{1}{32}+\ldots$ to ∞ is a GP of infinite terms having first term $\frac{1}{4}$ and common ratio $\frac{1}{2}$.

So, the product is $2^{\left(\frac{1/4}{1-1/2}\right)} = 2^{\left(\frac{1/4}{1/2}\right)} = 2^{1/2}$

Chapter 9 Straight Lines

1. ***(b)*** Let the given lines represent sides *AB*, *BC* and *CD* of a rectangle.

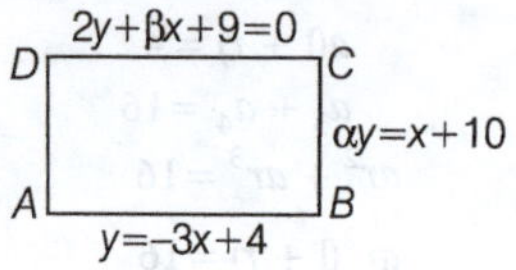

$\therefore AB \parallel CD$ and $AB \perp BC$

$\Rightarrow \quad \frac{-\beta}{2} = -3$ and $\frac{1}{\alpha} \times (-3) = -1$

$\Rightarrow \quad \beta = 6$ and $\alpha = 3$

$\therefore \quad \alpha\beta = 18$

2. ***(c)*** $x - 3y - a = 0, \alpha x + 2y - b = 0,$

$\alpha x + y = c$ form a right angled triangle.

If $x - 3y - a = 0$ and $\alpha x + 2y - b = 0$ are perpendicular, then

$$\frac{1}{3}\left(-\frac{\alpha}{2}\right) = -1 \Rightarrow \alpha = 6$$

If $x - 3y = a$ and $\alpha x + y = c$ are perpendicular, then

$$\frac{1}{3}(-\alpha) = -1 \Rightarrow \alpha = 3$$

$\alpha x + 2y - b = 0$ and $\alpha x + y = c$ can never be perpendicular because

$$\left(-\frac{\alpha}{2}\right)(-\alpha) = -1 \Rightarrow \alpha^2 = -2 \text{ (not possible)}$$

$\therefore \quad \alpha = 6$ or $\alpha = 3$

$\Rightarrow \quad (\alpha - 6)(\alpha - 3) = 0 \Rightarrow \alpha^2 - 9\alpha + 18 = 0$

3. ***(b)*** Point of intersection of given lines is $\left(\frac{12}{7}, \frac{12}{7}\right)$, then required line is

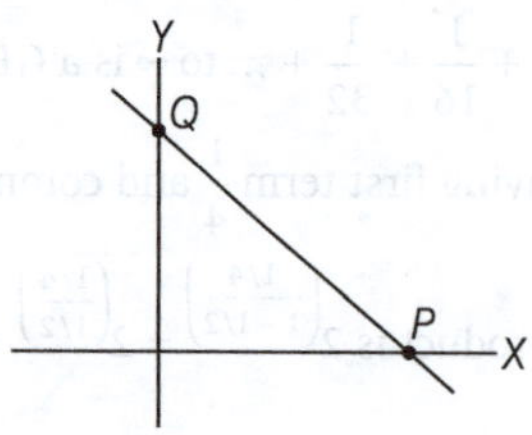

A variable line passes through $\left(\frac{12}{7}, \frac{12}{7}\right)$ and meets the coordinate axes at *P* and *Q*.

Then the equation becomes,

$$y - \frac{12}{7} = m\left(x - \frac{12}{7}\right)$$

Points $P\left\{\frac{12}{7}\left(1 - \frac{1}{m}\right), 0\right\}, Q\left\{0, \frac{12}{7}(1 - m)\right\}$

Coordinates of mid-point of

$$PQ = \left\{\frac{6}{7}\left(1 - \frac{1}{m}\right), \frac{6}{7}(1 - m)\right\}$$

Let $h = \frac{6}{7}\left(1 - \frac{1}{m}\right), k = \frac{6}{7}(1 - m)$

Eliminating *m*, we get

$7hk = 6(h + k) \Rightarrow$ Locus of mid-point of *PQ*.

$7xy = 6(x + y)$

4. ***(c)***

5. ***(d)*** $\alpha x + \beta y + \gamma = 0$ passes through first quadrant.

There can be 3 cases

(i) *x* and *y* are positive

(ii) Only *x* is positive

(iii) Only *y* is positive

$x\text{-intercept} = \frac{-\gamma}{\alpha} = \frac{-\gamma^2}{\alpha\gamma}$

$y\text{-intercept} = \frac{-\gamma}{\beta} = \frac{-\gamma^2}{\beta\gamma}$

For case (i), $\alpha\gamma < 0$ and $\beta\gamma < 0$

For case (ii), $\alpha\gamma < 0$ and $\beta\gamma > 0$

For case (iii), $\alpha\gamma > 0$ and $\beta\gamma < 0$

Hence, the common intersection is $\alpha\gamma < 0$ or $\beta\gamma < 0$.

6. ***(d)*** Let equation of line is $y = mx + c$

Here, $m = \tan 135° = -1$

$\therefore \quad y = -x + c$

$\Rightarrow \quad x + y - c = 0$

Distance from origin to the line

$$= \left|\frac{c}{\sqrt{1+1}}\right| = 5$$

$\Rightarrow \quad c = 5\sqrt{2}$

Hence, equation of line, $x + y = 5\sqrt{2}$

$$\Rightarrow \quad \frac{x}{5\sqrt{2}} + \frac{y}{5\sqrt{2}} = 1$$

7. ***(c)*** **8.** ***(c)***

9. ***(b)*** **10.** ***(c)***

11. *(b)* Given, lines are

$(1+\sqrt{3})y+(1-\sqrt{3})x=10,$ ...(i)

and $y=\sqrt{3}x+m$ ...(ii)

Slope of line (ii) is $\sqrt{3}$

Equation of line passing through origin and having slope $\sqrt{3}$ is $y=\sqrt{3}x$ ...(iii)

Solving for point of intersection of Eqs. (i) and (iii), we get

$$(1+\sqrt{3})\sqrt{3}x+(1-\sqrt{3})x=10$$

$$\Rightarrow \sqrt{3}x+3x+x-\sqrt{3}x=10$$

$$\Rightarrow x=\frac{10}{4}=\frac{5}{2}$$

$$\therefore y=\frac{5\sqrt{3}}{2}$$

Point of intersection is $\left(\frac{5}{2},\frac{5\sqrt{3}}{2}\right)$.

Distance of origin from this point

$$=\sqrt{\frac{25}{4}+\frac{75}{4}}=\sqrt{\frac{100}{4}}=5\text{ units}$$

12. *(c)*

13. *(a)* Given, diagonal (line) $7x-y+8=0$

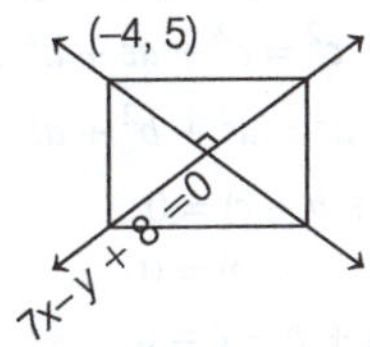

Given, point $(-4, 5)$ does not lie on given diagonal.

$\therefore$ Point $(-4, 5)$ is a point which lie on other diagonal.

Equation of line perpendicular to $7x-y+8=0$ is $x+7y+\lambda=0$

It passes through $(-4, 5)$.

$$\therefore -4+35+\lambda=0$$

$$\Rightarrow \lambda=-31$$

14. *(b)*

15. *(d)* Given lines,

$$x+y=p,\ x+y=pq,\ x+y=pq^2$$

$$\Rightarrow \frac{x}{p}+\frac{y}{p}=1,\ \frac{x}{pq}+\frac{y}{pq}=1,\ \frac{x}{pq^2}+\frac{y}{pq^2}=1$$

Intercepts cut-off by these lines between the axes are $p\sqrt{2}, pq\sqrt{2}, pq^2\sqrt{2}$.

Sum of intercepts $=\sqrt{2}(p+pq+pq^2)$

$$=p\sqrt{2}\left(1+\frac{1}{2}+\frac{1}{4}\right)=\frac{7\sqrt{2}}{4}p$$

16. *(d)* Length of side $=l$

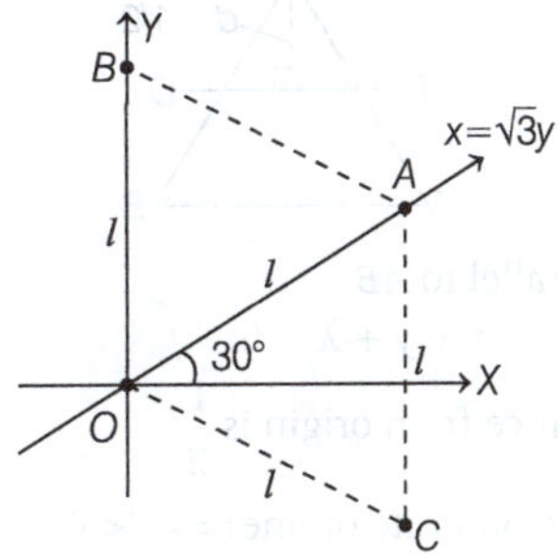

Coordinates of $A\ (l\cos 30°, l\sin 30°)=\left(\frac{\sqrt{3}}{2}l,\frac{l}{2}\right)$

Third vertex is either B or C.

Coordinate of $B\ (0, l)$.

Coordinate of $C\ \{l\cos(-30°), l\sin(-30°)\}$

$$C\left(\frac{\sqrt{3}}{2}l,\frac{-l}{2}\right).$$

17. *(a)* $\because$ Vertex $(1, 2)$ is not on line

$$3x+4y=7$$

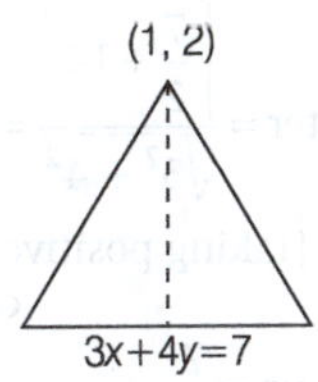

Let length of side be a, then

$$\frac{\sqrt{3}}{2}a=\left|\frac{3(1)+4(2)-7}{\sqrt{3^2+4^2}}\right|$$

[perpendicular distance of $(1, 2)$ from the $3x+4y=7$]

$$\Rightarrow \frac{\sqrt{3}}{2}a=\frac{4}{5}\Rightarrow a=\frac{8\sqrt{3}}{15}$$

18. *(a)* Let $\alpha=45°$, then $\sqrt{2}x-\sqrt{2}y=p$

and $\frac{x}{\sqrt{2}}+\frac{y}{\sqrt{2}}=0$

Length of perpendicular from origin

$$a=\frac{p}{\sqrt{4}}\text{ and } b=0$$

$$\Rightarrow 4a^2=p^2\text{ and } b^2=0\Rightarrow 4a^2+b^2=p^2$$

19. *(a)*

20. *(b)* Slope of $AB = \frac{-3+1}{-1+3} = -1$

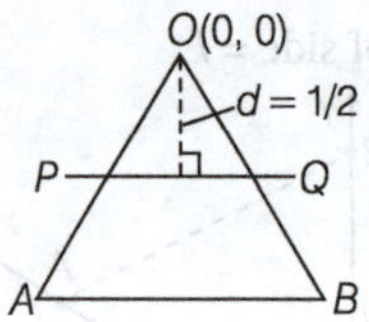

Line parallel to AB

$$x + y + \lambda = 0$$

Its distance from origin is $\frac{1}{2}$.

$(O, B$ are opposite of line$) \Rightarrow \lambda < 0$

$$\therefore \quad \frac{|\lambda|}{\sqrt{2}} = \frac{1}{2} \Rightarrow \lambda = -\frac{1}{\sqrt{2}}$$

$$\Rightarrow \quad x + y - \frac{1}{\sqrt{2}} = 0$$

21. *(a)* Lines $3x + 4y - 14 = 0$ and $6x + 8y + 7 = 0$ are parallel to each other.

$$3x + 4y - 14 = 0$$

$$3x + 4y + \frac{7}{2} = 0$$

Distance between lines = Diameter of circle

$$\Rightarrow \quad \text{Diameter} = \frac{\left|\frac{7}{2} + 14\right|}{\sqrt{3^2 + 4^2}} = \frac{35}{2 \times 5} = \frac{7}{2}$$

[taking positive value as diameter cannot be negative]

$$\therefore \quad \text{Radius} = \frac{7}{4}$$

22. *(b)* As, $L : \frac{x}{5} + \frac{y}{b} = 1$ passes through (13, 32),

we get $\frac{13}{5} + \frac{32}{b} = 1 \Rightarrow \frac{32}{b} = 1 - \frac{13}{5} = -\frac{8}{5}$

$$\Rightarrow \quad b = -20$$

$\therefore$ Equation of line L is $\frac{x}{5} - \frac{y}{20} = 1$

As, $K : \frac{x}{c} + \frac{y}{3} = 1$ is parallel to L.

$$\therefore \quad \frac{\frac{1}{5}}{\frac{1}{c}} = \frac{-\frac{1}{20}}{\frac{1}{3}}$$

$$\Rightarrow \quad \frac{c}{5} = -\frac{3}{20} \Rightarrow c = \frac{-3}{4}$$

Thus, equation of K is $\frac{-4x}{3} + \frac{y}{3} = 1$

$\therefore$ Equation of L and K are $4x - y - 20 = 0$ and $4x - y + 3 = 0$

Distance between L and K

$$= \frac{|-20-3|}{\sqrt{16+1}} = \frac{23}{\sqrt{17}} \text{ units}$$

23. *(a)* $(b - c)x + (c - a)y + (a - b) = 0$

and $(b^3 - c^3)x + (c^3 - a^3)y + (a^3 - b^3) = 0$

Both represents the same line.

$$\therefore \quad \frac{b^3 - c^3}{b - c} = \frac{c^3 - a^3}{c - a} = \frac{a^3 - b^3}{a - b}$$

$$\Rightarrow \quad \frac{(b-c)}{(b-c)(b^2 + c^2 + bc)} = \frac{c-a}{(c-a)(c^2 + ac + a^2)} = \frac{a-b}{(a-b)(a^2 + b^2 + ab)}$$

$$\Rightarrow \quad \frac{1}{b^2 + c^2 + bc} = \frac{1}{c^2 + ac + a^2} = \frac{1}{a^2 + b^2 + ab}$$

$$\Rightarrow \quad b^2 + bc + c^2 = c^2 + ac + a^2$$

and $c^2 + ac + a^2 = a^2 + b^2 + ab$

$$\Rightarrow \quad (a - b)(a + b + c) = 0$$

and $(b - c)(b + c + a) = 0$

$$\Rightarrow \quad a + b + c = 0 \quad [\because a \neq b \neq c]$$

24. *(c)* $x = \alpha + p$, $y = -2$ and $y = px$

By eliminating x, y from the three equations

$$-2 = p(\alpha + p)$$

$$\Rightarrow \quad p^2 + \alpha p + 2 = 0$$

$$\because \quad p \in R$$

$$\Rightarrow \quad \text{Discriminant} \geq 0$$

$$\Rightarrow \quad \alpha^2 - 8 \geq 0 \Rightarrow |\alpha| \geq 2\sqrt{2}$$

25. *(b)* $\alpha x + \beta y + \gamma = 0$, $\beta x + \gamma y + \alpha = 0$ and $\gamma x + \alpha y + \beta = 0$ are concurrent lines.

$$\Rightarrow \quad \begin{vmatrix} \alpha & \beta & \gamma \\ \beta & \gamma & \alpha \\ \gamma & \alpha & \beta \end{vmatrix} = 0$$

$$\Rightarrow \quad \alpha + \beta + \gamma = 0$$

$$\because \quad \alpha x + \beta y + \gamma = 0$$

$\therefore$ It passes through (1, 1).

26. ***(b)*** Given, $px + qy + r = 0$ is the equation of line such that

$$3p + 2q + 4r = 0$$

$$\frac{3p}{4} + \frac{2q}{4} + r = 0$$

$$\Rightarrow \quad p\left(\frac{3}{4}\right) + q\left(\frac{1}{2}\right) + r = 0$$

$\Rightarrow \left(\frac{3}{4}, \frac{1}{2}\right)$ satisfy $px + qy + r = 0$

So, the lines always pass through the point $\left(\frac{3}{4}, \frac{1}{2}\right)$.

27. ***(c)*** Let $(x_1, y_1) = (a, a+2)$ and $(x_2, y_2) = \left(\frac{3a}{2}, a^2\right)$

Points lie on the opposite sides of the line

$$L : 2x + 3y - 6 = 0$$

$$\Rightarrow \quad L_{(a, a+2)} \cdot L_{\left(\frac{3a}{2}, a^2\right)} < 0$$

$$\Rightarrow \quad 5a(3a + 3a^2 - 6) < 0$$

[putting points in the line L]

$$\Rightarrow \quad a(a+2)(a-1) < 0$$

$$\Rightarrow \quad a \in (-\infty, -2) \cup (0, 1)$$

28. ***(b)*** $L : 3x + 4y - 8 = 0$

$$(x_1, y_1) = (2, -5)$$

$$L_{(2,-5)} = 6 - 20 - 8 = -22$$

[putting (x_1, y_1) in the line L]

$$(x_2, y_2) = (-5, 2)$$

$$L_{(-5, 2)} = -15 + 8 - 8 = -15$$

[putting (x_2, y_2) in the line L]

$\because L_{(2,-5)} < 0$ and $L_{(-5,2)} < 0$, they have same signs.

$\therefore$ Both the points lie on the same side of L.

29. ***(b)*** $3x - 4y - 5 = 0$

$$5x + 12y - 26 = 0$$

$$a_1a_2 + b_1b_2 < 0, \; c_1c_2 > 0$$

$\therefore$ Using $\frac{a_1x + b_1y + c_1}{\sqrt{a_1^2 + b_1^2}} = \frac{a_2x + b_2y + c_2}{\sqrt{a_2^2 + b_2^2}}$

[$\because$ perpendicular distance of a point $(x_1 \; y_1)$ from both lines are equal]

$$\frac{3x - 4y - 5}{\sqrt{9+16}} = \frac{5x + 12y - 26}{\sqrt{25+144}}$$

$$\Rightarrow \quad 14x - 112y + 65 = 0$$

30. ***(a)*** Given, $x - 7y + 5 = 0$ and $5x + 5y - 3 = 0$

Bisector not containing origin using

$$\frac{a_1x + b_1y + c_1}{\sqrt{a_1^2 + b_1^2}} = \frac{a_2x + b_2y + c_2}{\sqrt{a_2^2 + b_2^2}}$$

[because c_1 and c_2 have opposite signs]

$$\Rightarrow \quad \frac{x - 7y + 5}{\sqrt{1+49}} = \frac{5x + 5y - 3}{\sqrt{25+25}}$$

$$\Rightarrow \quad x + 3y - 2 = 0$$

31. ***(c)*** Foot of the perpendicular of origin on the line is mid-point of $A(a\cos\alpha, b\sin\alpha)$ and $B(a\cos\beta, b\sin\beta)$.

$$\therefore \quad \left(\frac{a\cos\alpha + a\cos\beta}{2}, \frac{b\sin\alpha + b\sin\beta}{2}\right)$$

32. ***(b)*** Q is image of P w.r.t. $x - y - 5 = 0$

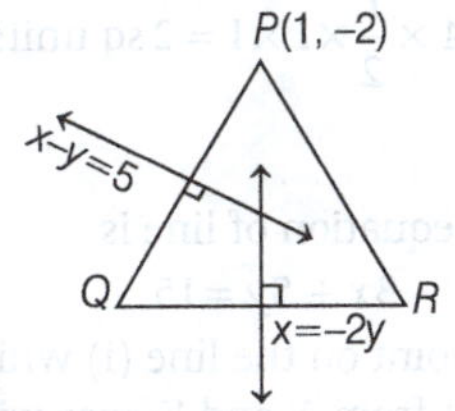

Let $Q(x_1, y_1)$

Then, $\frac{x_1 - 1}{1} = \frac{y_1 + 2}{-1} = \frac{-2(1 + 2 - 5)}{1+1}$

On solving, we get $Q(3, -4)$.

Image of Q is R w.r.t. $x + 2y = 0$

On solving, we get $R(5, 0)$.

33. ***(a)***

34. ***(a)*** Let the coordinates of A be $(a, 0)$. Then the slope of the reflected ray is

$$\frac{3-0}{5-a} = \tan\theta \text{ (say)} \qquad \text{...(i)}$$

Then the slope of the incident ray

$$= \frac{2-0}{1-a} = \tan(\pi - \theta) \qquad \text{...(ii)}$$

From Eqs. (i) and (ii),

$$\tan\theta + \tan(\pi - \theta) = 0$$

$$\Rightarrow \quad \frac{3}{5-a} + \frac{2}{1-a} = 0$$

$$\Rightarrow \quad 3 - 3a + 10 - 2a = 0; \; a = \frac{13}{5}$$

Thus, the coordinate of A is $\left(\frac{13}{5}, 0\right)$

35. *(c)* $y = |x| - 1$ and $y = -|x| + 1$

$\Rightarrow \quad y = x - 1, y = -x - 1$

and $\quad y = x + 1, y = -x + 1$

$\Rightarrow \quad x - y - 1 = 0, x + y + 1 = 0,$

$x - y + 1 = 0, x + y - 1 = 0$

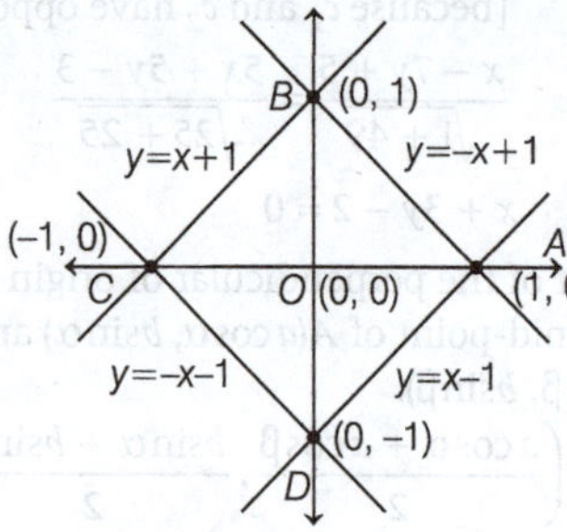

$\therefore$ Area $= 4 \times$ area of ΔOAB

$= 4 \times \frac{1}{2} \times 1 \times 1 = 2$ sq units

36. *(d)*

37. *(c)* Given, equation of line is

$$3x + 5y = 15 \qquad \dots (i)$$

Clearly, a point on the line (i) which is equidistant from X and Y-axes will lie on the line either on $y = x$ or $y = -x$.

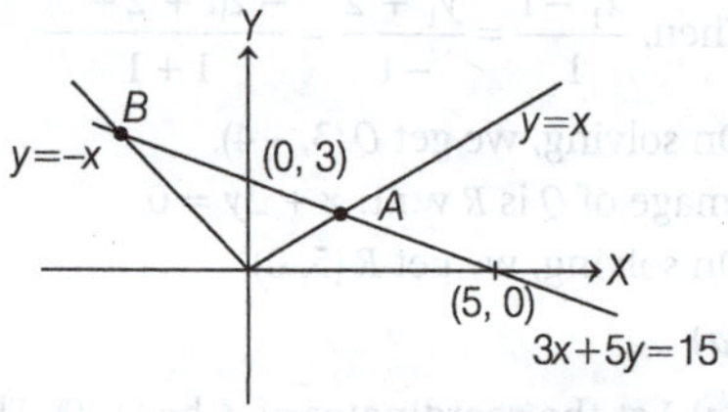

In the above figure, points A and B are on the line (i) and are equidistant from the coordinate axes.

On solving $y = x$ and the line (i), we get

$$A\left(\frac{15}{8}, \frac{15}{8}\right)$$

On solving $y = -x$ and the line (i), we get

$$A\left(-\frac{15}{2}, \frac{15}{2}\right).$$

So, the required points lie only in I and II quadrants.

38. *(d)* Given lines, $y = 3x + 1$,

$$2y = x + 3 \text{ and } y = mx + 4$$

Here, $m_1 = 3, m_2 = \frac{1}{2}, m_3 = m$

According to given condition,

$$\frac{m_1 - m_3}{1 + m_1 m_3} = \frac{m_3 - m_2}{1 + m_3 m_2}$$

$$\Rightarrow \quad \frac{3 - m}{1 + 3m} = \frac{m - \frac{1}{2}}{1 + \frac{m}{2}}$$

$$\Rightarrow \quad \frac{3 - m}{1 + 3m} = \frac{2m - 1}{2 + m}$$

$$\Rightarrow 6 + 3m - 2m - m^2 = -1 + 2m - 3m + 6m^2$$

$$\Rightarrow \quad 7m^2 - 2m - 7 = 0$$

$$\therefore m = \frac{2 \pm \sqrt{4 + 4 \times 49}}{14} = \frac{2 \pm \sqrt{200}}{14}$$

$$\Rightarrow \quad m = \frac{1 \pm 5\sqrt{2}}{7}$$

39. *(a)* Given, equation of circle is $x^2 + y^2 = 9$

So, let the diameter of PQ are $P(3\cos\theta, 3\sin\theta)$ and $Q(-3\cos\theta, -3\sin\theta)$.

Length of perpendicular from P on the straight line $x + y = 2$ is $(\alpha) = \frac{|3\cos\theta + 3\sin\theta - 2|}{\sqrt{2}}$

Length of perpendicular from Q to the straight line $x + y = 2$ is $(\beta) = \frac{|-3\cos\theta - 3\sin\theta - 2|}{\sqrt{2}}$

$$\alpha\beta = \frac{|(3\cos\theta + 3\sin\theta)^2 - 2^2|}{2}$$

$$\alpha\beta = \frac{|9 - 4 + 9\sin 2\theta|}{2} = \frac{|5 + 9\sin 2\theta|}{2}$$

$\because$ Maximum value of $\sin 2\theta = 1$

$$\therefore \quad \alpha\beta|_{max} = \frac{5 + 9}{2} = 7$$

40. *(b)*

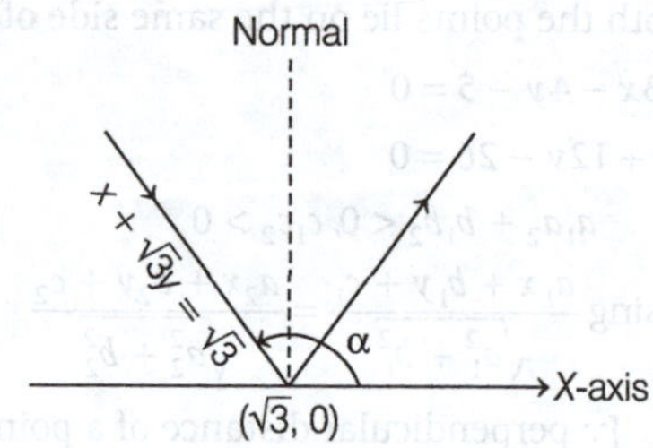

$$x + \sqrt{3}y = \sqrt{3}$$

$$\Rightarrow \quad y = -\frac{1}{\sqrt{3}}x + 1$$

$$\therefore \quad \tan\alpha = -\frac{1}{\sqrt{3}} \Rightarrow \alpha = 150°$$

So, this line makes 60° with the normal.
So, reflected light makes 30° with positive X-axis.

$\therefore$ Equation of reflected light is

$$y-0=\frac{1}{\sqrt{3}}(x-\sqrt{3})$$

41. ***(a)*** It is given that line L make x and y-intercepts as 3 and 1, respectively.

So, equation of line L is

$$\frac{x}{3}+\frac{y}{1}=1 \Rightarrow x+3y=3 \qquad \dots \text{(i)}$$

Now, let the image of point $(-1,-4)$ with respect to line (i) be (x_1, y_1), then

$$\frac{x_1+1}{1}=\frac{y_1+4}{3}=-2\left(\frac{-1-12-3}{1+9}\right)$$

$$\Rightarrow \quad x_1+1=\frac{y_1+4}{3}=+\frac{16}{5}$$

$$\Rightarrow \quad x_1=\frac{16}{5}-1=\frac{11}{5} \text{ and } y_1=\left(\frac{16}{5}\times 3\right)-4=\frac{28}{5}$$

$$(x_1, y_1)=\left(\frac{11}{5}, \frac{28}{5}\right)$$

42. ***(b)*** $\alpha x+\beta y=1$ will be bisector of given line.

Equation of bisector

$$\frac{3x+4y-5}{5}=\pm\left(\frac{5x-12y-10}{13}\right)$$

$$\Rightarrow 64x-8y=115 \text{ or } 14x+112y=15$$

$$\therefore \quad \alpha=\frac{64}{115}, \beta=\frac{-8}{115} \text{ or } \alpha=\frac{14}{15}, \beta=\frac{112}{15}$$

43. ***(d)*** $\because a=b^2 \Rightarrow A(b^2, b)$

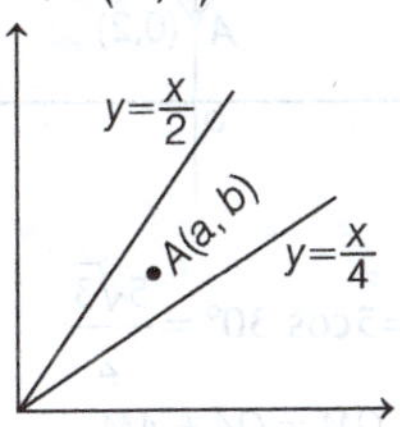

$\because b^2>0 \Rightarrow A$ lies in first quadrant.

The joint equation of two lines

$$x=2y \text{ and } x=4y$$

i.e. $u=x-2y=0$ and $v=x-4y=0$ is $u \cdot v=0$

i.e. $(x-2y)(x-4y)=0$

$\Rightarrow x^2-4xy-2xy+8y^2=0$

$\therefore S(x, y)=x^2-4xy-2xy+8y^2=0 \qquad \dots \text{(i)}$

If $A(b^2, b)$ lies in the interior of the acute angle formed by these lines, then the value of $S(x, y)$ at $A(b^2, b)$ is negative.

$$\Rightarrow \quad b^2(b^2-6b+8)<0$$

$$\Rightarrow \quad (b-2)(b-4)<0 \Rightarrow b \in (2, 4)$$

44. ***(a)*** Mid-point of $PR=(1, 2)$

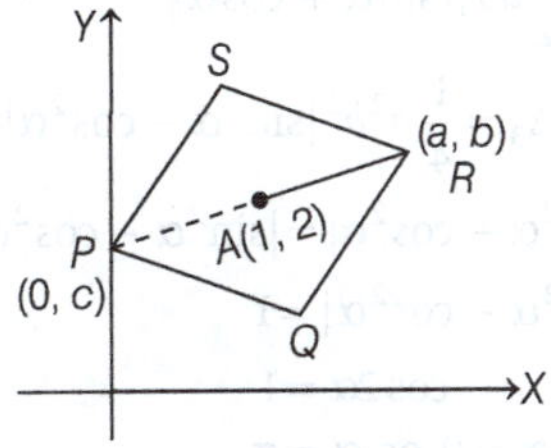

$$\frac{a}{2}=1 \Rightarrow a=2$$

$$\frac{b+c}{2}=2 \Rightarrow b+c=4$$

Sides are parallel to

$$x-y+2=0, 7x-y+3=0$$

$\therefore$ Equation of bisector of the angle between the lines

$$\frac{x-y+2}{\sqrt{2}}=\pm\frac{7x-y+3}{5\sqrt{2}}$$

$$\Rightarrow \quad 2x+4y-7=0$$

and $\quad 12x-6y+13=0$

$$\therefore \quad \text{Slope of } AP=\frac{-1}{2} \text{ or } 2$$

$$\therefore \quad \frac{2-c}{1-0}=\frac{-1}{2} \text{ or } 2$$

$$\Rightarrow \quad 2-c=\frac{-1}{2} \text{ or } 2$$

$$\Rightarrow \quad c=\frac{5}{2} \text{ or } 0$$

Ordinate of $P=\frac{5}{2}$

45. ***(d)*** $\Delta_1=\frac{1}{2}\begin{vmatrix} 0 & 0 & 1 \\ a\tan\alpha & b\cot\alpha & 1 \\ a\sin\alpha & b\cos\alpha & 1 \end{vmatrix}$

$$=\frac{1}{2}ab|(\sin\alpha-\cos\alpha)|$$

$$\Delta_2=\frac{1}{2}\begin{vmatrix} a & b & 1 \\ a\sec^2\alpha & b\operatorname{cosec}^2\alpha & 1 \\ a+a\sin^2\alpha & b+b\cos^2\alpha & 1 \end{vmatrix}$$

$$=\frac{1}{2}ab[\operatorname{cosec}^2\alpha-1-\cos^2\alpha+1+\sin^2\alpha$$
$$-\sec^2\alpha+\sec^2\alpha+1-\operatorname{cosec}^2\alpha-1]$$

$$=\frac{1}{2}ab[\sin^2\alpha-\cos^2\alpha]$$

$$\Delta_3 = \frac{1}{2}\begin{vmatrix} 0 & 0 & 1 \\ a\tan\alpha & -b\cot\alpha & 1 \\ a\sin\alpha & b\cos\alpha & 1 \end{vmatrix}$$

$$= \frac{1}{2}ab\,|(\sin\alpha + \cos\alpha)|$$

Now, $\Delta_1 \Delta_3 = \frac{1}{4}a^2b^2|\sin^2\alpha - \cos^2\alpha| = \Delta_2^2$

$\Rightarrow \quad |\sin^2\alpha - \cos^2\alpha| = |\sin^2\alpha - \cos^2\alpha|^2$

$\Rightarrow \quad |\sin^2\alpha - \cos^2\alpha| = 1$

$\Rightarrow \quad \cos 2\alpha = 1$

$\Rightarrow \quad \alpha = 0 \text{ or } \alpha = \pi$

But for these values of α, the triangles are not defined.

Hence, Δ_1, Δ_2, Δ_3 are in GP for no value of α.

46. ***(a)*** $3|x| + 2|y| \le 8$

$\Rightarrow \quad \dfrac{|x|}{\frac{8}{3}} + \dfrac{|y|}{4} \le 1$

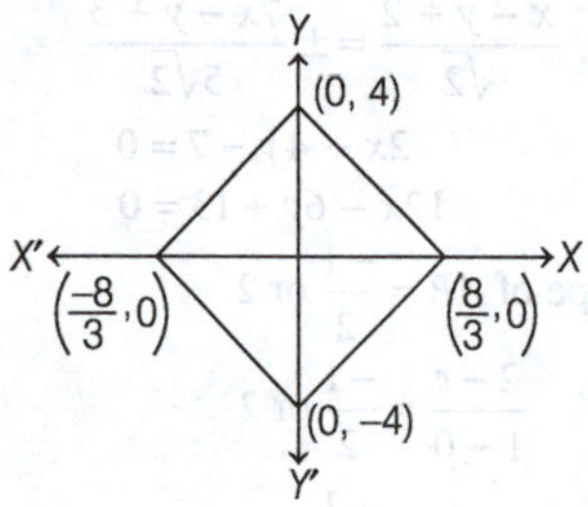

Required area $= 4 \times \frac{1}{2} \times \frac{8}{3} \times 4 = \frac{64}{3}$ sq units

$\because \quad f(1) = 2$

and $\quad f(x + y) = f(x)\,f(y)$

$f(1) = 2$ [given]

$f(2) = f(1) \cdot f(1) = 2 \times 2 = 4$

$\vdots \quad \vdots \quad \vdots$

$f(6) = 2f(5) = 4f(4) = 8f(3)$

$\therefore \quad f(x) = 2^x \Rightarrow f(6) = 2^6 = 64$

$\therefore \quad \text{Area} = \frac{1}{3} f(6)$ sq units

47. ***(b)*** $L_1 : x + y - 2 = 0$

$L_2 \perp L_1,\ L_2 : x - y + \lambda = 0$

L_2 passes through $\left(\frac{1}{2}, 0\right)$.

$\therefore \quad \frac{1}{2} - 0 + \lambda = 0$

$\Rightarrow \quad \lambda = \frac{-1}{2}$

$L_2 = 2x - 2y = 1$

$L_3 : Y\text{-axis, i.e. } x = 0$

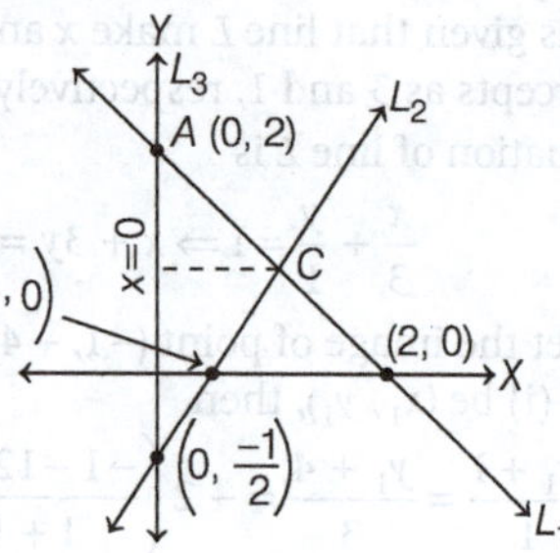

Solving L_1 and L_2 for C, we get

$$C\left(\frac{5}{4}, \frac{3}{4}\right).$$

$$\text{Area} = \frac{1}{2} \times \frac{5}{2} \times \frac{5}{4} = \frac{25}{16} \text{ sq units}$$

48. ***(b)***

49. ***(c)***

50. ***(a)*** $\because AP = 5$ unit

$\therefore$ in ΔAPM,

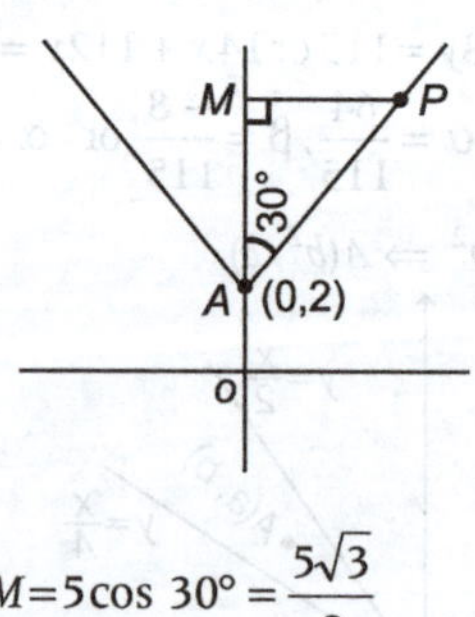

$$AM = 5\cos 30° = \frac{5\sqrt{3}}{2}$$

$\therefore \quad OM = OA + AM$

$$= 2 + \frac{5\sqrt{3}}{2}$$

$$= \frac{1}{2}(4 + 5\sqrt{3})$$

Hence, the coordinates of M are $\left(0, \frac{1}{2}(4 + 5\sqrt{3})\right)$.

Chapter 10 Conic Section

1. ***(b)*** $\because P$ lies on the circle and A and B are two points such that
$$\frac{PA}{PB} = \lambda$$
$\Rightarrow \quad \lambda \neq 1$ otherwise
$\Rightarrow \quad PA = PB.$
Then, P will lie on perpendicular bisector of AB.

2. ***(a)*** Centre of the circle is intersection of $2x + y - 7 = 0$ and $x + 3y - 11 = 0$ is $(2, 3)$.
If r is the radius, then
$$\pi r^2 = 16\pi \Rightarrow r = 4$$
Equation of circle
$$(x-2)^2 + (y-3)^2 = 4^2$$
$$\Rightarrow \quad x^2 + y^2 - 4x - 6y - 3 = 0$$

3. ***(b)*** Centre of the circle $(6, k)$.

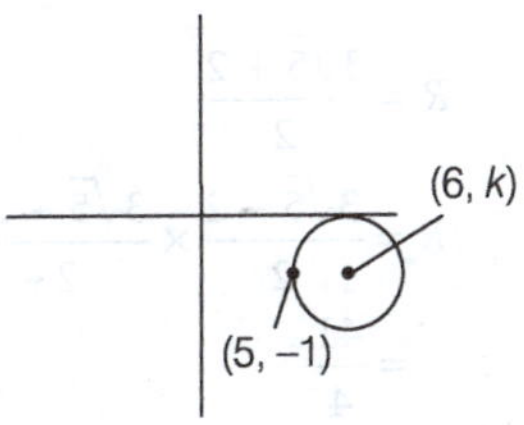

Radius $= k$
Equation of circle
$$(x-6)^2 + (y-k)^2 = k^2$$
It passes through $(5, -1)$
$$(5-6)^2 + (-1-k)^2 = k^2$$
$$\Rightarrow \quad k = -1$$
$\therefore$ Equation of circle
$$(x-6)^2 + (y+1)^2 = 1$$
It passes through the point $(7, -1)$.

4. ***(d)***

5. ***(a)*** Given, circle
$$x^2 + y^2 - 6x - 4y + 12 = 0$$
Centre $(3, 2)$
$$\text{Radius} = \sqrt{9 + 4 - 12} = 1$$
Image of $(3, 2)$ w.r.t. $x + y - 1 = 0$
$$\frac{h-3}{1} = \frac{k-2}{1} = \frac{-2(4)}{2}$$
$$h = -4 + 3 = -1$$
and $\quad k = -4 + 2 = -2$
$(-1, -2)$ is image of $(3, 2)$.
Equation of circle with centre $(-1, -2)$ and radius $= 1$
$$(x+1)^2 + (y+2)^2 = 1$$
$$\Rightarrow \quad x^2 + y^2 + 2x + 4y + 4 = 0$$

6. ***(b)*** $C_1 : x^2 + y^2 + 2ax + c = 0$
Centre $(-a, 0)$
$$\therefore \quad \text{Radius} = \sqrt{a^2 - c}$$
$C_2 : x^2 + y^2 - 2by - c = 0$
Centre $(0, b)$
$$\therefore \quad \text{Radius} = \sqrt{b^2 + c}$$
$\because$ Radii are equal.
$$\Rightarrow \quad \sqrt{a^2 - c} = \sqrt{b^2 + c}$$
On squaring both sides, we get
$$a^2 - c = b^2 + c$$
$$\Rightarrow \quad a^2 - b^2 = 2c$$
Locus of (a, b)
$$x^2 - y^2 = 2c$$

7. ***(c)*** $(1, 2)$ lies outside the circle.
$$\Rightarrow \quad 1^2 + 2^2 + 2(1) + 2(2) + p > 0$$
$$\Rightarrow \quad p > -11$$
$(-1, -2)$ lies inside the circle.
$$\Rightarrow \quad (-1)^2 + (-2)^2 + 2(-1) + 2(-2) + p < 0$$
$$\Rightarrow \quad p < 1$$
$$\therefore \quad p \in (-11, 1)$$

8. ***(c)*** Let tangent be $y = mx$
Length of perpendicular from the centre $(2, -1)$ on $y = mx$ and $3x + y = 0$ will be equal.
$$\therefore \quad \left|\frac{2m+1}{\sqrt{1+m^2}}\right| = \left|\frac{6-1}{\sqrt{9+1}}\right|$$
$$\Rightarrow \quad \frac{(2m+1)^2}{1+m^2} = \frac{25}{10}$$
$$\Rightarrow \quad 3m^2 + 8m - 3 = 0$$
$$\Rightarrow \quad (3m-1)(m+3) = 0$$
$$\Rightarrow \quad m = -3 \text{ or } \frac{1}{3}$$
$m = -3$ is the slope of given tangent.

$\therefore m = \frac{1}{3}$ is the slope of required tangent.

$\Rightarrow \quad y = \frac{1}{3}x$

$\Rightarrow \quad 3y = x$

Or $\quad x - 3y = 0$

9. *(b)*

10. *(a)* Line $hx + ky = 1$ touches the circle

$$x^2 + y^2 = k^2$$

$\Rightarrow$ Distance of line from the centre of circle will be equal to radius.

$$\Rightarrow \quad \left|\frac{1}{\sqrt{h^2 + k^2}}\right| = k$$

$$\Rightarrow \quad k(\sqrt{h^2 + k^2}) = 1$$

$$\Rightarrow \quad h^2 + k^2 = \frac{1}{k^2}$$

Locus of (h, k).

$$x^2 + y^2 = \frac{1}{k^2}$$

$$\Rightarrow \quad \text{Radius} = \frac{1}{k}$$

11. *(b)* Let (a, a) be the centre of circle and circle passes through vertex $(1, 1)$ of square of unit area.

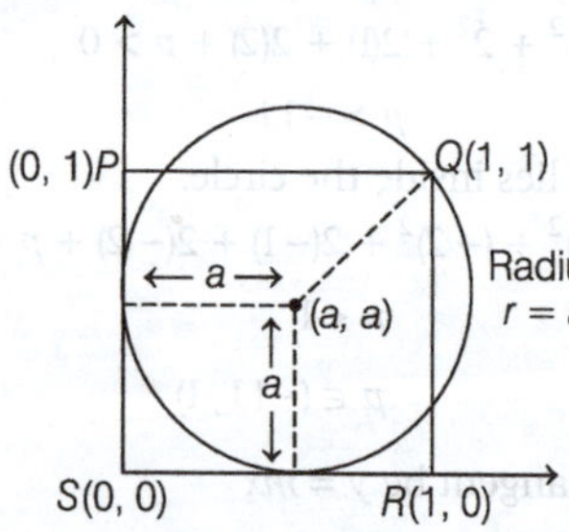

Then, $\sqrt{(1 - r)^2 + (1 - r)^2} = r$

On squaring both sides, we get

$$2(1 - r)^2 = r^2$$

On taking square root both sides, we get

$$\sqrt{2}(1 - r) = r$$

$$\Rightarrow \quad r = \frac{\sqrt{2}}{\sqrt{2} + 1}$$

$$= (2 - \sqrt{2}) \text{ units}$$

12. *(c)* $C_1 : (x - 2)^2 + y^2 = 4$

Centre $(2, 0)$ and radius $= 2$ units

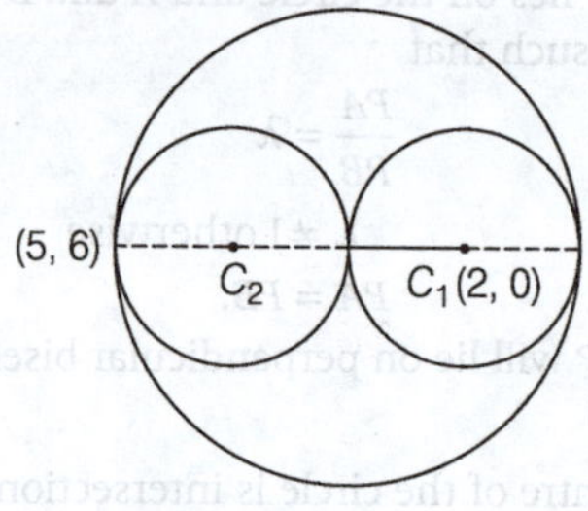

Distance between $(2, 0)$ and $(5, 6)$

$$= \sqrt{9 + 36}$$

$$= 3\sqrt{5} \text{ units}$$

$$\therefore \quad 2r + 2 = 3\sqrt{5}$$

$$\Rightarrow \quad r = \frac{3\sqrt{5} - 2}{2}$$

and $\quad 2R - 2 = 3\sqrt{5}$

$$\Rightarrow \quad R = \frac{3\sqrt{5} + 2}{2}$$

$$\therefore \quad rR = \frac{3\sqrt{5} - 2}{2} \times \frac{3\sqrt{5} + 2}{2}$$

$$= \frac{41}{4}$$

13. *(c)* Line $L : 5x - 2y + 6 = 0$

and circle $C : x^2 + y^2 + 6x + 6y - 2 = 0$

Line L intersects with tangent at A on the circle C on Y-axis at B $(0, 3)$.

$\therefore$ Tangent passes through $(0, 3)$

$\Rightarrow \quad AB =$ Length of tangent to circle from $(0, 3)$

$$= \sqrt{0 + 3^2 + 6(0) + 6(3) - 2}$$

$$= \sqrt{25} = 5 \text{ units}$$

14. *(c)*

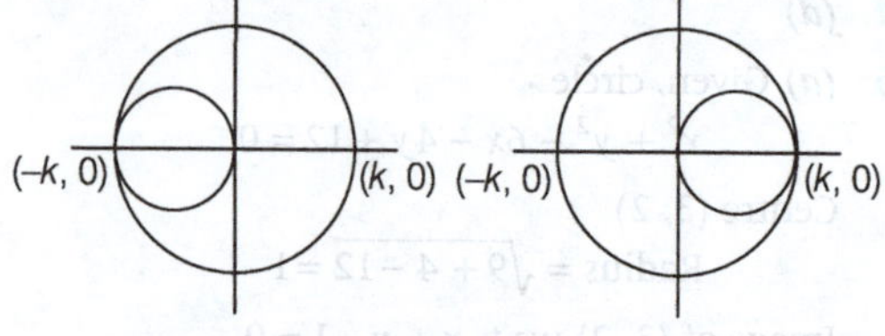

Circles touches each other internally, if

$$k = \lambda \text{ or } k = -\lambda \Rightarrow k = |\lambda|$$

15. ***(d)*** Let (x, y) be the point on $y^2 = 4x$ ...(i)

Comparing with $y^2 = 4ax$, we have

$$a = 1$$

Focal distance = 4

$\Rightarrow$ $x + a = 4$

$\Rightarrow$ $x = 4 - 1 = 3$

$y^2 = 4 \times 3 = 12$ [from Eq. (i)]

$\Rightarrow$ $y = \pm 2\sqrt{3}$

$\Rightarrow$ Coordinate = $(3, \pm 2\sqrt{3})$

16. ***(b)*** $\sqrt{\frac{x}{p}} + \sqrt{\frac{y}{q}} = 1 \Rightarrow \sqrt{\frac{x}{p}} = 1 - \sqrt{\frac{y}{q}}$

On squaring both sides, we get

$$\frac{x}{p} = 1 + \frac{y}{q} - 2\sqrt{\frac{y}{q}}$$

$\Rightarrow$ $\frac{y}{q} - \frac{x}{p} + 1 = 2\sqrt{\frac{y}{q}}$

Again, on squaring both sides, we get

$$\frac{y^2}{q^2} + \frac{x^2}{p^2} + 1 - \frac{2xy}{pq} - \frac{2x}{p} + \frac{2y}{q} = \frac{4y}{q}$$

$\Rightarrow$ $\frac{x^2}{p^2} - \frac{2xy}{pq} + \frac{y^2}{q^2} - \frac{2x}{p} - \frac{2y}{q} + 1 = 0$

Comparing with general equation of second degree, we have

$$a = \frac{1}{p^2}, h = \frac{-1}{pq} \text{ and } b = \frac{1}{q^2}$$

Here, $h^2 = ab$

$\therefore$ It is a parabola.

17. ***(a)***

18. ***(c)*** Circle : $x^2 + y^2 = 9$

Parabola : $y^2 = 8x$

Point of intersection

$$x^2 + 8x - 9 = 0$$

$\Rightarrow$ $x = -9$ or 1

For $y^2 = 8x, x > 0$

$\therefore$ $x = 1, y = \pm 2\sqrt{2}$

Point of intersection $(1, 2\sqrt{2}), (1, -2\sqrt{2})$

a = Length of common chord = $4\sqrt{2}$

and b = Length of latusrectum = 8

$\Rightarrow$ $a < b$

19. ***(b)*** Focus of parabola (2, 0)

Let equation of chord be $y = m(x - 2)$

Its distance from vertex (0, 0)

$$\left| \frac{-2m}{\sqrt{1 + m^2}} \right| = \sqrt{3}$$

$\Rightarrow$ $\frac{4m^2}{1 + m^2} = 3$

$\Rightarrow$ $4m^2 = 3 + 3m^2$

$\Rightarrow$ $m^2 = 3 \Rightarrow m = \sqrt{3}$

20. ***(b)*** Parametric form of parabola $y^2 = 4ax$

$$x = at^2 \text{ and } y = 2at$$

Point on parabola $P(at^2, 2at)$.

Focus $S(a, 0)$

$$\text{Slope of } SP = \tan\theta = \frac{2at}{at^2 - a}$$

$\Rightarrow$ $2\cot\theta = \frac{t^2 - 1}{t} = t - \frac{1}{t}$

Length of focal chord at t

$$a\left(t + \frac{1}{t}\right)^2 = a\left\{\left(t - \frac{1}{t}\right)^2 + 4\right\}$$

$$= a\{(2\cot\theta)^2 + 4\}$$

$$= 4a \operatorname{cosec}^2\theta$$

21. ***(c)*** Equation of common tangent

$$y = mx + \frac{1}{m}$$

of parabola $y^2 = 4x$

and circle $(x - 3)^2 + y^2 = 9$

whose centre (3, 0) and radius = 3 units

Then, $\left| \frac{3m + \frac{1}{m}}{\sqrt{1 + m^2}} \right| = 3$

$\Rightarrow$ $m = \pm \frac{1}{\sqrt{3}}$

$\because$ Angle is acute.

$\therefore$ $m = \frac{1}{\sqrt{3}}$

Equation of common tangent

$$y = \frac{1}{\sqrt{3}} x + \sqrt{3} \Rightarrow \sqrt{3}y = x + 3$$

22. *(d)* Equation of tangent to parabola is

$$y = mx + \frac{2}{m}$$

This is also a tangent to $xy = -1$

$$\therefore \quad x\left(mx + \frac{2}{m}\right) = -1$$

$$\Rightarrow \quad mx^2 + \frac{2}{m}x + 1 = 0$$

Condition of tengency

Discriminant = 0

$$\Rightarrow \quad \frac{4}{m^2} - 4m = 0 \Rightarrow m = 1$$

Common tangent is $y = x + 2$

23. *(b)* Solving C_1 and C_2, we have

$$x^2 - 2x + 1 = 0 \Rightarrow (x-1)^2 = 0$$

$$\Rightarrow \quad x = 1 \Rightarrow y = \pm 2$$

So, C_1 and C_2 touch at two points $(1, 2)$ and $(1, -2)$.

24. *(a)* Equation of normal

$$x = my - 2m - m^3$$

It passes through $(1, 2)$.

$$1 = 2m - 2m - m^3$$

$$\Rightarrow \quad m^3 = -1 \Rightarrow m = -1$$

Equation of normal

$$x = -y + 3 \Rightarrow x + y = 3$$

25. *(a)* For ellipse, $a^2 - a - 6 > 0$

$$\text{and} \quad a^2 - 6a + 5 > 0$$

$$\Rightarrow \quad (a-3)(a+2) > 0$$

$$\text{and} \quad (a-1)(a-5) > 0$$

$$\Rightarrow \quad a < -2 \text{ or } a > 3$$

$$\text{and} \quad a < 1 \text{ or } a > 5$$

$$\Rightarrow \quad a < -2 \text{ or } a > 5$$

$$\Rightarrow \quad a \in (-\infty, -2) \cup (5, \infty)$$

26. *(c)*

27. *(b)* $\sqrt{(5x+1)^2 + (5y+1)^2}$

$$= |\lambda - 1|\,|4x + 3y + 1|$$

$$\Rightarrow \sqrt{\left(x + \frac{1}{5}\right)^2 + \left(y + \frac{1}{5}\right)^2} = |\lambda - 1|\left|\frac{4x + 3y + 1}{\sqrt{25}}\right|$$

It represents an ellipse, if

$$|\lambda - 1| < 1 \Rightarrow -1 < \lambda - 1 < 1$$

$$\Rightarrow \quad 0 < \lambda < 2 \text{ but } \lambda \neq 1$$

$$\Rightarrow \quad \lambda \in (0, 2) - \{1\}$$

28. *(c)* Distance between foci = $2ae$

Length of latusrectum = $\dfrac{2b^2}{a}$

$$\because \quad 2ae = \frac{1}{2} \cdot \frac{2b^2}{a}$$

$$\because \quad 2e = \frac{b^2}{a^2} \quad [\because b^2 = a^2(1 - e^2)]$$

$$\Rightarrow \quad 2e = 1 - e^2$$

$$\Rightarrow \quad e = -1 \pm \sqrt{2}$$

$$\because \quad 0 < e < 1$$

$$\Rightarrow \quad e = \sqrt{2} - 1$$

29. *(a)* Ellipse: $\dfrac{x^2}{9} + \dfrac{y^2}{4} = 1$, $(a > b)$

$$e = \sqrt{\frac{a^2 - b^2}{a^2}} = \sqrt{\frac{9-4}{9}} = \frac{\sqrt{5}}{3}$$

$\therefore$ Required ratio = $(1 + e) : (1 - e)$

$$= \left(1 + \frac{\sqrt{5}}{3}\right) : \left(1 - \frac{\sqrt{5}}{3}\right)$$

$$= (3 + \sqrt{5}) : (3 - \sqrt{5})$$

30. *(c)* Ellipse : $\dfrac{x^2}{16} + \dfrac{y^2}{4} = 1$ ...(i)

Centre of circle $(1, 0)$

Let radius = r

Then, equation of circle,

$$(x-1)^2 + y^2 = r^2 \quad \text{...(ii)}$$

For intersection of Eqs. (i) and (ii),

$$(x-1)^2 + \frac{16 - x^2}{4} = r^2$$

$$\Rightarrow \quad 3x^2 - 8x + 20 - 4r^2 = 0$$

Circle lies inside the ellipse, then

discriminant ≤ 0

$$\Rightarrow \quad 64 + 12(4r^2 - 20) \leq 0$$

$$\Rightarrow \quad r \leq \sqrt{\frac{11}{3}}$$

Greatest radius = $\sqrt{\dfrac{11}{3}}$

Equation of circle, $(x-1)^2 + y^2 = \dfrac{11}{3}$

$$\Rightarrow \quad 3x^2 + 3y^2 - 6x - 8 = 0$$

31. *(b)* **32.** *(d)*

33. *(d)* Intersection of straight line $y = mx + c$ and ellipse

$$\frac{x^2}{a^2} + \frac{y^2}{b^2} = 1$$

$$\therefore \quad \frac{x^2}{a^2} + \frac{(mx+c)^2}{b^2} = 1$$

$$\Rightarrow x^2(b^2 + a^2m^2) + 2mc\, a^2x + a^2c^2 - a^2b^2 = 0$$

For intersection at real points,

Discriminant ≥ 0

$$4m^2c^2a^4 - 4(b^2 + a^2m^2)(a^2c^2 - a^2b^2) \geq 0$$

$$\Rightarrow \quad 4m^2c^2a^4 - 4[a^2b^2c^2 - a^2b^4 + a^4m^2c^2 - a^4m^2b^2] \geq 0$$

$$4m^2c^2a^4 - 4a^2b^2c^2 + 4a^2b^4 - 4a^4m^2c^2 + 4a^4m^2b^2 \geq 0$$

$$\Rightarrow \quad a^2m^2 \geq c^2 - b^2$$

34. *(c)*

35. *(a)* $e_1 = \dfrac{25 - b^2}{25}$ and $e_2 = \dfrac{16 + b^2}{16}$

$$\because \quad e_1e_2 = 1$$

$$\Rightarrow \quad \left(\frac{25-b^2}{25}\right)\left(\frac{16+b^2}{16}\right) = 1$$

$$\Rightarrow \quad 9b^2 - b^4 = 0$$

$$\Rightarrow \quad b^2 = 9 \Rightarrow b = \pm 3$$

36. *(b)* Equation of tangent

$$y = \frac{x}{\sqrt{5}} + \frac{c}{\sqrt{5}}$$

Equation of hyperbola

$$\frac{x^2}{5^2} - \frac{y^2}{2^2} = 1$$

We know that a line $y = mx + c$ touches the hyperbola

$$\frac{x^2}{a^2} - \frac{y^2}{b^2} = 1$$

Then, $c^2 = a^2m^2 - b^2$

$$\Rightarrow \left(\frac{c}{\sqrt{5}}\right)^2 = 25\left(\frac{1}{\sqrt{5}}\right)^2 - 4 \Rightarrow c = \pm\sqrt{5}$$

37. *(a)* Equation of tangent to the hyperbola $x^2 - y^2 = k^2$ is

$$y = mx + k\sqrt{m^2 - 1} \qquad \text{...(i)}$$

Equation of tangent perpendicular to Eq. (i), put $m = -\dfrac{1}{m}$, we get $y = \dfrac{-1}{m}x + k\sqrt{\dfrac{1}{m^2} - 1}$

$$\Rightarrow \quad my + x = k\sqrt{1 - m^2} \qquad \text{...(ii)}$$

$$\Rightarrow \quad m^2 - 1 \geq 0 \qquad \text{[from Eq. (i)]}$$

$$\text{and} \quad 1 - m^2 \geq 0 \qquad \text{[from Eq. (ii)]}$$

$$\text{So,} \quad 1 - m^2 = 0$$

$$m = \pm 1$$

$\therefore$ (a, b) lies on $y = \pm x$

38. *(a)* Let $e_1 =$ Eccentricity of ellipse

$e_2 =$ Eccentricity of hyperbola

$\because$ Hyperbola passes through the focus $(\pm ae_1, 0)$ of ellipse.

$$\Rightarrow \quad b = \pm ae_1$$

For ellipse, $b^2 = a^2(1 - e_1^2) \Rightarrow e_1 = \dfrac{1}{\sqrt{2}}$

For hyperbola, $\dfrac{x^2}{a_1^2} - \dfrac{y^2}{b_1^2} = 1$

$$b_1^2 = a_1^2(e^2 - 1)$$

$$\text{So,} \quad a^2 = b^2(e_2^2 - 1)$$

$$\Rightarrow \quad a^2 = a^2e_1^2(e_2^2 - 1) \Rightarrow 2 = e_2^2 - 1$$

$$\therefore \quad e_2 = \sqrt{3}$$

39. *(c)* For hyperbola,

$(\lambda + 3)$ and $(2 - \lambda)$ are of opposite signs.

$\Rightarrow$ $\lambda + 3 < 0$ and $2 - \lambda > 0$

Or $\lambda + 3 > 0$ and $2 - \lambda < 0$

$\Rightarrow$ $\lambda < -3$ and $\lambda < 2$

Or $\lambda > -3$ and $\lambda > 2$

$\Rightarrow$ $\lambda > 2$ and $\lambda < -3 \Rightarrow \lambda \notin (-3, 2)$

40. *(c)* Let $P(\alpha, \beta)$ be a point on $x^2 - y^2 = a^2$

Equation of tangent at P is

$$x\alpha - y\beta = a^2$$

$$\Rightarrow \quad \frac{x}{a^2/\alpha} + \frac{y}{-a^2/\beta} = 1 \Rightarrow x_1 = \frac{a^2}{\alpha}, y_1 = \frac{-a^2}{\beta}$$

Equation of normal at $P(\alpha, \beta)$ is

$$\frac{x}{\alpha} + \frac{y}{\beta} = 2 \Rightarrow \frac{x}{2\alpha} + \frac{y}{2\beta} = 1$$

$$\therefore \quad x_2 = 2\alpha,\ y_2 = 2\beta$$

Now, $x_1x_2 + y_1y_2$

$$= \frac{a^2}{\alpha}(2\alpha) + \left(\frac{-a^2}{\beta}\right)(2\beta) = 0$$

41. *(a)* It is given that the circle touches X-axis at (3, 0) and making an intercept of 8 on the Y-axis. Let the radius of the circle is r then the coordinates of centre of circle are $(3, r)$.

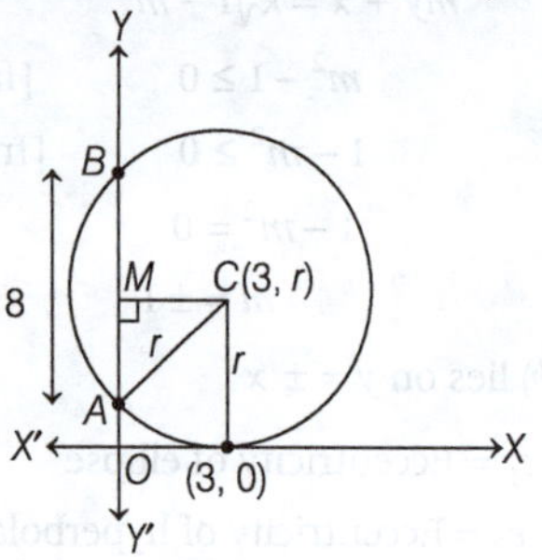

From the figure, we have

$$CM = 3 \Rightarrow CA = r$$

and $\quad AM = BM = \dfrac{AB}{2} = 4$

Then, in ΔCMA

$$r^2 = CM^2 + AM^2 = 9 + 16 = 25$$

$\Rightarrow r = \pm 5$

Now, the equation of circle having centre $(3, \pm 5)$ and radius = 5 is

$$(x-3)^2 + (y \pm 5)^2 = 25$$

Now, from the option (3, 10) satisfy the equation of circle $(x-3)^2 + (y-5)^2 = 25$

42. *(c)* Given, $C_1 : x^2 + y^2 - 16x - 20y + 164 = r^2$

$\Rightarrow \qquad (x-8)^2 + (y-10)^2 = r^2$

$$C_1\ (8, 10) \text{ and } r_1 = r$$

and $\quad C_2 : (x-4)^2 + (y-7)^2 = 36$

$$C_2(4, 7) \text{ and } r_2 = 6$$

Two circles intersect, if $|r_1 - r_2| < C_1C_2 < r_1 + r_2$

$$|r-6| < \sqrt{(8-4)^2 + (10-7)^2} < r+6$$

$\Rightarrow |r-6| < \sqrt{16+9} < r+6 \Rightarrow |r-6| < 5 < r+6$

Now, 5 is always less than $r+6$.

$\because |r-6| < 5 \Rightarrow -5 < r-6 < 5$

$$= -5+6 < r < 5+6 = 1 < r < 11$$

43. *(b)* Given, circles $C_1 : x^2 + y^2 - 2x - 2y - 2 = 0$

and $\qquad C_2 : x^2 + y^2 - 6x - 6y + 14 = 0$

are intersecting each other orthogonally because $2(1)(3) + 2(1)(3) = 14 - 2$

[$\because$ two circles are intersected orthogonally, if $2g_1\, g_2 + 2f_1 f_2 = C_1 + C_2$]

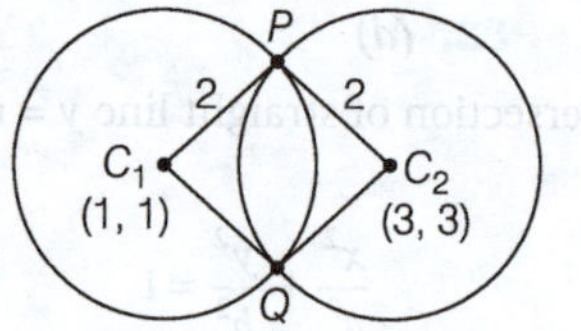

So, area of quadrilateral

$$PC_1QC_2 = 2 \times \text{area of } \Delta PC_1C_2$$

$$= 2 \times \frac{1}{2} \times 2 \times 2 = 4 \text{ sq units}$$

44. *(b)* Vertex of parabola

$$y^2 = -4(x - a^2) \text{ is } (a^2, 0)$$

For point of intersection with Y-axis put $x = 0$ in the given equation of parabola.

This gives, $y^2 = 4a^2 \Rightarrow y = \pm 2a$

Thus, the points of intersection are $(0, 2a)$ and $(0, -2a)$.

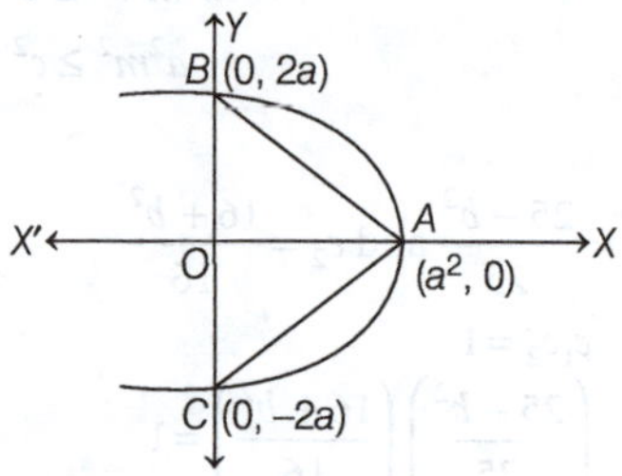

From the given condition,

Area of $\Delta ABC = 250$

$\Rightarrow \dfrac{1}{2}(BC)(OA) = 250$

$\Rightarrow \quad \dfrac{1}{2}(4a)(a^2) = 250$

$\Rightarrow \qquad a^3 = 125 \Rightarrow a = 5$

45. *(c)* Let the radius of circle with least area be r. Then, the coordinates of centre $= (0, 4-r)$

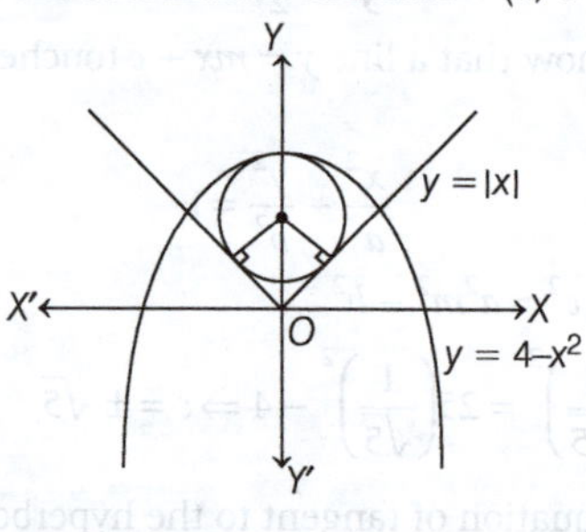

Since, circle touches the line $y = x$ in first quadrant.

$\therefore \quad \left|\dfrac{0-(4-r)}{\sqrt{2}}\right| = r \Rightarrow r - 4 = \pm\sqrt{2}r$

$\Rightarrow \quad r = \dfrac{4}{\sqrt{2}+1} \qquad [\because r > 0]$

$\Rightarrow \quad r = \dfrac{4(\sqrt{2}-1)}{(\sqrt{2}+1)(\sqrt{2}-1)} = 4(\sqrt{2}-1)$

46. ***(c)*** Since, equation of given parabola is $y^2 = 4\sqrt{2}x$ and equation of tangent line is $ax + y = c$ or $y = -ax + c$, then $c = \dfrac{\sqrt{2}}{m} = \dfrac{\sqrt{2}}{-a}$

[$\because$ line $y = mx + c$ touches the parabola $y^2 = 4ax$ if $c = a/m$]

Then, equation of tangent line becomes $y = -ax - \dfrac{\sqrt{2}}{a}$ which is also tangent to circle $x^2 + y^2 = 1$.

$\therefore \quad r = 1 = \left|\dfrac{-\sqrt{2}/a}{\sqrt{1+a^2}}\right| \Rightarrow \sqrt{1+a^2} = \left|-\dfrac{\sqrt{2}}{a}\right|$

$\Rightarrow \quad 1 + a^2 = \dfrac{2}{a^2}$

$\Rightarrow \quad a^4 + a^2 - 2 = 0$

$\Rightarrow \quad (a^2+2)(a^2-1) = 0$

$\Rightarrow \quad a^2 = 1 \text{ or } a^2 \neq -2$

$\therefore \quad |c| = \left|\dfrac{\sqrt{2}}{a}\right| = \dfrac{\sqrt{2}}{1} = \sqrt{2}$

47. ***(b)*** Let the equation of ellipse be $\dfrac{x^2}{a^2} + \dfrac{y^2}{b^2} = 1$

Then, according to the problem, we have

$\dfrac{2b^2}{a} = 8 \text{ and } 2ae = 2b$

$\Rightarrow \quad b\left(\dfrac{b}{a}\right) = 4 \text{ and } \left(\dfrac{b}{a}\right) = e$

$\Rightarrow \quad be = 4 \Rightarrow b = \dfrac{4}{e}$

Also, we know that

$b^2 = a^2(1-e^2)$

$\Rightarrow \quad \dfrac{b^2}{a^2} = 1 - e^2 \Rightarrow e^2 = 1 - e^2 \qquad \left[\because \dfrac{b}{a} = e\right]$

$\Rightarrow \quad 2e^2 = 1 \Rightarrow e = \dfrac{1}{\sqrt{2}}$

Now, $\quad b = \dfrac{4}{e} \Rightarrow b = 4\sqrt{2}$

$\Rightarrow \quad a^2 = \dfrac{b^2}{1-e^2} = \dfrac{32}{1-\dfrac{1}{2}} = 64$

$\therefore$ Equation of ellipse be

$\dfrac{x^2}{64} + \dfrac{y^2}{32} = 1$

Now, check all the option only $(4\sqrt{3}, 2\sqrt{2})$ satisfy the above equation.

48. ***(b)*** Equation of given ellipse is

$\dfrac{x^2}{a^2} + \dfrac{y^2}{b^2} = 1 \qquad \ldots(i)$

Now, equation of tangent at the point $\left(3, -\dfrac{9}{2}\right)$ on the ellipse (i) is $\dfrac{3x}{a^2} - \dfrac{9y}{2b^2} = 1 \qquad \ldots(ii)$

[$\because$ equation of tangent of ellipse $\dfrac{x^2}{a^2} + \dfrac{y^2}{b^2} = 1$ at point (x_1, y_1), is $\dfrac{xx_1}{a^2} + \dfrac{yy_1}{b^2} = 1$]

$\therefore$ Tangent Eq. (ii) represents the line

$x - y = 12$

So, $\dfrac{1}{3/a^2} = \dfrac{2}{9/b^2} = \dfrac{12}{1}$

$\Rightarrow \quad a^2 = 36 \text{ and } b^2 = 54$

Now, length of latusrectum

$= \dfrac{2b^2}{a} = \dfrac{2\times 54}{6} = 18 \text{ units}$

49. ***(c)***

50. ***(b)*** For the hyperbola $\dfrac{x^2}{a^2} - \dfrac{y^2}{b^2} = 1, e = \sqrt{1 + \dfrac{b^2}{a^2}}$

For the given hyperbola,

$e = \sqrt{1 + \dfrac{\sin^2\theta}{\cos^2\theta}} > 2$

$\Rightarrow \quad 1 + \tan^2\theta > 4$

$\Rightarrow \quad \tan^2\theta > 3$

$\Rightarrow \quad \tan\theta \in (-\infty, -\sqrt{3}) \cup (\sqrt{3}, \infty)$

But $\theta \in \left(0, \dfrac{\pi}{2}\right) \Rightarrow \tan\theta \in (\sqrt{3}, \infty)$

$\Rightarrow \theta \in \left(\dfrac{\pi}{3}, \dfrac{\pi}{2}\right)$

Now, length of latusrectum

$$= \frac{2b^2}{a} = \frac{2\sin^2\theta}{\cos\theta} = 2\sin\theta\tan\theta$$

Since, both $\sin\theta$ and $\tan\theta$ are increasing function.

$\therefore$ Least value of latusrectum

$$= 2\sin\frac{\pi}{3}\tan\frac{\pi}{3} = 2\times\frac{\sqrt{3}}{2}\times\sqrt{3} = 3$$

and greatest value is ∞.

Hence, latusrectum $= (3, \infty)$

51. *(a)* Reason is true.

Assertion Given, equation

$$y = -\frac{x^2}{2} + x + 1$$

$\Rightarrow \quad x^2 - 2x - 2 = -2y \Rightarrow x^2 - 2x + 1 = -2y + 3$

$\Rightarrow \quad (x-1)^2 = -2\left(y - \frac{3}{2}\right)$

which is parabola with axis as the line

$$x - 1 = 0$$

and its symmetric with respect to line $x = 1$

Assertion is true.

$\therefore$ Both Assertion and Reason are true and Reason is correct explanation of Assertion.

52. *(d)* Distance between two foci of the hyperbola

$$= 2ae$$

$\therefore \sqrt{(4+6)^2 + (1-1)^2} = 2ae$

$\Rightarrow \quad 10 = 2ae$

$\Rightarrow \quad 10 = 2a\left(\frac{5}{4}\right) \quad \left[\because e = \frac{5}{4}\right]$

$\Rightarrow \quad a = 4$

Hence, length of transverse axis

$$= 2a = 2\times 4 = 8 \text{ units}$$

So, Assertion is not true.

Distance between two foci $= 2ae$

$= $ Transverse axis $\times$ eccentricity

So, Reason is true.

53. *(c)* (A) $\frac{x^2}{9} + \frac{y^2}{16} = 1$

$\therefore \; c = \sqrt{16 - 9} = \sqrt{7}$

$\therefore$ Focus $= (0, \pm\sqrt{7})$

Equation of tangent at $\left(\frac{9}{4}, \sqrt{7}\right)$, the positive end of latusrectum is $\frac{x}{4} + \frac{\sqrt{7}y}{16} = 1$

$\Rightarrow \quad 4x + \sqrt{7}y - 16 = 0$

(B) $\frac{x^2}{16} - \frac{y^2}{25} = 1$

Positive end of latusrectum $= \left(\sqrt{41}, \frac{25}{4}\right)$

Equation of tangent $\sqrt{41}\,x - 4y - 16 = 0$

(C) $x^2 - y^2 = 4$

Positive end of latusrectum $(2\sqrt{2}, 2)$

Equation of tangent $2\sqrt{2}x - 2y = 4$

$\Rightarrow \quad \sqrt{2}x - y - 2 = 0$

(D) $y^2 = 8(x - 4)$

Focus $(6, 0)$

Positive end of latusrectum $(6, 4)$.

Equation of tangent at $(6, 4)$ is

$x - y - 2 = 0$.

Solutions. (Q. Nos. 54-55)

54. *(d)* **55.** *(d)*

Equation of bisectors of $x + 2y + 3 = 0$

and $\quad 2x + y + 3 = 0$ are given by,

$$x - y = 0$$

and $\quad x + y + 2 = 0$

Point of intersection of bisectors $P(-1, -1)$.

Thus, focus is the foot of perpendicular from P to line joining $(1, 1)$ and $(0, -2)$.

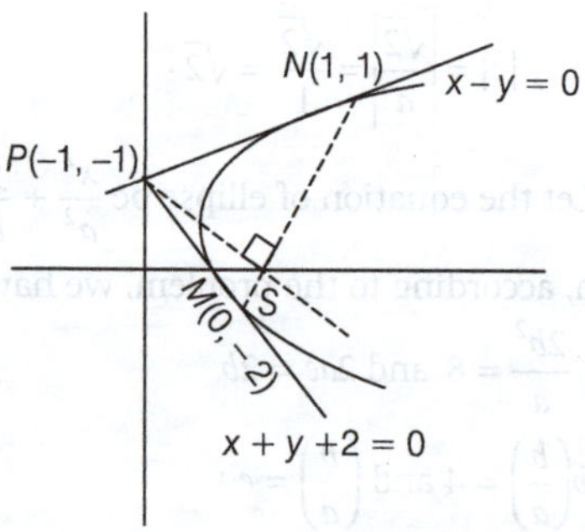

$MN : 3x - y - 2 = 0$ [equation of line passing through $(1, 1)$ and $(0, -2)$]

$PS : x + 3y + 4 = 0 \quad [\because MN \perp PS]$

$\therefore \quad$ Focus $S\left(\frac{1}{5}, \frac{-7}{5}\right)$

$MS = \sqrt{\frac{2}{5}}$ and $NS = 4\sqrt{\frac{2}{5}}$

$\because$ Harmonic mean of segments of focal chord is semi-latusrectum.

$$\therefore \text{Length of latusrectum} = 2\left[\frac{2\left(\sqrt{\frac{2}{5}}\right)\left(4\sqrt{\frac{2}{5}}\right)}{\sqrt{\frac{2}{5}}+4\sqrt{\frac{2}{5}}}\right]$$

$$= \frac{16\sqrt{2}}{5^{3/2}} \text{ units}$$

Solutions. (Q.Nos. 56-58)

56. *(c)* **57.** *(b)* **58.** *(d)*

Parabola : $y^2 = 2x$

Ellipse : $\frac{x^2}{9} + \frac{y^2}{4} = 1$

Point of intersection

$$\frac{x^2}{9} + \frac{2x}{4} = 1$$

$$\Rightarrow \quad 4x^2 + 18x - 36 = 0 \Rightarrow x = \frac{3}{2}, -6$$

But for $\quad y^2 = 2x, \; x > 0$

$$\therefore \quad x = \frac{3}{2} \Rightarrow y = \pm\sqrt{3}$$

$$P\left(\frac{3}{2}, \sqrt{3}\right)$$

and $\quad Q\left(\frac{3}{2}, -\sqrt{3}\right)$

Equation of tangent at P and Q to ellipse is

$$\frac{x}{9}\left(\frac{3}{2}\right) + \frac{y}{4}(\pm\sqrt{3}) = 1$$

$$\Rightarrow \quad \frac{x}{6} + \frac{\sqrt{3}y}{4} = 1 \text{ and } \frac{x}{6} - \frac{\sqrt{3}}{4}y = 1$$

Point of intersection of tangents $R(6, 0)$.

Equation of tangent at P and Q to parabola is

$$y(\pm\sqrt{3}) = x + \frac{3}{2},$$

which cuts X-axis at $x = \frac{-3}{2}$

Point $S\left(\frac{-3}{2}, 0\right)$

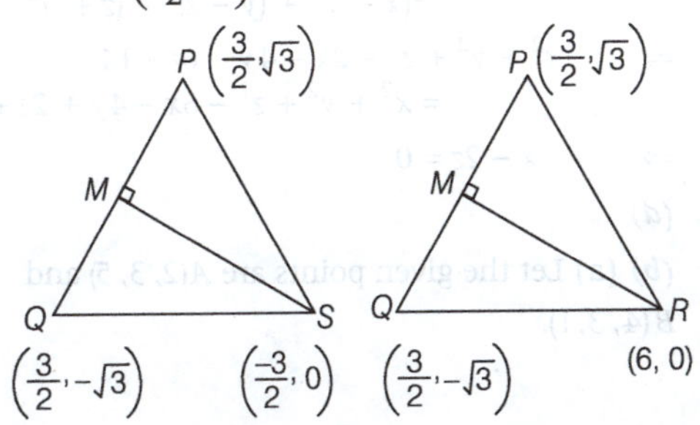

Here, $QS = PS = \sqrt{12}$

and $QR = PR = \sqrt{\frac{93}{4}}$

So, ΔPQS and ΔPQR are isosceles triangle.

$$\Rightarrow MP = MQ = \frac{PQ}{2} = \frac{2\sqrt{3}}{2} = \sqrt{3} \text{ (in } \Delta PQS)$$

$$\Rightarrow MP = MQ = \frac{PQ}{2} = \frac{2\sqrt{3}}{2} = \sqrt{3} \text{ (in } \Delta PQR)$$

So, in right angled triangles

i.e. ΔQSM and ΔQRM

By Pythagoras theorem,

$$QS^2 = MQ^2 + MS^2 \text{ and } QR^2 = MQ^2 + MR^2$$

$$\Rightarrow MS = 3 \text{ and } MR = \frac{9}{2}$$

$$\therefore \quad \frac{\text{Area of } \Delta PQS}{\text{Area of } \Delta PQR} = \frac{\frac{1}{2} \times PQ \times MS}{\frac{1}{2} \times PQ \times MR}$$

$$= \frac{MS}{MR} = \frac{3}{\frac{9}{2}} = \frac{2}{3}$$

$$\therefore \text{Area of quadrilateral} = \frac{1}{2}PQ(MS + MR)$$

$$= \frac{1}{2} \times 2\sqrt{3}\left(3 + \frac{9}{2}\right)$$

$$= \frac{15\sqrt{3}}{2} \text{ sq units}$$

Upper end of latusrectum of parabola is $\left(\frac{1}{2}, 1\right)$.

Equation of tangent at $\left(\frac{1}{2}, 1\right)$ to parabola

$$y = x + \frac{1}{2}$$

Equation of circle is

$$\left(x - \frac{1}{2}\right)^2 + (y-1)^2 + \lambda\left(y - x - \frac{1}{2}\right) = 0$$

Circle passes through vertex $(0, 0)$

$$\therefore \quad \frac{1}{4} + 1 - \frac{\lambda}{2} = 0$$

$$\Rightarrow \quad \lambda = \frac{5}{2}$$

$\therefore$ Equation of required circle is

$$\left(x - \frac{1}{2}\right)^2 + (y-1)^2 + \frac{5}{2}\left(y - x - \frac{1}{2}\right) = 0$$

$$\Rightarrow \quad 2x^2 + 2y^2 - 7x + y = 0$$

Chapter 11 Introduction to 3-D Geometry

1. ***(b)*** For the point *F*, the distance measured along *OY* is zero. Therefore, the coordinates of *F* are (2, 0, 5).

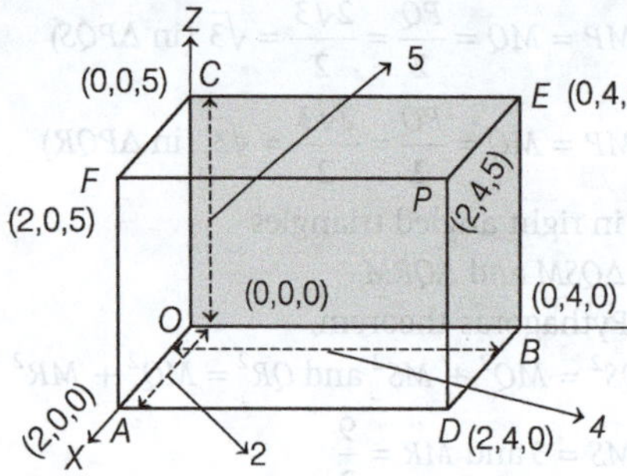

2. ***(b)*** Let the coordinates of point *P* be (x, y, z).
Here, $PA^2 = (x-3)^2 + (y-4)^2 + (z-5)^2$
and $PB^2 = (x+1)^2 + (y-3)^2 + (z+7)^2$
By the given condition $PA^2 + PB^2 = 2k^2$, we have
$$(x-3)^2 + (y-4)^2 + (z-5)^2 + (x+1)^2 + (y-3)^2 + (z+7)^2 = 2k^2$$
i.e. $2x^2 + 2y^2 + 2z^2 - 4x - 14y + 4z = 2k^2 - 109$

3. ***(b)*** In *YZ*-plane, $|x| = 0$
In *ZX*-plane, $|y| = 0$
$\Rightarrow \quad |x| = |y|$
$\Rightarrow \quad x^2 - y^2 = 0$

4. ***(d)*** $A(2, 1, 5), B(3, 2, 3), C(4, 0, 4)$
$AB = BC = CA$
Triangle is equilateral
$\Rightarrow$ Circumcentre = Orthocentre
$\Rightarrow$ Circumcentre – Othocentre = 0 unit

5. ***(d)*** Let $A(5, 0, 0), B(0, 5, 0), C(0, 0, 5)$.
Perimeter $= AB + BC + CA$
$= \sqrt{50} + \sqrt{50} + \sqrt{50}$
$= 3\sqrt{50} = 15\sqrt{2}$ units

6. ***(b)*** By Pythagoras theorem,
$AC^2 = AD^2 + DC^2$
$AC^2 = (\text{Side})^2 + (\text{Side})^2$
$AC^2 = 2\,\text{Side}^2$
$AC = \sqrt{2}\,\text{Side}$
$\because$ Length of diagonal = Side $\sqrt{2}$
$\Rightarrow \sqrt{(1-2)^2 + (-2+3)^2 + (3-5)^2} = \text{Side}\sqrt{2}$

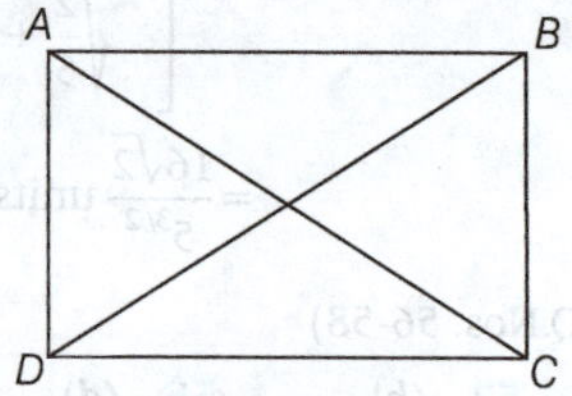

$\Rightarrow \quad \sqrt{1+1+4} = \text{Side}\sqrt{2}$
$\Rightarrow \quad \sqrt{6} = \text{Side}\sqrt{2}$
$\Rightarrow \quad \text{Side} = \sqrt{3}$ units

7. ***(c)*** $OA = \sqrt{1^2 + 2^2 + 3^2} = \sqrt{14}$ units
$OB = \sqrt{3^2 + 4^2 + 5^2} = \sqrt{50}$ units
$OC = \sqrt{1^2 + 0^2 + 1^2} = \sqrt{2}$ units
$OD = \sqrt{3^2 + 8^2 + 6^2} = \sqrt{109}$ units
Here, $\sqrt{2}$ is smallest of all.

8. ***(a)***

9. ***(b)*** Image of $P(x, y, z)$ in *ZX*-plane is $Q(x, -y, z)$.
$PQ = \sqrt{(x-x)^2 + (y+y)^2 + (z-z)^2}$
$= \sqrt{(2y)^2} = 2|y|$

10. ***(d)*** Let $A(-2, 3, 5), B(1, 2, 3)$ and $C(7, 0, -1)$.
$AB = \sqrt{3^2 + 1^2 + 2^2} = \sqrt{14}$ units
$BC = \sqrt{36 + 4 + 16} = \sqrt{56} = 2\sqrt{14}$ units
$CA = \sqrt{81 + 9 + 36} = \sqrt{126} = 3\sqrt{14}$ units
$AB + BC = CA$
Given points are collinear points.

11. ***(a)*** Let *P* be the point which is equidistant from *A* and *B*. i.e. $PA = PB$
$\Rightarrow \quad PA^2 = PB^2$
$\Rightarrow \quad (x-1)^2 + (y-2)^2 + (z-3)^2 = (x-3)^2 + (y-2)^2 + (z+1)^2$
$\Rightarrow \quad x^2 + y^2 + z^2 - 2x - 4y - 6z + 14 = x^2 + y^2 + z^2 - 6x - 4y + 2z + 14$
$\Rightarrow \quad x - 2z = 0$

12. ***(d)***

13. ***(b)*** (a) Let the given points are $A(2, 3, 5)$ and $B(4, 3, 1)$.

$\therefore$ Required distance

$$AB = \sqrt{(4-2)^2 + (3-3)^2 + (1-5)^2}$$
$$= \sqrt{4+0+16} = \sqrt{20} = 2\sqrt{5}$$

(b) Let the given points are $A(-3, 7, 2)$ and $B(2, 4, -1)$.

$\therefore$ Required distance

$$AB = \sqrt{[2-(-3)]^2 + (4-7)^2 + (-1-2)^2}$$
$$= \sqrt{(2+3)^2 + (4-7)^2 + (-1-2)^2}$$
$$= \sqrt{25+9+9}$$
$$= \sqrt{43}$$

(c) Let the given points are $A(-1, 3, -4)$ and $B(1, -3, 4)$.

$\therefore$ Required distance,

$$AB = \sqrt{(1+1)^2 + (-3-3)^2 + (4+4)^2}$$
$$= \sqrt{4+36+64}$$
$$= \sqrt{104} = 2\sqrt{26}$$

(d) Let the given points are $A(2, -1, 3)$ and $B(-2, 1, 3)$.

$\therefore$ Required distance

$$AB = \sqrt{(-2-2)^2 + (1+1)^2 + (3-3)^2}$$
$$= \sqrt{4^2 + 2^2 + 0}$$
$$= \sqrt{16+4} = \sqrt{20} = 2\sqrt{5}$$

14. ***(d)*** (a) Let $A(0, 7, -10)$, $B(1, 6, -6)$ and $C(4, 9, -6)$ are the vertices of a triangle. Then,

Side $AB = \sqrt{1+1+16} = \sqrt{18} = 3\sqrt{2}$

and side $BC = \sqrt{9+9+0} = \sqrt{18} = 3\sqrt{2}$

Clearly, $AB = BC$.

Hence, triangle is an isosceles triangle.

(b) Let $A(0, 7, 10)$, $B(-1, 6, 6)$ and $C(-4, 9, 6)$ are the vertices of a triangle. Then,

Side $AB = \sqrt{1+1+16} = \sqrt{18} = 3\sqrt{2}$

Side $BC = \sqrt{9+9+0} = \sqrt{18} = 3\sqrt{2}$

and side $CA = \sqrt{16+4+16} = \sqrt{36} = 6$

Now, $AB^2 + BC^2 = (3\sqrt{2})^2 + (3\sqrt{2})^2 = 6^2 = CA^2$

$\therefore$ ΔABC is right angled triangle at B.

(c) Let $A(-1, 2, 1)$, $B(1, -2, 5)$, $C(4, -7, 8)$ and $D(2, -3, 4)$ are the vertices of a quadrilateral $ABCD$.

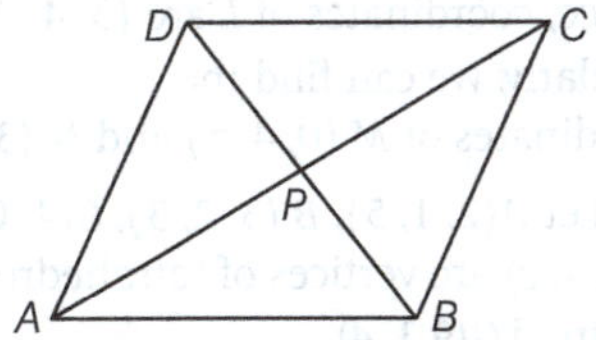

Then, mid-point of $AC = \left(\frac{3}{2}, \frac{-5}{2}, \frac{9}{2}\right)$

Mid-point of $BD = \left(\frac{3}{2}, \frac{-5}{2}, \frac{9}{2}\right)$

Mid-points of both the diagonals are same (i.e. they bisect each other.)

Hence, $ABCD$ is a parallelogram.

15. ***(b)*** Given, distance between points $(a, 0, 1)$ and $(0, 1, 2)$ is $\sqrt{27}$.

$$\therefore \sqrt{(a-0)^2 + (0-1)^2 + (1-2)^2} = \sqrt{27}$$
$$\Rightarrow \quad \sqrt{a^2 + 1^2 + 1^2} = \sqrt{27}$$
$$\Rightarrow \quad a^2 + 2 = 27$$

[$\because$ squaring both sides]

$$\Rightarrow \quad a^2 = 25 \Rightarrow a = \pm 5$$

16. ***(b)*** Let point be $P(x, y, z) = (1, 2, 3)$

$\therefore$ The distance from X-axis $= \sqrt{y^2 + z^2}$
$$= \sqrt{4+9} = \sqrt{13}$$

The distance from Y-axis $= \sqrt{x^2 + z^2} = \sqrt{1^2 + 3^2}$
$$= \sqrt{1+9} = \sqrt{10}$$

The distance from Z-axis $= \sqrt{x^2 + y^2} = \sqrt{1^2 + 2^2}$
$$= \sqrt{1+4} = \sqrt{5}$$

17. ***(b)*** Since, L is the foot of perpendicular segment from P on the XY-plane, z-coordinate is zero in the XY-plane.

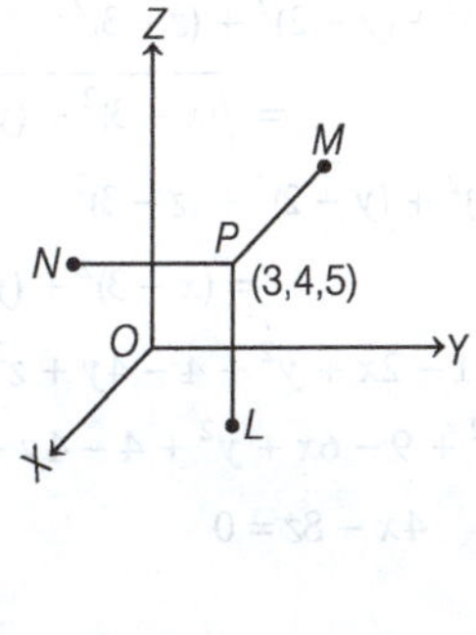

Hence, coordinates of L are (3, 4, 0). Similarly, we can find the coordinates of M (0, 4, 5) and N (3, 0, 5).

18. ***(a)*** Let $A(2, 1, 5)$, $B(3, 2, 3)$, $C(4, 0, 4)$, $D(x, y, z)$ are vertices of tetrahedron.

Centroid $G(9, 1, 4)$

$$G = \frac{A+B+C+D}{4}$$

$$\Rightarrow D = 4G - (A+B+C)$$
$$= 4(9,1,4) - [(2,1,5) + (3,2,3) + (4,0,4)]$$
$$= (36, 4, 16) - (9, 3, 12)$$
$$D = (27, 1, 4)$$

19. ***(b)*** P is centroid of ΔBCD.

So, G divides AP in 3 : 1 such that $AG = 3x$ and $GP = x$ i.e. $AP = AG + GP$

$$\Rightarrow \quad AP = AG + \frac{AG}{3}$$

$$\Rightarrow \quad AP = AG + \frac{AG}{3} = \frac{4}{3}AG$$

$$= \frac{4}{3}\sqrt{(2-2)^2 + (3-3)^2 + (4+1)^2}$$

$$= \frac{4\times 5}{3} = \frac{20}{3}$$

20. ***(b)*** Let the given points are A and B.

Let $P(x, y, z)$ be any point equidistant from A and B.

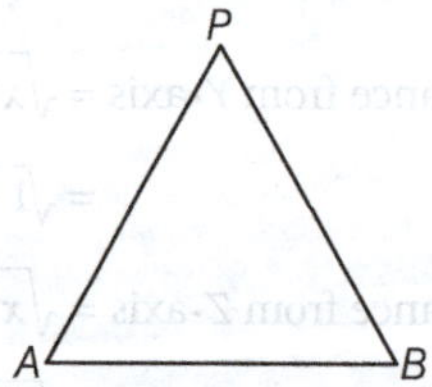

$$\therefore \quad PA = PB,$$

i.e. distance between P and A

= distance between P and B

$$\Rightarrow \sqrt{(x-1)^2 + (y-2)^2 + (z-3)^2}$$
$$= \sqrt{(x-3)^2 + (y-2)^2 + (z+1)^2}$$

$$\Rightarrow (x-1)^2 + (y-2)^2 + (z-3)^2$$
$$= (x-3)^2 + (y-2)^2 + (z+1)^2$$

$$\Rightarrow x^2 + 1 - 2x + y^2 + 4 - 4y + z^2 + 9 - 6z$$
$$= x^2 + 9 - 6x + y^2 + 4 - 4y + z^2 + 1 + 2z$$

$$\Rightarrow \quad 4x - 8z = 0$$

$$\Rightarrow \quad x - 2z = 0$$

which is the required equation.

21. ***(c)*** $\because$ Vertices of ΔABC are $A(-1, 3, 2)$, $B(2, 3, 5)$ and $C(3, 5, -2)$.

$$\Rightarrow \quad AB = \sqrt{9+0+9} = \sqrt{18}$$
$$CA = \sqrt{16+4+16} = 6$$

and $$BC = \sqrt{1+4+49} = \sqrt{54}$$

$$\because \quad AB^2 + CA^2 = BC^2$$

ΔABC is right angled triangle at A.

$$\therefore \quad \angle A = 90°$$

22. ***(a)*** $\therefore$ Distance from point $(x, y, \sqrt{1-x^2-y^2})$ to the origin.

$$= \sqrt{(x-0)^2 + (y-0)^2 + \sqrt{(1-x^2-y^2-0)^2}}$$
$$= \sqrt{x^2 + y^2 + 1 - x^2 - y^2}$$
$$= \sqrt{1+1-(1)} \quad [\because x^2 + y^2 = 1 \text{ given}]$$
$$= \sqrt{1} = 1$$

23. ***(a)*** The edge of a parallelopiped

$$= (3-5, 6-8, 8-10)$$
$$= (-2, -2, -2)$$

$$\therefore \text{Length of diagonal} = \sqrt{(-2)^2 + (-2)^2 + (-2)^2}$$
$$= \sqrt{4+4+4}$$
$$= 2\sqrt{3}$$

24. ***(b)*** Let $P(x, y, z)$ be any point in the plane.

According to the given condition,

(distance from P to X-axis)^2

+ (distance from P to Y-axis)^2

+ (distance from P to Z-axis)^2 = 36

$$\Rightarrow (\sqrt{y^2+z^2})^2 + (\sqrt{x^2+z^2})^2 + (\sqrt{x^2+y^2})^2 = 36$$

$$\Rightarrow \quad (y^2+z^2) + (x^2+z^2) + (x^2+y^2) = 36$$

$$\Rightarrow \quad 2(x^2+y^2+z^2) = 36$$

$$\Rightarrow \quad x^2+y^2+z^2 = 18 \quad \ldots(i)$$

$\therefore$ The distance from origin to the point (x, y, z) is

$$= \sqrt{x^2+y^2+z^2} = \sqrt{18}$$

[$\because$ from Eq. (i)]

$$= 3\sqrt{2}$$

25. ***(a)*** Now, $\Delta_{xy} = \frac{1}{2}\left\|\begin{matrix} 1 & -1 & 1 \\ 2 & -4 & 1 \\ 5 & -13 & 1 \end{matrix}\right\|$

$$= \frac{1}{2}|[1(-4+13)+1(2-5)+1(-26+20)]|$$

$$= \frac{1}{2}|[9-3-6]| = 0$$

$$\Delta_{yz} = \frac{1}{2}\left\|\begin{matrix} -1 & 3 & 1 \\ -4 & 5 & 1 \\ -13 & 11 & 1 \end{matrix}\right\|$$

$$= \frac{1}{2}|[-1(5-11)-3(-4+13)+1(-44+65)]|$$

$$= \frac{1}{2}|[6-27+21]| = 0$$

$$\Delta_{zx} = \frac{1}{2}\left\|\begin{matrix} 3 & 1 & 1 \\ 5 & 2 & 1 \\ 11 & 5 & 1 \end{matrix}\right\|$$

$$= \frac{1}{2}|[3(2-5)-1(5-11)+1(25-22)]|$$

$$= \frac{1}{2}|[-9+6+3]| = 0$$

$\therefore$ Area of triangle $= \sqrt{\Delta_{xy}^2 + \Delta_{yz}^2 + \Delta_{zx}^2}$

$$= \sqrt{0+0+0} = 0$$

Hence, given points are collinear.

26. ***(c)*** $\because$ $\Delta_{yz} = \frac{1}{2}\left\|\begin{matrix} y_1 & z_1 & 1 \\ y_2 & z_2 & 1 \\ y_3 & z_3 & 1 \end{matrix}\right\|, \Delta_{zx} = \frac{1}{2}\left\|\begin{matrix} z_1 & x_1 & 1 \\ z_2 & x_2 & 1 \\ z_3 & x_3 & 1 \end{matrix}\right\|$

$$\Delta_{xy} = \frac{1}{2}\left\|\begin{matrix} x_1 & y_1 & 1 \\ x_2 & y_2 & 1 \\ x_3 & y_3 & 1 \end{matrix}\right\|$$

$$\therefore \quad \Delta_{yz} = \frac{1}{2}\left\|\begin{matrix} 1 & 1 & 1 \\ 1 & 2 & 1 \\ 0 & 1 & 1 \end{matrix}\right\|$$

$$= \frac{1}{2}|[1(2-1)-1(1-0)+1(1-0)]|$$

$$= \frac{1}{2}|[1-1+1]|$$

$$= \frac{1}{2}$$

$$\Delta_{zx} = \frac{1}{2}\left\|\begin{matrix} 1 & 2 & 1 \\ 2 & 3 & 1 \\ 1 & -4 & 1 \end{matrix}\right\|$$

$$= \frac{1}{2}|[1(3+4)-2(2-1)+1(-8-3)]|$$

$$= \frac{1}{2}|[7-2-11]| = 3$$

$$\Delta_{xy} = \frac{1}{2}\left\|\begin{matrix} 2 & 1 & 1 \\ 3 & 1 & 1 \\ -4 & 0 & 1 \end{matrix}\right\|$$

$$= \frac{1}{2}|[2(1-0)-1(3+4)+1(0+4)]| = \frac{1}{2}$$

$\therefore$ Area of triangle,

$$\Delta = \sqrt{\Delta_{yz}^2 + \Delta_{zx}^2 + \Delta_{xy}^2}$$

$$= \sqrt{\left(\frac{1}{2}\right)^2 + (3)^2 + \left(\frac{1}{2}\right)^2}$$

$$= \sqrt{\frac{1}{4} + 9 + \frac{1}{4}} = \frac{\sqrt{38}}{2} \text{ sq units}$$

Solutions (Q. Nos. 27 and 28) Here, P is any point in the space, not in a coordinate plane, and through P pass planes parallel to the coordinate planes YZ, ZX and XY meeting the coordinate axes in the points A, B, and C, respectively.

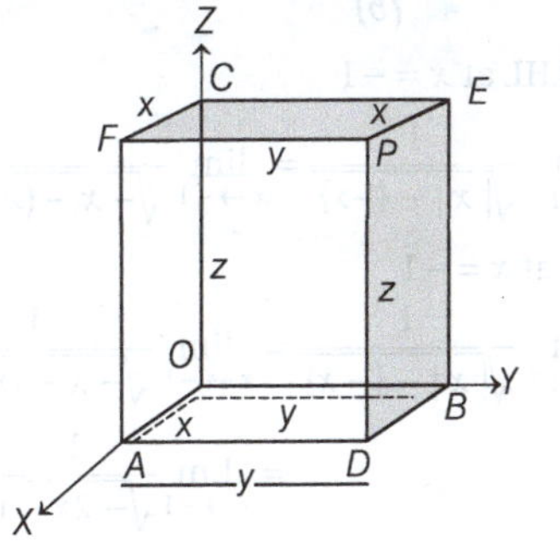

27. ***(d)*** So, three planes are
(i) $ADPF \parallel YZ$-plane
(ii) $BDPE \parallel XZ$-plane
(iii) $CFPE \parallel XY$-plane

28. ***(c)*** These planes determine a rectangular parallelopiped which has three pairs of rectangular faces ($ADPF$, $OBEC$), ($BDPE$, $CFAO$) and ($AOBD$, $FPEC$)

Chapter 12 Limits and Derivatives

1. *(c)* LHL at $x = 5$

$$\lim_{x\to 5^-}\frac{|x-5|}{x-5}=\lim_{h\to 0}\frac{|5-h-5|}{5-h-5}=\lim_{h\to 0}\frac{h}{-h}=-1$$

RHL at $x = 5$

$$\lim_{x\to 5^+}\frac{|x-5|}{x-5}=\lim_{h\to 0}\frac{|5+h-5|}{5+h-5}=\lim_{h\to 0}\frac{h}{h}=1$$

LHL $\neq$ RHL

$\therefore$ Limit does not exist.

2. *(c)* $$\lim_{y\to 0}\frac{y\sqrt{x^2-(x-y)^2}}{\{\sqrt{8xy-4y^2}+\sqrt{8xy}\}^3}$$

$$=\lim_{y\to 0}\frac{y\sqrt{2xy-y^2}}{\{\sqrt{y}\,(\sqrt{8x-4y}+\sqrt{y}\sqrt{8x})\}^3}$$

$$=\lim_{y\to 0}\frac{y\sqrt{y}\,\sqrt{2x-y}}{y\sqrt{y}\{\sqrt{8x-4y}+\sqrt{8x}\}^3}$$

$$=\lim_{y\to 0}\frac{\sqrt{2x-y}}{\{\sqrt{8x-4y}+\sqrt{8x}\}^3}$$

$$=\frac{\sqrt{2x}}{(2\sqrt{8x})^3}=\frac{\sqrt{2x}}{8\times 8x\sqrt{8x}}$$

$$=\frac{1}{128x}$$

3. *(d)** **4.** *(b)*

5. *(d)* LHL at $x = -1$

$$\lim_{x\to -1^-}\frac{1}{\sqrt{|x|-\{-x\}}}=\lim_{x\to -1}\frac{1}{\sqrt{-x-(x+2)}}=\infty$$

RHL at $x = -1$

$$\lim_{x\to -1^+}\frac{1}{\sqrt{|x|-\{-x\}}}=\lim_{x\to -1}\frac{1}{\sqrt{-x-(x+1)}}$$

$$=\lim_{x\to -1}\frac{1}{\sqrt{-2x-1}}=1$$

LHL $\neq$ RHL

$\therefore$ Limit does not exist.

6. *(c)* $$\lim_{x\to 2}\frac{5^{\frac{x}{2}}-5}{5^x-25}=\lim_{x\to 2}\frac{5^{\frac{x}{2}}-5}{(5^{x/2})^2-5^2}$$

$$=\lim_{x\to 2}\frac{(5^{x/2}-5)}{(5^{x/2}-5)\,(5^{x/2}+5)}$$

$$=\lim_{x\to 2}\frac{1}{5^{x/2}+5}=\frac{1}{10}$$

7. *(a)* $$\lim_{x\to 1^+}\frac{\sqrt{x^2-1}+\sqrt{x-1}}{\sqrt{x^2-1}}$$

$$=\lim_{x\to 1^+}\frac{\sqrt{x-1}(\sqrt{x+1}+1)}{\sqrt{x-1}\,\sqrt{x+1}}$$

$$=\frac{\sqrt{2}+1}{\sqrt{2}}$$

$$=1+\frac{1}{\sqrt{2}}$$

8. *(b)*

9. *(a)* $$\lim_{x\to 0}\frac{a^x-1}{\sqrt{1+x}-1}$$

$$=\lim_{x\to 0}\frac{a^x-1}{(\sqrt{1+x}-1)}\times\frac{(\sqrt{1+x}+1)}{(\sqrt{1+x}+1)}$$

$$=\lim_{x\to 0}\frac{(a^x-1)\,(\sqrt{1+x}+1)}{x}$$

$$=\lim_{x\to 0}\frac{a^x-1}{x}\cdot\lim_{x\to 0}\sqrt{1+x}+1$$

$$\left[\begin{array}{l}\because \lim\limits_{x\to a}[f(x)\,g(x)]\\ =\lim\limits_{x\to a}[f(x)\lim\limits_{x\to a}g(x)]\end{array}\right]$$

$$=\log_e a\cdot(2)=2\log_e a$$

10. *(a)* $$\lim_{x\to 1}\frac{\sqrt[3]{7+x^2}-\sqrt{3+x^2}}{x-1}$$

It is an indeterminate $\left(\frac{0}{0}\right)$ form.

On applying L' Hospital's rule, we get

$$\lim_{x\to 1}\frac{\frac{1}{3}(7+x^2)^{\frac{-2}{3}}\cdot 2x-\frac{1}{2}(3+x^2)^{\frac{-1}{2}}\cdot 2x}{1-0}$$

$$=\frac{1}{3}(8)^{\frac{-2}{3}}\cdot 2-\frac{2}{2}(4)^{\frac{-1}{2}}=\frac{2}{3}(2)^{-2}-\frac{2}{2}(2)^{-1}$$

$$=\frac{2}{3}\left[\frac{1}{4}\right]-\frac{1}{2}=-\frac{1}{3}$$

11. *(c)* $$\lim_{x\to 2}\frac{\sqrt{x-2}+\sqrt{x}-\sqrt{2}}{\sqrt{x^2-4}}$$

At $x\to 2$, it is an indeterminate $\left(\frac{0}{0}\right)$ form.

On applying L' Hospital's rule, we get

$$= \lim_{x \to 2} \frac{\frac{1}{2\sqrt{x-2}} \cdot 1 + \frac{1}{2\sqrt{x}} - 0}{\frac{1}{2\sqrt{x^2-4}} \cdot 2x}$$

$$= \lim_{x \to 2} \frac{\frac{1}{2}\left[\frac{1}{\sqrt{x-2}} + \frac{1}{\sqrt{x}}\right]}{\frac{x}{\sqrt{x-2}\sqrt{x+2}}}$$

$$= \lim_{x \to 2} \frac{\frac{1}{2}\left[\frac{\sqrt{x}+\sqrt{x-2}}{\sqrt{x}\sqrt{x-2}}\right]}{\frac{x}{\sqrt{x-2}\sqrt{x+2}}}$$

$$= \lim_{x \to 2} \frac{1}{2}\left[\frac{\sqrt{x}+\sqrt{x-2}}{x\sqrt{x}}\right]\sqrt{x+2}$$

$$= \frac{1}{2}\left[\frac{\sqrt{2}}{2\sqrt{2}}\right]\sqrt{2+2} = \frac{1}{2} \cdot \left[\frac{1}{2}\right] \cdot 2 = \frac{1}{2}$$

12. *(c)* Given, $\lim_{x \to \infty} \frac{1^2 + 2^2 + 3^2 + \ldots + x^2}{x^3}$

$$= \lim_{x \to \infty} \frac{x(x+1)(2x+1)}{6x^3}$$

[using sum of special series]

$$= \lim_{x \to \infty} \frac{\left(1 + \frac{1}{x}\right)\left(2 + \frac{1}{x}\right)}{6} = \frac{1}{3}$$

13. *(b)* Given, $\lim_{x \to \infty} \left[\frac{1}{1-x^2} + \frac{2}{1-x^2} + \ldots + \frac{x}{1-x^2}\right]$

$$= \lim_{x \to \infty} \left(\frac{1+2+\ldots+x}{1-x^2}\right)$$

$$= \lim_{x \to \infty} \frac{x(x+1)}{2(1-x)(1+x)}$$

[using sum of special series]

$$= \lim_{x \to \infty} \frac{1}{2\left(\frac{1}{x} - 1\right)} = \frac{-1}{2}$$

14. *(b)* Let $x = \lim_{n \to \infty} \left[\frac{n!}{n^n}\right]^{\frac{1}{n}}$

$$\Rightarrow \quad x = \lim_{n \to \infty} \left[\frac{1}{n} \cdot \frac{2}{n} \cdot \frac{3}{n} \cdots \frac{n}{n}\right]^{\frac{1}{n}}$$

Taking log on both sides, we get

$$\log x = \lim_{n \to \infty} \frac{1}{n}\left[\log\frac{1}{n} + \log\frac{2}{n} + \log\frac{3}{n} + \ldots + \log\frac{n}{n}\right]$$

$$= \lim_{n \to \infty} \sum_{r=1}^{n} \frac{1}{n} \log\frac{r}{n}$$

$$\log x = \int_0^1 \log x\, dx = (x \log x - x)_0^1 = -1$$

$$\Rightarrow \quad x = \frac{1}{e}$$

15. *(c)* $\lim_{x \to 0} \frac{(1 - \cos 2x)\sin 3x}{x^2 \sin 5x}$

$$= \lim_{x \to 0} \left(\frac{2\sin^2 x}{x^2}\right) \cdot \left(\frac{\sin 3x}{\sin 5x}\right)$$

$$= \lim_{x \to 0} 2\left(\frac{\sin x}{x}\right)^2 \cdot \left(\frac{\sin 3x}{3x}\right) \cdot \left(\frac{5x}{\sin 5x}\right) \frac{3}{5}$$

$$= 2 \times (1)^2 \times (1) \times (1) \times \frac{3}{5} = \frac{6}{5}$$

$$\left[\because \lim_{x \to 0} \frac{\sin ax}{ax} = 1\right]$$

16. *(c)* $\lim_{x \to 1} (1-x)\tan\left(\frac{\pi x}{2}\right)$

Let $1 - x = t \Rightarrow x = 1 - t$

As $x \to 1$, then $t \to 0$

$$\therefore \quad \lim_{t \to 0} (t) \tan\left(\frac{\pi(1-t)}{2}\right)$$

$$= \lim_{t \to 0} t \tan\left(\frac{\pi}{2} - \frac{t\pi}{2}\right)$$

$$= \lim_{t \to 0} t \cot\frac{t\pi}{2}$$

$$= \lim_{t \to 0} \frac{t}{\tan\frac{t\pi}{2}} = \lim_{t \to 0} \frac{\frac{t\pi}{2} \cdot \frac{2}{\pi}}{\tan\frac{t\pi}{2}}$$

$$= (1)\left(\frac{2}{\pi}\right) = \frac{2}{\pi} \quad \left[\because \lim_{x \to 0} \frac{\tan ax}{ax} = 1\right]$$

17. *(b)* $\lim_{x \to \frac{\pi}{2}} \left[\frac{1 - \tan\frac{x}{2}}{1 + \tan\frac{x}{2}}\right] \frac{(1 - \sin x)}{(\pi - 2x)^3}$

$$= \lim_{x \to \frac{\pi}{2}} \tan\left(\frac{\pi}{4} - \frac{x}{2}\right) \cdot \frac{(1 - \sin x)}{(\pi - 2x)^3}$$

Let $\frac{\pi}{2} - x = t$

$\Rightarrow \quad x = \frac{\pi}{2} - t$

As $\quad x \to \frac{\pi}{2}$,

then $\quad t \to 0$

$$\therefore \quad \lim_{t\to 0} \tan\frac{t}{2}\frac{(1-\cos t)}{(2t)^3}$$

$$= \lim_{t\to 0} \tan\frac{t}{2} \cdot \frac{2\sin^2\frac{t}{2}}{8t^3}$$

$$= \lim_{t\to 0} \frac{1}{32} \frac{\tan\frac{t}{2}}{\frac{t}{2}} \cdot \left(\frac{\sin\frac{t}{2}}{\frac{t}{2}}\right)^2$$

$$= \frac{1}{32} \times 1 \times (1)^2$$

$$\left[\because \lim_{t\to 0}\frac{\sin t}{t} = 1, \lim_{t\to 0}\frac{\tan t}{t} = 1\right]$$

$$= \frac{1}{32}$$

18. *(c)* Put $x = \frac{\pi}{2} - h$, as $x \to \frac{\pi}{2}, h \to 0$

$$\text{Given, limit} = \lim_{h\to 0} \frac{1-\tan\left(\frac{\pi}{4}+\frac{h}{2}\right)(1-\cos h)}{1+\tan\left(\frac{\pi}{2}+\frac{h}{2}\right)(2h)^3}$$

$$= \lim_{h\to 0} \tan\left(\frac{h}{2}\right) \lim_{h\to 0} \frac{2\cdot\sin^2\left(\frac{h}{2}\right)}{8h^3}$$

$$= \lim_{h\to 0} \frac{1}{4}\left(\frac{\tan\frac{h}{2}}{2\times\frac{h}{2}}\right) \times \lim_{h\to 0}\left(\frac{\sin\frac{h}{2}}{\frac{h}{2}}\right)^2 \times \frac{1}{4}$$

$$= \frac{1}{32}$$

19. *(d)* $\because$ Roots of $ax^2 + bx + c = 0$ are α and β.

So, roots of $cx^2 + bx + a = 0$ are $\frac{1}{\alpha}$ and $\frac{1}{\beta}$.

$$\therefore \quad cx^2 + bx + a = c\left(x - \frac{1}{\alpha}\right)\left(x - \frac{1}{\beta}\right)$$

$$\text{Now, } \lim_{x\to\frac{1}{\alpha}} \frac{\sin\left[c\left(x-\frac{1}{\alpha}\right)\left(x-\frac{1}{\beta}\right)\right]}{\alpha c\left(x-\frac{1}{\alpha}\right)\left(x-\frac{1}{\beta}\right)} \cdot c\left(x-\frac{1}{\beta}\right)$$

$$= \frac{c}{\alpha} \lim_{x\to\frac{1}{\alpha}} \left[\frac{\sin\left\{c\left(x-\frac{1}{\alpha}\right)\left(x-\frac{1}{\beta}\right)\right\}}{c\left(x-\frac{1}{\alpha}\right)\left(x-\frac{1}{\beta}\right)}\right] \cdot \lim_{x\to\frac{1}{\alpha}}\left(x-\frac{1}{\beta}\right)$$

$$= \frac{c}{\alpha}\left(\frac{1}{\alpha} - \frac{1}{\beta}\right)$$

20. *(a)* $\lim_{x\to\frac{\pi}{2}} \left(\frac{2^{\cot x} - 2^{\cos x}}{\cot x - \cos x}\right)$

$$= \lim_{x\to\frac{\pi}{2}} \left(\frac{2^{\cos x}(2^{\cot x - \cos x} - 1)}{\cot x - \cos x}\right)$$

$$= 2^{\cos\frac{\pi}{2}} \lim_{x\to\frac{\pi}{2}} \left(\frac{2^{\cot x - \cos x} - 1}{\cot x - \cos x}\right)$$

$$\left[\because \lim_{x\to a}[f(x)\, g(x)] = \lim_{x\to a} f(x) \cdot \lim_{x\to a} g(x)\right]$$

$$= \log 2 \qquad \left[\because \lim_{x\to 0}\frac{a^x - 1}{x} = \log a\right]$$

21. *(a)* $\because 2\pi^2 = 19.71$

$[-2\pi^2] = -20$

$$\therefore \lim_{x\to 0} \frac{\tan([-2\pi^2]x^2) - x^2\tan([-2\pi^2])}{\sin^2 x}$$

$$= \lim_{x\to 0} \frac{\tan(-20x^2) - x^2\tan(-20)}{\sin^2 x}$$

$$= \lim_{x\to 0} -\frac{\tan(20x^2)}{\sin^2 x} + \lim_{x\to 0} \tan 20 \cdot \frac{x^2}{\sin^2 x}$$

$$= \lim_{x\to 0} -20\frac{\tan(20x^2)}{20x^2}\left(\frac{x}{\sin x}\right)^2 + \tan 20 \lim_{x\to 0}\left(\frac{x}{\sin x}\right)^2$$

$$= -20 + \tan 20$$

22. *(d)* $\lim_{x \to 0} \frac{e^{ax} - e^{bx}}{x}$

$$= \lim_{x \to 0} \frac{(e^{ax} - 1) - (e^{bx} - 1)}{x}$$

$$= \lim_{x \to 0} \frac{e^{ax} - 1}{x} - \lim_{x \to 0} \frac{e^{bx} - 1}{x}$$

$[\because \lim_{x \to a} [f(x) - g(x)] = \lim_{x \to a} f(x) - \lim_{x \to a} g(x)]$

$$= \lim_{x \to 0} \frac{\left(1 + ax + \frac{(ax)^2}{2!} + \dots \infty\right) - 1}{x} - \lim_{x \to 0} \frac{\left(1 + bx + \frac{(bx)^2}{2!} + \dots\right) - 1}{x}$$

$= a - b$

23. *(a)* $\lim_{x \to 0} \frac{\log_e(1 + 2x) - 2\log_e(1 + x)}{x^2}$

$$= \lim_{x \to 0} \frac{\left(2x - \frac{4x^2}{2} + \frac{8x^3}{3} - \dots \infty\right) - 2\left(x - \frac{x^2}{2} + \frac{x^3}{3} - \dots \infty\right)}{x^2}$$

$$= \lim_{x \to 0} \frac{-x^2 + 2x^3 - \dots}{x^2}$$

$$= \lim_{x \to 0} (-1 + 2x - \dots)$$

$= -1$

24. *(d)* $\lim_{x \to 0} \frac{xe^x - \log(1 + x)}{x^2}$ $\left[\frac{0}{0} \text{ form}\right]$

Using L' Hospital's rule,

$$= \lim_{x \to 0} \frac{e^x + xe^x - \frac{1}{1 + x}}{2x} \quad \left[\frac{0}{0} \text{ form}\right]$$

$$= \lim_{x \to 0} \frac{e^x + e^x + xe^x + \frac{1}{(1 + x)^2}}{2}$$

$$= \frac{1 + 1 + 0 + 1}{2} = \frac{3}{2}$$

25. *(c)* $\lim_{x \to 2} \frac{xf(2) - 2f(x)}{x - 2}$

$$= \lim_{x \to 2} \frac{xf(2) - 2f(2) + 2f(2) - 2f(x)}{x - 2}$$

$$= \lim_{x \to 2} \frac{f(2)(x - 2) - 2[f(x) - f(2)]}{x - 2}$$

$$= \lim_{x \to 2} f(2) - \frac{2[f(x) - f(2)]}{x - 2}$$

$$= f(2) - 2\lim_{x \to 2} \frac{f(x) - f(2)}{x - 2}$$

$= f(2) - 2f'(2)$

$= 4 - 2(4)$

$= 4 - 8 = -4$

26. *(d)*

27. *(c)* $f(x) = |x - 1| + |x + 1|$

$$f(x) = \begin{cases} -(x - 1) - (x + 1), & x < -1 \\ -(x - 1) + (x + 1), & -1 \le x < 1 \\ (x - 1) + (x + 1), & x \ge 1 \end{cases}$$

$$= \begin{cases} -2x, & x < -1 \\ 2, & -1 \le x < 1 \\ 2x, & x \ge 1 \end{cases}$$

For $x \ge 1$, $f(x) = 2x$

$\therefore$ $f'(x) = 2, \forall x \ge 1$

$\therefore$ $f'(2) = 2$

28. *(b)* $2f(x) + f\left(\frac{1}{x}\right) = x + 2$ ...(i)

$\Rightarrow 2f\left(\frac{1}{x}\right) + f(x) = \frac{1}{x} + 2$ ...(ii)

On solving Eqs. (i) and (ii), we get

$$3f(x) = 2x - \frac{1}{x} + 2$$

As, $y = 3f(x)$

$\therefore$ $y = 2x - \frac{1}{x} + 2$

$$\frac{dy}{dx} = 2 + \frac{1}{x^2}$$

$$\Rightarrow \left(\frac{dy}{dx}\right)_{x=1} = 2 + 1 = 3$$

29. *(a)* $x^y = e^{x - y}$

Taking log on both sides, we get

$y \log x = (x - y)$ ...(i)

$[\because \log_b(m^k) = k \cdot \log_b(m)]$

$$y \cdot \frac{1}{x} + \log x \frac{dy}{dx} = 1 - \frac{dy}{dx}$$

$$\Rightarrow (1 + \log x)\frac{dy}{dx} = 1 - \frac{y}{x}$$

$$\Rightarrow \frac{dy}{dx} = \frac{x-y}{x(1+\log x)}$$

$$= \frac{y \log x}{x(1+\log x)} \quad \text{[using Eq. (i)]}$$

$$= \frac{\log x}{(1+\log x)^2} \quad \text{[using Eq. (i)]}$$

30. *(a)* $\frac{d}{dx}(\sin\sqrt{x})^{\frac{1}{2}} = \frac{1}{2\sqrt{\sin\sqrt{x}}} \times \frac{d}{dx}(\sin\sqrt{x})$

$$= \frac{1}{2\sqrt{\sin\sqrt{x}}} \times \cos\sqrt{x}\,\frac{d}{dx}\sqrt{x}$$

$$= \frac{1}{2\sqrt{\sin\sqrt{x}}}\cos\sqrt{x}\cdot\frac{1}{2\sqrt{x}}$$

$$= \frac{\cos\sqrt{x}}{4\sqrt{x\sin\sqrt{x}}}$$

31. *(c)* $\cos^2 x + \cos^4 x + \cos^6 x + \dots \infty$

$$= \frac{\cos^2 x}{1-\cos^2 x} = \frac{\cos^2 x}{\sin^2 x} = \cot^2 x$$

[using sum of infinite series of GP]

$\therefore \quad y = e^{\cot^2 x}$

$$\frac{dy}{dx} = \frac{d}{dx}(e^{\cot^2 x}) = e^{\cot^2 x}\frac{d}{dx}(\cot^2 x)$$

$$= y\cdot 2\cot x\,\frac{d}{dx}(\cot x)$$

$$= -2y\cdot\cot x\,\text{cosec}^2 x$$

32. *(b)* $f(x) = \log_x(\log x) = \frac{\log(\log x)}{\log x}$

$$f'(x) = \frac{\frac{1}{x} - \frac{1}{x}\log(\log x)}{(\log x)^2}$$

At $x = e$, $f'(e) = \frac{\frac{1}{e} - \frac{1}{e}\log(\log e)}{(\log e)^2} = \frac{1}{e}$

33. *(b)* We have, $\lim_{x\to 0}\left[1 + x + \frac{f(x)}{x}\right]^{1/x} = e^3$

$$\Rightarrow e^{\lim_{x\to 0}\left\{1+x+\frac{f(x)}{x}-1\right\}\frac{1}{x}} = e^3$$

$$\Rightarrow e^{\lim_{x\to 0}\left[1+\frac{f(x)}{x^2}\right]} = e^3$$

$$\Rightarrow \lim_{x\to 0}\frac{f(x)}{x^2} = 2$$

Now, $\lim_{x\to 0}\left[1 + \frac{f(x)}{x}\right]^{1/x} = e^{\lim_{x\to 0}\left[1+\frac{f(x)}{x}-1\right]\frac{1}{x}}$

$$= e^{\lim_{x\to 0}\frac{f(x)}{x^2}} = e^2$$

34. *(b)* $\lim_{x\to 1}(\log_2 2x)^{\log_x 5}$

$$= \lim_{x\to 1}(\log_2 2 + \log_2 x)^{\log_x 5}$$

$$= \lim_{x\to 1}\left[(1+\log_2 x)^{\frac{1}{\log_2 x}}\right]^{\log_2 x \log_x 5}$$

$$= e^{\lim_{x\to 1}\log_2 5} = e^{\log_2 5}$$

35. *(a)* $y = \cos x\cos 2x\cos 2^2x\cos 2^3x\cos 2^4x$

$\because \cos A\cdot\cos 2A\cos 2^2A \dots \cos 2^{n-1}A$

$$= \frac{\sin 2^n A}{2^n \sin A}$$

$$\Rightarrow y = \frac{\sin 2^5 x}{2^5\sin x} = \frac{\sin 32x}{32\sin x}$$

$$\Rightarrow \frac{dy}{dx} = \frac{32\sin x\cos 32x - \cos x\sin 32x}{32\sin^2 x}$$

At $x = \frac{\pi}{4}$, $\frac{dy}{dx} = \frac{32\cdot\sin\frac{\pi}{4}\cos 8\pi - \cos\frac{\pi}{4}\sin 8\pi}{32\left(\sin\frac{\pi}{4}\right)^2}$

$$= \frac{32\cdot\frac{1}{\sqrt{2}}\cdot 1 - 0}{32\cdot\frac{1}{2}} = \sqrt{2}$$

36. *(b)* $y = \sqrt{\frac{1+\cos\theta}{1-\cos\theta}}$

$$= \sqrt{\cot^2\frac{\theta}{2}}$$

$$\Rightarrow y = \left|\cot\frac{\theta}{2}\right|$$

$$\Rightarrow y = \cot\frac{\theta}{2}$$

$$\therefore \frac{dy}{d\theta} = \frac{-1}{2}\text{cosec}^2\frac{\theta}{2}$$

$$= \frac{-1}{2\sin^2\frac{\theta}{2}} = \frac{-1}{1-\cos\theta}$$

At $\theta = \frac{3\pi}{4}, \frac{dy}{d\theta} = -\frac{1}{1 - \cos\frac{3\pi}{4}}$

$$= -\frac{1}{1 + \cos\frac{\pi}{4}} = \sqrt{2} - 2$$

37. ***(a)*** Let $f(x) = \tan^{-1}\left(\frac{\sin x - \cos x}{\sin x + \cos x}\right)$

Dividing numerator and denominator by cos *x*, where

$$\cos x > 0, x \in \left(0, \frac{\pi}{2}\right)$$

$$= \tan^{-1}\left(\frac{\tan x - \tan\frac{\pi}{4}}{1 + \left(\tan\frac{\pi}{4}\right)(\tan x)}\right)$$

$$= \tan^{-1}\left(\tan\left(x - \frac{\pi}{4}\right)\right)$$

$\because \quad x \in \left(0, \frac{\pi}{2}\right)$

$\Rightarrow \quad x - \frac{\pi}{4} \in \left(-\frac{\pi}{4}, \frac{\pi}{4}\right)$

Then, $f(x) = \tan^{-1}\left(\tan\left(x - \frac{\pi}{4}\right)\right) = x - \frac{\pi}{4}$

Now, derivative of $f(x)$ w.r.t. $\frac{x}{2}$ is

$$\frac{d(f(x))}{d(x/2)} = \frac{2df(x)}{d(x)} = 2 \times \frac{d}{dx}\left(x - \frac{\pi}{4}\right) = 2$$

38. ***(a)***

39. ***(a)*** $y = (\log x)^x$

Taking log on both sides, we get

$$\log y = x \log(\log x)$$

$$\Rightarrow \quad \frac{1}{y}\frac{dy}{dx} = x \cdot \frac{1}{\log x} \cdot \frac{1}{x} + \log(\log x) \cdot 1$$

$$\Rightarrow \quad \frac{dy}{dx} = y\left[\log(\log x) + \frac{1}{\log x}\right]$$

40. ***(a)*** $\lim_{x \to 0} \frac{2^x - 3^x}{x(2^x + 3^x)}$ $\quad \left[\frac{0}{0} \text{ form}\right]$

Using L' Hospital's rule,

$$\lim_{x \to 0} \frac{2^x \log 2 - 3^x \log 3}{x(2^x \log 2 + 3^x \log 3) + (2^x + 3^x)}$$

$$= \frac{\log 2 - \log 3}{2} = \frac{1}{2}\log\left(\frac{2}{3}\right)$$

41. ***(a)*** We have, $a_{n+1} = \frac{4 + 3a_n}{3 + 2a_n}$

$$\lim_{n \to \infty} a_{n+1} = \lim_{n \to \infty} \frac{4 + 3a_n}{3 + 2a_n}$$

$\Rightarrow \quad a = \frac{4 + 3a}{3 + 2a}$

$\Rightarrow \quad 2a^2 = 4 \Rightarrow a = \pm\sqrt{2}$

$\because \quad$ Each $a_n > 0$

$\therefore \quad \lim_{n \to \infty} a_n = a > 0$

$\Rightarrow \quad a = \sqrt{2}$

[as $a \neq -\sqrt{2}$ because each $a_n > 0$]

42. ***(d)***

43. ***(b)*** Given, $\lim_{x \to \frac{\pi}{2}} \frac{\cot x - \cos x}{(\pi - 2x)^3}$ $\quad \left[\frac{0}{0} \text{ form}\right]$

$$= \lim_{x \to \frac{\pi}{2}} \frac{1}{8} \cdot \frac{\cos x(1 - \sin x)}{\sin x\left(\frac{\pi}{2} - x\right)^3}$$

Taking $x \to \frac{\pi}{2} - h$ and $h \to 0$

$$= \lim_{h \to 0} \frac{1}{8} \frac{\cos\left(\frac{\pi}{2} - h\right)\left[1 - \sin\left(\frac{\pi}{2} - h\right)\right]}{\sin\left(\frac{\pi}{2} - h\right)\left(\frac{\pi}{2} - \frac{\pi}{2} + h\right)^3}$$

$$= \frac{1}{8}\lim_{h \to 0} \frac{\sin h}{\cos h}\left(\frac{1 - \cos h}{h^3}\right)$$

$$= \frac{1}{8}\lim_{h \to 0} \frac{\sin h}{\cos h}\left(\frac{2\sin^2\left(\frac{h}{2}\right)}{h^3}\right)$$

$$= \frac{1}{8}\lim_{h \to 0} \frac{\sin h \cdot \left(2\sin^2\left(\frac{h}{2}\right)\right)}{h^3 \cos h}$$

$$= \frac{1}{4}\lim_{h \to 0} \frac{\sin h \cdot \sin^2\left(\frac{h}{2}\right)}{h^3 \cos h}$$

$$= \frac{1}{4}\lim_{h \to 0}\left(\frac{\sin h}{h}\right)\left(\frac{\sin h/2}{h/2}\right)^2 \cdot \frac{1}{\cos h} \cdot \frac{1}{4}$$

$$= \frac{1}{4} \times \frac{1}{4} = \frac{1}{16}$$

44. *(b)* Given, $y = \sum_{k=1}^{6} k\cos^{-1}\left(\frac{3}{5}\cos kx - \frac{4}{5}\sin kx\right)$

Let $\frac{3}{5} = \cos\theta$ and $\frac{4}{5} = \sin\theta$

So, $\frac{3}{5}\cos(kx) - \frac{4}{5}\sin(kx) = \cos(kx+\theta)$

Also, $\tan\theta = \frac{4}{3}$

$$\therefore \quad y = \sum_{k=1}^{6} k\cos^{-1}\cos(kx+\theta)$$

$$= \sum_{k=1}^{6} k(kx+\theta) = \sum_{k=1}^{6} k^2x + k\theta$$

$$= x\sum_{k=1}^{6} k^2 + \theta\sum_{k=1}^{6} k$$

$$= x\left(\frac{6\times 7\times 13}{6}\right) + \left(\frac{6\times 7}{2}\right)\theta$$

[using sum of special series]

$$y = 91x + 21\theta$$

$$\therefore \quad \left.\frac{dy}{dx}\right|_{x=0} = 91$$

45. *(d)*

46. *(c)* Given, equation

$p(x) = x^2 - x - 2 = (x-2)(x+1)$ having positive root α, so $\alpha = 2$.

Now, $\lim_{x\to\alpha^+} \frac{\sqrt{1-\cos(p(x))}}{x+\alpha-4}$

$$= \lim_{x\to 2^+} \frac{\left|\sqrt{2}\sin\left(\frac{p(x)}{2}\right)\right|}{x-2}$$

$$= \lim_{x\to 2^+}\left[\frac{\sqrt{2}\sin\left(\frac{(x-2)(x+1)}{2}\right)}{x-2}\right]$$

$[\because \sin\theta > 0, \text{ if } \theta\to 0^+]$

$$= \lim_{x\to 2^+}\left[\frac{\sqrt{2}\sin\left(\frac{(x-2)(x+1)}{2}\right)}{\frac{(x-2)(x+1)}{2}}\times\left(\frac{x+1}{2}\right)\right]$$

$$= \sqrt{2}\left(\frac{3}{2}\right) = \frac{3}{\sqrt{2}}$$

47. *(a)* $\lim_{x\to 0^+} x^m(\log x)^n = \lim_{x\to 0^+}\frac{(\log x)^n}{x^{-m}} \quad \left[\frac{\infty}{\infty}\text{ form}\right]$

By L' Hospital's rule, we have

$$= \lim_{x\to 0^+}\frac{n(\log x)^{n-1}\frac{1}{x}}{-mx^{-m-1}} \quad \left[\frac{\infty}{\infty}\text{ form}\right]$$

$$= \lim_{x\to 0^+}\frac{n(\log x)^{n-1}}{-mx^{-m}} \quad \left[\frac{\infty}{\infty}\text{ form}\right]$$

$$= \lim_{x\to 0^+}\frac{n(n-1)(\log x)^{n-2}\frac{1}{x}}{-m(-m)\,x^{-m-1}}$$

[by L' Hospital's rule]

$$= \lim_{x\to 0^+}\frac{n(n-1)(\log x)^{n-2}}{(-m)^2x^{-m}} \quad \left[\frac{\infty}{\infty}\text{ form}\right]$$

$$= \lim_{x\to 0^+}\frac{n!}{(-m)^n x^{-m}}$$

[differentiating numerator and denominator n times]

$$= 0$$

48. *(d)* $\lim_{x\to 2}\frac{\sin(e^{x-2}-1)}{\log(x-1)}$

Let $\quad x-2 = t \Rightarrow \quad x-1 = t+1$

As $x\to 2$, then $t = 0$

$$= \lim_{t\to 0}\frac{\sin(e^t-1)}{\log(t+1)} = \lim_{t\to 0}\frac{\sin(e^t-1)}{(e^t-1)}\cdot\frac{e^t-1}{\log(t+1)}$$

Since, $\lim_{x\to a}[f(x)\,g(x)] = \lim_{x\to a} f(x)\lim_{x\to a} g(x)$

$$= 1\cdot\lim_{t\to 0}\frac{e^t-1}{\log(1+t)} \quad \left[\because \lim_{x\to 0}\left(\frac{\sin x}{x}\right) = 1\right]$$

$$= \lim_{t\to 0}\frac{\left(1+t+\frac{t^2}{2!}+\frac{t^3}{3!}+\dots\right)-1}{\left(t-\frac{1}{2}t^2+\frac{1}{3}t^3-\dots\right)}$$

$$= \lim_{t\to 0}\frac{1+\frac{t}{2!}+\frac{t^3}{3!}+\dots}{1-\frac{1}{2}t+\frac{1}{3}t^2-\dots} = 1$$

49. *(c)* Given,

$$\lim_{x\to 0}\frac{((729)^x-(243)^x-(81)^x+9^x+3^x-1)}{x^3} = \lambda(\ln 3)^3$$

$$\Rightarrow \lim_{x\to 0}\frac{(3^x-1)(9^x-1)(27^x-1)}{x^3}=\lambda(\ln 3)^3$$

$$\Rightarrow \lim_{x\to 0}\frac{(3^x-1)}{x}\cdot\frac{(9^x-1)}{x}\cdot\frac{(27^x-1)}{x}=\lambda(\ln 3)^3$$

$$\Rightarrow (\ln 3).(\ln 9)(\ln 27)=\lambda(\ln 3)^3$$

$$\Rightarrow (\ln 3^2).(\ln 3)(\ln 3^3)=\lambda(\ln 3)^3$$

$$\Rightarrow 2\times 3(\ln 3)^3=\lambda(\ln 3)^3$$

On comparing both sides, we get

$$\lambda = 6$$

50. *(b)* Given, equation is

$$(2x)^{2y}=4e^{2x-2y} \quad \dots\text{(i)}$$

On applying $\log_e$ both sides, we get

$$\log_e(2x)^{2y}=\log_e 4+\log_e e^{2x-2y}$$

$$\Rightarrow 2y\log_e(2x)=\log_e(2)^2+(2x-2y)$$

$$[\because \log_e n^m = m\log_e n \text{ and } \log_e e^{f(x)}=f(x)]$$

$$\Rightarrow (2\log_e(2x)+2)y=2x+2\log_e(2)$$

$$\Rightarrow y=\frac{x+\log_e 2}{\log_e(2x)+1}$$

On differentiating y w.r.t. x, we get

$$\frac{dy}{dx}=\frac{(1+\log_e(2x))(1)-(x+\log_e 2)\left(\frac{2}{2x}\right)}{(1+\log_e(2x))^2}$$

$$=\frac{1+\log_e(2x)-1-\frac{1}{x}\log_e 2}{(1+\log_e(2x))^2}$$

$$\Rightarrow \frac{dy}{dx}=\frac{x\log_e(2x)-\log_e 2}{x(1+\log_e(2x))^2}$$

51. *(a)* Let $y=\tan^{-1}\left(\frac{\sqrt{2ax-x^2}}{a-x}\right)$

On putting $x=2a\sin^2\theta$ $\quad\dots$(i)

$$y=\tan^{-1}\left(\frac{2a\sin\theta\cos\theta}{a\cos 2\theta}\right)$$

$$=\tan^{-1}(\tan 2\theta)=2\theta$$

$$=2\sin^{-1}\sqrt{\frac{x}{2a}} \qquad \text{[from Eq. (i)]}$$

$$\frac{dy}{dx}=2\cdot\frac{1}{\sqrt{1-\frac{x}{2a}}}\times\frac{1}{\sqrt{2a}}\times\frac{1}{2\sqrt{x}}$$

$$=\frac{1}{\sqrt{2ax-x^2}}$$

52. *(c)* $x=\sin^{-1}2^y$

$$\Rightarrow 2^y=\sin x \quad \dots\text{(i)}$$

$$\Rightarrow 2^y\log 2\frac{dy}{dx}=\cos x$$

$$\Rightarrow \sin x\log 2\frac{dy}{dx}=\cos x \qquad \text{[from Eq. (i)]}$$

$$\Rightarrow \frac{dy}{dx}=\frac{\cot x}{\log 2}$$

53. *(d)*

54. *(c)* $x=t+\sin t$ and $y=1-\cos t$

$$\frac{dx}{dt}=1+\cos t \text{ and } \frac{dy}{dt}=\sin t$$

$$\therefore \frac{dx}{dy}=\frac{dx/dt}{dy/dt}=\frac{1+\cos t}{\sin t}$$

$$=\frac{2\cos^2\frac{t}{2}}{2\sin\frac{t}{2}\cos\frac{t}{2}}=\cot\frac{t}{2}$$

$$\therefore p=\frac{t}{2}$$

55. *(a)* $x=t-\frac{1}{t}$ and $y=t+\frac{1}{t}$

$$\frac{dx}{dt}=1+\frac{1}{t^2} \text{ and } \frac{dy}{dt}=1-\frac{1}{t^2}$$

$$\therefore \frac{dy}{dx}=\frac{dy/dt}{dx/dt}=\frac{1-\frac{1}{t^2}}{1+\frac{1}{t^2}}=\frac{t^2-1}{t^2+1}=\frac{tx}{ty}=\frac{x}{y}$$

56. *(a)* $\lim_{x\to 0}\frac{\sqrt{(1-\cos 2x)}}{x}$

$$=\lim_{x\to 0}\frac{\sqrt{2\sin^2 x}}{x}=\sqrt{2}\lim_{x\to 0}\frac{|\sin x|}{x}$$

$$=\sqrt{2}\begin{cases}\lim_{x\to 0}\frac{\sin x}{x}, & 0<x<\frac{\pi}{2}\\ -\lim_{x\to 0}\frac{\sin x}{x}, & -\frac{\pi}{2}<x<0\end{cases}$$

$$=\sqrt{2}\begin{cases}1, & 0<x<\frac{\pi}{2}\\ -1, & -\frac{\pi}{2}<x<0\end{cases}$$

$$=\begin{cases}\sqrt{2}, & 0<x<\frac{\pi}{2}\\ -\sqrt{2}, & -\frac{\pi}{2}<x<0\end{cases}$$

$\therefore$ LHL $= -\sqrt{2}$ and RHL $= \sqrt{2}$

$\Rightarrow$ LHL $\neq$ RHL

So, Assertion and Reason both are true and Reason is the correct explanation of Assertion.

Solutions. (Q.Nos. 57-61)

$\because \lim_{x \to 0^+} f(x) = \text{finite}$

$\Rightarrow \lim_{h \to 0} f(0 + h) = \text{finite}$

$$\Rightarrow \lim_{h \to 0} \frac{\sin h + ae^h + be^{-h} + c\ln(1+h)}{h^3} = \text{finite}$$

At $h \to 0$, Numerator $\to a + b$

and Denominator $\to 0$

$\because$ RHS is finite,

$\therefore \quad a + b = 0$

$\Rightarrow \quad b = -a \quad \ldots \text{(i)}$

$$\text{Now, } \lim_{h \to 0} \frac{\sin h + ae^h - ae^{-h} + c\ln(1+h)}{h^3} = \text{finite}$$

$$\Rightarrow \lim_{h \to 0} \frac{\frac{\sin h}{h} + \frac{a(e^h - 1)}{h} - a\frac{(e^{-h} - 1)}{h} + \frac{c\ln(1+h)}{h}}{h^2} = \text{finite}$$

At $h \to 0$, Numerator $\to 1 + a + a + c$

and Denominator $\to 0$

$\because$ RHS is finite.

$\therefore \quad 1 + 2a + c = 0$

$\Rightarrow \quad c = -1 - 2a \quad \ldots \text{(ii)}$

$$\therefore \lim_{h \to 0} \frac{\sin h + ae^h - ae^{-h} - (1+2a)\ln(1+h)}{h^3} = \text{finite}$$

$$\left[\text{form}\left(\frac{0}{0}\right)\right]$$

By L'Hospital's rule, we have

$$= \lim_{h \to 0} \frac{\cos h + ae^h + ae^{-h} - \frac{(1+2a)}{(1+h)}}{3h^2} \left[\text{form}\left(\frac{0}{0}\right)\right]$$

Applying L' Hospital's rule,

$$= \lim_{h \to 0} \frac{-\sin h + ae^h - ae^{-h} + \frac{(1+2a)}{(1+h)^2}}{6h}$$

Numerator must be $= 0$

$$\Rightarrow 0 + a - a + \frac{1+2a}{(1)^2} = 0$$

57. ***(a)*** $a = -\frac{1}{2}$

58. ***(b)*** From Eq. (i), $b = \frac{1}{2}$

59. ***(c)*** From Eq. (ii), $c = -1 + 1 = 0$

60. ***(d)*** $\lim_{x \to 0^+} f(x) = \lim_{h \to 0} f(h) \quad [x \to 0 + h, h \to 0]$

$$= \lim_{h \to 0} \frac{\sin h - \frac{1}{2}e^h + \frac{1}{2}e^{-h}}{h^3} \quad \left[\frac{0}{0}\text{form}\right]$$

Using L' Hospital's rule, we get

$$= \lim_{h \to 0} \frac{\cos h - \frac{e^h}{2} - \frac{e^{-h}}{2}}{3h^2} \quad \left[\frac{0}{0}\text{form}\right]$$

On applying L' Hospital's rule,

$$= \lim_{h \to 0} \frac{-\sin h - \frac{e^h}{2} + \frac{e^{-h}}{2}}{6h} \quad \left[\frac{0}{0}\text{form}\right]$$

$$= \lim_{h \to 0} \frac{-\cos h - \frac{e^h}{2} - \frac{e^{-h}}{2}}{6}$$

[by L' Hospital's rule]

$$= \frac{-1 - \frac{1}{2} - \frac{1}{2}}{6} = -\frac{1}{3}$$

61. ***(a)*** $\lim_{x \to 0^+} x^2 f(x) = \lim_{h \to 0} h^2 f(h) \, [x \to 0 + h, h \to 0]$

$$= \lim_{h \to 0} \frac{\sin h + ae^h + be^{-h} + c\ln(1+h)}{h}$$

$$= \lim_{h \to 0} \frac{\sin h - \frac{1}{2}e^h + \frac{1}{2}e^{-h}}{h}$$

$$\left[\because a = -\frac{1}{2}, b = \frac{1}{2}, c = 0\right]$$

$$= \lim_{h \to 0} \left[\frac{\sin h}{h} - \frac{1}{2}\frac{(e^h - 1)}{h} + \frac{1}{2}\frac{(e^{-h} - 1)}{h}\right]$$

$$= 1 - \frac{1}{2} - \frac{1}{2}$$

$$\left[\because \lim_{h \to 0} \frac{\sin h}{h} = 1, \lim_{h \to 0} \frac{e^h - 1}{h} = 1\right]$$

$$= 0$$

Chapter 13 Statistics

1. ***(b)*** $\because (1+x)^n = {}^nC_0 + {}^nC_1 x + {}^nC_2 x^2 + {}^nC_3 x^3 + \ldots + {}^nC_n x^n$

On putting $x=1$, we get

$${}^nC_0 + {}^nC_1 + {}^nC_2 + {}^nC_3 + \ldots + {}^nC_n = 2^n$$

$$\text{Arithmetic mean} = \frac{{}^nC_0 + {}^nC_1 + {}^nC_2 + \ldots + {}^nC_n}{n+1} = \frac{2^n}{n+1}$$

2. ***(b)***

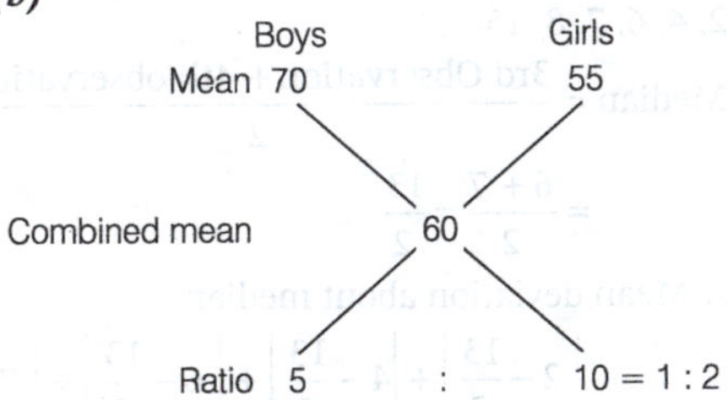

3. ***(a)*** Given, $\text{AM} = \dfrac{a_1 + a_2 + \ldots + a_n}{n} = K$

Now, new observations are

$a_1 + 1, a_2 + 2, a_3 + 3, \ldots, a_n + n$

$$\text{AM} = \frac{(a_1+1)+(a_2+2)+(a_3+3)+\ldots+(a_n+n)}{n}$$

$$= \frac{a_1 + a_2 + a_3 + \ldots + a_n}{n} + \frac{1+2+3+\ldots+n}{n}$$

$$= K + \left(\frac{n+1}{2}\right)$$

4. ***(b)***

5. ***(d)*** We have, modal class = 100-150

Mode = 140

$$\therefore \quad \text{Mode} = l + \frac{f_0 - f_{-1}}{2f_0 - f_{-1} - f_1} \times h$$

where, $l = 100, f_0 = 37, f_{-1} = 33, f_1 = b, h = 50$

$$\therefore \quad 140 = 100 + \left[\frac{37-33}{2\times 37 - 33 - b}\right] \times 50$$

$$\Rightarrow \quad 5740 = 4300 + 40b$$

$$\Rightarrow \quad b = 36$$

6. ***(d)*** We have, $0 < y < x < 2y$

$\Rightarrow \quad x < 2y$

Also, $x - y < \dfrac{x}{2}$ and $2y < 2x + y$

$\Rightarrow \quad \dfrac{x}{2} < y$

$\therefore \quad x - y < y < x < 2x + y$

$\text{Median} = \dfrac{x+y}{2} = 10$

$\Rightarrow \quad x + y = 20$ ...(i)

and range $= (2x+y) - (x-y) = 28$

$\Rightarrow x + 2y = 28$ ...(ii)

$$\therefore \quad \text{Mean} = \frac{(x-y)+y+x+(2x+y)}{4}$$

$$= \frac{4x+y}{4} \quad \text{...(iii)}$$

On solving Eqs. (i) and (ii), we get

$x = 12$ and $y = 8$

$$\therefore \quad \text{Mean} = \frac{4\times 12 + 8}{4} = 14$$

7. ***(a)*** $\because \text{Median} = l + \dfrac{\frac{N}{2} - cf}{f} \times h$

Given, median = 35, $N = 100$, $cf = 45$ $h = 10$ and $l = 30$

$$\therefore \quad 35 = 30 + \frac{50-45}{f} \times 10$$

$$\Rightarrow \quad 5 = \frac{50}{f} \Rightarrow f = 10$$

8. ***(a)***

9. ***(a)*** Given, $n = 27$

$$\therefore \text{Median observation} = \left(\frac{27+1}{2}\right)\text{th term}$$

$$= 14\text{th term} = 18$$

Three new observations are added 16, 18, 50, one is less than median, one is greater than median, one is equal to median which makes number of observations 30 in number.

$$\text{Median} = \frac{15\text{th term} + 16\text{th term}}{2}$$

$$= \frac{18+18}{2} = 18$$

10. *(d)*

Class interval	f	cf
0.5-5.5	3	3
5.5-10.5	7	10
10.5-15.5	6	16
15.5-20.5	5	21
Total	21	

$\because \quad N = 21$

$\Rightarrow \quad \frac{N}{2} = 10.5$

$\therefore$ Median class = 10.5-15.5

$$\text{Median} = l + \frac{\frac{N}{2} - cf}{f} \times h$$

$$= 10.5 + \frac{10.5 - 10}{6} \times 5 = 10.917$$

Modal class = 5.5-10.5

Thus, median is not contained in the modal class and distribution is not bell-shaped.

11. *(d)*

12. *(c)* Mean

$$= \frac{1 + (1 + d) + (1 + 2d) + \ldots + (1 + 100d)}{101}$$

$$= 1 + 50d$$

MD about mean = 295

$$\Rightarrow \frac{|1 - (1 + 50d)| + |(1 + d) - (1 + 50d)| + |(1 + 2d) - (1 + 50d)| + \ldots + |(1 + 100d) - (1 + 50d)|}{101} = 295$$

$$\Rightarrow \quad 2d \times \frac{50 \times 51}{2} = 101 \times 295$$

$$\Rightarrow \quad d = \frac{101 \times 295}{50 \times 51} = 11.68$$

13. *(b)* Mean $= \dfrac{a + (a + d) + (a + 2d) + \ldots + (a + 2nd)}{(2n + 1)}$

$$= \frac{\frac{2n + 1}{2}[2a + 2nd]}{(2n + 1)}$$

$$= a + nd$$

$\therefore$ Mean deviation about mean

$$= \frac{1}{2n + 1}[|(a - a - nd)| + |a + d - a - nd| + |a + 2d - a - nd| + \ldots + |a + 2nd - a - nd|]$$

$$= \frac{2}{2n + 1}[(1 + 2 + 3 + \ldots + n)d]$$

$$= \frac{2}{2n + 1} \cdot \frac{n(n + 1)d}{2} = \frac{n(n + 1)d}{(2n + 1)}$$

14. *(b)* Given, mean = 7

$$\therefore \quad 7 = \frac{4 + 7 + 2 + 8 + 6 + x}{6} \Rightarrow x = 15$$

Arranging observations in ascending order 2, 4, 6, 7, 8, 15.

$$\text{Median} = \frac{\text{3rd Observation} + \text{4th observation}}{2}$$

$$= \frac{6 + 7}{2} = \frac{13}{2}$$

$\therefore$ Mean deviation about median

$$= \frac{\left|2 - \frac{13}{2}\right| + \left|4 - \frac{13}{2}\right| + \left|6 - \frac{13}{2}\right| + \left|7 - \frac{13}{2}\right| + \left|8 - \frac{13}{2}\right| + \left|15 - \frac{13}{2}\right|}{6}$$

$$= \frac{18}{6} = 3$$

15. *(c)* Given, observations $a, 2a, 3a, \ldots, 50a$

$$\text{Median} = \frac{\text{25th term} + \text{26th term}}{2} \qquad [n = 50]$$

$$M = \frac{25a + 26a}{2} = 25.5a$$

$$\text{Mean deviation about median} = \frac{\sum_{i=1}^{50} |x_i - M|}{50}$$

$$\because \quad 50 = \frac{1}{50}[|a - 25.5a| + |2a - 25.5a| + |3a - 25.5a| + \ldots |50a - 25.5a|]$$

$$\therefore \quad 50 = \frac{1}{50}[2 \times |a|(0.5 + 1.5 + 2.5 + \ldots + 24.5)]$$

$$1250 = |a|\left[\frac{25}{2}(0.5 + 24.5)\right]$$

$$|a| = \frac{1250 \times 2}{25 \times 25}$$

$$\Rightarrow \quad |a| = 4$$

16. ***(b)*** Given, SD of $y = \sigma_y$

$$\text{SD of } \frac{cy+d}{a} = \left|\frac{c}{a}\right|$$

$$\text{SD of } y = \left|\frac{c}{a}\right| \sigma_y$$

17. ***(c)***

Classes	f	x	$u = x - 15$	fu	fu^2
0-10	1	5	– 10	– 10	100
10-20	3	15	0	0	0
20-30	4	25	10	40	400
30-40	2	35	20	40	800
Total	10			$\Sigma fu = 70$	$\Sigma fu^2 = 1300$

$$\text{SD} = \sqrt{\frac{\Sigma fu^2}{\Sigma f} - \left(\frac{\Sigma fu}{\Sigma f}\right)^2} = \sqrt{\frac{1300}{10} - \left(\frac{70}{10}\right)^2}$$

$$= \sqrt{130 - 49} = \sqrt{81} = 9$$

18. ***(b)*** $\text{Mean} = \frac{-1+1+0+k}{4} = \frac{k}{4}$ and $\text{SD} = \sqrt{8}$

$$\Rightarrow \quad \frac{\Sigma x^2}{4} - (\bar{x})^2 = 8$$

$$\Rightarrow \quad \frac{2+k^2}{4} - \frac{k^2}{16} = 8 \Rightarrow \frac{8+4k^2-k^2}{16} = 8$$

$$\Rightarrow \quad 3k^2 = 8 \times 16 - 8$$

$$\Rightarrow \quad k^2 = \frac{8 \times 15}{3} \Rightarrow k = \sqrt{40}$$

19. ***(c)*** Scores: 40, 45, 43, 42, 45, x

$\bar{x} = \text{Mean} = 45$

$$\Rightarrow \quad \frac{40+45+43+42+45+x}{6} = 45 \Rightarrow x = 55$$

x	$x - \bar{x} = x - 45$	$(x - \bar{x})^2$
40	– 5	25
45	0	0
43	– 2	4
42	– 3	9
45	0	0
55	10	100
		$\Sigma(x - \bar{x})^2 = 138$

$$\text{SD} = \sqrt{\frac{138}{6}} = \sqrt{23}$$

20. ***(b)***

21. ***(c)*** $\text{Mean} = \bar{x} = 20$, $\text{SD} = \sigma = 2$

New mean $= a\bar{x} - b$

$$\Rightarrow \quad 10 = a(20) - b$$

$$\Rightarrow \quad 20a - b = 10 \qquad \text{...(i)}$$

New $\text{SD} = |a|\sigma$

$$1 = |a|(2)$$

$$\Rightarrow \quad |a| = \frac{1}{2} \Rightarrow a = \pm\frac{1}{2}$$

If $\quad a = \frac{1}{2}$, then $b = 0$

If $\quad a = -\frac{1}{2}$, then $b = -20$

22. ***(a)*** $\text{Mean} = \frac{np + nq}{2n}$

$$= \frac{p + (-p)}{2} = 0$$

$$\text{SD} = \sqrt{\frac{\Sigma x^2}{2n} - \Sigma(\bar{x})^2}$$

$$\Rightarrow \quad 4 = \sqrt{\frac{p^2(2n)}{2n}}$$

$$\Rightarrow \quad 4 = \sqrt{p^2} \Rightarrow |p| = 4$$

23. ***(b)*** Variance of first n natural numbers $= \frac{n^2-1}{12}$

$\therefore$ Variance of first 5 natural numbers $= \frac{5^2-1}{12} = 2$

24. ***(d)*** For 5 students, Average height = 150

Total height = 150 × 5 = 750 cm

Variance = 18

$$\Rightarrow \quad \frac{\Sigma x^2}{5} - (150)^2 = 18 \Rightarrow \Sigma x^2 = 112590$$

For 6 students,

$$\text{Average height} = \frac{750+156}{6} = 151$$

$$\text{Variance} = \frac{112590 + (156)^2}{6} - (151)^2 = 20$$

25. ***(a)*** Given, $\sigma_x^2 = 4$, $\sigma_y^2 = 5$, $\bar{x} = 2$, $\bar{y} = 4$,

$n_1 = 5$ and $n_2 = 5$

$$\sigma_x^2 = \frac{\Sigma x^2}{n_1} - \left(\frac{\Sigma x}{n}\right)^2$$

$$\Rightarrow \quad 4 = \frac{\Sigma x^2}{5} - 4$$

$\Rightarrow \quad \Sigma x^2 = 40$

$$\sigma_y^2 = \frac{\Sigma y^2}{n_2} - \left(\frac{\Sigma y}{n}\right)^2 \Rightarrow 5 = \frac{\Sigma y^2}{5} - 16$$

$\Rightarrow \quad \Sigma y^2 = 105$

Sum of square of both data sets

$$= \Sigma x^2 + \Sigma y^2 = 145$$

Sum of both data sets $= \Sigma x + \Sigma y = 30$

Variance of combined data $= \dfrac{145}{10} - \left(\dfrac{30}{10}\right)^2 = \dfrac{11}{2}$

26. ***(b)*** Given, $\Sigma x = 170$, $\Sigma x^2 = 2830$ and $n = 15$

New $\Sigma x = 170 - 20 + 30 = 180$

New $\Sigma x^2 = 2830 - 20^2 + 30^2 = 3330$

New variance $= \dfrac{\Sigma x^2}{n} - \left(\dfrac{\Sigma x}{n}\right)^2$

$$= \frac{3330}{15} - \left(\frac{180}{15}\right)^2 = 222 - 144 = 78$$

27. ***(a)*** Since, both the observations are consecutive integers.

∴ Both have same standard deviation

∴ Variance is equal.

$\therefore \quad \dfrac{\sigma_x}{\sigma_y} = 1$

28. ***(b)*** Variance, $\sigma^2 = \dfrac{1}{n}\Sigma x_i^2 - (\bar{x})^2$

$$\bar{X} = \frac{\Sigma x_i}{n} = \frac{2+4+6+8+\ldots+100}{50}$$

$$= \frac{50 \times 51}{50} = 51$$

$[\Sigma\, 2n = n\,(n+1)$, here $n = 50]$

$$\sigma^2 = \frac{1}{50}(2^2 + 4^2 + \ldots + 100^2) - (51)^2 = 833$$

29. ***(c)*** $(\bar{x}) = \dfrac{\text{Sum of quantities}}{n} = \dfrac{\frac{n}{2}(a+l)}{n}$

$$= \frac{1}{2}[1 + 1 + 100\,d] = 1 + 50\,d$$

$\therefore \quad \text{MD} = \dfrac{1}{n}\Sigma|x_i - \bar{x}| \Rightarrow \; 255$

$$= \frac{1}{101}[50d + 49d + 48d + \ldots + d + 0 + d + \ldots + 50d]$$

$$= \frac{2d}{101}\left(\frac{50 \times 51}{2}\right)$$

$\therefore \quad d = \dfrac{255 \times 101}{50 \times 51} = 10.1$

30. ***(d)*** Mean of $ax_1, ax_2, \ldots, ax_n$

$$= \frac{ax_1 + ax_2 + \ldots + ax_n}{n}$$

$$= a\left(\frac{x_1 + x_2 + x_3 + \ldots + x_n}{n}\right)$$

$$= a\bar{x} \qquad \left(\because \bar{x} = \frac{x_1 + x_2 + \ldots + x_n}{n}\right)$$

Variance of $ax_1, ax_2, \ldots, ax_n$

$$= \frac{\Sigma(ax_i - a\bar{x})^2}{n}$$

$$= \frac{(ax_1 - a\bar{x})^2 + (ax_2 - a\bar{x})^2 + \ldots + (ax_n - a\bar{x})^2}{n}$$

$$= \frac{a^2[(x_1 - \bar{x})^2 + (x_2 - \bar{x})^2 + \ldots + (x_n - \bar{x})^2]}{n}$$

$$= a^2\frac{\Sigma(x_i - \bar{x})^2}{n} = a^2\sigma^2 \left[\because \sigma^2 = \frac{\Sigma(x_i - \bar{x})^2}{n}\right]$$

31. ***(b)*** Given, frequency distribution of 20 students are

Marks	2	3	5	7
Frequency	$(x+1)^2$	$2x - 5$	$x^2 - 3x$	x

$\because \quad \Sigma f_i = (x+1)^2 + (2x-5) + (x^2 - 3x) + x$

$\Rightarrow \quad 20 = x^2 + 2x + 1 + 2x - 5 + x^2 - 3x + x$

$\Rightarrow \quad 20 = 2x^2 + 2x - 4$

$\Rightarrow \quad 2x^2 + 2x - 24 = 0$

$\Rightarrow \quad x^2 + x - 12 = 0$

$\Rightarrow \quad (x+4)(x-3) = 0$

$\Rightarrow \quad x = 3 \qquad [\because x > 0]$

Now, mean $= \dfrac{\Sigma f_i x_i}{\Sigma f_i}$

$$\Rightarrow \bar{x} = \frac{2(3+1)^2 + 3\{2(3) - 5\} + 5\{3^2 - 3(3)\} + 7(3)}{20}$$

$$\Rightarrow \bar{x} = \frac{32 + 3 + 0 + 21}{20} = \frac{56}{20} = 2.8$$

∴ Mean = 2.8

32. ***(b)*** Mean = 15

$\Rightarrow \bar{x} = 15 \Rightarrow \Sigma x = 15 \times 20 = 300$

$\therefore \quad$ Incorrect sum = 300

Correct sum = 300 − 3 − 6 + 8 + 4
= 300 + 3 = 303

$\therefore$ Correct mean $= \frac{303}{20} = 15.15$

33. *(a)* Given ten numbers are
10, 22, 26, 29, 34, *x*, 42, 67, 70, *y*

$$\text{Median} = \frac{(5\text{th} + 6\text{th})\text{ observation}}{2}$$

$$\Rightarrow 35 = \frac{34 + x}{2} \quad [\because \text{median} = 35]$$

$$\Rightarrow x = 70 - 34 = 36$$

$$\text{Mean} = \frac{10 + 22 + 26 + 29 + 34 + x + 42 + 67 + 70 + y}{10}$$

$$\Rightarrow 45 = \frac{300 + x + y}{10} \quad [\because \text{mean} = 45]$$

$$\Rightarrow 450 = 300 + 36 + y \quad [x = 36]$$

$$\Rightarrow y = 450 - 336 = 114$$

$$\therefore \frac{y}{x} = \frac{114}{36} = \frac{19}{6}$$

34. *(d)* $\text{SD} = \sqrt{\frac{\Sigma(x_i - 5)^2}{n} - \left[\frac{\Sigma(x_i - 5)}{n}\right]^2}$

$$= \sqrt{\frac{5n}{n} - \left(\frac{n}{n}\right)^2} = \sqrt{4}$$

35. *(d)* Mean = 16 = SD

$$\therefore \frac{\Sigma x}{50} = 16$$

$$\Rightarrow \Sigma x = 16 \times 50$$

and $\sqrt{\frac{\Sigma x^2}{50} - (16)^2} = 16$

$$\Rightarrow \Sigma x^2 = 2 \times (16)^2 \times 50$$

$$\therefore \text{Required mean} = \frac{\Sigma(x - 5)^2}{50}$$

$$= \frac{\Sigma x^2 + \Sigma 5^2 - 2 \times 5\Sigma x}{50}$$

$$= \frac{2 \times (16)^2 \times 50 + 25 \times 50 - 10 \times 16 \times 50}{50}$$

$$= 512 + 25 - 160 = 377$$

36. *(b)* $a + b + c + d + e = 25$

$$\Rightarrow 1 + 3 + 8 + d + e = 25$$

$$\Rightarrow d + e = 13 \quad \text{...(i)}$$

and $\frac{a^2 + b^2 + c^2 + d^2 + e^2}{5} - 5^2 = 9.20$

$$\Rightarrow \frac{1 + 9 + 64 + d^2 + e^2}{5} = 9.2 + 25$$

$$\Rightarrow d^2 + e^2 = 97 \quad \text{...(ii)}$$

$$\because (d + e)^2 - 2de = d^2 + e^2$$

$$\therefore (13)^2 - 2de = 97$$

$$\Rightarrow de = 36 \quad \text{...(iii)}$$

Using Eqs. (i) and (iii), we get

$$d : e = \frac{4}{9} \text{ or } \frac{9}{4}$$

37. *(b)* Sum = $\Sigma x = 400$ and $\Sigma x^2 = 2475$

Three observations 3, 4 and 5 are removed.

Then, sum = $\Sigma x = 400 - 3 - 4 - 5$
= 388

$$\Sigma x^2 = 2475 - 3^2 - 4^2 - 5^2 = 2425$$

$$\text{Variance} = \frac{\Sigma x^2}{97} - \left(\frac{\Sigma x}{97}\right)^2 = \frac{2425}{97} - \left(\frac{388}{97}\right)^2 = 9$$

38. *(b)* We know, $\text{SD} = \sqrt{\frac{\Sigma x_i^2}{n} - \left(\frac{\Sigma x_i}{n}\right)^2}$

$$\Rightarrow (3.5)^2 = \frac{2^2 + 3^2 + a^2 + (11)^2}{4} - \left(\frac{2 + 3 + a + 11}{4}\right)^2$$

$$\Rightarrow 12.25 = \frac{4 + 9 + a^2 + 121}{4} - \left(\frac{16 + a}{4}\right)^2$$

$$\Rightarrow \frac{49}{4} = \frac{134 + a^2}{4} - \frac{256 + a^2 + 32a}{16}$$

$$\Rightarrow \frac{49}{4} = \frac{4a^2 + 536 - 256 - a^2 - 32a}{16}$$

$$\Rightarrow 49 \times 4 = 3a^2 - 32a + 280$$

$$\Rightarrow 3a^2 - 32a + 84 = 0$$

39. *(a)* Given, $\bar{x} = 10$ and $\sigma = 3$

$$\bar{x} = \frac{\sum_{i=1}^{5} x_i}{5} \Rightarrow \Sigma x_i = 5 \times 10 = 50$$

$$\sigma^2 = \frac{\Sigma x_i^2}{5} - \left(\frac{\Sigma x_i}{5}\right)^2$$

$$\Rightarrow 9 = \frac{\Sigma x_i^2}{5} - \left(\frac{50}{5}\right)^2$$

$$\Rightarrow \frac{\Sigma x_i^2}{5} = 9 + 100 = 109 \Rightarrow \sum_{i=1}^{5} x_i^2 = 109 \times 5 = 545$$

Now, variance of 6 observations x_1, x_2, x_3, x_4, x_5 and -50 is

$$\sigma^2 = \frac{\sum_{i=1}^{5} x_i^2 + (-50)^2}{6} - \left(\frac{\sum_{i=1}^{5} x_i - 50}{6}\right)^2$$

$$= \frac{545 + 2500}{6} - \left(\frac{50 - 50}{6}\right)^2 = \frac{3045}{6} = 507.5$$

40. *(c)* Given, $\bar{x}$ is the mean and σ^2 is the variance of n observation $x_1, x_2, x_3, \dots, x_n$

Mean of $2x_1, 2x_2, 2x_3, \dots, 2x_n$

$$= \frac{2x_1 + 2x_2 + 2x_3, \dots, + 2x_n}{n}$$

$$= \frac{2(x_1 + x_2 + x_3 + \dots x_n)}{n} = 2\bar{x}$$

Hence, Reason is false.

Now, variance of $2x_1, 2x_2, 2x_3, \dots, 2x_n$

$2x_i = 2^2$ (variance of x_i) $= 4\sigma^2$

Hence, Assertion is true.

Chapter 14 Probability

1. *(d)* $P(A) = P(B) = 3P(C)$

$\because \quad P(A) + P(B) + P(C) = 1$

$\Rightarrow \quad 3P(C) + 3P(C) + P(C) = 1$

$\Rightarrow \quad P(C) = \frac{1}{7}$

2. *(b)* Total coins $= n$

Out of n coins, K are heads and $(n - K)$ are tails.

$n(E) =$ Getting K heads $= {}^nC_K$

$n(S) = 2^n$

$\therefore$ Probability $= \frac{{}^nC_K}{2^n}$

3. *(a)*

4. *(a)* $E_1 = \{(1, 1)\}, P_1 = P(E_1) = \frac{1}{36}$

$E_4 = \{(1, 4), (2, 2), (4, 1)\},$

$P_4 = P(E_4) = \frac{3}{36}$

$E_6 = \{(1, 6), (6, 1), (2, 3), (3, 2)\},$

$P_6 = P(E_6) = \frac{4}{36},$

$E_{30} = \{(6, 5), (5, 6)\}, P_{30} = P(E_{30}) = \frac{2}{36},$

$\therefore \; P_1 < P_{30} < P_4 < P_6$

5. *(c)* $P(E_k) \propto K \Rightarrow P(E_K) = cK$

$P(E_1) + P(E_2) + P(E_3) + P(E_4) + P(E_5) + P(E_6) = 1$

$\Rightarrow c + 2c + 3c + 4c + 5c + 6c = 1$

$\Rightarrow \quad c = \frac{1}{21}$

$\therefore \quad P(E_1) + P(E_3) + P(E_5) = \frac{1}{21} + \frac{3}{21} + \frac{5}{21} = \frac{3}{7}$

6. *(c)* $n(S) = (12)^5$

$n(E) = {}^{12}P_5$

$\therefore \quad P(E) = \frac{{}^{12}P_5}{12^5}$

7. *(d)* Given, system of equations

$px + qy = 0$

and $\quad rx + sy = 0$

has unique solutions,

if $\quad \Delta \neq 0$

$\Rightarrow \quad ps - qr \neq 0$

$\Rightarrow \quad ps = 1$ and $qr = 0$

or $\quad ps = 0$ and $qr = 1$

$n(S) = 2 \times 2 \times 2 \times 2 = 16$

$n(E) = 6$

$\therefore \quad P(E) = \frac{6}{16} = \frac{3}{8}$

8. *(d)* $n(S) = (366)^2$

$n(E) = 1 \times 365 + 365 \times 1 = 2 \times 365$

$\therefore \quad P(E) = \frac{365 \times 2}{366 \times 366} = \frac{365}{366 \times 183}$

9. *(d)* $P(K) =$ Probability of getting a number k

$P(K) \propto K$

$\Rightarrow \quad P(K) = aK$

$\because \quad P(1)+P(2)+P(3)+\ldots+P(2n)=1$

$\Rightarrow \quad a+2a+3a+\ldots+2na=1$

$\Rightarrow \quad \dfrac{a\{(2n(2n+1)\}}{2}=1$

[using sum of special series]

$\Rightarrow \quad a=\dfrac{1}{n(2n+1)}$

$\therefore$ Required probability

$$=P(2)+P(4)+\ldots+P(2n)$$
$$=2a(1+2+3+\ldots+n)$$
$$=\frac{2}{n(2n+1)}\cdot\frac{n(n+1)}{2}$$
$$=\frac{n+1}{2n+1}$$

10. ***(c)*** Probability of selecting a month $=\dfrac{1}{12}$

13th day of a randomly selected month is Friday if its first day is Sunday.

So, probability of this event $=\dfrac{1}{7}$

$\therefore$ Required probability $=\dfrac{1}{12}\times\dfrac{1}{7}=\dfrac{1}{84}$

11. ***(a)*** Let ellipse be $\dfrac{x^2}{a^2}+\dfrac{y^2}{b^2}=1$

Then, circle is $x^2+y^2=a^2$

$\therefore$ Area of ellipse $=\pi ab$

Area of circle $=\pi a^2$

$\therefore$ Required probability $=\dfrac{\pi a^2-\pi ab}{\pi a^2}$

$$=1-\frac{b}{a}$$
$$=1-\sqrt{1-e^2}$$
$$=1-\frac{1}{3} \qquad \left[\because e=\frac{2\sqrt{2}}{3}\right]$$
$$=\frac{2}{3}$$

12. ***(d)***

13. ***(b)*** Probability (India wins a match) $=\dfrac{1}{3}$

Probability (India losses a match) $=\dfrac{2}{3}$

I. Probability (India wins atleast one match)

$=1-$ Probability (India losses all matches)

$$=1-\left(\frac{2}{3}\right)^3=\frac{19}{27}$$

II. Probability (India losses all the three matches)

$$=\left(\frac{2}{3}\right)^3=\frac{8}{27}$$

14. ***(c)*** Number of ways each can apply

$$=4^4=256$$

All four may opt for any one of the 4 houses.

$\therefore$ Required probability $=\dfrac{4}{256}=\dfrac{1}{64}$

15. ***(c)***

16. ***(b)*** $n(S)={}^{P}C_2$

$n(E)=P-1$

$\therefore \quad P(E)=\dfrac{P-1}{{}^{P}C_2}$

17. ***(c)*** Both selected squares are either in a row or column

$n(E)=2\times 8\times 7=56\times 2=112$

$n(S)={}^{64}C_2$

$\therefore \quad P(E)=\dfrac{112}{{}^{64}C_2}$

18. ***(c)*** Probabillty (room is lighted)

$=1-$ Probability (room is not lighted)

$$=1-\frac{{}^{3}C_3}{{}^{8}C_3}$$
$$=1-\frac{1}{56}=\frac{55}{56}$$

19. ***(a)*** Vowel $\rightarrow$ O, E

Consonant $\rightarrow$ H, M

Probability (atleast one is consonant)

$=1-P$(all are vowels)

$$=1-\frac{{}^{2}C_2}{{}^{4}C_2}=1-\frac{1}{6}=\frac{5}{6}$$

20. ***(a)*** $n(S)={}^{52}C_4$

$n(E)={}^{13}C_1\times{}^{13}C_1\times{}^{13}C_1\times{}^{13}C_1=(13)^4$

$\therefore \quad P(E)=\dfrac{(13)^4}{{}^{52}C_4}$

21. ***(d)***

22. ***(a)*** $n(S)={}^{52}C_2$

$n(E)={}^{2}C_1\cdot{}^{50}C_1$

$\therefore\ P(E) = \dfrac{^2C_1 \times {^{50}C_1}}{^{52}C_2}$

$= \dfrac{2 \times 50 \times 2}{52 \times 51} = \dfrac{50}{663}$

23. *(a)*

24. *(c)*

Odd digits = 1, 3, 5, 7, 9
Even digits = 0, 2, 4, 6, 8
Since, odd digits should be at odd place and even digits should be at even place.
$\therefore$ Places of odd digits = 3
and places of even digits = 2
$\Rightarrow$ Favourable ways = $^5P_3 \times {^5P_2}$

$\therefore$ Required probability $= \dfrac{^5P_3 \times {^5P_2}}{9 \times 9 \times 8 \times 7 \times 6}$

$= \dfrac{25}{567}$

25. *(d)* Total number of ways = 2^n

A person is odd man out if he is alone in getting a head or tail.
Then, the number of favourable ways
= Number of ways in which there is exactly one tail (head) and rest are heads (tails)

$^nC_1 + {^nC_1} = 2n$

$P(E) = \dfrac{2n}{2^n} = \dfrac{1}{2}$ [given]

$\Rightarrow\ n = 2^{n-2}$

$\Rightarrow\ n = 4$ [by hit and trial method]

26. *(a)* Total number of ways of choosing 3 tickets out of 30 is $^{30}C_3$.
$\therefore$ We can choose x_1 in 14 ways, x_3 in 10 ways.
$\therefore$ Probability of the required events

$= \dfrac{(14)\,(10)}{^{30}C_3} = \dfrac{1}{29}$

27. *(a)*

28. *(d)* $P(E_1) = P(\geq 100) = 0.7$

$P(E_2) = P(\leq 120) = 0.8$

$P(E_1 \cap E_2) = P(\text{between 100 and 120})$
$= P(E_1) + P(E_2) - P(E_1 \cup E_2)$
$= 0.7 + 0.8 - 1.0$
$= 0.5$

29. *(a)* Given, $P(A) = \dfrac{2}{5}$, $P(B) = \dfrac{1}{3}$, $P(C) = \dfrac{1}{2}$

and $P(A \cap C) = \dfrac{1}{5}$

$\therefore\ P(A' \cap C') = 1 - P(A \cup C)$
$= 1 - [P(A) + P(C) - P(A \cap C)]$
$= 1 - \left(\dfrac{2}{5} + \dfrac{1}{2} - \dfrac{1}{5}\right) = \dfrac{3}{10}$

30. *(d)* $\dfrac{3}{4} \leq P(A \cup B) \leq 1$

$\Rightarrow\ \dfrac{3}{4} \leq P(A) + P(B) - P(A \cap B) \leq 1$

$\Rightarrow\ \dfrac{3}{4} + \dfrac{1}{8} < P(A) + P(B) \leq 1 + \dfrac{3}{8}$

$\Rightarrow\ \dfrac{7}{8} \leq P(A) + P(B) \leq \dfrac{11}{8}$

31. *(b)* A wins, if getting a total of 6

$P(A \text{ wins}) = P(A) = \dfrac{5}{36}$

B wins, if getting a total of 8

$P(B \text{ wins}) = P(B) = \dfrac{5}{36}$

A starts the game and wins in third throw.

$\therefore$ Required probability
$= P(\bar{A})P(\bar{B})P(A)$
$= \dfrac{31}{36} \times \dfrac{31}{36} \times \dfrac{5}{36} = \dfrac{(31)^2 \times 5}{(36)^3}$

32. *(b)* $\because A \cup A = A$ and $A \cap A = A$
Given, $P(A \cup B) = P(A \cap B)$
which is only possible when $P(A) = P(B)$
$\therefore P(A \cup B) = P(A \cap B)$
$\Rightarrow P(A) + P(B) - P(A \cap B) = P(A \cap B)$
$\Rightarrow \{P(A) - P(A \cap B)\} + \{P(B) - P(A \cap B)\} = 0$
Since, both brackets are positive which is only possible only when
$P(A) - P(A \cap B) = 0 = P(B) - P(A \cap B)$
$\Rightarrow\ P(A) = P(B) = P(A \cap B)$

33. *(b)* Let $x = r$, then $y = 2n - r$
Then, $r \in \{1, 2, \ldots 2n - 1\}$
Total number of ways in which $x + y = 2n$, $x, y \in N = (2n - 1)$
From $(2n - 1)$ ways, there is only one point (n, n) that lies on the line $y = x$

$\therefore$ Required probability $= 1 - \dfrac{1}{2n - 1} = \dfrac{2n - 2}{2n - 1}$

34. *(c)* $\begin{vmatrix} a & b \\ c & d \end{vmatrix} = ad - bc$

Each of the element can only take 2 values.

$\therefore$ Total number of ways $= 16$

But $ad - bc \neq 0$ if and only if $ad = x^2$ and $bc = -x^2$ or $ad = -x^2$ and $bc = x^2$

But $ad = x^2$ and $bc = -x^2$

$\Leftrightarrow (a = d = x$ or $a = d = -x)$

and $(b = x, c = -x$ or $b = -x, c = x)$

i.e. there are four ways.

Similarly, $ad = -x^2$ and $bc = x^2$ in four ways.

$\therefore$ Required probability $= \dfrac{4+4}{16} = \dfrac{1}{2}$

35. *(c)* Let $y = \sqrt{\dfrac{x-15}{(x-10)(x-20)}}$,

which is a positive real number.

$\Rightarrow \quad y = \dfrac{x-15}{(x-10)(x-20)} > 0$

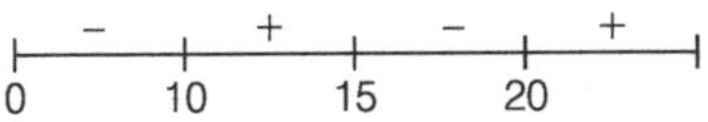

$\Rightarrow \quad y > 0$

$\Rightarrow \quad 11 \le x \le 14$ or $x \ge 21$

Therefore, there are 84 favourable cases.

Hence, required probability $= \dfrac{84}{100} = \dfrac{21}{25}$

36. *(c)* It is given that a person wins ₹ 15 for throwing a doublet (1, 1) (2, 2), (3, 3), (4, 4), (5,5), (6, 6) and win ₹ 12 when the throw results in sum of 9 i.e. when (3,6), (4, 5), (5, 4), (6, 3) occurs.

Also, losses ₹ 6 for throwing any outcome i.e. when any of the rest $= 36 - 6 - 4 = 26$

$\therefore$ Outcomes expected gain/loss

$= 15 \times P$ (getting a doublet)

$+ 12 \times P$ (getting sum 9)

$- 6 \times P$ (getting any rest 26 outcomes)

$$= 15 \times \frac{6}{36} + 12 \times \frac{4}{36} - 6 \times \frac{26}{36}$$

$$= \frac{15 + 8 - 26}{6}$$

$= -\dfrac{1}{2}$ means loss of ₹ $\dfrac{1}{2}$

37. *(c)* Let $p = P(\text{drawing a white ball}) = \dfrac{x}{x+y}$

and $q = P(\text{drawing a black ball}) = \dfrac{y}{x+y}$

$P(B \text{ wins}) = p + q^2p + q^4p + \ldots \infty$

$$= \frac{p}{1-q^2} = \frac{\frac{x}{x+y}}{1 - \left(\frac{y}{x+y}\right)^2}$$

$$= \frac{\frac{x}{x+y}}{(x+y)^2 - y^2} \times (x+y)^2$$

$$= \frac{x(x+y)}{x^2 + y^2 + 2xy - y^2}$$

$$= \frac{x(x+y)}{x(x+2y)} = \frac{x+y}{x+2y}$$

38. *(a)*

39. *(b)* Possible situations

$(WWR), (WBR), (BBR), (BWR)$

Required probability

$$= \frac{3}{8} \times \frac{2}{7} \times \frac{2}{6} + \frac{3}{8} \times \frac{3}{7} \times \frac{2}{6} + \frac{3}{8} \times \frac{2}{7} \times \frac{2}{6} + \frac{3}{8} \times \frac{3}{7} \times \frac{2}{6}$$

$$= \frac{12 + 18 + 12 + 18}{8 \times 7 \times 6} = \frac{60}{8 \times 7 \times 6} = \frac{5}{28}$$

40. *(c)* $P(\text{getting black ball}) = \dfrac{2}{6} \times \dfrac{3}{7} + \dfrac{4}{6} \times \dfrac{4}{7} = \dfrac{11}{21}$

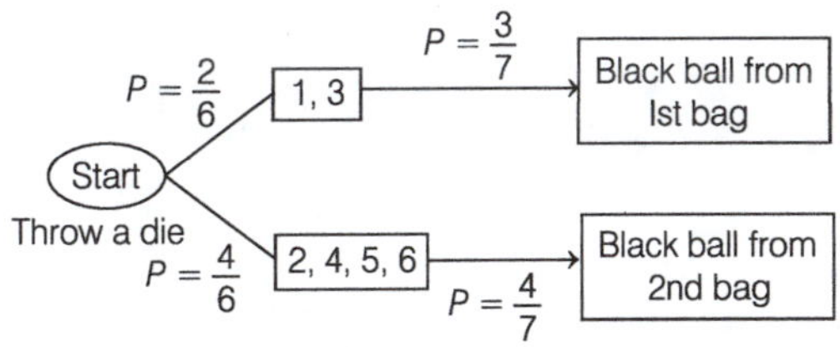

41. *(b)* Given, probability of speaking truth are

$$P(A) = \frac{4}{5} \text{ and } P(B) = \frac{3}{4}$$

and their corresponding probability of not speaking truth are

$$P(\bar{A}) = \frac{1}{5}\ P(\bar{B}) = \frac{1}{4}$$

$\therefore$ Required probability

$$= P(A)P(\bar{B}) + P(\bar{A})P(B)$$

$$= \frac{4}{5} \times \frac{1}{4} + \frac{1}{5} \times \frac{3}{4} = \frac{7}{20}$$

42. *(a)* Let A = Akash will qualify exam
and B = Anil will qualify exam

$P(A) = 0.10$

$P(B) = 0.05$

$P(\overline{A}) = 0.9$

$P(\overline{B}) = 0.95$

$P(A \cap B) = 0.02$

Only one will qualify the exam

$= P[(A \cap \overline{B}) \cup (\overline{A} \cap B)]$

$= P(A \cap \overline{B}) + P(\overline{A} \cap B)$

$= P(A) - P(A \cap B) + P(B) - P(A \cap B)$

$= 0.10 - 0.02 + 0.05 - 0.02 = 0.11$

43. *(b)* P (exactly one of A or B occurs)

$= P(A \cup B) - P(A \cap B) = P(A) + P(B) - 2P(A \cap B)$

According to question,

$$P(A) + P(B) - 2P(A \cap B) = \frac{1}{4} \quad \text{... (i)}$$

$$P(B) + P(C) - 2P(B \cap C) = \frac{1}{4} \quad \text{... (ii)}$$

$$P(C) + P(A) - 2P(C \cap A) = \frac{1}{4} \quad \text{... (iii)}$$

On adding Eqs. (i), (ii) and (iii), we get

$$P(A) + P(B) + P(C) - P(A \cap B) - P(B \cap C) - P(C \cap A) = \frac{3}{8}$$

$\therefore$ Required probability

$= P(A \cup B \cup C)$

$= P(A) + P(B) + P(C) - P(A \cap B) - P(B \cap C) - P(C \cap A) + P(A \cap B \cap C)$

$= \frac{3}{8} + \frac{1}{16} = \frac{7}{16}$

Practice Set 1

1.	(b)	**2.**	(d)	**3.**	(d)	**4.**	(d)	**5.**	(c)	**6.**	(c)	**7.**	(d)	**8.**	(a)	**9.**	(d)	**10.**	(c)
11.	(a)	**12.**	(a)	**13.**	(d)	**14.**	(c)	**15.**	(a)	**16.**	(a)	**17.**	(a)	**18.**	(d)	**19.**	(c)	**20.**	(d)
21.	(d)	**22.**	(b)	**23.**	(b)	**24.**	(b)	**25.**	(c)	**26.**	(d)	**27.**	(b)	**28.**	(c)	**29**	(c)	**30.**	(c)
31.	(b)	**32.**	(b)	**33.**	(c)	**34.**	(d)	**35.**	(d)	**36.**	(b)	**37.**	(b)	**38.**	(a)	**39.**	(c)	**40.**	(d)
41.	(b)	**42.**	(a)	**43.**	(d)	**44.**	(d)	**45.**	(d)	**46.**	(d)	**47.**	(b)	**48.**	(c)	**49.**	(c)	**50.**	(a)

Practice Set 2

1.	(d)	**2.**	(c)	**3.**	(c)	**4.**	(d)	**5.**	(d)	**6.**	(b)	**7.**	(c)	**8.**	(c)	**9.**	(b)	**10.**	(a)
11.	(b)	**12.**	(c)	**13.**	(a)	**14.**	(c)	**15.**	(b)	**16.**	(c)	**17.**	(b)	**18.**	(a)	**19.**	(b)	**20.**	(b)
21.	(b)	**22.**	(b)	**23.**	(d)	**24.**	(a)	**25.**	(a)	**26.**	(b)	**27.**	(a)	**28.**	(b)	**29**	(c)	**30.**	(a)
31.	(b)	**32.**	(d)	**33.**	(c)	**34.**	(b)	**35.**	(c)	**36.**	(a)	**37.**	(c)	**38.**	(d)	**39.**	(d)	**40.**	(a)
41.	(b)	**42.**	(d)	**43.**	(b)	**44.**	(a)	**45.**	(a)	**46.**	(d)	**47.**	(b)	**48.**	(b)	**49.**	(b)	**50.**	(d)

Practice Set 3

1.	(a)	**2.**	(d)	**3.**	(a)	**4.**	(c)	**5.**	(b)	**6.**	(c)	**7.**	(c)	**8.**	(c)	**9.**	(c)	**10.**	(c)
11.	(a)	**12.**	(b)	**13.**	(c)	**14.**	(a)	**15.**	(d)	**16.**	(c)	**17.**	(d)	**18.**	(c)	**19.**	(b)	**20.**	(a)
21.	(c)	**22.**	(d)	**23.**	(b)	**24.**	(c)	**25.**	(d)	**26.**	(b)	**27.**	(b)	**28.**	(d)	**29**	(c)	**30.**	(c)
31.	(c)	**32.**	(d)	**33.**	(b)	**34.**	(b)	**35.**	(a)	**36.**	(c)	**37.**	(a)	**38.**	(b)	**39.**	(c)	**40.**	(b)
41.	(b)	**42.**	(b)	**43.**	(c)	**44.**	(c)	**45.**	(b)	**46.**	(a)	**47.**	(d)	**48.**	(a)	**49.**	(b)	**50.**	(a)